Readings and Problems in
Accounting Information Systems

Readings and Problems in Accounting Information Systems

L. Murphy Smith, D.B.A., CPA
Associate Professor

Robert H. Strawser, D.B.A., CPA
Arthur Andersen & Co. Former Students Professor

Casper E. Wiggins, Jr., D.B.A., CPA
Associate Professor

All of
Department of Accounting
Texas A&M University

IRWIN

Homewood, IL 60430
Boston, MA 02116

© *RICHARD D. IRWIN, INC., 1991*

Senior sponsoring editor: Ron Regis
Project editor: Karen Murphy
Production manager: Carma W. Fazio
Cover designer: Laurie Entringer
Compositor: Weimer Typesetting Inc.
Typeface: 10/12 Times Roman
Printer: R. R. Donnelley & Sons Company

Library of Congress Cataloging-in-Publication Data

Smith, L. Murphy.
    Readings and problems in accounting information systems / L.
Murphy Smith, Robert H. Strawser, Casper E. Wiggins.
        p.   cm.
    ISBN 0-256-07040-7
    1. Electronic spreadsheets.   2. Accounting—Data processing.
3. Accounting—Data processing—Problems, exercises, etc.
4. Electronic spreadsheets—Problems, exercises, etc.   I. Strawser,
Robert H.   II. Wiggins, Casper E.   III. Title.
HF5679.S647   1991
657′.0285—dc20   90–23291

Printed in the United States of America
2 3 4 5 6 7 8 9 0   DOC   8 7 6 5 4 3 2

Contents in Brief

Contents

Chapter 8   The New Office Technology—LANs and Desktop Publishing   *302*

Chapter 9   Expert Systems—Taking an Expert to the Field   *331*

Chapter 10   Microcomputers   *367*

Appendix A   Microcomputer Spreadsheets   *409*

Appendix B   DBASE III +   *433*

Introduction

The need to introduce accounting students to computer concepts, as well as to specific computer applications (e.g., spreadsheets), has led many universities to add the Accounting Information Systems (AIS) course to their curriculums. Other universities have integrated the computer-related material within various existing courses. Using either approach, there is much material to be covered. Developments in the AIS area have substantially affected accounting practice and, consequently, accounting education.

The AIS area encompasses many potential topics (e.g., general systems theory, control structure, and specific computer applications). No consensus has been reached on the exact topics that should be covered in the AIS course. A major purpose of this readings and problems book is to provide instructors with a supplement to the basic AIS textbook. The readings may provide coverage of additional topics or more complete coverage of topics included in the basic textbook. This book may also be used stand-alone to provide AIS coverage in a non-AIS course, such as auditing.

The chart inside the cover of the teacher's manual cross-references the readings and problems chapters in this book with appropriate chapters in six AIS textbooks and two auditing textbooks.

The readings and problems are divided among ten chapters, covering such subjects as controlling the development of information systems, computer crime, and expert systems, among others. Each chapter provides an introduction to the subject matter, which is then addressed by several professional journal articles. Several short problems (discussion questions or short cases) are provided in each chapter. At the end of the book are appendixes on microcomputer spreadsheets and data base software. The appendixes are provided to allow students with little or no knowledge of these software tools to quickly acquire a working knowledge.

CHAPTER 1

The Information Revolution

Being an accounting professional today requires far more than just a textbook understanding of debits and credits, journaling and posting steps, and the latest accounting and auditing pronouncements. The accounting professional of the 1990s must also stay abreast of the many technological advances which continually reshape the business world. These advances have sparked an information revolution which in the past two decades has transformed almost every aspect of accounting. Perhaps the greatest impact of the information revolution has been on the accounting system itself; indeed, accounting systems and the world of computers and data processing have become inseparable. Recognition of this fact has given rise to a new accounting specialty area known as accounting information systems.

Most accounting information systems (AIS) today involve elements of computer processing, and the complexity of computer processing is steadily increasing. For example, in the 1960s the early computers enabled many organizations to replace manual systems with batch processing systems. As equipment costs declined in the 1970s, many of these early batch systems were displaced by more complex on-line systems, some with real-time and/or data base applications. The advent of microcomputers and continuing reductions in overall equipment costs in the 1980s made computer processing affordable to almost all businesses. Today, real-time applications, data base applications, computer networks, electronic data interchange (EDI), and many other sophisticated features are becoming commonplace in accounting information systems.

Such technology permits, for example, the rapid processing of huge volumes of transactions, the immediate updating of on-line files, point-of-sale (POS) transaction entry, rapid access to data in integrated data bases, instantaneous data communications within geographically distributed computer networks, and an increased level of computer resource sharing. To a decision maker this translates into more accurate, reliable, and timely information to support tough economic decisions made in an ever more competitive environment. This enhances planning and control at all organizational levels and for all aspects of business activity.

This technological revolution has also produced radical changes in the design and manufacturing activities of many businesses. For example, computer-aided drafting, design, and manufacturing (CAD/CAM technology) has totally restructured the drafting, design, and manufacturing industries. CAD/CAM has virtually eliminated the iterative manual drafting process and has dramatically reduced the labor hours required for the design of new automobiles, aircraft, buildings, factories, and many other products. Complete material and labor cost schedules are also automatically produced from computer designs. Thus, CAD/CAM technology both automates and integrates design, manufacturing, and production processes. Benefits include significant gains in productivity and savings in cost, as well as a shortening of the design, development, and production cycles. In addition, related technologies permit the real-time monitoring of manufacturing processes, reducing labor and waste costs and greatly enhancing quality control.

Advancing technology also has significant implications for the auditors of these ever more complex systems. Gone are the traditional paper audit trails which auditors can easily follow. Instead of the customary segregation of duties, auditors find that duties have been concentrated in computer programs. Files of information once stored conveniently in file cabinets now reside in computer files which cannot be read by humans. Indeed, the information revolution has created an unfamiliar and imposing audit environment for auditors. Fortunately, the profession has responded to this challenge and has developed new tools and techniques for auditing in computer environments. However, as technology continues to change, so also must audit technology and strategies.

The three readings included in this chapter establish a framework for the remaining topics of this text by exploring both present and future implications of the information revolution for the accounting profession. The initial article, "Commentary on Information Systems," by Gordon B. Davis, describes the intimate relationship which exists today between information systems and the accounting profession. Professor Davis's comments underscore the critical importance of accounting information systems knowledge in basic education as well as in continuing education for accounting professionals.

The second article, "The Corporate Financial Planning Workstation and Software Tools," provides an overview of the corporate financial planning philosophy, the computing environment, and some appropriate computer software tools. The chapter's final article, "The CPA in the Information Age: Today and Tomorrow," surveys the emerging technologies which are reshaping the public accounting profession, and presents a glimpse of an audit system of the future.

CHAPTER 1 READINGS

1. Gordon B. Davis, "Commentary on Information Systems," *Accounting Horizons,* March 1987, pp. 75–79.
2. L. Murphy Smith and James A. Sena, "The Corporate Financial Planning Workstation and Software Tools," *Journal of Accounting and EDP*, Fall 1989, pp. 48–56.

3. Robert S. Roussey, "The CPA in the Information Age: Today and Tomorrow," *Journal of Accountancy*, October 1986, pp. 94–107.

CHAPTER 1 QUESTIONS

Article 1

1. Describe the roles often provided by accounting professionals which suggest a strong affinity between accounting and information systems. Why is it advisable for an accountant to be involved with systems developers in the design and testing of new applications?

Article 2

2. What are the key levels of planning?
3. List personal software tools.
4. List the software tools used for managerial processing and comprehensive analysis.

Article 3

5. Which aspects of the audit process are most adaptable to and benefit most from automation? Why are benefits (productivity gains) from audit automation somewhat difficult to measure?
6. What are the implications of audit automation for: (*a*) auditors; (*b*) their clients? Some say that auditing will never be the same. Do you agree?
7. How has the role of accounting changed in the information age? Will trained accountants still be needed in 10 years? Are accountants the primary purveyors of information in today's business world?

General

8. What is CAD/CAM technology? In what ways has this new technology increased productivity in manufacturing industries such as the automobile industry?
9. How can the value of information be measured? What are some of the costs and benefits of information to a typical business? Are the costs of information easier or more difficult to assess than the value of information?

Case 1–1

GREASY BBQ

The Greasy BBQ has served Casper, Wyoming, customers for over two decades and has gained a reputation for its truly fine BBQ. The specialty of the house is fajitas marinated in a special sauce which, according to the owner, Fred Frijole, attracts customers "from as far away as Mexico." While business has been steadily increasing, Fred is very concerned because the BBQ's profits do not seem to be increasing.

Fred fears that his accounting system may be inadequate, especially in the area of control structure. Fred's cousin Joe Bob made a C– on his first test in high school accounting and was the natural choice to set up the BBQ's accounting system. The BBQ operates on a cash basis because Joe Bob left high school before "they got to the accrual basis." Besides, in Joe Bob's opinion, "We're all in it for the cash anyway." Joe Bob also does the books for the BBQ during the rodeo off-season. Fred cannot reach Joe Bob now, since it is rodeo season, and he has called you in for help since he heard that you are taking accounting information systems in college. Fred is particularly interested in improving his accounting system, increasing profits, and learning more about effective control structure. He is also concerned that the IRS might criticize his accounting system should the BBQ ever be audited. This was not a worry in the past because Fred just filed the BBQ's first-ever tax return last month.

Customers enjoy a casual atmosphere at the Greasy BBQ, which operates as follows. Customers enter the front door and select one of the 20 tables or 12 booths, and seat themselves. Menus are painted on signs posted on each wall so that a menu is always in sight. One of the six waiters or waitresses, all of whom are students at the local university, quickly takes customers' orders on a plain white order pad. The table number is marked on each order before it is taken to the kitchen.

The three cooks, also university students, then fill the orders, always giving generous portions. (The BBQ is cooked slowly the night before by a university student who is also responsible for cleaning the restaurant.) When the table order is ready, one of the cooks will holler out, and the first available waiter or waitress will serve the food to the appropriate table. All orders are served on butcher paper which adds to the homey atmosphere and virtually eliminates dishwashing. When customers are finished with their meal they go to the cashier stand located at the back of the restaurant, tell Fred what they had, and pay accordingly. Part of the atmosphere of the BBQ is the 1875 cash drawer which is still in daily use.

Fred is very proud that the BBQ has operated on the honor system successfully for all these years. Many of his best customers are university students and truckers, and in Fred's opinion, "if you can't trust your customers, who can you trust?" He always takes checks from his customers and does not worry about bad checks because "all my meals are cheap and, besides, the bank takes care of bad checks, that's their job."

Fred also orders all of the meat and the other items used in the restaurant. His orders are based on his many years of experience, the season of the year, and the day of the week. He feels this "seat of the pants" method works well for the BBQ and brags that he has never run out of food to serve his customers. In addition, he believes the amount of wasted food is not excessive. Leftover food is regularly sold to a local kennel and feed ranch.

REQUIRED

1. What are the likely causes of the BBQ's "lean" profits?
2. Identify any weaknesses noted in Greasy's accounting system which may contribute to a loss of profits.
3. What improvements might you suggest to overcome any of the weaknesses cited above?
4. Should the BBQ convert from the cash to the accrual basis? What are the pros and cons?
5. What information might Fred utilize in order to better manage the BBQ? How might the accounting information system be modified to generate this management information?

Case 1–2

AQUALUNG, INC.

John Arend, President of Aqualung, Inc., a small Miami-based underwater construction and marine salvage company, sat back in his chair and pondered an investment opportunity which had unexpectedly presented itself. Earlier in the week, John had received a telephone call from Mike Brown, a former college fraternity brother, who wanted to discuss a possible business venture. Over lunch the next day, John learned that Mike was organizing a group of investors to finance a search for the wreck of a Spanish galleon, the *Toledo,* which sank off the coast of Bermuda during the 18th century. The *Toledo* had been carrying gold and silver bullion mined in Mexico, none of which had ever been recovered. Mike had contacted John because of his expertise in underwater salvage work. Aqualung's investment would consist of providing a boat, several teams of divers, and their equipment. Other investors would provide the working capital and specialized knowledge needed for day-to-day operations.

As John considered Brown's proposition, he realized that he needed additional quantitative information regarding the risk/return trade-off that the investment offered. To this end he scheduled a meeting the next afternoon with Mike Brown. John asked you, Aqualung's controller, to join him at the meeting. During the meeting, Mike informed John that his best estimate of Aqualung's share of the search costs was $1.5 million. Mike also estimated that the probability of finding the *Toledo* and recovering the majority of the bullion before the hurricane season began was only 20 percent. However, since gold prices were at an all-time high due to strong inflation in the world economy, a successful search should result in a net gain to Aqualung of approximately $8 million. The probability that the venture would be a failure was 80 percent.

REQUIRED:

a. Summarize Mike's cost and probability estimates in a decision tree and calculate the expected values of John's alternatives regarding the investment.

b. John notes that because the net expected value of the decision to invest is higher than that of not investing, the best decision, based on the available information, might be to invest. However, he still hesitates because of the high probability and cost of failure. While John realizes, of course, that perfect information as to the existence of underwater treasure is not available, he asks you to calculate the net expected value of the venture, given perfect information (i.e., John would know for certain in advance whether treasure existed or not). In other words, you are to determine how much John would be willing to pay for perfect information.

Reading 1–1

COMMENTARY ON INFORMATION SYSTEMS

By Gordon B. Davis

Should every accountant be a computer expert? Is it reasonable to expect that a "normal" person can be a good accountant and a computer-based information processing expert as well? If the answer is "not an expert," there still remains a need for accountants to have a fairly good understanding of computers and information systems. But what does this mean in terms of basic education and continuing professional education? This column will describe some of the differences and affinities that characterize the relationship of accounting and information systems. With this background (and a definition of information systems), three computer and information system literacies vital to professional accountants will be explained. These literacies provide a basis for being an accountant with adequate skills in information systems without taking on the requirement of being an expert.

ACCOUNTANTS AND INFORMATION PROCESSING SYSTEMS WORK

The world was simpler for accountants before there were computers. In the olden days, accountants needed to understand the bookkeeping systems that processed the transactions and maintained the accounting files, but that was

---

Reprinted with permission from *Accounting Horizons,* March 1987, pp. 75–79.

rarely a problem. The bookkeeping files were visible, the procedures were observable from start to finish (and in any case, there was a person there to explain what they did), and there tended to be very little change from one period to the next.

Accounting systems topics were rarely taught to accountants, and if the subject was taught, it was not considered to be a subject that excited the intellect. Committees of the American Accounting Association regularly indicated the importance of accounting systems as a topic for instruction, but it failed the market test, and accountants learned about accounting systems "on the job."

Until the advent of computers, accounting provided *the* formal financial information systems for organizations. When computers were applied to information processing in organizations, starting in about 1954, it seemed very natural for computer data processing systems to be incorporated in the domain of accounting, both organizationally and academically. Sometimes it happened, but frequently it did not.

A new function, *data processing* or *information systems,* arose to manage the technology of information processing. Why did this happen? Three major reasons that information systems did not remain a simple subfield of accounting (as an expanded accounting systems function) are the demands of a changing technology, new development methods, and specialization.

- Computer technology for information processing has been changing at such a pace that it requires significant ongoing effort to maintain real expertise.

- The development methodologies for information systems (requirements determination, development, design, and implementation) use techniques that are new or are significantly changed from past accounting systems development methods.

- Specialization in computer-based information processing has provided the basis for a new professional identity. Many of the people with this professional identification have little background in accounting and do not identify with it.

DEFINITION OF INFORMATION SYSTEMS

Many accountants equate information systems with computers, but when the field is viewed more broadly, the relationship to accounting becomes more significant. Information systems as a business function can be termed data processing, management information systems, information systems, etc. For the purposes of this article, "information systems" will be used to refer to both the organizational function and its related professional and academic fields. Information systems is defined as the function that performs the design, construction, and maintenance of human/machine systems that

- utilize information processing technology (computers, telecommunications, and office automation)
- to support the information processing needs and information access requirements
- of the management and the various functions within an organization.

Note that the purpose of the function is to support the rest of the organization (including accounting) with information processing and information access; the systems are characterized by a combination of information processing technology and humans (as both operators and users). The hardware ranges from large mainframes to small personal computers. The facilities are located in computer centers, information centers, and individual workstations. The systems are designed not just to process transactions but also to provide information processing and information access to a broad spectrum of users, from clericals to managers. The systems provide support for transaction processing and for the various activities in operations, management control, and strategic planning. The information systems applications range from large corporate transaction and reporting systems to individual support systems and end-user computing.

THE AFFINITY OF ACCOUNTING AND INFORMATION SYSTEMS

Even though there are differences between accounting and information systems, there is a significant affinity. Accountants have very real reasons for a continuing interest and involvement in information systems. Four important reasons are the role of information systems as processing support for accounting, the role of information systems as the custodian of data bases utilized by accountants, the use of information technology by accountants, and the importance of information systems knowledge for performance of the audit function.

- The professional role of accountants is analysis and interpretation. When complex computer-based systems provide the raw material for analysis and interpretation, there is a need to understand the systems that process and store data. When accountants prepare reports containing important financial data, they make implied representations about the quality of the reports; to make valid representations of quality requires a knowledge of the processing systems and the controls included in them.
- Computer-based systems provide a richer supply of data than was feasible in manual or mechanical systems. There are large numbers of data bases (both internal and external) from which data may be extracted for analysis and interpretation. To retrieve the data needed for accounting assignments (and evaluate the quality of the data obtained), ac-

countants need to have a reasonable understanding of data base systems, data base integrity controls, and data base retrieval capabilities.

- Until recently, accountants were insulated from the computer by the requirement that all requests for data processing, retrievals, or report preparation (no matter how small) had to go through the information processing function. The situation has not changed dramatically. The accountant can use the computer directly, either working with a stand-alone personal computer or working through a terminal or personal computer connected to the mainframe. This direct access to processing power and data requires some skill in user-oriented software such as spreadsheet packages, retrieval software, and report generators. The accountant also needs to apply procedures to control this end-user processing and assure its quality.

- It is important to understand the processing system to evaluate internal control and to design and perform compliance tests and substantive testing procedures. Therefore, auditors must have an understanding of computer-based processing systems and the methods for accessing and processing data required for the audit.

These four accounting activities with their requirement for an understanding of information systems suggest the need for accountants to have both academic preparation in fundamentals of information systems and a continuing professional education effort to maintain an adequate level of expertise. The issue is not whether an accountant should include information systems in the scope of collegiate and continuing professional education; the issue is what to include from the many topics that might be studied.

BEYOND COMPUTER SYSTEM LITERACY

There is general agreement that every person in society today should be computer literate. But the world of accounting is intertwined with computer-based information systems, and therefore every accountant should be literate in three areas with respect to computers and information processing, and this basic knowledge should be maintained and strengthened during a career in accounting:

1. *Computer literacy*
   Computer literacy encompasses an elementary knowledge of basic hardware, software, and telecommunications technology.

2. *Skills in using accountant's knowledge work tool kit*
   The computer workstation (hardware, software, and data communications) can be described as a professional tool kit. The workstation, when configured for an accountant, supports both improved productivity and enhanced capabilities for accounting and auditing work.

3. *Accountant's information systems literacy*

This literacy is the ability to access, use, and manage information resources and to advise others with respect to these resources. Information systems literacy is of general importance for those who study business and management; its importance is enhanced and its scope is broadened for accountants.

Computer literacy is an interesting topic in itself, but the main objective here is to discuss the last two: what an accountant should be able to do relative to computer use, and the roles relative to information systems in which an accountant should be able to perform professionally.

ACCESS AND USE SKILLS FOR THE ACCOUNTANT'S KNOWLEDGE WORK TOOL KIT

Accountants are knowledge workers. One of the major issues of society relative to productivity is to improve productivity of knowledge workers. One source of productivity improvement is through computer hardware and software to support knowledge work by professionals such as accountants. This trend has started with the almost universal adoption of the spreadsheet processor (such as Lotus 1-2-3). The criterion for applying computer software to knowledge work is to allow existing activities to be performed more efficiently (less time, less errors, etc.) and to promote new, innovative applications.

The computer access and use skills are based on the existence of a personal computer workstation for every accountant. The workstation can be used as a stand-alone computer or as a terminal to access the larger corporate mainframe. Gone are the days when the support for an accountant consisted of some pencils and green pads; adequate support now includes the accountant workstation and software.

Examples of the knowledge work support software that should be included in the accountant's professional tool kit are the following:

Spreadsheet processor for spreadsheets and simple analytical modeling.

Statistical software for performing statistical analyses.

Graphics software for presentation graphics.

Modeling software for more complex modeling.

Electronic mail for internal and external communications.

Data base management systems for supporting special accounting files and for accessing organizational files.

Software to access and use external data bases and data banks for comparative analysis.

Software to support audit working papers, sampling, etc.

INFORMATION LITERACY FOR ACCOUNTANTS

What accountants should know about computers and information systems is usually described in terms of topics. Instead of a topics approach, seven roles or activities are described which an accountant should be able to perform, both because of university education and because of continuing professional skill maintenance. The roles define the topics to be studied and maintained.

1. *User* role as a supplier of data or recipient of outputs from predefined applications. This is the simplest role, but to perform it effectively, there needs to be an introductory understanding of processing systems.

2. *User-developer* role in which the accountant formulates retrievals, develops information processing routines, and writes processing commands using end-user facilities. These are small applications for which the accountant takes full responsibility.

3. *Large application development participant* role in which the accountant is an active member of a project team. In this role, the accountant is involved in the development life cycle, management of the project, and political and social dimensions of specifications and implementation.

4. *Information requirements specifier* role in which the accountant specifies information requirements to be implemented in either small end-user developed applications or in large applications. The requirements include direct inputs and outputs, plus controls, audit trail requirements, and security needs.

5. *Data base designer and user* role in which the accountant builds and uses accounting area data bases or aids in defining, building, and using large corporate data bases. The ability to access and use data bases encompasses both internal data bases and external data banks.

6. *Data and information evaluator* role in which the accountant evaluates for a given use the quality and appropriateness of data available from data bases or provided by applications.

7. *Information systems controls and audit* role in which the accountant as auditor evaluates data processing system controls and collects evidence for evaluation. These activities include using the computer where appropriate.

These roles or activities provide the rationale for topics to include in the professional education of all accountants and for the design of a program of continuing education to maintain and enhance ability to perform them and to keep abreast of new developments affecting the roles.

SUMMARY

Accounting has an unusual relationship to information systems. Although the domain of accounting is information, it is frequently differentiated from information systems by technology, methodology, and specialization. But the field of accounting, both professionally and academically, has a continuing interest in and affinity with information systems. This close tie occurs because the information processing systems provide the raw material for accounting analysis; computer-based systems provide sources of data not otherwise available; accountants are direct users of information processing technology for retrieval and analysis; and auditing of an organization requires an understanding of the processing systems.

To the question of how much every accountant should know about computers and information systems, three "literacies" were specified: computer literacy, skill in using an accountant's knowledge work tool kit, and information literacy. The focus is on the latter two.

The professional tool kit consists of a computer workstation to support accounting work. The computer and communications capabilities, when combined with appropriate software, improve productivity and enhance capabilities of accountants.

Information literacy for accountants (which has more breadth and depth than literacy for other functions) is defined in terms of seven roles that accountants perform. These are a user of predefined applications, user-developer of small end-user applications, participant in large application development projects, specifier of requirements (including controls, auditability, and security), data base designer and user, evaluator of data and information, and auditor. The roles provide the basis for topics to be included in both basic and continuing professional education.

Reading 1–2

THE CORPORATE FINANCIAL PLANNING WORKSTATION AND SOFTWARE TOOLS

By L. Murphy Smith and James A. Sena

Financial planning is a critical part of a corporation's overall strategy. Corporate survival requires all functions of a company to coordinate their financial operations and planning. Corporate planning is an analytical process whereby the corporation makes an assessment of its future in terms of financial and other resource requirements. This article will discuss the planning philosophy, the computing environment, and the necessary software tools.

Reprinted from *Journal of Accounting and EDP* (New York: Auerbach Publishers). © 1989 Warren, Gorham, and Lamont. Used with permission.

PLANNING PHILOSOPHY

Corporate planning tasks require that a company possess the capabilities to accomplish the key levels of planning:

- Strategic planning.
- Functional planning.
- Organizational planning.
- Systems planning.

Each of the planning levels is directly related to corporate financial planning.

The development of a corporate planning system can be approached by either a top-down or bottom-up process or a combination. Top-down is also called decision analysis; bottom-up is called data analysis. The top-down approach begins at the top level of management. This approach starts with clearly establishing objectives and policies. The bottom-up approach begins at the bottom, or operational, level where the transaction systems are located. For either approach, there are three distinct methodological options used by a typical corporation in the planning process. Each option addresses one of the following questions:

1. What if?
2. What to achieve?
3. What is best?

The question most emphasized by management will determine the planning methodology and lead to the modeling structure that will provide the foundation for the corporate planning process.

What If?

The what-if option has become a common term among U.S. businesses, as evidenced by Hewlett-Packard's media blitz and the popularity of Lotus software. This option examines the effect of alternative assumptions about a firm's external environment. What-if analysis is also called sensitivity analysis because it measures the sensitivity of certain objectives (e.g., net income) to changes in other variables (e.g., an increase in sales price).

There are a variety of software tools to perform this type of analysis, the most common being the spreadsheet. On a higher level, modeling languages, such as IFPS, are decision support system generators that provide the ability to construct models to test a wider range of decision analysis.

What to Achieve?

Under the what-to-achieve question, frequently called goal setting, the planning methodology calls for specifications of numerical targets such as return on investment, market share, and sales growth. The question becomes "What strategies will yield the desired results?"

This approach is system analytical. The strategy options are represented as a set of equations that are solved in terms of a given target variable. In 1-2-3 and other spreadsheets, this process is tedious; IFPS, on the other hand, has a built-in goal seek facility. The financial planning workstation can be connected to the corporate mainframe and serve as a terminal (e.g., IBM 3270 mode). Connection to the mainframe allows the use of software like Application System, which can be used for model construction—sensitivity analysis, goal setting, interfaces to data base systems (e.g., Structure Query Language and DB2), report generation, graphics, and project management.

What Is Best?

This question represents the optimization or management science approach to corporate planning. Planning models are formulated to provide management with a set of strategies approaching optimality. Return on investment, cash flow, or profitability measures are examples of areas where optimization techniques are being applied. From a corporate planning perspective, the optimization option is the most difficult to implement. This option is appropriately suited for well-defined operational planning (e.g., production scheduling for a major oil refinery). The financial planning aspect is not as easily reduced to such models.

IFPS has a software extension called Optimum that handles linear and nonlinear programming. There are a number of software products available on the microcomputer that can handle these types of problems (e.g., Borland's Eureka and TK Solver). The main problem is placing the models into the required form.

STRATEGIC PLANNING

By using a computer, the planning staff can improve the productivity and effectiveness of the planning process by providing capabilities for:

- Strategic issues development.
- Critical success factor application.
- What-if evaluations.
- Risk assessment.
- Strategic implementation.

Computer software products could facilitate the planner's definition and determination of the final impact of external threats and internal concerns.

BUSINESS FUNCTION PLANNING

The financial planning function ranges from strategic planning to business planning. The computer can assist in the planning process by providing new ways to describe, analyze, and forecast:

- Current and future business unit missions and functional strategies.
- Critical management functions required for satisfaction of strategic issues and critical success factors.
- Organizational accountability.
- Actions with quantifiable results.

With the computer tools and a planning workstation the planner can rank key issues and responsibilities for business units in order of their importance. By analyzing the relationships, he or she can focus on the critical areas for improving key management functions: managerial effectiveness, policy administration, resource management, organizational accountability, and management productivity.

ORGANIZATIONAL PLANNING

As the planning staff focuses on organizational effectiveness, computer tools can improve productivity by providing capabilities to:

- Plan improvements for the current and future periods.
- Develop organizational structures that support and further the functional and strategic objectives.
- Plan responsibilities for specific positions and establish accountability.
- Ensure that critical success factors are adequately addressed.

By using the modeling features provided by the software tools, the planning staff can integrate the modeling and relational analysis to tie these structures together.

SYSTEMS PLANNING

As decision support, expert systems, and financial modeling efforts are devised, the computer can assist the planning staff in ensuring that the systems are properly developed. Competitive systems can be developed to:

- Identify the information needed to support the firm's high-leverage opportunities.
- Plan future system architectures.
- Ensure that the needed information is directed and supported by the appropriate functional area.

- Plan the technology for the organization's information processing, communication, and office automation needs.
- Export the top-level system requirements to a system design tool.

Once the planning staff has identified the organization's priorities and established their relationships to various systems, the computer can be used in evaluating the system development priorities. In this way, an effective information resource management strategy can be implemented to show what information is needed and the person responsible for compiling it.

SPECIFICATION OF GOALS AND OBJECTIVES

In many cases, a corporate planning model is built without determining the corporation's primary objectives. This, however, is not the best approach. The model needs to respond to specified well-defined financial planning problems. Here are some considerations to be addressed in the model design:

- What types of decisions are to be made based on information from the planning model?
- What are the financial stakes involved?
- Are large dollar investments to be evaluated by the model?
- How important is forecasting precision?
- What are the possible risks and consequences associated with inaccurate forecasts generated by planning models?
- What will be the use of computer-based planning models?
- Is the information derived from the model of sufficient value to justify the cost of acquisition and model development?

THE CORPORATE PLANNING COMPUTING ENVIRONMENT

The primary managerial task of senior managers is to develop and maintain the corporate financial plan. To support the corporate plan, senior management needs an information system. A study on executive information systems recommends the development of computerized, interactive systems that:

- Provide a time-series oriented data storage facility—For example, the executive could examine the progress of a promising R&D project from inception through field test.
- Facilitate the ability to accommodate external as well as internal data sources coming from manual or automated systems, simplifying the collection and use of personal, external, and corporate data bases in a uniform manner.

- Are interactive—These systems would provide decision makers with features that allow posing and reposing of crucial questions, communicating directly with data, and evaluating alternatives.

- Provide flexibility of analysis to accommodate spontaneity as well as scheduled, prescribed analysis—A variety of software tools should be used to extract data from corporate data bases, external information, and working data. The data could be analyzed by spreadsheets, modeling languages, analytical data bases, and statistical and econometric techniques.

- Adapt to a changing environment through an accommodating system environment and thus provide a modular approach with the ability to customize on request—Such a system would allow the manager to construct a support environment to respond to new demands in decision situations.

THE FINANCIAL PLANNING WORKSTATION

The corporate financial planning environment can be served by a computerized workstation. Staff members would be responsible for information entry, retrieval, analysis, and reporting.

Exhibit 1 describes typical computer hardware requirements. For data entry and inquiry, there is the keyboard containing function keys and some pointing device or stylus, such as a joystick, mouse, or digitizer pad. A color display with high-resolution graphics is desirable, especially when operated by senior management. Storage systems for extracted data are necessary to accommodate internal and external data requirements. A hard disk, permitting faster access, reliability, and more permanent files, is recommended along with diskette drives for temporary or transient files.

Communication with the corporate mainframe or minicomputer is desirable for accessing data and management information systems and for saving archive data from the hard disk drive. However, the storage on the corporate system needs to be protected from unauthorized user access. This is accomplished by proper security definition in the data base definition. In addition, interfaces to a local area network are becoming the norm for electronic mail and data transfer between staff members. External communication facilities are necessary to acquire needed data from on-line and dialed sources, as well as facsimile transmission. There is also a need to have CD ROM storage to access financial data base information from an archive. An optical reader that accepts and digitizes printed documents is also desirable.

Software and an operating system are needed to accompany the hardware. The use and design of software may require the services of a software development specialist. The following data and software facilities need to be established to support corporate financial planning:

EXHIBIT 1
Computer Hardware Requirements

Entry Devices

Keyboard
Joystick, mouse, or touchpad

Display Device

A color monitor with high-resolution graphics, such as EGA or VGA

Storage Devices

A hard disk of at least 40M to 50M bytes
Two diskette drives
Exclusive and protected space on the central computing facility

External Communication Devices and Media

Hard-wired connection to the central computing facility and participation in
    a local area network
An external data line (modem) to external data sources

Output Devices

A dot matrix printer
A letter-quality printer
A graphics, laser, or ink-jet printer

Processor

286 or 386 with extended memory (up to 6 million characters)—Necessary to
    run presentation graphics and certain mainframe equivalent products
    (e.g., PC/application system)

Facsimile Transmission

An Optical Scanner or Reading Device

A CD-ROM Storage Unit

- External environment data bases.
- Internal data bases and management information systems.
- A personal data base.
- A set of tools to utilize the workstation.

This software and data configuration is presented in Exhibit 2.

EXHIBIT 2   Software and Data Configuration

```
┌─────────────────┐                    ┌─────────────────────┐
│ External        │                    │ Internal corporate  │
│ data base       │                    │ data bases          │
└─────────────────┘                    └─────────────────────┘
              ╲                        ╱
               ╲                      ╱
┌─────────────────┐   ┌─────────────┐   ┌─────────────────────┐
│ Personal        │───│ Computer    │───│ Internal management │
│ data base       │   │ workstation │   │ information systems │
└─────────────────┘   └─────────────┘   └─────────────────────┘
```

Tools	
Personal computing	Managerial processing and analysis

Memo writer   Spreadsheet
 	
Calculator   Data base
     (microcomputer
Calendar   management)
 	
Appointments   Data communications
dialer
    Expert systems
Word processing
	Electronic mail Modeling language
	or messages
	     Decision support
	Data base (mainframe)
	access facility: Statistical and
	• File and record management
	  transfer science
	• Query or browse
	• Report generator Image processing

External Environment Data Bases

To maintain the corporate plan in a changing environment involves an ongoing review of external indicators. Arrangements can be made to periodically transmit data on selected areas of interest to the financial planning staff. Many personal computers can be activated by an external computer system permitting this transfer of data.

In external information acquisition, selectivity and filtering are of more concern than information availability. There is a need to translate data received in an electronic form to a readable and usable medium. Newspapers and summary reports are routinely provided electronically. For example, real-time stock quotations and trade information (*Broker's Notebook*), financial time-series data (*Data Resources' Financial Time Series Data*), and Dow-Jones news and retrieval (*Dow Jones Spreadsheet Link*) are obtained through automatic link systems from the PC to commercial communication services.

To work with the acquired data, the information has to be placed into an accessible form. As part of the software development process, the corporate financial planners will define the necessary external monitoring and search behavior. The description could take on the form of data definitions entered into a data dictionary system for entry to a data base manager software package. Once the procedure for electronic acquisition has been established, a process for transferring selected data on a periodic or as-needed basis to the external data base can be established.

Internal Data Bases and MIS Systems

The typical management information system (MIS) is formed along such functional lines as finance, marketing, production, or human resources. Information in these various MIS systems needs to to be accessible in summary form for maintenance of the corporate plan. This process of information acquisition and reporting is frequently called the corporate information system (CIS).

There are circumstances when the financial planning staff requires access to other operational and specific MIS data. In these cases, an executive information system (EIS) may be employed. An EIS permits the manager access to timely and critical mainframe data, using a microcomputer. More importantly, an EIS compresses mainframe data, allowing the executive to review information in graphic form and make decisions based on the trends and relationships revealed.

Query report generator facilities on the corporate computer system may also be used to readily obtain pertinent operational and MIS data. In this case, the workstation serves as a terminal for data transfer by downloading from the mainframe to the micro. The corporate information system contains data that has been formally defined and is operational in a data base management system framework. This data and information obtained through selective access can be retrieved and stored in a financial planning data base.

Personal Data Base

As the financial planning staff uses the workstation, the need to build and store models, memos, ideas, and personnel records will arise. A corporate decision memory bank will be needed. Functions that have been performed manually may be computerized. There are desk management software packages available for this process, such as Sidekick. However, these packages are only accessories and would not be capable of meeting detailed data combination requirements.

The staff may use an integrated package such as Framework or Symphony to assist in the combination process. These software packages incorporate word processing, spreadsheet, data base, and communications capabilities into an integrated set. Data from the external or internal data bases can be exported or imported into these systems. The staff member could then manipulate and analyze the data according to the financial planner's needs. These systems have tended not to be used extensively. Instead, more powerful stand-alone software programs such as dBASE IV and Lotus 1-2-3, with add-on packages facilitating interfaces and communications, have been developed and are more widely used.

To be compatible with the superstructure of data base definitions, a selection of frequently used data elements from the personal data base should be defined. The elements would be part of the financial planning workstation's data structure. Using either an integrated package or a fourth-generation language product such as Focus, queries, reports, and graphs can be produced. An SQL or DB2 base is desirable since SQL now appears to be the emerging standard for user interfaces. A data base management package with an SQL component, such as Oracle or dBASE IV, could be used on the workstation, and a similar system like SQL or DB2 could be used on the mainframe.

Workstation Software Tools

There are two levels of software tools needed to support the financial planning process. These are shown in Exhibit 2. The first level is the personal software tools. The other level addresses support tools for managerial processing and analysis. These second-level tools were only available on mainframe and specialty time-sharing services but are now also available on the PC. Advanced technologies such as the ability to combine data and video images from video recording are also included.

PERSONAL SOFTWARE TOOLS

The first level of personal software tools consists of:

- Word processing and memo writing.
- Spreadsheet and business graphics.
- The data base manager.
- Communications.
- Decision support and expert systems.

These tools are used by most employees and are not exclusive to the realm of senior management. Properly organized, they assist the corporate staff in day-to-day activities and less rigorous analysis.

Word Processing and Memo Writing

With office automation, many support functions have been assumed by the information management function. Publishing based on the use of laser printers as well as local letter-quality printers and graphics is available to corporate system users. Through the workstation, corporate planners can access this equipment.

For this local use of the workstation as a stand-alone system, there are a number of word processing packages available. For many mainframe users and those accustomed to stand-alone word processors, the Display Writer series of word processing packages can also be used on the microcomputer. Those users who initially used word processing on the microcomputer are more familiar with first-generation packages, such as Wordstar. Today, depending on their specific needs, such as letter writing and manuscript production, there are many packages available. The most popular is Word Perfect. Other systems, such as Lotus Manuscript, provide an interface with spreadsheet or data base packages.

For planning purposes, the ability to record ideas in note fashion is an important feature of the workstation. Sidekick Plus and other desktop organizers provide a quick way to record notes and attach or clip them to spreadsheets, data bases, or letters. Other features of the desktop organizer provide phone directories, automatic dialing, calculator functions, appointment calendars, and communication capabilities.

The financial planning staff needs to maintain a record of documented development and staff communications. It is important that staff members standardize on a selected set of software. A standardized system of recording and naming the documents should be established to facilitate retrieval and document access.

Spreadsheet and Business Graphics

Spreadsheets are the basic workhorse of financial executives. The basic analysis and data construction begins at this level. There are a number of spreadsheet packages that function on a microcomputer system. The most widely used are Lotus 1-2-3 and SuperCalc 4.

For the mainframe, Lotus has announced a Version G that has all of the microcomputer capabilities as well as enhanced features to access the corporate data bases. There are also a number of mainframe spreadsheet packages (e.g., Boeing Calc) that provide two- and three-dimensional features and a number of specialized macros or functions.

Alternatives to the tabular spreadsheet are packages such as Reflex that provide different views of the data—form, list, graph, or cross-tabular computations. Packages that are directly tied to financial analysis, such as Javelin, provide for time-series, periodic, and specialized financial functions as well as modeling features that approximate the capabilities of the decision support or modeling language generators, IFPS and Model.

There are many types of financial planning packages. They range from simple spreadsheet products to intricate decision-support systems that include connections to mainframe data bases.

At the low end of the spectrum, financial planning packages are generally less expensive and easier to use than first-rate spreadsheets. In addition, they are often customized for specific jobs. Managers or other staff members may find them useful for tasks such as budgeting projections.

In most cases, spreadsheet packages (e.g., Lotus or SuperCalc) are customized for one or more tasks. These custom spreadsheets, which require little computer expertise to use, are sometimes referred to as templates. Templates are dataless spreadsheets that contain the calculation formulas for a particular job. A typical template might determine whether equipment should be leased or purchased. The user would simply supply the loan and equipment costs. All of the calculations and formulas would be provided by the program.

The presentation of computations and financial data in graphical form is important. For a financial planning workstation, the spreadsheet and graphics software must be of a high quality to meet the needs of sophisticated corporate users. The major spreadsheet vendors offer graphical display facilities with their package (e.g., PrintGraph on 1-2-3). These facilities are satisfactory for basic data presentation but not for detailed graphic display at the corporate level. Lotus Freelance is one of several add-on packages with professional graphics capabilities. There are also presentation graphics programs, such as Harvard Presentation Graphics, that can accept data from a variety of sources (e.g., Lotus or dBASE III).

Many software companies offer integrated packages that include word processing, spreadsheet, graphics, data base, and communication capabilities. Virtually all of these integrated packages' individual modules are inferior to the stand-alone products. However, there are some exceptions. Symphony features Lotus 1-2-3 as a spreadsheet; Framework has a strong data base manager similar to dBASE III.

Data Base Managers

For the storage of personal data and information extracted from external and corporate data bases that have been manipulated for reporting and analysis purposes, data base managers expressly developed for the microcomputer can be used. These data managers do not yet have the power and capabilities of their counterparts on the mainframe—the data base management system.

Microcomputer data base managers or file managers can be divided into two categories: flat file managers and relational managers. Flat file managers, or simply file managers, can manipulate only one file at a time. They organize data into simple two-dimensional tables that resemble spreadsheets. They can be thought of as electronic index cards. Many of the memo managers and information retrieval systems use this type of file manager. Of special interest to financial executives are such packages as Simantek's Q&A, which provides a natural language interface, allowing the planner to create or style a tailored retrieval of information stored in working files. Other variations are forms-driven systems, such as Ability and First Choice, that specify the data content by painting a screen to resemble a communication form or analysis worksheet.

The relational managers allow the user to manipulate or work with more than one file. These data base managers more closely resemble their counterparts on the mainframe. In most cases, they are still single-user systems, do not provide for data integrity and security, and do not have the elaborate data dictionary (logical view alternatives) provided by mainframe DBMSs. For the microcomputer, the most widely used data base manager is Ashton-Tate's dBASE III. This system has set the standard for most microcomputer data base managers and data base compilers.

Using a data base manager, the planning staff can create and maintain data bases, generate reports, query and browse selected records using direct commands, or employ a series of help screens. There are procedural programming features that allow the user to perform more detailed analysis, reporting, and data manipulation.

The trend in the development of data base managers is SQL compatibility. Ashton-Tate released dBASE IV in the fall of 1988. One of the main features was an SQL interface. Oracle, a minicomputer relational DBMS, also available on the microcomputer, features an SQL interface. Focus, a fourth-generation language designed to interface with various DBMSs operating on a mainframe (e.g., IBM's IMS), has a microcomputer product, PC/Focus, that allows the user to interface with the mainframe data base in a manner similar to the mainframe product.

The user could also run IBM's Application System (AS). AS has data base management, modeling, graphics, and project management features. It can directly interface with SQL to access data stored on corporate data bases.

Communications Software

Microcomputer-based telecommunications is a rapidly growing field. The technology involves the combination of a microcomputer, modem, software, and a telephone line to connect the equipment to external data bases. Internally, communication between microcomputers, minicomputers, and mainframes is accomplished by direct connections to other computers or communication devices or by participation in one or more local area networks. The microcomputer, when functioning in this mode, serves as a terminal for a mainframe or participates in a network in which a communication manager accepts and sends signals between devices.

For external communications, there are a number of programs available (e.g., Crosstalk). These programs offer a variety of features, such as automatic communications-parameter adjustments, unattended operation, automatic callback, and data encryption.

When the financial planning workstation is used to communicate between the microcomputer and other computer systems, especially a mainframe, data translations must be handled. The primary mode of operation is IBM's 3270 terminal emulation. A circuit board can be placed in the microcomputer that allows communication of this nature. Alternatively, software (e.g., Kermit) could be used to perform the function of the board.

For communications between the microcomputer and other systems, some connection method must be established. The ability to download and upload files is also important. The advent of the electronic office dictates that messages, scheduling, conferencing, and transmissions have these connections.

Decision Support and Expert Systems

An expert system is a computer program that manipulates knowledge to solve problems within a narrow problem domain, such as financial statement analysis. For the planner, expert systems would take on the guise of consultative or quasi-decision support systems because the scope of work at the executive level is usually unstructured and is not directly tenable to an expert system application.

Expert systems are available that are already programmed to solve specific problems. Also available are general-purpose expert systems, called expert system shells, which can be programmed by a user to solve a specific problem. Financial planners can use stand-alone expert shells (e.g., M–1 from Tecknowledge), application development systems (e.g., Guru from Micro Data Base Systems), and mainframe system development (e.g., Expert System Environment from IBM).

A general-purpose shell, like M–1, is intended for end-user developers. Development of expert system applications is similar to development of spreadsheet applications in 1-2-3. The staff can use these shells to quickly and easily develop an expert system to solve specific problems.

Use of a microcomputer expert system development package is similar to the integrated packages (e.g., Framework). Guru incorporates a spreadsheet, relational data base, graphics, report writing, text processing, procedural programming, remote communications, and an expert system shell. This particular system is very tightly integrated—allowing the developer to access all of the functions within the expert system shell.

The mainframe expert system shells allow users to interface with external programs and data. Expert System Environment was the first expert system development offered by IBM. One of its features is an SQL interface. For the financial planning workstation, a wide range of expert system development tools are available. If access to corporate data bases on a large scale is needed, then a product like Expert System Environment is recommended. For small projects with little data manipulation, the basic shell (e.g., M–1) is recommended. For the application requiring consolidation of a number of data bases, a package like Guru is an alternative.

MANAGERIAL DECISION SUPPORT SOFTWARE TOOLS

The second level of tools is software used in managerial processing and comprehensive analysis. The second-level tools include:

1. Modeling languages.
2. Statistical and management science products.
3. Fourth-generation languages supporting data base systems.
4. Decision support and expert systems.
5. Image processing systems.

Modeling Languages

Modeling languages are planning and modeling software tools used to develop decision support systems. These systems are a bridge between the procedural languages (e.g., COBOL) and the nonprocedural (e.g., fourth-generation languages). On many occasions, these modeling languages serve as the basis for planning packages sold by vendors.

A modeling language, such as Execucom's IFPS, provides features for model definition, what-if analysis, goal-seeking analysis, statistical analysis, graphic analysis, and report preparation. Modeling software packages are available for either the microcomputer or the mainframe. The planning workstation can use either type, depending on the size of the model, amount of data to be manipulated, and the extent of data acquisitions required. For the mainframe, there are more than 60 model languages (DSS generator software packages) available. Many of these vendors offer similar packages on the microcomputer.

Usually the microcomputer versions do not offer all of the features found in their mainframe counterparts. For example, IFPS does not provide the statistical and probabilistic features (e.g., Monte Carlo simulation) in the microcomputer version. The advantages of the microcomputer version, especially in the case of the IFPS, is ease-of-use and the ability to create a simple, quick model that can be manipulated in ways not available in spreadsheet analysis.

Statistical and Management Science Products

The modeling, statistical, and management science products provide powerful analysis tools. Many products have both statistical and management science capabilities embedded in their makeup (e.g., Guru has a statistical analysis feature for analysis of data bases or spreadsheets that can be used in conjunction with the expert system analysis).

Using communication facilities, the planning workstation could access these products. Alternatively, many of the mainframe software packages now have microcomputer versions. Statistical packages are available for descriptive, inferential, parametric, and nonparametric statistical analysis. The most widely used systems are SAS and SPSS. Both of these packages offer microcomputer versions. SAS also provides a wide range of add-on components, including interfaces to SQL and Lotus.

There are several hundred management science packages available for models ranging from inventory control to project management. Many of the packages have interfaces to 1-2-3 and dBASE III and IV. Some of the modeling language DDS generators have optimization and simulation capabilities (e.g., IFPS/Optimum).

There are also several software packages that are decision aids. These packages can be incorporated into models or spreadsheets or can be used to supplement them by providing input data or by massaging the output data from a model or spreadsheet. For example, Lightyear enables the user to weigh different factors in a decision-making process and present the information graphically.

Fourth-Generation Languages

Nonprocedural or fourth-generation language products facilitate accessing and using consolidated data bases through a composite data dictionary. Data from external, corporate, MIS, personal, and derived sources can be combined into a composite system.

There are a number of fourth-generation languages available. Many of these languages offer similar products on the microcomputer. For example, Focus offers a cut-down version, PC/Focus, for the microcomputer. Information Builders, the developer of Focus, encourages users to use both products. Data bases can be established and fine-tuned on the microcomputer and then uploaded to the mainframe for shared use.

Decision Support and Expert Systems

Decision support and expert systems can be applied to certain problem-solving or opportunity-enhancing situations. Decision support systems use extracted data by formulating models. The user can consider various alternatives in a what-if mode. Expert systems are not being widely used in business at the strategic level. As their use increases, however, certain applications will be established to support the executive in a consultative rather than expert decision-making mode.

Image Processing

An image processing system includes microfilm and record retrieval as well as image and video storage and retrieval. Apple has developed several applications for its SE series that combine video and computer displays on a common screen. This image processing capability could be useful in presentations and report preparation.

CONCLUSION

The first-level tools focus on local or immediate tasks. The second-level tools allow the user to address external, corporate, MIS, and personal data bases. They also provide the staff with in-depth analysis capabilities on a comprehensive corporate scale.

Many organizations have information centers, end-user assistance personnel, or information services specialists who have the knowledge of the software tools, the computer hardware capabilities, and the ability to create the workstation. Software products also exist that help this effort.

However, the most important ingredient is the executive and his or her staff, who are willing to participate in the development and operation of the financial planning workstation.

Reading 1–3

THE CPA IN THE INFORMATION AGE: TODAY AND TOMORROW

By Robert S. Roussey

Traditional. Conservative. Slow to change. These labels may have characterized the CPA of yesteryear, but they don't today. The accounting profession is undergoing a dynamic evolution of change.

The rise of technology is, of course, only one of many factors altering the profession, but it will continue to have a significant impact on how CPAs do business in the future. Technological innovations will be available that far surpass any thing now used in performing the traditional and newer services. These innovations will encompass the electronic review, filing, storage, retrieval and telecommunication of data; the linking of practice systems to entitywide accounting and office automation systems; and the development of the electronic audit, tax, and consulting systems of the future.

MANAGING CHANGE: PLANNING AND IMPLEMENTATION

The present-day microcomputer and related technologies will evolve over the next several years to become even more useful—and at lower costs. Besides developing the necessary skills, however, CPAs must also develop plans to grow with the technology. No organization can afford to keep changing to new products because those in charge didn't plan for innovation.

Probably the most important aspect of technological innovation is psychological—becoming comfortable with it. CPAs must get acquainted with technology by reading about and studying specific areas and applications of interest; talking about it with others; analyzing how it can be used in CPA firms and industry. But most of all the profession must continue implementing the new technology. The faster this is done, the faster new accounting and auditing concepts can be developed—and the faster CPAs can develop significant new service opportunities using innovative methods and practices.

A SNAPSHOT OF THE FUTURE

Figure 1 illustrates how the auditor may use technology in the not-too-distant future. To get the day going, the auditor uses digital voice exchange technology, then quickly moves to the firm's executive support system, which allows, among other things, access to electronic mail, shared data bases of information, data base research, the office systems, and the practice systems for review of engagement data. The auditor feels comfortable using this technology. But it not only "feels right"—it also gives the auditor access to information technology not possible otherwise.

Is this scenario farfetched? Is it something out of science fiction? Not by a long shot. Virtually all the technology described is available today, although in some cases it needs to be fitted into integrated systems. But this isn't an insurmountable problem, for technology is evolving at a dizzying pace. To illustrate the point: The stand-alone microcomputer environment of today, when compared with the integrated systems technology of the future, may appear like the Wright brothers' first biplane when compared with today's Earth-orbiting satellites. The increase in the processing speed of computer microprocessors, greater memory and data storage, faster telecommunication speed—all point to more cost effective and easier-to-use systems of the future.

FOR SMALL FIRMS AND SOLE PRACTITIONERS, TOO

One wonderful advantage of this technology is that it can be used cost-effectively by sole practitioners and smaller firms, as well as by the national and international firms. The individual tax practitioner, for example, can use low-cost microcomputers and data bases to maintain client data and tax due

FIGURE 1   Auditing in the Electronic Age: A Look at Tomorrow

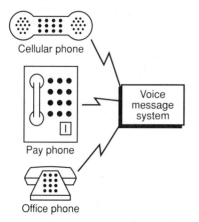

Cellular phone

Pay phone

Office phone

While driving to work the auditor calls the office voice messaging network, listens to various messages and responds to them—all with the push buttons of a cellular car phone. Similarly, the system may be accessed from a pay phone or from the office phone.

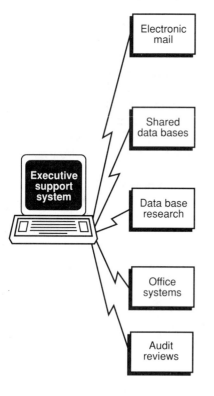

In the office the auditor uses the firm's executive support system to

• **Access electronic mail (letters and memorandums sent and stored in electronic form).** The current day's mail is read and answered by the auditor on the system; some is answered directly; for others a hard copy is printed for later dictation. Certain electronic mail is saved for later search and retrieval.

• **Access shared data bases (information stored in data base files).** In connection with a new client proposal, the auditor accesses the client information data base to determine how many clients the firm has in a certain industry and stratifies them according to size.

• **Perform data base research (information on external or internal research data bases).** A client calls with a complex question on leveraged leasing; while on the phone, the auditor researches the firm's interpretation of leases on the internal research data base and finds the answer.

• **Access the office accounting system.** The auditor has just cleared a billing with a client, so the client job information data base is accessed on the firm's microcomputer system and the billing is prepared.

• **Perform an audit review.** A staff person, 200 miles from the office, calls to advise the auditor that a forecast schedule is ready for review. The schedule is teleprocessed to the auditor's computer, where it is reviewed on the screen. Then the "follow-up points" are typed and transmitted to the staff person's micro.

Note: The thunderbolt symbol signifies either a direct or telecommunication link, depending on the circumstances.

dates, special software to prepare tax returns, and a laser printer to print out the actual tax forms, together with the tax return data. The smaller firm will use similar technology but might use it in a network environment in which several professionals have their microcomputers linked so as to share the data base, tax preparation software, and laser printer resources. The larger firms will also use this technology, plus more of what has been described and more of what is discussed later.

WHERE WE ARE TODAY AND WHERE WE'RE HEADING

What are some of the innovations available now? They range from the simple use of voice messaging to the sophisticated use of expert systems. They include low-cost items that can be easily implemented as well as high-cost options that require careful planning and substantial resources—financial as well as human resources.

"Capital-intensive" is a phrase much in use nowadays, and we CPAs are moving from a people-intensive business to a capital-intensive one. Just as the large corporations used computerization to grow to mammoth sizes in the 1970s, CPAs will use technology to change and improve the delivery of services. We will still require highly qualified, skilled personnel, but we will need new capital and greater capital recovery in our fees to move into this world of technology. Let's turn now to some of these innovations and explore how the profession might use them.

Voice Messaging.   Voice messaging, or digital voice exchange (DVX), is a fast, efficient way to exchange thoughts, ideas, and instructions in a personal manner. Proper use can eliminate a good deal of the "telephone tag game." With this technology, a computer that runs a voice exchange system is linked to the telephone system. The voice system provides many options to users: Access can be from office telephones and from outside, so messages can be left and accessed from virtually any push-button telephone. Users have message boxes available to callers. The computer stores a message for later retrieval or transfer to another in the system in such a manner that, when later retrieved, the playback is in the natural voice of the caller.

Use of voice exchange is instant; there is no delay for typing messages or mail delivery. Messages are clear and not left to the interpretation (or misinterpretation) of others. Messages can be left for associates, and clients can leave messages for practitioners. But most important, DVX is easy to learn and use because it involves technology that is familiar to all of us—the unthreatening telephone.

Personal Computing.   Undoubtedly the technological change having the greatest current impact on the accountant and auditor is the ability to do personal computing with the microcomputer. This phenomenal hardware device, in combination with software programs developed for it, has enabled the profession to enter a new world: In hours the CPA can develop break-even analyses, cash-flow projections, budgets and merger analyses, all of which used to take days or weeks, using mainframe or time-sharing computers, if they were done at all. Professionals are already delivering more timely and cost-effective new services to clients.

We can do some of our own word processing (this article, for example, was written on a personal computer and transmitted to the American Institute of CPAs on a diskette for direct entry into the *Journal of Accountancy*'s word processing equipment). We can also set up electronic worksheets and develop data bases of key information available for management decision making and other purposes—all at the touch of a key.

As the accountant and auditor master the skills of personal computing, the use of other technologies comes to be seen as a necessity rather than as something that's nice to have around. And these other technologies won't seem so formidable or imposing: Skilled professionals will be able to set up systems to access these technologies in ways that are easy, user friendly, and fast.

Data Bases.   It wasn't too many years ago that the profession had only the NAARS system as its key accounting and auditing research data base. And it was available only through a special terminal. Now, with the use of the microcomputer and low-cost telecommunication equipment (modems) and software, many more data bases of financial and research information, including the NAARS system, are available efficiently and at low cost.

In addition, internal data bases of information and statistics are being developed and used. And some firms are putting their own accounting, auditing, and other policy reference materials on external "private" or internal data bases so that research is done in an electronic environment.

The development of the new optical-disk memory system technology promises to revolutionize the use of data bases. These small, laser-read disks can hold an enormous amount of data (the equivalent of up to 1,500 floppy disks), which can be retrieved at blinding speeds. A firm will be able to put all of its policy and procedure manuals, microcomputer programs, and other data on one optical disk, with much room left over, for access by its staff using microcomputers.

Decision Support Systems.   Decision support systems can be characterized as an organized way to accumulate, process and present information to a user, who then has the information available to make informed decisions. Such systems have been in use for a number of years, but the recent development of the so-called knowledge software (special program generators) should expand their capabilities dramatically over the next several years.

Decision support systems can be programmed, using programming languages, data base systems, electronic worksheets, and the new third-party knowledge software. For example, simple staffing systems can provide information on a timely basis for making decisions on staff use. Or more elaborate systems can analyze information or financial trends, provide reasons or explanations for variances or trends and even suggest recommended courses of action or suggested procedures.

The CPA doesn't, of course, have to follow the recommendations or suggestions of such a system, but the output can quickly provide valuable information that should at least be considered in making decisions. Decision support systems are usually developed because the professional, skilled in microcomputer technology, recognizes the potential, sees the opportunities and has enough knowledge to develop or direct the development of such systems.

Office Automation.   Much ballyhooed in the early 1980s, office automation is starting to come of age. Without going into the arguments about its present or future status, it can be said that office automation is an important force to reckon with, and CPAs need to address its potential for their practices.

Office automation can include aspects of word processing, electronic mail, data base storage, and retrieval of letters and reports. Office automation can also include search capabilities on data bases, personal and group calendaring, laser printing of data and forms on blank paper, desktop printing of brochures through automatic "typesetting," and laser printing from word processing and graphics files, as well as access in executive support systems to accounting information and other documents on mainframe and minicomputer systems.

How many of these office automation features are used isn't important. What is important is that CPAs start preparing for the future by thinking about how to start using office automation to make the workplace more productive and how it can provide new and more efficiently produced services to clients.

Other Technologies.   There are, of course, many other developments that will substantially affect the accountant and auditor. One of them, expert systems, is described in the box on page 34. Some others, to name only a few, include multiuser and multitasking microcomputer systems, telecommunications, and networking of microcomputers. These technologies will be important in the firm office, in client offices, and in "remote" auditing. Although there are indeed more learning opportunities at this stage, their integration with some of the other technologies will be important in more efficient delivery of new services.

COSTS OF AVAILABLE TECHNOLOGY

As the capability and capacity of these new technologies have increased rapidly, costs have declined almost as rapidly.

The Challenge of Expert Systems

Probably one of the most interesting innovations but also one of the most difficult systems to develop is the so-called expert system, which stores the knowledge and reasoning of an expert. As information is put into the expert system, the system analyzes the data and presents to the user a suggested solution or answer to the problem at hand. These systems often are used to help in the performance of some task or duty by those who don't have the knowledge contained in the system.

Expert systems are already used in medical diagnoses and are starting to be used in accounting and auditing on a limited basis. CPA firms and academics are conducting ongoing, significant research, however, in this important area.

The practice potential for these systems is enormous, especially when technological advances make the expert systems programs more feasible to run in the microcomputer environment. The introduction of reduced instruction set computer (RISC) microcomputers has already started the transition of the more sophisticated expert system software from minicomputers to the new RISC microcomputers.

Low-cost, easy-to-use telecommunication modems, to transfer data between computers using the telephone system, have transitioned, for example, from 300 baud (bits per second) in the early 1980s to 1,200 and 2,400 baud today. And a quantum jump can occur if low-cost modems, with 4,800 and 9,600 speeds for the microcomputer, can be developed in the future.

The heart of the microcomputer, the microprocessor chip, has also seen dramatic changes since the early 1980s. The increase in processing speed and functionality of the microprocessor, together with dramatic increases in memory and data storage, have made the microcomputer a real powerhouse.

We are now at a low point in the cost curve for current technology. Investments in certain microcomputer technology can be made today—economically—with little fear that later enhancements for this technology will be available at significantly lower costs. This means that good, usable technology can be acquired, learned, and used today. There is no good reason to delay implementation.

The costs related to the use of current technology can be recovered in increased efficiency and, perhaps more important, in the performance of new services that wouldn't be practical without the technological innovations. A caveat, nevertheless, must be offered here: Even current technology shouldn't be acquired without planning, as the box on page 35 makes clear.

Strategic Planning for Technology

Strategic financial planning has been the rage these past several years. Now technology must be included in the planning and capital-budgeting process.

Years ago, either the EDP manager or someone with EDP expertise was the driving force in bringing computer technology into business organizations and into CPAs' practices. Today, management must be the driving force in setting the organizational plans on which technology to use and how it is to be implemented in the organization.

A long-range strategic plan for technology is a must. Management, whether a sole practitioner or the leadership group of a CPA firm, needs to look into the future to determine if it wants to use microcomputers, office automation, and other technology that is available today—and to consider how its use will likely evolve over the next several years.

Management needs to develop a plan for translating its vision of the future into a reality. If management doesn't set the agenda, rest assured that others in the organization will do it by bringing in technology piecemeal. When this happens, there is a high probability that the various pieces of technology won't fit together, communicate or be compatible with each other, or meet the future needs of the organization.

Research and study are the two first steps in developing a strategic plan for technology. And goals for standardization and evolution of the technology over a period of years are critical features of any strategy.

Once the long-range picture is put together, a short-range strategy can be devised and implemented. This can include encouraging personnel gradually to become familiar with microcomputer hardware and software, encouraging experimentation in the use of microcomputers and certain other technology, such as telecommunications for the performance of practice services, and providing proper and sufficient training. All of this can go on while further plans are made for the innovative use and future development of new practice systems and procedures.

TECHNOLOGY FOR DEVELOPING PRACTICE SYSTEMS

For all the increases in speed, power, and storage provided by today's technologies, they would be less than fully useful if they couldn't be combined as integrated systems. When talking about integrated systems, one needs to think about practice systems and how they can be linked to office automation and office accounting systems, client systems, and third-party systems. (A summary of the discussion below is treated graphically in Figure 2.)

How might these systems evolve? Let's look at practice systems first.

Practice Systems. A practice system is a system designed for a specific practice area to help the professional perform client services. An audit system

FIGURE 2 An Integrated Practice System of the Future

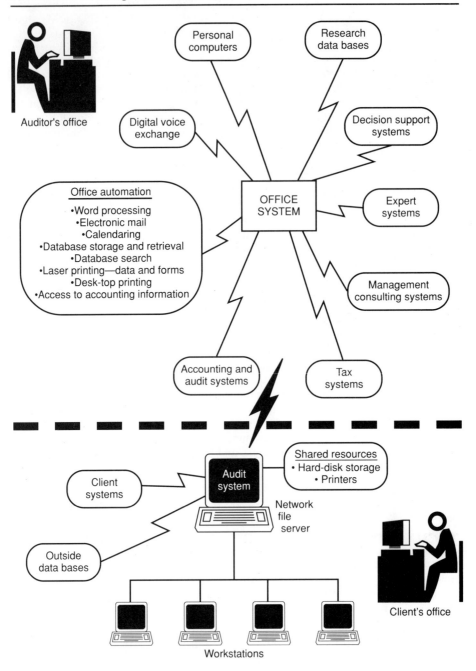

Auditor's office

Personal computers

Research data bases

Digital voice exchange

Decision support systems

OFFICE SYSTEM

Expert systems

Office automation
•Word processing
•Electronic mail
•Calendaring
•Database storage and retrieval
•Database search
•Laser printing—data and forms
•Desk-top printing
•Access to accounting information

Management consulting systems

Accounting and audit systems

Tax systems

Client systems

Audit system

Shared resources
• Hard-disk storage
• Printers

Network file server

Outside data bases

Client's office

Workstations

Note: The thunderbolt symbol signifies either a direct or telecommunication link, depending on the circumstances.

for the auditor or a tax system for the tax consultant are illustrations. These systems generally are a collection of software programs (applications) that work together in an integrated fashion. A number of firms have developed or are working on such systems and, to cite another example, the Internal Revenue Service is developing an automated examination system for use by its agents in tax audits and examinations. There is no doubt that this trend will accelerate.

The so-called practice systems will develop and evolve over a period of years in several stages. The initial stage will be the development of integrated systems using third-party vendor windowing programs; such programs allow the user to combine the programs of greatest interest and need. Developers will combine the separate functional programs of several discrete third-party programs under the control of the windowing environment into an integrated program designed for the specific needs of the practice system.

Also at this stage the developer will use the windowing program as a system control program and will start to write special applications. Here the developer is designing and programming systems to incorporate many special functions not included in the software programs combined under the windowing software. This special programming starts to set these systems off from the other types of integrated systems.

Probably the ultimate stage of practice system development will be when special programs are designed to act as operating environments, under which fully functioning practice application programs can be programmed.

Linking with Office Systems.   As practice systems are being developed, there must be planning to integrate these systems with the office systems. If the practitioner is planning or implementing office automation, management needs to determine how the two systems will interact. How will word processing documents created on the practice systems operate in the office systems? Will conversion be necessary? How will the data be transferred— by media (diskette or tape) or electronically? How will financial statements be transmitted back and forth? How will practice systems access electronic mail, data base and accounting systems in the office? These are but a few of the many planning questions that need to be considered in linking together the practice and office systems.

Linking with Client Systems.   An important aspect of the development of practice systems will be their ability to access data on client computers. Just as businesses are finding that access to shared data bases is important to management information systems, CPAs are finding that greater access to client data is important. The need for quick direct and indirect access by the microcomputer to such data is important to eliminate key entry—and to access data for the application of new tests or procedures not possible or practical in a manual environment.

AN AUDIT SYSTEM OF THE FUTURE

Let's now take a look at a practice system of the future—one that might be developed for the auditor. What might it include? How might it operate? How might it help move the auditor into the world of the future?

First of all, the microcomputer system will probably be built around a central unit, the network file server. This unit will have in excess of 4 megabytes (1 megabyte equals 1 million characters of information) of main random access memory; hard-disk storage of over 200 megabytes; an optical disk with over 500 megabytes of storage available; a 32-bit microprocessor; systems software that will allow more than one application to run on the server at the same time; and telecommunication facilities. The unit will be small, portable, and equipped with a built-in modem that can send and receive data at 9,600 baud. And individual auditor workstation units will easily connect to the server in a network.

In the field, the audit team will take the units to the client's location and quickly set up the audit network so that all audit staff on the team can access and work on the data and programs residing in the file server, as well as access the shared printer attached to the server. In the field, access to the auditor's office systems will be through telecommunications, whereas in the office, the team will connect the practice systems directly to the office automation network.

Some of the key elements of an audit system might include

• Electronic work files. All the key files and schedules, traditionally kept in working paper format, will be developed, maintained and stored in electronic form. A new term will have to be developed to describe audit working papers in computer-readable format. Perhaps "electronic work files," "audit data files" or "audit working files" will fill the bill. Which phrase is ultimately selected isn't important. What is important is that audit information and support will be—and even at this moment is being—put into computer-readable format and stored on disk or tape for later retrieval and use.

• A specialized operating system. The audit system might need a special operating system to control all aspects of system operations.

• Application software. Special-application software will be developed and used with third-party software to provide the unique functionality required for efficient use of the audit system.

• Audit tools. For the audit system to be efficient, it would have to include many powerful decision support, expert systems, and application programs. These will help the auditor organize information, assess risk, set audit scope, perform audit work and calculations, document the work done, and prepare financial statements and management recommendations.

How might the auditor use such a system? The following scenario illustrates the possible uses, while further describing the functionality of such a system:

• Initially the auditor downloads the prior-year electronic data files from the firm's office automation computer system storage files into the file server of the audit system (or transfers the files from a 5¼-inch optical disk, where it has been stored since the last audit).

• The prior-year planning audit program is called up from the data base and modified to fit the current situation. The auditor uses the audit program generator to make the modifications. In doing so, the auditor searches the accounting and disclosure system on the firm's central data base to look for any changes in accounting and auditing requirements from the prior year and reviews them for applicability to the client. When changes are needed, the auditor accesses the standard program file for applicable audit procedures, copies them into the planning program file, and modifies them.

• The planning process starts with the auditor obtaining data on current operations, industry statistics, risk considerations, and similar information and entering them into the expert system scope-setting module. When this is completed, the system develops a proposed audit scope. The auditor reviews the proposed scope, discusses it with the partner, and makes any necessary modifications.

• Internal control systems are reviewed and updated. Prior-year flowcharts and documentation are called up from disk storage and modified. Changes are made in the evaluations, and the results are added to the expert system scope-setting module for updates to the audit scope.

• The audit program is updated, using the audit program generator as described.

• Current-year financial data are downloaded from the client's systems and entered into the audit system data files. Some data are transmitted electronically, some by media transfer, some using optical character-recognition equipment, some by digital image processing, some by key entry.

• Audit work is performed and documented in the electronic audit data files with the use of electronic note and tickmark reference tracking software.

• Adjusting and reclassifying entries are recorded, using other functional software designed for the system, which keeps track of the entries and the schedules to which they are associated.

• Partner, manager, and staff reviews are made and review points maintained in the system by the person and the schedule with which the points are associated.

- Research is performed using both outside electronic data bases and the firm's policy and research files on its central computer systems (or on 5¼-inch optical disks supplied by the firm to its staff).

- Arrangements are made with other offices using electronic mail to do work at subsidiaries, and audit data are transmitted electronically back and forth. The staff in the field access their electronic mail through telecommunication links with the office.

- Partner review of audit work at remote field locations is performed through a telecommunications link to the audit system at the remote site.

- Financial statements are transmitted to the office for printing on a laser printer.

- At the end of the audit the electronic audit data files are stored in the firm's office automation system storage files.

YESTERDAY, TODAY, AND TOMORROW

Yesterday, just a few years ago, CPAs could only dream about having audit working papers in a computer-readable format and using electronic audit systems. As technology moved forward and microcomputers and related hardware and software were incorporated in accounting and audit work, some of the dream became reality.

Today the profession is taking giant strides in using this new technology for the performance of new practice services—and even for day-to-day work. The concept is no longer vague, hard to describe. On the contrary, there is now sufficient computer hardware, software, and related equipment to design and develop new systems to use in our practices. We can take the vision and translate it into functioning, integrated systems that improve productivity.

But no one should be lulled into thinking that developing even today's practice system is easy. They are extremely challenging and difficult to achieve. Their development requires capital resources as well as human resources in the form of the energy, knowledge, and goals of highly skilled and dedicated professionals.

Tomorrow promises even more in the way of advances in technology. Because of what we are doing today, we have a much better understanding of what can and will be developed, approximately when it will be delivered, and how we will use it.

Our planning has become more concrete. Indeed, planning is perhaps the most important thing we can do today as we move toward tomorrow. With skillful strategic planning, we can determine how we will use technology and integrate it in our work in the years ahead. And we can develop and implement systems now that can be used as building blocks in the as yet undreamed-of systems of the future.

CHAPTER 2
Controlling the Development of Information Systems

Traditionally, the systems development process includes five components or stages: system analysis, system design, system selection, system implementation, and follow-up. These stages may be described as follows:

1. *System Analysis*. In this stage, the current system is carefully evaluated. Problems and strengths are identified. In some cases, the old system may be found to be adequate after only minor changes, and system development would terminate here.

2. *System Design*. The new system is designed based on problems and strengths of the old system determined from system analysis. Basically this stage involves designating the features desired in the new system. The most essential features of the system should be identified; less essential features may be dropped following cost–benefit analysis in the next stage. Several alternative system designs are usually developed.

3. *System Selection*. Alternative systems are evaluated, using cost–benefit analysis. The optimum system is selected and acquired. If a new computer system is to be purchased, the alternative system designs should be demonstrated by vendors and discussed with current users prior to acquisition.

4. *System Implementation*. In this stage, the analyst installs the new system. The firm's personnel must be adequately trained before, during, and after the installation of the new system.

5. *Follow-Up*. The new system must be continually reviewed. Periodically, modifications may be required due to changing needs.

Analyzing and designing systems require a thorough understanding of both existing and proposed new systems. Analysis and design require accountants to describe and document systems under consideration. Several techniques are available to assist the accountant in this documentation process. The most commonly used techniques include narrative descriptions, flowcharts, and data flow diagrams. Flowcharts are typically associated with the traditional approach to system analysis and design. Data flow diagrams are generally associated with the structured approach to system analysis and design. Both flowcharts and data flow diagrams are widely used to document systems.

A narrative description is simply a sentence-by-sentence discussion of the system's components and their interrelationships. Quite often, a system or application (such as accounts receivable update or payroll preparation) can be more effectively described by an illustration than by words. Flowcharts and data flow diagrams are two especially effective pictorial techniques for describing systems.

There are several types of flowcharts, such as program, system, and document flowcharts. Program flowcharts illustrate the major steps in computer programs, such as input/output, process, decision, and start/stop. A system flowchart illustrates the major input, processing, and output components of the system. A document flowchart illustrates the document flow in a system or application. Specialized system and document flowchart symbols include the following and other items: physical flow of goods, report or document, file symbols (off-line, disk, and tape), process, and data input device.

The "physical flow of goods" symbol (a dolly) is used strictly in document flowcharts. Additionally, document flowcharts place activities of key individuals or departments into separate columns which may be designated by vertical lines. The document flowchart effectively presents where important documents or reports originate and how they move through the system. The first article in this chapter presents additional information on flowcharts and graphs.

Data flow diagrams (DFDs) show the data used and provided by processes within a system. DFDs make use of four basic symbols:

Symbol	*Represents*
1. Open-ended rectangles	Data collection points (e.g., accounts receivable master file).
2. Ovals	Processes (e.g., order entry).
3. Open-ended rectangles with "horns"	Interfaces with other applications (e.g., a billing interface with the accounts receivable processing system).
4. Rectangles	Processing reports (e.g., schedule of accounts receivable).

Since only four types of symbols are used in DFDs, they may be more easily understood by the casual user. The limited number of symbols also makes it easier to learn how to prepare DFDs. An example of a DFD concerning payroll preparation is shown in Figure 2–1.

Data flow diagrams are a relatively new tool used by accountants to describe systems. DFDs are a key component of "structured systems develop-

FIGURE 2–1

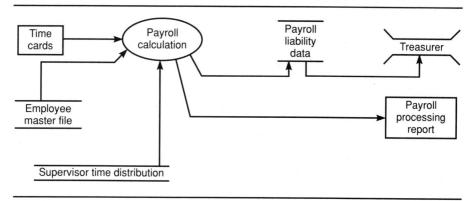

ment." Structured techniques were pioneered by well-known author and consultant Ed Yourdon. In structured systems development, DFDs are used to present the overall perspective or macro-level view of a system. These macro-level DFDs are supported by more detailed (micro-level) DFDs or other types of logical flow diagrams. Besides DFDs, other characteristics of the structured approach to systems development include the following:

1. Thorough documentation of the existing system.
2. In-depth systems analysis stage.
3. Detailed description of the logic of the proposed system.
4. Cost–benefit analysis of the proposed system.
5. Modular systems design.

The structured approach offers a more efficient approach to systems development for many systems development projects. However, the structured approach is not a panacea for systems development. As a relatively new approach, it requires personnel to learn new skills. Additionally, systems developed using the structured approach typically require more computer storage and processing time because modular program code is longer than traditional code. The accountant embarking on a systems development project should carefully consider the advantages and disadvantages of the structured approach before beginning the project.

One of the biggest controversies facing accountants, specifically CPAs, in the systems development field is not how to analyze or to design systems, but whether CPAs should even offer such services. If a public accounting firm provides consulting services, such as designing accounting systems for their clients, then there is some concern that the accountants will not maintain their objectivity when they evaluate those systems during auditing engagements.

The question of whether CPAs should offer both auditing and consulting services to the same client is a thorny issue facing the profession. Do consulting services impair an auditor's independence? The AICPA ethics code requires auditors to have independence in mental attitude. The code does not specifically prohibit CPAs from providing audits and consulting engagements for the same client. In any case, CPA firms continue to offer both types of services to the same client.

Systems development projects are a major category of consulting services provided by CPAs (i.e., external accountants). Systems development projects are also done by management accountants (i.e., internal accountants). Whether done by internal or external accountants, for a project to be successful it must involve, not just the accountants, but all the people affected by the new system.

The five basic stages in systems development are generally the same in all projects, but the practical details may vary widely, depending on the individual circumstances. Individual projects may include modifications made to manual accounting systems, installation of computerized accounting systems, or improvements in nonaccounting systems. The second article in this chapter, "Control Guidelines for Systems under Development," offers specific control guidelines for accounting systems development.

Changes in technology have permitted system designers to substantially automate the analysis and design processes. Selected software tools are discussed in the third article, "Are Automated Tools Changing Systems Analysis and Design?" The fourth article, "Use of System Development Methodology and Tools," reports on the tools and methodologies used by a sample of companies. The final article, "Using the Microcomputer for Project Management," presents how project management software can be of invaluable assistance in managing large projects with numerous interrelated activities. Accountants can utilize such software in management consulting projects (e.g., for systems development) or even in traditional tasks, such as auditing and tax services.

CHAPTER 2 READINGS

1. Steven Golen, James Worthington, Greg Thibadoux, William D. Cooper, and Ira S. Greenberg, "Flowcharts and Graphics," *The CPA Journal,* March 1986, pp. 12–14, 17, 18, 20–23.
2. Terry L. Kruger, "Control Guidelines for Systems under Development," *The Internal Auditor,* June 1985, pp. 41–42.
3. John C. Windsor, "Are Automated Tools Changing Systems Analysis and Design?" *Journal of Systems Management,* November 1986, pp. 28–32.
4. Jane M. Carey and Raymond McLeod, Jr., "Use of System Development Methodology and Tools," *Journal of Systems Management,* March 1988, pp. 30–35.
5. L. Murphy Smith, "Using the Microcomputer for Project Management," *Journal of Accounting and EDP,* Summer 1989, pp. 30–37.

CHAPTER 2 QUESTIONS

Article 1

1. What is the purpose of flowcharts?
2. What types of data are best suited for graphs?

Article 2

3. As an alternative to direct participation in the development of a computer system, EDP auditors may provide a list of internal control guidelines to the system development team. Should these guidelines be general or detailed? Why?
4. List these control guidelines.

Article 3

5. List the techniques that have been developed to improve the cost effectiveness of developing and maintaining systems.
6. Describe systems engineering packages.

Article 4

7. What system development tools are receiving consistent use?
8. Describe system flowcharts and data flow diagrams.

Article 5

9. List three project management techniques.
10. What is meant by "resource leveling"?

Case 2–1

KATHY TAKEN TRUCKING CO.

Kathy Taken Trucking Co. is an independent contractor that delivers goods for anyone, anywhere. Customers are billed following shipment. Customer payments are received in the mailroom once per day. The amount of each payment is entered into a magnetic tape file, called "customer payments transaction file," immediately after the mail is opened. The actual customer payments, that is, checks or money orders, are sent from the mailroom to the treasurer for deposit.

The customer payments transaction file is then sent to the accounts receivable department where the file is sorted, using a sort program. The sorted customer payments transaction file, along with the accounts receivable master file (also on tape), is used as input to a program called "post customer accounts." This program credits the customer accounts for the amount of each payment.

The output from the post program is an updated master file and two copies of a report entitled "List of Customer Payments," which includes a total of all payments processed that day. One copy is filed by date in the accounts receivable department; the other copy is forwarded to the treasurer.

REQUIRED:

1. Prepare a system flowchart for the customer payments processing as described above.

2. Prepare a document (columnar) flowchart.

3. Prepare a data flow diagram.

4. Why would the treasurer need a copy of the "List of Payments" report?

Reading 2-1

FLOWCHARTS AND GRAPHICS

Part I—Flowcharts, by Steven Golen, Ph.D., and James Worthington, CPA

Part II—Graphics, by Greg Thibadoux, Ph.D., William D. Cooper, CPA, Ph.D., and Ira S. Greenberg, CPA, Ph.D.

FLOWCHARTS/INTRODUCTION

When flowcharts or flowcharting is mentioned, each of us develops a mental image of lines and symbols and how they are connected. If the images were converted to paper, there would probably be no two flowcharts alike, because of our varied backgrounds and relationships to flowcharts. This article will look at the basic concepts of flowcharting, show how flowcharts are used, and illustrate some examples of preparing them.

Reprinted with permission of *The CPA Journal* (March 1986), © 1986.

DEFINITION OF FLOWCHARTS

A flowchart can be defined as a graphic representation of a process, system, or operation which demonstrates, through symbols, lines, and arrows, the sequence and interrelationship of activities and documents to complete a specific process, system, or operation.

PURPOSE OF FLOWCHARTS

Flowcharts can be used for a number of purposes. More common uses are:

- Serves to document in an easily used and understood format abstract thoughts, processes, or systems.
- Gives a means to present visually an accounting system, trace a check or voucher through a system, or present the logic of solving a problem.
- Allows more than one person to discuss the problems with an assurance that they are discussing the same problem.
- Provides an opportunity to analyze facts and present ideas.

TYPES OF FLOWCHARTS

Although there are many types of flowcharts, the following are frequently used:

- *Logic flowcharts.* Used to chart the logic of a computer program prior to writing it.
- *Document flowcharts.* Used to follow either a specific document or a group of documents through a particular process.
- *System flowchart.* Used to portray the documents used, decisions made, processes performed, or actions taken within a certain department or company.
- *Decision flowchart.* Used to trace the decision-making and approval process through a given system.

FLOWCHART FORMATS

Flowcharts can be displayed visually in several formats. They can be from top to bottom, left to right, or in a columnar format.

A vertical flowchart is the form typically used by computer personnel in charting logic flow. The flow of thought and symbols is from top to bottom, hence the name vertical flowchart.

A horizontal flowchart is widely used by management and systems analysts. The flow is from left to right. The central logic or operation is in the center with subordinate or supportive operations entering above or below the center line. The horizontal flowchart also can be used to demonstrate interrelationships.

A columnar flowchart is used to demonstrate the flow of documents or actions through several departments. The departments are represented as columns. Activity or documents flow from left to right through the departments.

FLOWCHART SYMBOLS

Flowcharts are prepared for use in a variety of industries and professions. As such, symbols have been introduced which are peculiar to a particular field or industry. Flowchart templates have been developed for use by computer systems designers, engineers, management specialists, architects, and other professionals. However, some symbols are basic and are used by all who have responsibility for flowcharting. Some of the most widely used symbols in systems flowcharting are illustrated in Figure 1.

1. *Process/operation*—any operation or process other than sorting which causes a change in value, form, or location of information. The type of operation is indicated in the box.
2. *Documents, records, ledger, etc.*—any document or record from which data is taken or on which data is placed. The document name is placed in the symbol. The simultaneous preparation of a document is indicated by multiple symbols, one for each document to be traced.
3. *Decision*—any decision in the system which affects the flow of documents or activity. Used to branch off at a decision, either yes or no, or some other parameter which should be shown.
4. *File*—any copy or document sent to file. Type of file, either temporary or permanent, should be indicated on the symbol.
5. *Retrieval*—indicates when documents reenter the system or are retrieved from file. Source file should be indicated on the symbol.
6. *Sort*—indicates the sorting of data and the subsequent branching, if applicable. Parameter of sorting should be indicated on the symbol.
7. *Flow direction*—indicates the flow of logic or direction or movement of documents.
8. *Transmittal*—indicates the addition of source document of a transmittal form or adding machine tape. Notation may be made on or next to the symbol.
9. *Connectors*—used to connect two separate portions of the flowchart. A number in this symbol indicates transfer to a similarly numbered symbol elsewhere.
10. *Offpage connectors*—indicates transfer to a flowchart on another page.

FIGURE 1   Standard Symbols Used in Systems Flowcharting

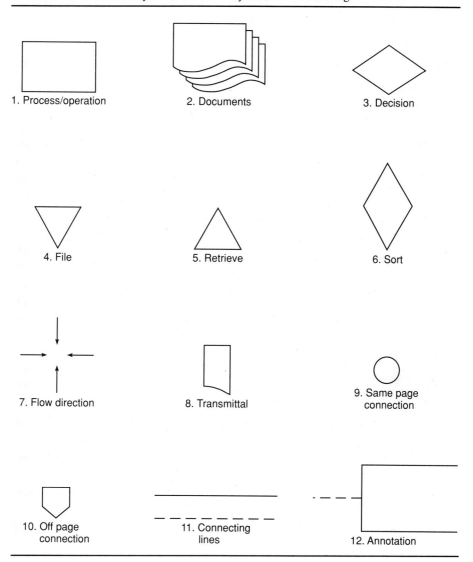

11. *Connecting lines*—the main flow is shown by connecting the relevant symbols with a solid line. Supplementary flow or authority is indicated by a broken line.

12. *Annotation*—the addition of descriptive comments or explanatory notes for clarification.

BASIC PROCEDURES FOR PREPARING FLOWCHARTS

When preparing flowcharts, follow these procedures.

- Define the area or topic to be flowcharted.
- Chart the complete system.
- Indicate all forms, documents, and ledgers used and account for all form copies.
- Chart what is done as opposed to how it is done.
- Make the chart clear, neat, and easy to follow.
- Avoid cross flow lines.
- Work at a consistent detail level.
- Cross-reference other charts as necessary.
- Use a summary chart for several detailed charts.

Also, it is a good idea to write each step in the process as if one were giving instructions to complete the flowchart. Use the imperative mood, action verbs, active voice, and simple sentences. Key each step to the flowchart by writing the number next to the symbol it describes. By writing out each step, a written documentation of the entire flowchart results.

EXAMPLES OF FLOWCHARTS

Three examples have been prepared that illustrate the types of flowcharts that can be used. The illustrations are of a logic flowchart, columnar flowchart, and a system flowchart. They are described as follows:

Logic Flowchart

This logic flowchart describes the process of filling out a timesheet, tracing the logic and describing what is done while maintaining a consistent level of detail. Flowchart shows a vertical flow (see Figure 2).

1. Make decision as to whether a time sheet is due. If no, go to end of process. If yes, go to step 2.
2. Fill in name and date on time sheet from document.
3. List time for firm.
4. List client billable time.
5. Make decision as to client number. If client number is not available, go to step 6. If client number is available, go to step 7.
6. Look up client number on master client list.
7. Enter client numbers on time sheet.
8. Prepare adding machine tape of client numbers and total.

FIGURE 2 Example of Logic Flowchart Showing Preparation of Timesheet

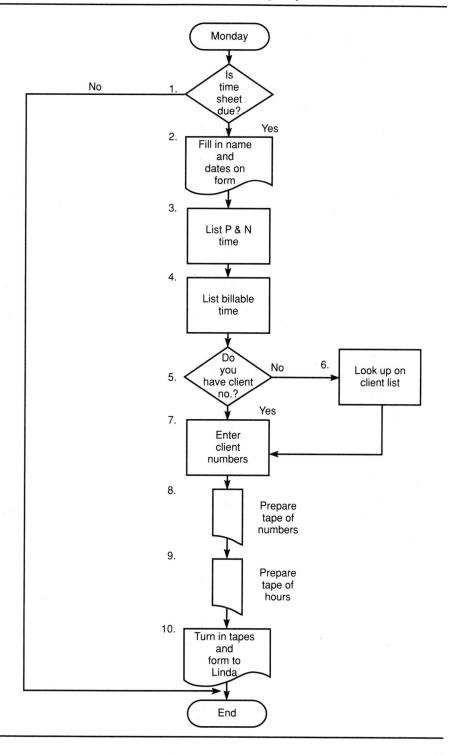

9. Prepare adding machine tape of hours and total.

10. Turn in time sheet form and tapes to payroll supervisor.

Columnar Flowchart

This columnar flowchart describes the process of filling a shipping order. Example shows use of document flowchart in a columnar format (see Figure 3).

1. Receive order from customer.
2. Prepare six-part shipping order.
   a. Send copy no. 2 to customer as an acknowledgment of order received.
   b. File copies 3, 4, 5, 6.
3. Send shipping order copy no. 1 to shipping department.
4. Fill order.
5. Date shipping order document.
6. Retrieve copies 3, 4, 5, 6 from sales department.
7. Send copy no. 3 to customer with order.
8. Send copy no. 4 to inventory control department.
   a. File copy no. 4 in inventory control department.
9. Send copy no. 5 to accounts receivable department for billing.
   a. File copy no. 5 in A/R department.
10. File copies no. 6 and 1 in sales department.

System Flowchart

This system flowchart traces the process in the shipping department when the shipping order is received. This example illustrates a system flowchart with a horizontal flow (see Figure 4).

1. Receive shipping order.
2. Make decision as to whether material is in stock.
3. Issue back order if material is not in stock.
4. Attach back order to shipping order and return to sales department.
5. Fill order from stock.
6. Wrap order for shipping.
7. Label package.
8. Date shipping order.
9. Return shipping order to sales department.

FIGURE 3 Document Flowchart in Columnar Format Showing Flow of Filling a Customer Order

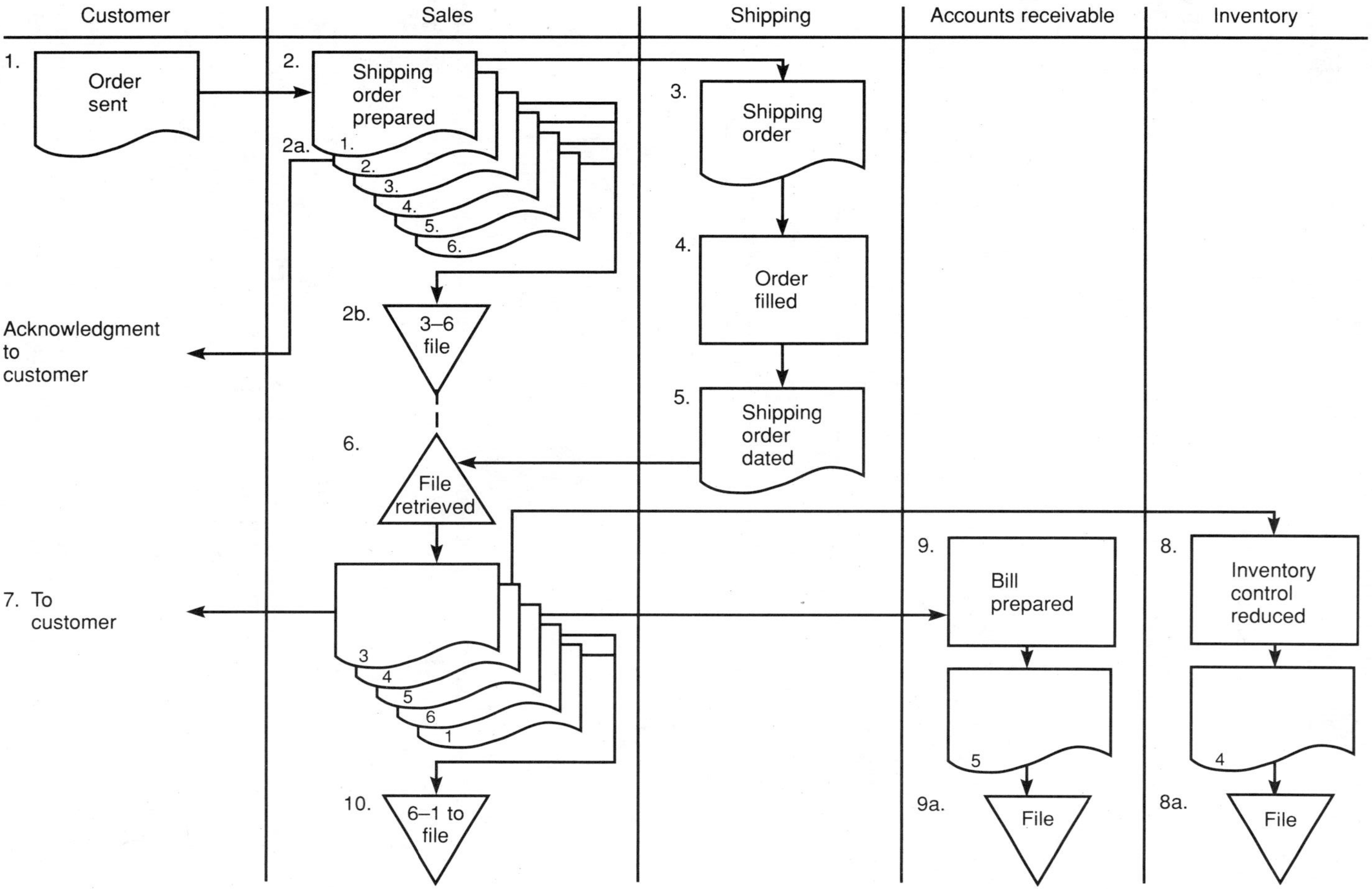

53

FIGURE 4   System Flowchart in Horizontal Format Showing Process of
Shipping Order in Shipping Department

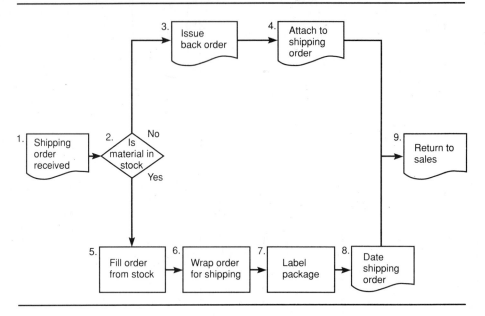

SUMMARY

There are many uses of flowcharts, with a corresponding number of styles
and symbols. The basic purpose, however, is to present an idea, process, or
system in a picture that easily describes what happens. Whether the style is
vertical, horizontal, or columnar depends on the preparers who must remember that their purpose is to communicate to their audience. Therefore, they
must make their charts as simple as possible, easy to follow and interpret, yet
get their message across.

GRAPHICS

Accountants often forget that although we can understand traditional accounting information with little difficulty, many other users of financial statements are not so adept. The FASB in its conceptual framework states that
one of the primary objectives of financial reporting is to provide useful information to statement users. One technique that can be used to make financial
data more apparent to users is a graphic presentation.

Graphics represent a useful and flexible medium for explaining, interpreting and analyzing quantitative data. They make possible the presentation of
such data in a clear and effective manner which is often not the case with
tabular or textual forms of presentation. Probably, the most important advan-

tage graphics have over other media is they are highly effective in creating and holding audience attention. Secondly, they are better tools for portraying relationships and trends that can be hidden if among tables or narrative. This is particularly important when presenting a large quantity or mass of statistical data. Finally, graphics can provide a comprehensive overview of a problem that can not often be derived from tabular or textual presentation. Graphs can provide financial information about any aspect of a firm's operation. Examples include: revenue and expenditure breakdowns, cash flow analysis, inventory management, divisional performance, and performance over time.

Accountants and other business professionals have long been aware of the potential value of graphics. In the past, however, their use has been limited by the time, effort, and expertise required in their design and construction. Frequently, graphs had to be designed by a specialist and drawn to specifications by a draftsman. Today, however, with the widespread availability of powerful graphic software packages, the accountant can inexpensively incorporate elaborate graphs into any report or presentation.

But as with any tools, there always exists the potential for misuse. We would like to briefly discuss some basic initial considerations for using graphics, how to choose the most appropriate graph, and guidelines for constructing three of the most commonly used graphs.

INITIAL CONSIDERATIONS

Before beginning to design any particular graphic, it is necessary to complete certain preliminary steps. First, the designer should become familiar with the data set. He or she must be aware of exactly what aspects of the data can be incorporated into graphic form and what aspects are not as amenable to visual presentation.

This analysis leads directly to the second consideration; a decision has to be made about whether a graphic is indeed the best form for communicating the data. The fact that certain data can be visually treated does not mean that a graph is the most effective manner for presenting the data. Factors in determining the usefulness of graphic communication include the following: (1) the nature of the data set, (2) presentation medium, (3) purpose of the tool, and (4) audience for whom the use of the graph is intended.

Nature of the Data Set

Certain types of data do not lend themselves to effective graphic display. Graphs are best used to display multivariate data where a certain piece of data is related to another piece (e.g., unemployment rates vs. the CPI). Univariate and simple data sets usually can be more effectively presented in tabular form. If the data can be incorporated into data maps, time series plots, space-time designs, or relational displays, the use of a graph is probably appropriate.

Presentation Medium

Graphs may be effectively used in (1) books, periodicals, or written reports, (2) exhibit presentations, (3) slides, (4) lectures, and (5) television. The only constraint on the use of graphics in these media relates to the design. Care must be given to the size of the graph, thickness of lines, and lettering styles. But if care is taken in design, graphics can be effectively used in most visually oriented media.

Purpose of the Graph

A graph should primarily be used to emphasize new or significant relationships. It may also be useful in presenting new facts or developing hypotheses. In order to fulfill these functions, the graph must meet certain criteria: it must (1) accurately represent the facts, (2) be clear and easily understood, and (3) hold attention. If a graph can not meet these criteria, then it will not be an effective medium for presenting new ideas or relationships.

Audience

The education level and professional interest of the audience for whom the graph is intended should be given primary consideration. A well prepared graph that does not address these concerns will be of little use and may result in a loss of audience attention.

CHOOSING THE APPROPRIATE GRAPH

There is no absolute criterion for selecting a particular graph for use. Selection depends in part on the four initial considerations: (1) data set, (2) presentation medium, (3) purpose, and (4) the audience. Additionally, a primary consideration relates to how to focus attention on a particular aspect of the data set. Complex data sets can be presented in as many as 20 different graphic forms. There are, however, certain data sets that can be best presented by particular graphics. Three of the most commonly used graphs are the bar chart, the pie (sector) graph, and the line (curve) graph.

To compare magnitude or the size of items or parts of a total the preparer might consider using a bar chart. There are two basic types of bar charts: vertical (column) charts and horizontal charts. These two types of charts represent the most frequently used graphic because they can visually convey a comparison of a larger number of data points. The bars may represent a single value or may be used to represent several values, in which case various sections of the bar will be segmented by different coloring or shading. In a bar chart, comparison is based on linear values; the length of the bar is directly proportional to the value or amount in each category.

Generally, magnitudes or item size relationships that are appropriate for bar charts can also be displayed in pie (sector) charts. Pie graphs display data in the form of a circle divided into sections proportional in size to the data represented. Although sector charts rank high in popular appeal, they are not considered as effective as bar graphs. The eye can compare linear measures more accurately than sector areas of arcs of a circle.

Line (curve) charts are most appropriately used to display time series data such as movements or trends over a period of years or months, weeks, days, or hours. Values for each point in time are plotted (the x-axis representing time units and the y-axis the value) and the points are joined to form a continuous line or curve.

After having decided on the appropriateness of using a graph and having chosen a particular graphic form, the preparer is then ready to design and to construct the chart. A good deal of attention must be given to this final phase since a poorly designed graph may look grotesque and be incompatible with the overall tone of the presentation. There are five concerns that need to be addressed in designing a graph: (1) arranging the data, (2) spacing, (3) scaling, (4) labeling, and (5) shading. Each of these is discussed in regard to the bar chart, the pie chart, and the line graph.

DESIGN CONSIDERATIONS

Bar Charts

Arranging the data—The bars should be arranged in some analytical pattern. If one is showing magnitude differences, then the bars should be arranged in size order beginning with the largest bar. Other arrangement schemes include time sequences, geographical groupings, and alphabetical ordering.

Spacing—Bar charts are easier to read and interpret if space is left between the bars. Ideally, the distance between bars should be ½ the width of the bar. In special cases, it may be appropriate to lay out the space as little as ¼ the width or as much as the entire width. In any case, the bars should be of uniform width and evenly spaced.

Scaling—The scale for a bar chart should begin with zero and generally remain unbroken. The number of intervals on a scale should help in measuring of distances but too many scale numbers can create confusion. Generally, intervals should be in round numbers in units of 1s, 10s, 100s, 1,000s, etc. Odd unit scale numbers should be avoided. The intervals should be marked off with lines or ticks.

Labeling—On vertical (column) bar graphs, scale numbers should appear at the left of the chart. For horizontal bar charts, the scale is usually placed at the top of the chart. In some cases it is desirable to include figures inside the bars.

This is often not a good practice, because it can lead to a distortion in the interpretation of comparative lengths. If such figures are included, they should be small and not placed near the end of the bar. Finally, writing between bars should be avoided.

Shadings—It is customary to use some shading of the bars. Black is appropriate if the bars are not extremely wide. Diagonal line shading or crosshatching may be best for large size bars. For segmented bars (those representing more than one value), the bottom segments of the bar should be solid colored topped off with other patterns. Avoid using horizontal and vertical shadings in segmented bars because these lines may affect the perceived width and shape of the bar. If crosshatching is used, care should be taken not to create optical illusions.

Pie Charts

Arranging the data—Begin the largest sector at the central point of the upper right half of the circle. The sectors should then follow clockwise from right to left in descending size order. If the graph contains a "miscellaneous" sector with a small number of components, it should be placed last in the series regardless of its rank in order of size.

Spacing—Generally, spacing is not a concern in pie chart design. However, the importance of an individual sector can be emphasized by separating it from the rest of the pie.

Scaling—The scale of the pie chart is simply the size of the sector or angle of the arc. One should, however, limit the number of sectors to no more than five or six, since a greater number can be visually confusing.

Labeling—Generally, the only labeling needed on a pie chart is an identification of each sector and the percentage value the sector represents out of a 100 percent total. Lettering should be either placed horizontally in the sectors or in a contiguous position outside the circle with an arrow pointing to the appropriate sector.

Shading—Sector charts do not require strong contrasts. The sectors should be lightly shadowed with dots, diagonal lines, or crosshatching or with no shading.

Line Graphs

Arranging the data—The data is plotted according to time and the associated amount and the points are connected to form the curve. If the data represents specific points of time, it should be plotted from the point of time on the x-axis (plotted to line). If the data represents values over a time period, it should be plotted midway between points of time on the x-axis (plotted to space). In general, the data points should be connected with straight lines unless the lines have been smoothed by mathematical techniques.

Scaling—In a line graph, the horizontal scale represents the independent variable, usually time, and the vertical scale, the dependent variable, the value or amount. The time divisions on the x-axis are indicated by scale lines extending the height of the graph or by ticks. The time scale should begin with the earliest plotting period and end with the most recent. The scale of the y-axis, which shows amount, should begin with zero and be marked off in even numbers or multiples of five. The vertical scale values are either indicated by lines extending the length of the graph or by tick marks.

Labeling—Scale figures for time appear at the bottom of the horizontal axis. Because of space limitations, it is often necessary to abbreviate or apostrophize time scale figures. Three letter abbreviations are common for the days of the week and months. Yearly scales may be apostrophized such as 1920, '30, '40, '50, etc. Scale figures for the vertical axis should be placed to the left side of the graph and in the case of large charts may appear on both vertical sides.

Spacing and shading—If a line chart has more than one curve, the curves should be spaced far enough apart so that they can be differentiated. Often, however, the plotting of the data will bring the curves close together or even cause them to cross. In this case, the curves can be differentiated by the use of colors or shading. Another way to differentiate curves is to represent each curve by a different pattern. These may include the solid line, dash line, dotted lines, dot-dash line, and the line and dot.

There is one final issue that relates to the design of bar and line charts that needs to be discussed, that is, the proportioning of the graph. In general, graphics that use horizontal and vertical scale lines should be proportioned so that the horizontal scale is greater in length than the height. There are several reasons for favoring the horizontal over the vertical. First, the eye is accustomed to detecting deviations from the horizon. Secondly, it is easier to label a horizontally stretched plotting field. Finally, a longer horizontal scale helps to demonstrate the independent or causal variable. While there is no standard proportion, a commonly used ratio is 1 (vertical scale) to 1.5 (horizontal scale).

These basic guidelines should help in designing graphics. But the most important advice in designing graphics is to simply make sure that the graph gives visual access to and revelation of the complex data set.

Reading 2–2

CONTROL GUIDELINES FOR SYSTEMS UNDER DEVELOPMENT

By Terry L. Kruger, RIA

EDP auditors are often asked to participate in the design of internal controls during the development stages of a computer system. In many cases, the internal auditing department may not be able to supply the necessary resources when they are requested. This may be due to a variety of reasons, some of which involve departmental policy regarding participation in systems development.

For example, a current controversy exists in our profession: Some auditors feel that full participation at this stage could result in a loss of independence and an abdication by management from its responsibilities. Other auditors feel that participation is the best way to ensure that the project team is control conscious.

Regardless of its position, the internal auditing department may simply not have enough trained EDP auditors. This is common. One alternative which will still satisfy the request to participate is to supply a list of internal control guidelines for the system-development team to use as a base to work from. In many situations, these guidelines would also form part of the system development methodology, most likely developed by controls analysts from the data processing department with input from EDP auditors. If the guidelines are well prepared and thought out, they can serve to make the project team aware of the fundamental principles of control in the absence of direct participation from the internal auditing department.

As systems vary in design, scope, purpose, and other areas, the internal control guidelines can be quite general in nature. General or more conceptual guidelines do not require constant revision, are easier to follow, and have a better chance of covering all of the situations prevalent in today's complex systems.

Obviously, these guidelines should be followed with common sense. The idea is not to simply "check off" the guidelines without considering the integration and relationship between the control points. It is precisely this relationship that makes for a control subsystem and set of control loops that ensure reasonable data integrity.

This article was reprinted with permission from the June 1985 issue of *The Internal Auditor*, published by The Institute of Internal Auditors, Inc.

Here's one example of the many suitable formats for guidelines to be used as part of a system-development methodology. This example is broken down into seven categories that make up the functions of a typical system. There is some overlapping between the categories so that the control areas or loops are complete and all major aspects are covered.

TRANSACTIONS

Controls should ensure the integrity of transactions before and after entry into the system:

- Controls should ensure complete and accurate transaction input. Only authorized sources should initiate transactions and transactions should not be altered before entry.
- Controls should provide for adequate separation of transaction-handling duties where practical. However, the transaction flow or passage of transactions from one responsibility group to the other should be conducted in a controlled environment.
- If the transaction flows are fully automated (using on-line terminals), controls should ensure the integrity of the data-input function. This includes monitoring staff input of transactions.
- All transactions that enter the system should be controlled throughout the entire system cycle. Those transactions validated according to pre-defined system specifications should stay intact within the system (unaltered except through authorized and tested system processing) until final output. Rejected transactions must be controlled to ensure that they are corrected and resubmitted.

AUDIT TRAIL/SYSTEM BACKUP

Master files should be connected with valid audit trails (the route by which the processing of data can be traced either forward or backward through the system cycle).

- Master files of different generations should be connected only by complete blocks of authorized, validated transactions.
- Where practical or for high-risk transactions, retain hard-copy source as backup.
- Blocks of updating transactions should, for a reasonable period, remain intact and unaltered to re-create the master files if necessary. The retention criteria, however, should be related to a formal management-authorization/deletion policy and not *only* to a specified time period.
- The master files should be the sum of their parts and the system should be able to recombine the original parts to re-create the master. Where

destructive updating (transactions are changed or deleted) occurs, backup should be retained of the master file before and after updating and of the updating transactions themselves. For on-line, random-update situations, a separate log should be retained of the master records influenced *before and after* and of the updating transactions.

MASTER-FILE INTEGRITY

Controls should be in place to ensure that validated data on a master file remain intact and are never altered in any unauthorized manner.

STANDING-DATA-FILE INTEGRITY

All standing-data files should comprise only authorized, validated data and should remain intact and unaltered except by authorized means.

TOTAL-SYSTEM RECONCILIATION

Monitoring devices which will form part of the controls should be developed that ensure total-system reconciliation:

- Controls independent of the main system's processing should be as close to the source of the transaction as possible and carried through the entire system. These controls should be designed to ensure system integrity for each run and from run-to-run over the entire operating cycle.
- Devices should be in place to ensure total-system reconciliation.

OUTPUT CONTROLS

Controls should be maintained so that system output is not misplaced, mis-handled, or dispersed to unauthorized personnel.

SYSTEM-USER CONTROLS

Controls maintained in the user areas should be developed as part of the overall-development process:

- User-control interfaces should be manageable and workable.
- Consider system-function timeliness when developing controls. If system functions which depend on each other get out-of-step, the system controls may fail to function properly.
- Monitoring devices should be in place to ensure system users are fulfilling their system-control responsibilities.

CONCLUSION

Principles of control remain the same regardless of the basic design of the system or the style or mode of inputting transactions, resubmitting rejected errors, or updating files. The main objective of control guidelines is to make systems analysts, programmers, and users aware of control principles. The guidelines should enable project-team members to "think controls," integrate them into their system design, and recognize and guard against areas of exposure. These guidelines are the base any organization must have in the absence of direct participation from EDP auditors.

Reading 2–3

ARE AUTOMATED TOOLS CHANGING SYSTEMS ANALYSIS AND DESIGN?

By John C. Windsor, Ph.D., CSP

It is unusual to find a data processing center that is not behind in its work. The data processing manager commonly has more requests for new systems or improvements on existing systems than the department can handle. The systems analyst is usually faced with deadlines that cannot be met if he or she is to do a professional job. Programmers are commonly forced to release programs that have not been fully tested. Faced with these types of pressures, it is unlikely that these professionals are going to remember that their job is to provide, in a cost-effective manner, a system that will transform data into information in order to aid managers.

Coincidentally, most managers who are waiting on the new or improved system to enhance their decision making forget that there are two measures of effectiveness. They are generally concerned with only one measure: How long it takes to get the system on line. While this measure is important, and indeed may be critical, it completely ignores the second measure: how long will the system effectively accomplish its objectives—which may be even more critical to the business.

Besides all the implied benefits of a system that has a long survival time (e.g., client satisfaction) there are explicit benefits to the data processing cen-

---

Reprinted with permission from *Journal of Systems Management*, November 1986, pp. 28–32.

ter and to the entire organization. The longer a system survives, the fewer resources the center will have to devote to it. Therefore, more resources will be available to deal with new requests by the clients. When this happens the organization receives a greater return on its investment in data processing.

Over the entire history of data processing, attempts have been made to improve the cost-effectiveness of developing and maintaining client systems. Documentation standards were established to, among other things, shorten system development time and make maintenance faster and easier. Structured programming standards were developed to speed program development time and reduce maintenance time, as well as make documentation easier. All of the structured analysis and design techniques were developed to formalize the development life cycle. This resulted in spreading the documentation throughout the entire life cycle, providing better documentation at each stage of the system's development, and shortening the programming and maintenance time for the systems. A formal testing step was proposed to improve the life of the system. Prototyping, one of the newest entries in the tool box of the analyst and designer is designed to shorten the development life cycle and involve the client more directly. Prototyping thus delivers a working model of the system as early as possible while delaying the finished system until the client is able to determine that the system is exactly what they want.

While all of these techniques have improved the delivery of a new or improved system, most managers have been able to recognize new needs or improvements faster than the data processing professional can deliver them. Also, these techniques have never delivered everything they were supposed to, in part because they were oversold and in part because of the learning time needed to implement them. One of the newest aids for analysis and design to be put forth is automated tools for analysis and design. These tools, usually called workbenches or system engineering packages, will add their part to the cost-effectiveness of a system, but the real question is exactly what these packages will do for the systems professional.

SYSTEMS ENGINEERING PACKAGES

Systems engineering packages and workbenches are available with a wide range of capabilities and run on a wide range of computers. Although generally found on minicomputers, there are products that are designed for use on large mainframes (for almost all vendors), and more recently very complete packages have become available for microcomputers (usually IBM PC XTs and TI Professionals). No matter where they are found these packages are designed to aid the analyst and designer in their decision-making activities during systems development.

At the very least these packages provide a structure for system investigation, data and process definition, and they automate the documentation process at each step of the development life cycle. While all of this is a great help to the analyst many of these packages, even those found on microcomputers, go far beyond these basic capabilities. Typically, a complete systems engineering package will use as input the information gathered by the analyst and produce the following output:

Analysis Phase

- A leveled data flow diagram to functional primitives.
- Full definition of the processes.
- Full definition of the data stores.
- A complete data dictionary.
- Initial design of input forms.
- Initial design of output forms.

Design Phase

- System and program specifications in the form of Structure charts of HIPO charts.
- Program logic flowcharts.
- A complete data dictionary.
- Complete file specifications.
- Logical data base design.
- Final input form design.
- Final output form design.

Development Phase

- Pseudo code for each program in the system.
- Executable code (through the use of a code generator).
- A set of test standards for each program.

Systems engineering packages are in general more complete than workbenches; however, no package will do everything for the analyst. In addition, for a package to provide all of these features, the problem definition and initial information requirements must be extensive. In some cases these systems require information that the analyst would not normally collect or have access to. Finally, the package will impose its standards on the analyst, standards that may not match those of the organization.

IMPACT OF ANALYSIS AND DESIGN LIFE CYCLE

Before looking at the impact of systems engineering packages on the development life cycle it would be worthwhile to recognize what these packages will not do for the analyst. First, the analyst is a data collector. Through the use of interviews, observation, and experience the analyst works with a client to define the scope of a system. This definition usually includes the identification of the basic needs of the system, the problem it is to address, and its boundaries. While a system engineering package will provide a highly structured set of initial information needs, it will not aid in the collection of information or the synthesis of this information into a clear definition of the system.

Second, the analyst is usually a manager. He or she will be the first to investigate the economic and technical feasibility of the system, a task that is not even addressed by system engineering packages. In addition the analyst is usually responsible for the development of implementation and conversion strategies. While the performance of these two tasks is critical to the success of any system, a workbench or system engineering package will not provide any help toward their accomplishment.

Just because these packages do not provide help in some of the most critical activities of an analysis is no reason to abandon them. Remember that they are designed to aid in the preliminary and detailed design of a system, and in addition, to shorten the development time. Most of these packages are very good at exactly what they were designed to do. When used correctly these packages can have a dramatic impact on the development life cycle and on the survival time and maintenance cost of the resulting system.

The use of a system engineering package will impact the total life cycle of a system in seven major areas. First, while the package will not collect and synthesize information about a system, it will provide structure to the task. The process of simply collecting the information and making the decisions needed to meet the input requirements of the package will lead the analyst through the definition of the system. In order for the package to be of any use the analyst must provide the problem definition and a complete functional analysis of the system. Through an iterative process working with the package the analyst can quickly generate an initial design of algorithms, data needs, data flows, data dictionary and data base descriptions, and the contents of the input and output forms.

Because there are always conflicting objectives and trade-offs to be made when designing a system, an analyst needs to be able to investigate alternative designs. This is the second area of major impact of system engineering packages. Normally, an analyst only has time to generate one basic design and then make adjustments to that design to handle the conflicting objectives and special problems. Through the use of system engineering packages alternative designs can be generated by simply changing the initial input requirements. Additionally, the analyst can make changes directly to the data flow diagrams, data stores, or the input and output forms, and then allow the package to make all the adjustments to the system needed to incorporate these changes. Through the use of the ability to quickly and easily investigate alternatives, the analyst is capable of generating a "best" system, a system that will most closely meet the need of the client.

Since these packages make the investigation of alternative systems an easy operation, the analyst is able to address additional concerns in the systems design. For example, error handling routines, system auditability, and security issues are usually addressed after the system has been designed. Using a system engineering package allows the analyst to incorporate these issues in the initial design steps. Making these concerns an integral part of the system design allows for a more efficient final product, one that has not lost all of its advantages because processes that it was not originally designed to handle had to be "tacked on."

As a result of the capability to investigate alternative systems and the ability to incorporate concerns about error handling, auditability, and security into the design process the finished system should be more comprehensive. This is the fourth major impact of using system engineering packages. A more carefully thought-out system should have a longer survival time avoiding the cost of major maintenance work and the cost of having to redesign the system because of initial design errors. This longer survival time does not avoid the need to redesign the system due to changes in the procedures and requirements on the client. However, when changes are needed for these reasons they will be much easier to make, unless, of course, the changes are so extreme that they require a totally new system, an event that is very rare.

The fifth major impact area is in the development of the code needed to implement the system. Even without a code generator these packages deliver a complete set of documentation to the programmer. This documentation makes the system easier to understand and therefore it is faster and easier to generate the code. The inclusion of code generators in these packages make significant changes in the development time for a system. ". . . Code generators can make today's programmers significantly more productive, with gains up to 50:1 as compared to manual coding."[1]

Through the use of these system engineering packages a standard is established for documentation of the system and the code that is generated. When the package is used to develop a system, not only is a standard set for documentation but the documentation is complete. The analyst and maintenance programmers are no longer faced with the problems of trying to discover the purpose of a particular program, module, or subroutine. The characteristics and definitions of the data being used anywhere in the system are readily available. This represents the sixth major area of impact for system engineering packages.

Finally, because of the forced standards, documentation and structured code system maintenance becomes easier and faster. Almost 80 percent of the cost of a software system is in maintenance. Reductions in this cost will significantly reduce the cost of the system. In addition, over 50 percent of the nonoperating budget of a DP shop is devoted to maintenance. Therefore any reduction in this cost will free resources that can be used to handle the backlog of new and improved systems requests sitting on the DP manager's desk.

DISADVANTAGES

The primary disadvantages of systems engineering packages lie in their strengths. First, the standards that can be helpful in system maintenance are enforced standards. Despite the fact that these standards may not meet your needs or may place requirements on the developer that are in conflict with the way the organization normally performs its systems development, these standards must be met. Because of the required standards the organization must either change its policies and procedures or run the risk of having the tool (system engineering packages) ignored.

Once the standards of systems engineering packages have been accepted and they are used in systems development, there is no guarantee that the development time will be shortened. With the ability to investigate alternatives quickly and easily the systems professional may try all possible alternatives in an attempt to find the best system possible. *There are no rules to tell you when to stop investigating alternative systems.* The investigation of alternative systems to this extreme will cancel one of the major advantages of systems engineering packages.

Along with the ability to investigate alternative systems these packages allow the developer to include development issues that traditionally have been ignored until the final stages of implementation. The result of this capability is a more complex system. This system would normally require more coding time, except when code generators are used, and make the job of testing both the modules and the system more difficult and time-consuming. In addition the more complex system is more difficult to explain to the client, requiring more time and effort on the part of the developer.

The disadvantages of code generators have already been well documented by other authors.[1] The code generators in systems engineering packages still suffer from the same problems. Generators are unable to deal with every function of an application requiring programmer time to finish the code. Also, code generators have difficulty integrating with other parts of the complete system, for example the DBMS, report generator, and query language.

Finally, the use of systems engineering packages also creates a problem in maintenance of the system. When making small changes to a system which was developed using systems engineering packages, are the changes made manually or is the entire system redeveloped? If the entire system is redeveloped then small changes to the system can become very time-consuming. If the changes are made manually without the aid of systems engineering packages, then the original system documentation becomes out-of-date, and there is a risk that it will not be usable when major design changes are required.

IMPACT ON PROTOTYPING

One of two assumptions is being made whenever a decision is made to use prototyping as a strategy for systems development. The first assumption is that any system produced will be better than the current system. The second assumption is that client and developer cannot specify the requirements of the system completely enough to use the traditional development life cycle. If either or both of these assumptions are true, then prototyping offers the best chance of success in development of the system. Prototyping in effect shortens the analysis and design time for initial system development at the cost of extending the implementation time for the completed system.

If prototyping is done correctly, the use of systems engineering packages will not significantly decrease the time required to introduce the initial system. However, these packages will have a major impact on the time required to deliver the completed system. Because of the nature of these packages, already discussed, the prototype system will be more complete than a system developed without them. In addition, the prototype system will be completely documented with very little additional effort on the part of the developer.

Once an initial prototype system has been developed using systems engineering packages, the iterative procedure of implementing revisions and enhancements is greatly simplified.[2] Since the system is already defined within the systems engineering package, revisions can be made on-line and their effects traced through the complete system. This provides major time and cost savings in the prototyping step that is usually the most expensive for the organization.

SUMMARY

Despite all the advances being made in computer technology and methods for systems development, it is still impossible for the systems professional to meet the demands of management. While there are many tools that can help the systems professional deliver a new or improved system to management to aid in decision making, the time needed to employ these tools is not available. System engineering packages have come a long way in providing the professional with a means of using these tools and delivering working systems to management in a cost-effective manner.

While there are disadvantages to using software engineering packages, the potential gains from their use far exceed any problems that might arise. Through the use of system engineering packages many of the mechanical time-consuming activities can be automated. This automation frees the developer to do the more critical job of working with the manager to better analyze the requirements of a system. Because of this, the manager can receive the right system sooner and at lower cost.

Notes

1. Lee L. Gremillion and Timothy P. Shea, "Cobol Application Code Generators," *Journal of Systems Management,* December 1985.
2. Ralph Harrison, "Prototyping and the Systems Development Life Cycle," *Journal of Systems Management,* August 1985.

Reading 2–4

USE OF SYSTEM DEVELOPMENT METHODOLOGY AND TOOLS

By Jane M. Carey, Ph.D., and Raymond McLeod, Jr., DBA

Over the past several years various tools and methodologies have been created to aid in the system development process (see Appendixes A and B). The manager of the software development process is faced with the dilemma of selecting appropriate tools to fit the particular development situation. Managers who elect to remain with traditional techniques may feel some anxiety when they hear their colleagues tossing around tool jargon that they don't understand. What is really happening in industry? Which tools are being utilized? Which tools enhance productivity? If your company does not use the structured design aid tools, are you doomed to failure?

Although tool utilization has been studied and correlated with descriptive variables such as budget and length of existence of organizations,[2,4,5,7] little attempt has been made to determine the effectiveness of these tools in regard to productivity enhancement. Has the "structured revolution" really hit the industry? Which tools are being utilized in organizations? Which tools are considered to be effective? These questions should be addressed if:

1. System developers, end users, and computer specialists are to intelligently select tools and methods appropriate to their needs.

2. Computer specialists are to gain expertise in those tools most valuable in achieving user satisfaction and career goals.

Two hundred and fifty questionnaires were mailed to information resource directors of companies randomly selected from the *Directory of Computer Facilities in Texas* (1983).[3] The response rate was 48.4 percent, very high for an industrial sample. The variables measured by the questionnaire covered three main areas:

1. Descriptive or demographic information (tenure, number of personnel, budget, existence of an information center, and so forth).

2. Performance information (user satisfaction, employee morale, deadline and cost overruns, post-implementation bugs).

3. Tool and methodology usage (eleven tools and methodologies measured on a 5-point Likert scale from "never utilized" to "frequently utilized").

Reprinted with permission from *Journal of Systems Management,* March 1988, pp. 30–35.

FINDINGS

Since all of the companies are Texas based, using this sample may hamper generalization to all organizations. However, there is no reason why Texas organizations would be expected to be much different from those in the other states or in any other country where computer-based business systems are the norm.

Table 1 contains the means of frequency analysis of the study. Taking these findings and creating from them a "typical" organization using the *arithmetic means* of each demographic response yields a composite profile that includes the following facts:

- The "typical" organization obtained its first computer in 1971.
- The data processing staff includes 1.2 systems analysts, 4.9 programmers, 6.6 operations personnel, and .87 data base administrators.

TABLE 1   Profile of "Average" Company

Approximately when did your organization get its first computer? Mean: 1971.
Approximately how many personnel do you have in the following categories?

Number of People	
Systems analysis	Mean 1.2
Programming	Mean 4.9
Operations	Mean 6.6
Data base	Mean 0.87

About how long does it take to complete the average computer project?
Mean: 2.8 months.
Approximately how many micros do you have? Mean: 20.3
If you have micros, are any networked?

Yes: 16 (13.2%)
No: 98 (81%)
No response: 7 (5.8%)

Approximately what percent of departmental time (person days) is devoted to the following system life cycle phases?

Analysis	Mean 15.5%
Design	Mean 19.5%
Implementation	Mean 27.8%
Maintenance	Mean 31.9%

Has your company established an information center?

Yes: 34 (28.1%)
No: 86 (71.1%)
No response: 1 (.8%)

- The organization has an IBM mainframe or minicomputer and 20.3 microcomputers that are not networked.
- 2.8 months are required to complete the average project.
- Increasing proportions of departmental time are incurred as the system life cycle proceeds—in analysis (15.5 percent), design (19.5 percent), implementation (27.8 percent), and maintenance (31.9 percent).
- The organization has not established an information center.

Table 2 lists the tools and methodologies (described in the appendixes) along with the breakdown of responses. These usage patterns reveal that systems flowcharts and data flow diagrams are the only tools receiving consistent use ("always" or "very frequently"). A second tier of usage includes structured English, decision tables, and structure charts. Tools receiving scant mention are HIPO, Nassi-Schneiderman, and Warnier-Orr. Of the methodologies, top-down analysis enjoys consistent use, with structured walkthroughs and prototyping fairly close behind. All in all, the usage patterns, especially for the more publicized structured tools and methodologies, are disappointing. These usage patterns are also reflected in Table 3, which lists the tools in order of utilization from the most highly utilized to the least utilized.

Only 5 percent of the organizations utilize all 11 tools on a frequent basis. Almost 16 percent of the organizations do not use any of the tools at all. The mean number of tools used by organizations is 3.

TABLE 2   Tool Usage

Please indicate how often your personnel use the following tools on a system development project.

Tool	Always	Very Frequently	Frequently	Seldom	Never
1. Systems flow charts	12.0%	21.0%	26.0%	17%	21%
2. Decision tables	.8	5.1	13.0	37	41
3. Data flow diagrams	9.1	14.9	29.0	25	21
4. Structured English	5.0	13.0	22.0	23	32
5. HIPO charts	.8	1.7	1.7	29	62
6. Structure charts	6.0	5.0	18.0	22	47
7. Nassi-Schneiderman diagrams	3.0	.8	.8	15	77
8. Warnier-Orr diagrams methodology	0	0	3.0	16	75
9. Top-down analysis	8.0	24.0	16.0	19	30
10. Structured walkthroughs	5.0	15.0	24.0	19	35
11. Prototyping	2.5	13.0	16.0	25	41

Note: Percentages may not always add up to 100% due to lack of response and/or rounding.

TABLE 3   Utilization of Tools and Methodologies

	Percent of Organizations Utilizing Tool
1. Data flow diagrams	79%
2. Systems flowcharts	75
3. Top-down analysis	70
4. Structured walkthroughs	65
5. Structured English	61
6. Prototyping	49
7. Structure charts	43
8. Warnier-Orr diagrams	25
9. HIPO charts	25
10. Nassi-Schneiderman diagrams	7
11. Decision tables	5

TOOLS AND PRODUCTIVITY

In an effort to gauge the impact of productivity tools on performance variables, correlation analysis is conducted between all of the performance variables and the individual tools, between the demographic variables and the individual tools, and between the performance variables and the demographic variables. The most important findings are:

1. Top-down analysis (TDA) correlates negatively with the number of post-implementation bugs in delivered systems. The number of bugs decreases as the utilization of TDA increases (Pearson Product Moment Correlation $= .2470$, $p = .003$). Top-down analysis places early emphasis on the detection and correction of interface bugs which are often the most difficult to resolve. Also, in TDA the lowest level modules are developed last, focusing on high levels of module cohesiveness and low levels of coupling between modules.

2. Utilization of systems flowcharts also correlates with the number of post-implementation bugs, but the correlation is positive. The number of bugs increases with an increase in the utilization of systems flowcharts (PPMC $= .2122$, $p = .010$). This finding is rather puzzling. Since the data do not provide an answer, we can only hypothesize as to the correlation. The systems flowchart is a technique which describes the physical, device-specific flow of data through the system. Bugs are often due to lack of modularity at the lowest level. The systems flowchart does not address the logic or often even the purpose of these functional primitives. Therefore, there is no reason for bugs in logic to have any relationship with systems flowcharts at all. Also, systems flowcharts are representative of the older, more traditional techniques which seem to serve quite well as specification

tools for simple, small systems, but lack sufficient power for large, complex systems.

3. The level of morale of data processing employees also correlates negatively with the utilization of Warnier-Orr diagrams (PPMC = 1.1779, p = .025). As the usage of Warnier-Orr diagrams increases, the morale of the employees decreases. This is a strange and totally unexpected finding. It is our opinion that this correlation is due to some intervening or confounding variable such as size of the organization. The smaller organizations did not use or even recognize some of these techniques, including Warnier-Orr diagrams. It may be that the morale level of the data processing employees is lower in larger organizations and therefore seems to correlate with the use of such techniques as Warnier-Orr diagrams.

4. The Anova technique reveals a significant main effect between budget levels and the number of tools utilized (f = 3.18, p = .016). As the budget level increases, the number of tools utilized also increases. This is a logical finding. While many of these tools are off-line and in themselves are not expensive, training the DP staff to utilize these tools is an expensive process and thus larger budgets are needed.

CONCLUSIONS

If this sample can be generalized, tool utilization in industry is lower than expected. Only 5 percent of the organizations studied utilize all 11 tools on a frequent basis. Almost 16 percent of the organizations do not use any of the tools. The ranking of the tools and methodologies in terms of utilization identifies data flow diagrams, system flowcharts, and several of the structured methodologies as the most popular. Decision tables and Nassi-Schneiderman diagrams are almost never used. Prototyping is utilized by 49 percent of the organizations to some degree. Prototyping has become more popular with the advent of fourth generation tools that lead to easy prototypes.

The research findings of Lientz and Swanson (1980)[7] are confirmed with the significant effect of budget levels of organizations on the number of tools utilized. As the budget level increases, the number of utilized tools also increases. This makes sense, because while the tools themselves are not expensive, they may require large amounts of machine overhead and require a sophisticated computer staff.

The impact of productivity tools on performance is disappointing. Very few of the performance variables correlate favorably with the individual tools or number of tools used by organizations. Top-down analysis does seem to contribute to fewer post-implementation bugs.

What information can data processing professionals draw from this study?

1. The study provides a means of comparing tool selection and utilization levels with general practice.

2. The study suggests that DP professionals are in the majority rather than the minority if they do not use (or possibly even understand) many of these tools.

3. The study shows that companies with large DP budgets are using more tools than are companies with low budgets, but it is not clear whether the tools contribute to the growth of the company or are acquired after growth and profitability are achieved.

4. The study provides a profile of computing facilities for comparative purposes.

The bottom line is that current tools have not proven to be the panacea that many anticipated. There is still a need for tools that increase the productivity of the systems analysis, design, and maintenance.

APPENDIX A
DEVELOPMENT TOOLS

The most popular systems development tools are systems flowcharts, decision tables, data flow diagrams, structured English, HIPO charts, structure charts, Nassi-Schneiderman diagrams, and Warnier-Orr diagrams.

SYSTEMS FLOWCHARTS

Systems flowcharts are system-level graphic charts that illustrate the physical flow (device-specific) of information through the system. This tool is part of the traditional approach to analysis and design and has been used for many years. Several of the symbols have been standardized on a national and international basis.

DECISION TABLES

Decision tables are logic design aids that serve to decompose a complex problem into its component conditions and actions. There are four sections to each decision table; the upper two deal with conditions, and the lower two deal with actions. The strength of the decision table is that all possible conditions and their resultant actions can be taken into consideration.

DATA FLOW DIAGRAMS

Data flow diagrams (DFDs) are graphical in nature. They present a pictorial representation of the logical flow of information through a system. In this respect, they are similar to systems flowcharts. DFDs have only four symbols (Figure 1), making them especially easy for users to understand. A set of DFDs can be constructed that begins at the overview level, and through step-

FIGURE 1   Data Flow Diagram

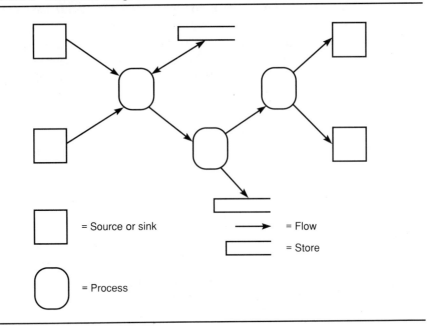

= Source or sink   ⟶ = Flow

                        = Store

= Process

wise refinement, ends at a very detailed level. Together with data dictionaries and process descriptions in structured English, DFDs comprise the main tools of Yourdan's structured approach to system analysis and design.[8]

STRUCTURED ENGLISH

Structured English (SE) is pseudocode that is confined to the three basic control structures of sequence, selection, and repetition. Structured English uses cryptic, English-like phrases that are confined to a limited set of verbs such as WRITE, COMPUTE, ADD, and so forth as well as the data elements defined in the data dictionary.

HIPO CHARTS

HIPO stands for Hierarchy plus Input, Process, Output. There are two parts of this technique—both of them are graphic. The first part is a visual table of contents (VTOC) that sets up the modules in a hierarchy that looks much like an organization chart. The second part is a three-section diagram (Figure 2) that lists all input, all processes, and all output, and frequently is called an "IPO" chart. Upper level IPO charts are called overview diagrams; those on the bottom level are called detail diagrams.

FIGURE 2   Functional HIPO Chart

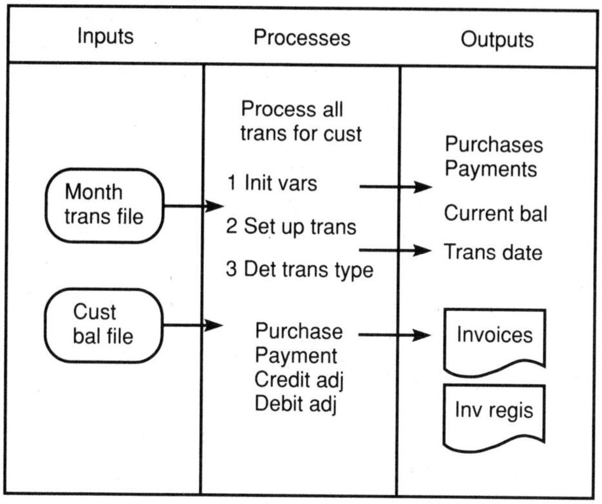

Inputs	Processes	Outputs

Process all trans for cust

Month trans file

1 Init vars

2 Set up trans

3 Det trans type

Cust bal file

Purchase
Payment
Credit adj
Debit adj

Purchases
Payments

Current bal

Trans date

Invoices

Inv regis

STRUCTURE CHARTS

Structure charts are the same as a VTOC in the HIPO methodology. They lay out the hierarchy of the modules within a system including the span of control of modules. The only difference between the two tools is that the VTOC is always accompanied by a HIPO functional chart whereas the structure chart may stand alone.

NASSI-SCHNEIDERMAN DIAGRAMS

The Nassi-Schneiderman diagram (also called a structured flowchart) is a graphic logic aid tool that forces the analyst to work in a modular, top-down mode (Figure 3). There are three basic elements (process, decision, and iteration) contained within a box structure that represents the entire module.

WARNIER-ORR DIAGRAMS

Warnier-Orr diagrams resemble hierarchical charts laid on their sides so that the output or detail modules are on the right side and the control modules are on the left side. The symbols include braces that delineate each level of modules, " + "s to show alteration, and parentheses with numbers to show interaction (Figure 4).

FIGURE 3 Nassi-Schneiderman Diagram

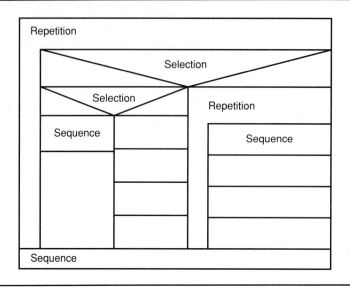

FIGURE 4 Warnier-Orr Diagram

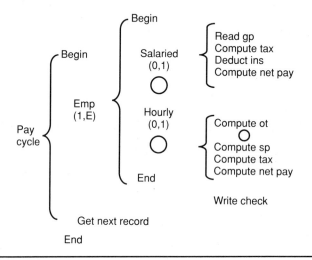

APPENDIX B
STRUCTURED DESIGN APPROACHES

The structured design approaches that are used include top-down analysis, structured walkthroughs, and prototyping.

TOP-DOWN ANALYSIS

Top-down analysis occurs when the analyst begins at the overview or general level and makes stepwise refinements to end up at the lowest level of detail. This is an interactive process. The analysis, design, coding, testing, and installation steps occur at each level. The greatest advantage to this technique is that the difficult interface bugs are found early in the development process rather than at the end when deadlines draw near. This is the opposite of the traditional bottom-up development process.

STRUCTURED WALKTHROUGHS

Structured walkthroughs require programmers and/or analysts to meet on a routine basis and "walk-through" their designs or codes with other members of the team. The walkthroughs are meant to provide constructive criticism, consistency, and an opportunity to catch logic errors that typically are not detected until the testing phase. One beneficial side effect is that well-handled walkthroughs promote synergism and elevate team morale. Poorly handled walkthroughs actually can decrease morale primarily due to ego problems.

PROTOTYPING

Prototyping is concerned with developing a shell version of a system where most of the user interfaces such as screens and reports are developed very quickly in order to ensure that the user approves of the output. Many fourth-generation tools such as application generators and code libraries have facilitated prototyping. The problem with prototyping is that the user sees the shell and cannot understand why the end system takes so long. Users do not understand that the modeling and building of the data underlying the shell is the time-consuming and critical portion of system development.

Notes

1. Brooks, F. P. *The Mythical Man-Month*. Reading, MA; Addison-Wesley, 1975.
2. Colter, M. A. "A Comparative Examination of Systems Analysis Techniques." *MIS Quarterly* 8, March 1984, pp. 51–66.
3. *Directory of Computer Facilities in Texas*, 1983. College of Business Administration, Texas A & M University.

4. Ferguson, G. T. "Making Productivity Tools Work." *Infosystems* 30, December 1983, pp. 58ff.
5. Guimaraes, T. "The Study of Application Program Development Techniques." *Communications of the ACM* 28, May 1985, pp. 494–499.
6. Hackman, J. R., and G. R. Oldham. "Development of the Job Description Survey." *Journal of Applied Psychology* 55, June 1971, pp. 259–286.
7. Lientz, B. P., and E. B. Swanson. "Impact of Development Productivity Aids on Application System Maintenance." *Proceedings Conference on Application Development Systems,* 1980, ACM, pp. 114–120.
8. Yourdan, E. *Managing the Structured Techniques.* New York: Yourdan Press, 1976.

Reading 2–5

USING THE MICROCOMPUTER FOR PROJECT MANAGEMENT

L. Murphy Smith

Project management guidelines make project teams accountable for deadlines and help them examine their performance successes and failures. Project management techniques, which include the program evaluation review technique (PERT) chart, Gantt chart, and critical path method (CPM) diagram, help control timing and reduce the cost of projects. This article provides an overview of recent developments in project management software, including specific information regarding several software packages, and discusses how other applications can be linked to project management software.

Before the age of computers, it was extremely difficult to keep track of the numerous details of planning and completing large projects. Project management software was initially expensive and developed for mainframe computers. Today, there are a number of relatively inexpensive microcomputer project management software packages available. Project management microcomputer software sales were recently estimated at $40 million and estimates indicate they will be as high as $70 million by the early 1990s.

Project management techniques are extremely helpful in coordinating projects that involve many persons. As microcomputer network systems expand and proliferate, allowing a number of users to work together in an integrated system, project management software sales will continue to increase.

At this time, however, most microcomputer users do not have project management software, because these applications are not as obvious or well known as spreadsheets, word processing, and data base applications. This situation is changing, as micocomputer users learn more about the features, ease of use, and benefits of project management software. Those who have used these software packages indicate that the time and effort involved in becoming proficient were well spent.

THREE PROJECT MANAGEMENT TECHNIQUES

The three most common project management techniques are the Gantt chart, the PERT chart, and the CPM diagram.

The Gantt Chart

Time-event network analysis is used for planning and controlling time relationships between the events or stages of a program or project. The first time-event network analysis was developed by Henry L. Gantt early in the 20th century. The Gantt chart, although simple in concept, is considered revolutionary in management. Gantt understood that project objectives should be regarded as a series of interdependent events that people can comprehend and follow.

The Gantt chart is a bar chart that has been adapted to project planning and control. Tasks are shown on the left side of the chart and units of time (e.g., days and weeks) are shown across the top. For each task, a bar is drawn showing the period during which that task is expected to be completed. As the project proceeds, a marking procedure (e.g., shading in the open space for each bar) is used to record the progress toward completion of each task.

Exhibit 1 shows a Gantt chart for a computer system implementation project with seven tasks, or events, labeled A to G. Task A, ordering the necessary software and hardware, must be completed during the first week. By the end of the sixth week, the new system should be completely installed and operating.

The PERT Chart

PERT was developed by the U.S. Navy Special Projects Office during the Polaris missile system project in the late 1950s. PERT worked very well in coordinating the thousands of contractors and subcontractors involved in the Polaris project, and for years afterward PERT was widely used throughout the defense and aerospace industries. The same principles of network planning and control continue to be used in many defense and aerospace programs, although the PERT acronym is disappearing. Since its origin in the defense industry, PERT has expanded into numerous business applications

EXHIBIT 1   Gantt Chart for a New Computer System Implementation

				Week			
Event	1	2	3	4	5	6	

A
B
C
D
E
F
G

EVENTS:

A = Order computer hardware and software
B = Prepare physical site
C = Train personnel
D = Install computer hardware and software
E = Test new system
F = Phase out old system
G = Operate and maintain new system

and is now used for planning, coordinating, and controlling large and complex projects such as computer systems development and implementation.

The PERT chart is a diagrammatical representation of a project, using arrows and nodes. The arrows represent project tasks that require an expenditure of time and resources. The nodes represent milestone points, indicating the completion of one or more tasks and the initiation of one or more subsequent tasks. The PERT chart indicates which projects must be done before others. The chart may be used to calculate the minimum time needed to complete a project, based on the chart's critical (longest time) path. Slack time for noncritical path tasks can also be determined. PERT does not actually do planning; it forces managers to plan. Although PERT does not make control automatic, it creates an environment in which control principles can be effectively applied.

Exhibit 2 shows a PERT diagram for the same project illustrated in the Gantt chart in Exhibit 1. The PERT diagram clearly shows the relationship of predecessor activities to successor activities (e.g., A to C). The critical (longest) path in this diagram is six weeks (B-F-G), so the shortest time in which the project can be completed is six weeks.

The CPM Diagram

CPM was developed by DuPont and Remington Rand about the same time as PERT. Like PERT, CPM was developed to help manage large projects with many interrelated activities. CPM was designed for industrial projects in which activity (event) times were known with virtual certainty, unlike PERT, which originally incorporated uncertainty (probability estimates) into activity completion dates. CPM also differed from PERT by its focus on the costs incurred to shorten the times of individual activities by adding more resources. Today, however, there is no practical distinction between PERT and CPM—computer software created for time-event network analysis usually includes features permitting analysis based on both uncertain activity times and time versus cost trade-offs.

ACCOUNTING APPLICATIONS OF PROJECT MANAGEMENT

Project management applications, which include both PERT and Gantt diagrams, can readily be applied to accounting projects, such as audits, management consulting projects, and tax services. Exhibit 3, an example of a PERT

EXHIBIT 2   PERT Chart for a New Computer System Implementation

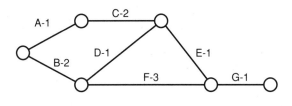

EVENTS:

A = Order computer hardware and software
B = Prepare physical site
C = Train personnel
D = Install computer hardware and software
E = Test new system
F = Phase out old system
G = Operate and maintain new system

EXHIBIT 3 PERT Chart of Audit of Willie's Bricks, 5/3/89

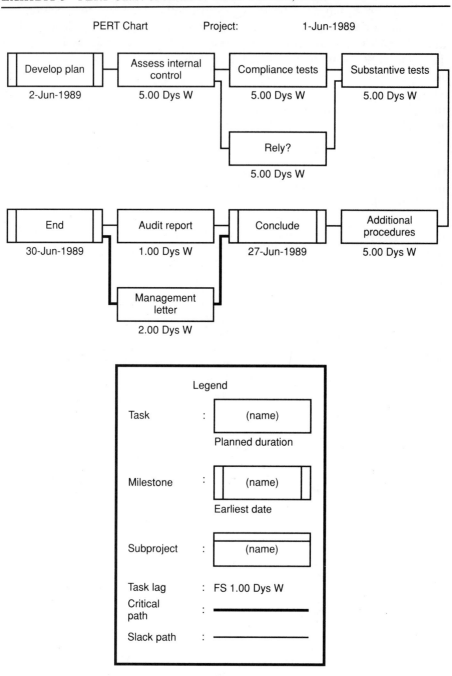

diagram for an audit engagement, was prepared using Harvard Total Project Manager II.

For illustration purposes, only the major audit tasks are shown. The first step is to develop the audit plan, officially beginning on June 2, 1989. Then the internal controls must be assessed to determine which controls to rely on during the audit. Next, compliance tests are conducted while the auditor determines whether reliance can be placed on these controls. Following compliance tests, the auditor plans and conducts substantive tests and additional procedures, if needed. Finally, the auditor reaches the summary conclusions and prepares the audit report and the management letter to the audit.

The process of creating the PERT diagram with Harvard Total Project Manager II is relatively easy because the system is menu driven. As tasks are added or deleted from the project, the software automatically recalculates the dates for the beginning and ending tasks, as well as for the overall project.

After the data is entered, other textual and graphic reports are immediately available, such as the Gantt chart, the PERT Zoom, a work breakdown graph, a task and milestone list, and a task work summary. An example of the PERT Zoom is shown in Exhibit 4; it provides a quick visual image of the steps in the project. Additional information about Harvard Total Project Manager II and other project management software packages is provided in Exhibit 5.

EXHIBIT 4   PERT Zoom

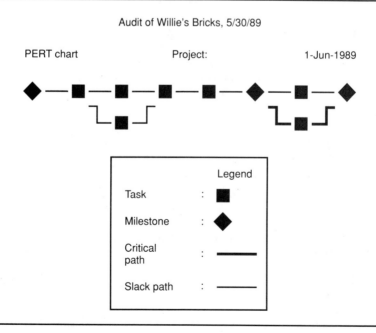

Audit of Willie's Bricks, 5/30/89

PERT chart   Project: 1-Jun-1989

EXHIBIT 5   Project Management Software Vendors

Product	System Specificaitons	List Prices ($)
Insta Plan InstaPlan Corp Suite 311 655 Redwood Highway Mill Valley CA 94941 (415) 389-1414	512K bytes of RAM Tasks per project are limited by memory	99
Microsoft Project 3.0 Microsoft Corp 16011 NE 36 St PO Box 97017 Redmond WA 98073-9717 (206) 882-8080	256K bytes of RAM Tasks per project are limited by memory	395
PROMIS Strategic Software Planning Corp 245 First St Cambridge MA 02142 (617) 577-8800	512K bytes of RAM Tasks per project are limited by disk space	2,995
Primavera Project Planner Primavera Systems Inc 2 Bala Plaza Bala Cynwyd PA 19004 (215) 667-8600	512K bytes of RAM Tasks per project are 10,000 maximum	2,500
ProTrac Timberline Software 9405 SW Gemini Beaverton OR 97005 (503) 626-6775	256K bytes of RAM Tasks per project are 999 maximum	4,110 (single user) 6,111 (multiuser)
Pertmaster Advance Westminster Software Inc 3235 Kifer St Santa Clara CA 95051 (408) 736-6800	320K bytes of RAM Tasks per project are limited by memory	1,495
Harvard Total Project Manager II Software Publishing Corp 1901 Landings Dr PO Box 7210 Mountain View CA 94039 (415) 962-8910	512K bytes of RAM Tasks per project are limited by memory	595

THE COST MANAGEMENT PROCESS

The cost management process involves estimating, project management, and job costing. The first step in the process is to develop an estimate for the project and to integrate that information with a schedule to create a cost plan. Most businesses seek contracts in a fiercely competitive environment, which results in a low profit margin. The careful completion of the cost management process is crucial because there is usually little margin for error.

Whether estimating the cost of building a bridge or of providing an audit, cost management means covering all costs and providing the firm with the best chance of making a profit. After the job is acquired, the firm must control job costing, which involves determining actual costs as they occur and comparing these costs to budgeted costs (from the estimate).

Project management is integral to both estimating and job costing. Outlining and scheduling the tasks of a project form the basis for estimating the project cost. After a job is acquired, controlling job costs depends largely on effective project management.

Managing many people effectively is critical for the successful completion of a project. Resource leveling is a technique that permits a project supervisor, such as an audit manager, to examine, track, and plan resources (including both people and materials). Resource leveling permits the project supervisor to use what-if analysis and examine various approaches in planning the project.

SOFTWARE FOR PROJECT MANAGEMENT

Several project management software packages, including Pertmaster Advance, InstaPlan, and Primavera Project Planner, offer menu-driven systems similar to Lotus. Users familiar with Lotus, therefore, will have little difficulty learning to use these project planners. Pertmaster uses input screens in which all data can be entered at one time and both activities and resources can be seen together on one screen. Other software packages can present only one activity at a time. InstaPlan provides an outlining capability for activities. The project supervisor can initially enter the major tasks and include details later by adding up to 12 levels of indented tasks.

The outline approach permits a project supervisor to see the broad structure of the project; detailed tasks can be summarized without losing the ability to interconnect tasks and time sequencing can be used to link each task or group of tasks to predecessor tasks. As with other project management software, InstaPlan includes a resource leveling feature. Exhibit 6 compares features available among the project management software packages. ProTrac can make Gantt and PERT charts; the others can also make CPM diagrams. As noted earlier, both PERT and CPM use the same basic principles, so either approach can be effectively used to solve the same time-event planning problem.

EXHIBIT 6 Project Management Software Summary of Features

Product / Features	InstaPlan	Microsoft Project 3.0	PROMIS	Primavera Project Planner	ProTrac	Pertmaster Advance	Harvard Total Project Manager II
Gantt, PERT, or CPM	All	All	All	All	Gantt, PERT	All	All
Resource loading report	Yes	Yes	Yes	Yes	Yes	Yes	Yes
Variable schedule units	Years, quarters, months, weeks, days, hours	Months, weeks, days, hours, minutes	Years, months, weeks, days	Months, weeks, days	Days	Years, months, weeks, days, hours, minutes	Years, months, weeks, days, hours, minutes
On-line help	Yes	Yes	Yes	Yes	No	Yes	Yes
User interface is similar to Lotus	Yes	No	No	Yes	No	Yes	No

Note: The resource loading report feature allows users to generate reports based on people, equipment, or costs.

88

PROJECT MANAGEMENT SOFTWARE LINKS TO OTHER SOFTWARE

Because project management (in particular scheduling) is closely related to job estimating, it is not surprising that there are now links between these two types of software. Constructive Computing, for example, offers direct links between its two estimating packages (i.e., QuickEst Basic for $795 and QuickEst Advanced for $3,995) and three of the project management packages (i.e., Project Management Integrated System, or PROMIS, from Strategic Software Planning Corp., Microsoft Project from Microsoft Corp., and Primavera). Currently, most estimating done on microcomputers uses spreadsheets, but this situation is changing as more microcomputer-based estimating software becomes available.

Project management software must be linked with other applications, such as accounting, job costing, and forecasting; creating these interfaces is crucial to the efficient use of the project software. Version 2.0 of Pertmaster Advance from Westminster Software Inc. offers new importing and exporting features; it can directly read and create Lotus 1-2-3, Borland's Paradox, and dBASE III files. The majority of the more popular project management packages permit the importing and exporting of dBASE III and Lotus 1-2-3 files.

Strategic Software provides direct interfaces to Lotus, dBASE, and ASCII data formats with its Project Management Integrated system. Robert Monroe, a software product marketing manager, states:

> Ultimately, true integration of project management and accounting is where the industry is heading. The differences between the sciences of accounting and project management may keep their functions separate, but data will be joined through links.[1]

Exhibit 7 illustrates how project management software packages can be interfaced with other applications.

CONCLUSIONS

More and more traditionally manual jobs are being performed with microcomputer software applications. Project management software packages, now available for as little as $99, can prepare Gantt, PERT, and CPM diagrams and help achieve more efficient time and resources management. In addition, project management software can be linked with job estimating software to further control the job management process (i.e., estimating, project management, and job costing).

Using project management software, accountants can more effectively plan and control audit engagements, management consulting projects, and tax services. Project management software packages are increasingly user friendly—many have menu-driven systems similar to Lotus to facilitate ease of use. Interfaces have been developed that permit the importing and export-

EXHIBIT 7   Project Management Software Interfaces to Other Applications

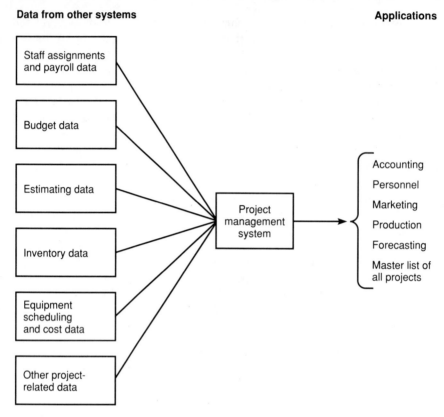

Data from other systems   **Applications**

Staff assignments and payroll data

Budget data

Estimating data

Inventory data

Project management system

Equipment scheduling and cost data

Other project-related data

Accounting
Personnel
Marketing
Production
Forecasting
Master list of all projects

Note:
Data from other systems may be in the form of Lotus, dBASE III, or ASCII files for selected project management software packages.

ing of data between project management software packages and other applications, such as dBASE III and Lotus 1-2-3. Project management software is an increasingly useful tool for planning and controlling projects.

Notes

1. Kristina B. Sullivan, "Software Developers Are Beginning to Meet the Connectivity Needs of Users," *PC Week*, February 23, 1988, pp. 87–89.

CHAPTER 3

Data Base Systems

The traditional approach to data management is characterized by separate and frequently overlapping file structures maintained by various units within an organization. The media and file storage techniques employed often vary widely among departments and functional areas. For example, one department might utilize immediate-access, on-line computer files, another might use sequential computer files accessible only through periodic batch processing runs, while others might use paper files maintained in file cabinets and desk drawers. Departments are often unaware of data items maintained by other departments, and many common data items are stored (redundantly and perhaps inconsistently) by more than a single department. Furthermore, even if data availability is known, accessing the data might be very difficult due to media incompatibilities, format differences, definitional reasons, or proprietary attitudes. Thus, sharing of data in the traditional file management environment was very difficult and often simply not feasible.

The data base approach to data management seeks to overcome these and other primary limitations of the traditional approach. In contrast to the traditional departmental or application-oriented view of information, the data base approach views information as a firmwide resource which is to be shared by the various units within the organization. The data base approach involves integrating related traditional files into a single logical data structure which is maintained in direct access storage. Data redundancy and data inconsistency are reduced because a data element is normally stored only once in the integrated data base. Data accessibility is enhanced because the data base can be quickly accessed via on-line computer terminals. Another advantage of the data base approach is that the complexities of data storage and retrieval are handled by the system itself. This feature, known as data independence, greatly simplifies applications software development and maintenance, and promotes flexibility.

These and other data base features are made possible by software packages known as data base management systems (DBMS). DBMS provide links between users and the physical data base, which facilitates user access, manipulation, and retrieval of stored data. From a user standpoint, a major advantage of DBMS is increased accessibility to data and reporting flexibility. DBMS typically provide user-friendly, almost English-like, data manipulation languages. These languages allow users to retrieve selected data from the data base and develop their own specialized reports. This is particularly important to managers, who no longer have to wait to the end of the week or month for a special report. Thus, for the first time, managers may have special reports tailored to a particular decision on a timely basis.

The increased accessibility of data provided by data bases poses potential internal control problems for accountants and auditors. Fortunately, many of these concerns are alleviated by access controls which are typically an integral part of the DBMS. Most DBMS provide a means of limiting the set of data elements which can be viewed by each DBMS user. This "data window" can then be tailored to the particular information needs of an individual user. The data base administrator (DBA) is responsible for establishing the data windows for each user, defines the data elements to be included in the data base, and organizes and formats the data. These tasks are accomplished by the DBA using the data definition language component of the DBMS.

From a more technical standpoint, DBMS may be described as providing linkages between the physical storage of data and a user's logical view of data (i.e., the DBMS link the physical data base and the logical data base). Numerous physical storage and retrieval techniques are used in DBMS and, fortunately, such complexities are the domain of the DBA and are transparent to DBMS users. However, in order to become more effective users, accountants and managers must be familiar with the three logical data models currently employed in DBMS: the hierarchical, network, and relational models.

This chapter focuses on the relational model since virtually all recently developed commercial DBMS are based on it. In 1986 the American National Standards Institute (ANSI) adopted SQL (structured query language) as the official standard for relational languages. Since that time SQL has become the de facto standard interface for relational data base systems. A primary advantage of the SQL standard is that applications written with SQL can be easily transported from one computer platform to another and can be easily linked across different platforms in a network. Despite the current popularity of the relational model and SQL, many DBMS experts believe that a new data base technology, object-oriented data bases (OODBMS), will replace the relational model in the 1990s.

The readings included in this chapter address the fundamentals of DBMS from both a practical and a conceptual perspective. The initial article, "DBMS Basics," provides a primer on the data base concept and related terminology and introduces the three principal logical models presently utilized in commercial DBMS. The second article, "Using the Relational Data Base," demonstrates the operation of a relational DBMS and describes the advantages of the relational model to management accountants by direct comparison on a network model. The final article, "Current Trends in Transaction Processing Systems," reports on the current state of transaction processing technology and examines the special problems encountered in designing high-volume transaction processing systems.

CHAPTER 3 READINGS

1. Jeff Farin and Amor Nazario, "DBMS Basics," *Infosystems,* June 1986, pp. 42–47.
2. James F. Smith and Amer Mufti, "Using the Relational Data Base," *Management Accounting,* October 1985, pp. 43–54.
3. Vijay Kumar, "Current Trends in Transaction Processing Systems," *Journal of Systems Management,* January 1990, pp. 33–37.

CHAPTER 3 QUESTIONS

Article 1

1. Compare the data base approach to the traditional file-oriented approach to data management.
2. A major advantage of the data base approach is that data independence is provided. What is meant by data independence and what are the implications for users?
3. What is a data dictionary? How is it used?

Article 2

4. What are the key advantages to users of relational DBMS?
5. What are the basic differences between the relational models and previous models (hierarchical, network)?
6. Cite examples of 1:1, 1:n, and m:n relationships from the perspective of your college or university setting.

Article 3

7. Give three examples of industries which have a critical need for high-performance transaction processing systems. What are the special problems encountered in these systems?
8. Describe several potential solution approaches to the problems associated with high-performance transaction processing systems.

General

9. From an audit standpoint, what advantages and disadvantages do DBMS offer?

Case 3-1

DBMS BASICS

In the last two decades progress in the design and development of computer-based accounting information systems has been impressive. Traditionally, computer-based data-processing systems were arranged by departments and applications. Computers were applied to single, large-volume applications such as inventory control or customer billing. Other applications were added once the first applications were operating smoothly.

As additional applications were added, problems in data management developed. Businesses looked for ways to integrate the data-processing systems to make them more comprehensive and to achieve shorter response times. As a consequence, a data base system was developed which was composed of the data base itself, the data base management system, and the individual application programs.

REQUIRED:

a. Explain the basic difference between the traditional approach to data processing and the data base approach in terms of: (1) file structure, and (2) the processing of data.

b. Identify and discuss the favorable and unfavorable issues which a company should consider prior to implementing a data base system.

c. From a programming point of view, one of the purported advantages of DBMS is data independence. What is meant by data independence and how does it make a programmer's job easier?

(CMA Adapted)

Case 3-2

THE SIMS PROJECT

Your university is planning to develop a student information management system (SIMS) to facilitate the processing of student records and information. Presently student information is maintained on diverse file media in five locations on campus:

1. Registrar's office—courses and grade records.
2. Library—books charged out and unpaid overdue fines.

3. Medical clinic—medical records and unpaid medical fees.

4. Public Safety department—records of student parking tickets.

5. Major department—records of student activities, honors, and awards.

The primary objective of the SIMS project is to facilitate the "clearing" of students for registration for classes and for graduation. Due to the state budget crunch, it has become critical that students be barred from registration and graduation until all fees, fines, and other penalties have been paid in full. The university has been losing over a million dollars each year due to such overlooked or ignored charges and has consequently adopted a "get tough" policy. A secondary objective is to facilitate the granting of student awards at graduation. The cost of developing the project is expected to be $250,000.

You have been retained as a consultant to help develop a conceptual or logical data base for the SIMS project.

REQUIRED:

1. The five original file systems were developed independently by the respective units. What resistance, if any, might you expect from the individual units?

2. What data elements in each original file system would likely be stored redundantly (and probably inconsistently)?

3. What key data elements would you recommend to be included in the data base?

4. Given the system requirements above, what logical data model would you recommend for the data base? Why?

5. Assume that the administration also desires that in addition to generating student course schedule reports for each student, SIMS be able to generate student rosters for each section of each course. What logical data model would you recommend for SIMS now?

Case 3–3

INVERTED FILES

Inverted files are a physical means of data association often utilized in DBMS. Inverted files may be accessed using multiple keys (i.e., multiple-key retrieval). Invert the Employee Data File appearing below for the DEPT field by building a DEPT INDEX in good form.

Employee Data File

Disk Address	NAME	DEPT	AGE	SKILL
1000	Smith	FAB	25	1
1100	Jones	CUT	35	3
1200	Tom	PAINT	25	4
1300	Sally	CUT	45	2
1400	Jim	FAB	55	2
1500	Joe	PAINT	35	3
1600	Pam	FAB	25	1
1700	Pat	CUT	35	1
1800	Laura	ASM	55	4

DEPT
INDEX

DEPT	DISK ADDRESS

Reading 3–1

DBMS BASICS

By Jeff Farin and Amor Nazario

A data base management system (DBMS), which is playing an increasingly major role in the development of computer systems, isolates data structures from program structures to provide a flexibility in the design and implementation of application software.

A DBMS also provides an environment in which data can be accessed efficiently by multiple applications with a minimum of redundancy.

When properly used, a DBMS is a powerful tool that can benefit both system developers and users. By understanding the functions, capabilities, and limitations of a DBMS, people can build systems to take advantage of this technology.

WHAT IS A DBMS?

A data base is a set of user data organized to serve one or more application systems efficiently by centralizing the data and minimizing redundant data. What makes a data base different is the data base management system, or operational software, that permits application programs to access the stored information.

A DBMS also provides data independence so that application programs can manipulate data rather than files.

A DBMS achieves its independence by defining data sets for general use. Instead of including a description of each data set in each program, the DBMS stores a single data base definition that can be used by any authorized program. This avoids unnecessary redundancy in programs. Neither an environment section nor file descriptions are necessary in programs that use a DBMS. By eliminating file descriptions, programs become flexible when a data base record layout is modified. Instead of modifying and recompiling every program, only a single data base definition requires modification.

A DBMS also performs housekeeping functions to protect the integrity of an organization's data. DBMS software handles transaction logging of data base updates, security editing, and sophisticated backup and recovery procedures. Each function, centrally executed by the DBMS, frees application programs from these tasks.

The purpose of a DBMS is to manipulate and maintain files, allowing application programs to manipulate and maintain data items that make up the file's records.

DATA DICTIONARY

A data dictionary is an automated device for storing definitions of data elements (fields) and data-element groupings to standardize the meaning of terms.

In its basic form, a data dictionary is simply a place to store definitions and data characteristics such as usage, physical representation, ownership, authorization, and security. More sophisticated data dictionaries contain data definitions to form data base segments and records.

A number of freestanding and DBMS-integrated data dictionary products exist. Functions generally include an on-line facility for maintaining data characteristics, a report generator for listing data-element groupings, and a data description generator that produces high-level language files and definitions.

These functions are passive in nature. No changes or output processed by the data dictionary are directly applied to existing program logic. In many

---

Evolution of DBMS

DBMS technology has its roots in the 1960s, but it was neither developed sufficiently nor used actively until the late 1970s.

DBMS development rests on three foundation stones: the advancement of direct access techniques (disk data storage devices and access methods); the maturity of on-line systems; and requirements voiced by users and application developers.

Direct access and on-line technologies allowed DBMS to be developed, but user and programmer requirements spurred that development. Users quickly grasped the potential of on-line capabilities such as real-time data updating and ad hoc management reporting. Programmers and other application developers perceived a need for flexible systems that could accommodate their users' requirements.

In addition, organizations became aware that the data are a resource. Information about entities—personnel, clients, vendors, inventories—is what organizations require to perform day-to-day tasks.

Well-managed data sharpen a company's competitive edge and enable an organization to coordinate its services efficiently. With this perspective, it makes a lot of sense to keep one set of data in one location, instead of maintaining multiple sets of the same data in many locations.

These requirements fueled the growth of DBMS software. Primary DBMS goals were data independence and flexibility. Once these goals were attained, ad hoc reporting and other features could be addressed, such as the relegation of file housekeeping to the DBMS.

Later, data dictionaries and other productivity tools were developed as additional DBMS features.

---

instances, programs must be modified and recompiled to accommodate data-element modifications.

By comparison, an active data dictionary would cause all data description changes to update any affected program immediately. Unfortunately, no truly active data dictionary currently exists.

Systems software developers continue to enhance existing DBMS products and introduce new ones. Generally, newer DBMS generations consist of more powerful software that makes applications and data bases easier to create.

For example, the Application Development Facility (ADF) from IBM, Armonk, New York, enables an analyst to develop simple data base structures and processing modules quickly. The IDMS from Cullinet Software, Westwood, Massachusetts, features a data dictionary that can be used actively to define data base components.

Optimization packages can be used to fine-tune the physical data base design for processing efficiency.

DATA BASE DESIGN AND MODELING

Under traditional system development efforts, files were constructed to furnish programs unique sets of data, arranged and sequenced in the manner easiest for each program to use. This gave rise to the creation and maintenance of a large number of files: extract files, re-sorted files and the like.

Often, several files contained duplicate data and caused problems for users and programmers because of the need to maintain the same information in more than one place. Because DBMS technology eliminates the need to establish redundant data files and promotes the organization of data for use by multiple applications, system designers and theorists developed the concept of data base design.

Data base design is the technique of developing logical and physical arrangements of data that can be accessed through a DBMS. It is essentially a three-step process: gather data requirements, develop logical data relationships, and implement the physical representation of data.

In gathering data, a designer must identify all information requirements of a user community. Past, present, and future uses of data must be considered in establishing a data base that will serve a universe of potential applications.

The key is in identifying the entities that are significant to an organization, such as clients, vendors, or automobiles, and identifying the attributes that relate to those entities: client name, vendor ID, or automobile color.

The designer then must determine which attributes, often more than one, identify an entity. Social Security number, for instance, identifies an individual, but so does address, home telephone number, and blood type.

Next, the designer must organize the logical relationships between entities, a step known as "data modeling." The designer must consider whether and how entities are related: Can a client own more than one automobile? Can more than one vendor serve the same client?

The designer also must consider whether a relationship has any value to the user community. Clearly, an auto insurer must know whether a single policyholder possesses more than one automobile, while the Division of Motor Vehicles might concern itself only with each individual owner-automobile relationship.

The last step in data base design is to physically develop the data bases that optimally organize the data and their logical relationships.

This is a balancing act in which the designer must consider the design rules set by the installation's DBMS; the benefits of keeping physical representations in parallel with logical relationships; the benefits of keeping structures simple; the maximization of flexibility; and the optimization of system performance.

The designer also must determine how data base records are to be accessed. What is the best "key" for a record? Are alternate indices required or will performance be hindered by creating them?

APPROACHES TO A DBMS

System software companies offer DBMS packages based on one of three approaches: hierarchical, relational, or inverted list.

A hierarchical DBMS, such as IBM's Information Management System, presents data to users in a tree-like structure. Within each record, data elements are organized into pieces of records called segments.

To the user, each record resembles an organization chart in which segments fit into a well-defined hierarchy or tree and there is only one segment at the top level known as the "root." It contains information that identifies the record, as well as some of the most commonly accessed information in the record.

At lower levels are "child" or dependent segments that each contain some set of data elements that are logically related to each other.

The Commission Information segment, for instance (Figure 1), might contain commission goals and actual commissions for the current and prior years. The Policyholder Information segment might contain the policyholder's Social Security number, name, and address. Multiple levels of dependent segments are possible.

The hierarchical model also supports the generation of twin segments or is the means by which multiple occurrences may be recorded and maintained. For instance, if a policy covers two automobiles, a multiple number of Automobile segments can be placed beneath the Insurance Policy segment.

This model allows for variable-length records that consist of one root segment plus any number of dependent segments, with or without twin segments for multiple-occurring pieces of data.

FIGURE 1   Hierarchical Data Base

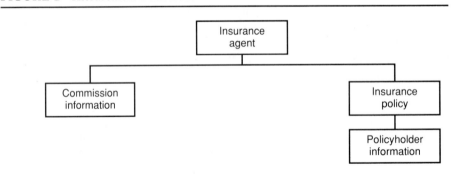

Insurance agent, commission, information, insurance policy, and policyholder information are "segments."
Insurance agent is the "root segment."
Commission information and insurance policy are "children" of insurance agent.
Policyholder information is a "child" of insurance policy.
Commission information and policyholder information are "leaves."

The DBMS accomplishes this flexibility by using a set of pointers, chains, physical positioning, directories, and bit maps that indicate connections.

It is up to the data base designer to establish physical data base representations that result in processing efficiencies, to group data elements that are logically related, and to create segments by considering how data will be accessed by application programs.

High-volume data, for example, are placed in segments that are nearest to the head of the record, to reduce access time.

The hierarchical model allows for an application program to access all or part of a data base record. Access is generally restricted by a data base administrator who authorizes one or more paths for a particular program to use.

Paths, or logical views, are defined by the types of data base segments that can be accessed and by the kind of access that is permitted, such as read only, read/write, and the like.

Application programs process hierarchical data bases one record at a time and must explicitly add, modify, or delete individual records.

A related DBMS type is the network model. Its organization is similar to the hierarchical structure in that the same terminology defines the relationships between segments. The primary difference is that the network model allows a segment to have more than one parent.

This concept provides the facility to model "many-to-many" relationships and makes possible a much greater number of relationships in which a segment can participate.

The relationship between an insurance agent and insurance policy, for example, is defined as a "one-to-many" relationship. The relationship between policyholder information and insurance policy is also defined as "one-to-many." In this model, Insurance Policy is the connector segment that provides the many-to-many link between Insurance Agent and Policyholder Information.

An insurance agent can have many policyholders as clients. A policyholder can deal with many insurance agents; a policyholder can have many policies written by many insurance agents. IDMS from Cullinet Software is an example of a network model DBMS.

In a hierarchical structure, all potential access paths are explicitly defined by the data base designer and the data base administrator. Any application program that accesses the data base must work through a predefined and preauthorized access path. These paths are a major strength of the hierarchical data base.

Data bases can be designed to maximize the efficiency of access by placing the most frequently accessed segments in the top, left side of the hierarchy. This places the segments close to the head of the computerized record for easy access.

When a data base has been designed to optimize access paths, then access will be more efficient compared to other DBMSs. The tree structure also is better suited for transaction-oriented applications.

In a hierarchical DBMS, there is a need to make the data base design as complete and correct as possible at the outset. Unlike other DBMSs, a hierarchical one is more time-consuming and difficult to install. Design errors also are difficult and costly to remedy in a tree structure.

This is the major weakness of the hierarchical approach. It is not as flexible as a relational or inverted list DBMS.

Generally, a hierarchical DBMS is relatively programming intensive. In most cases, record processing depends upon conventional application programs. This type of DBMS does not work well for ad hoc or natural English languages. Instead, the DBMS is treated as an extension of an application program.

The strength of a hierarchical DBMS is in the organization of and access to data, not in the rapid development of query-based systems.

RELATIONAL APPROACH

A relational DBMS presents data to users in the form of tables of rows and columns often called "flat files." The user is isolated from the physical storage of data. A file is represented as a table in which each record in the file is a row, and each field is a column (Figure 2).

A relational DBMS uses a very simple file structure. Each table consists of one record type housing a fixed number of fields. Duplicate records are not allowed, meaning each record in the table is unique. There is no explicit sequence by which records are organized.

Within each record, repeating groups are not allowed, so that each field is uniquely defined. Values are derived from a domain of possible field values. There is no restriction from using the same domain for other field types. For example, an automobile's interior and exterior colors can both have the same value of black.

Once constructed, a set of tables can be accessed by specifying relationships between tables in order to develop useful sets of data.

FIGURE 2 Relational Data Base

Table 1—Auto Insurance Policies

	A Policy Number	B Policyholder	C Soc. Security No.	D License Plate
1	56M1784	SMITH	079–23–8492	JPG–592
2	72X2562	JONES	132–65–3527	696–ZAK
3	89Y3652	WHITE	121–05–3690	292–BFO

Table 1 is equivalent to a file; rows 1, 2, and 3 are records; columns A, B, and C are fields.

There are three basic operations that a user can specify in a relational data base: Select, Project, and Join. In each, one or more tables are manipulated, resulting in the formation of a new table. The user then extracts information of interest from this final table.

The Select operation creates a subset of all records in a table, resulting in a table of records matching a stated criterion. By isolating these records, a user restricts subsequent operations to specific records of interest.

The Project operation creates a subset of the columns in the original table. This operation then could be used to constrain a user's access to data for security or need-to-know limitations.

The Join operation combines relational tables to provide the user with more information than is available in individual tables. The DBMS relates tables by matching fields that appear in more than one table.

The Join operation best illustrates the power of a relational DBMS. It takes full advantage of the segmentation of data into usable pieces (tables) that can be retrieved and combined when necessary.

Unlike hierarchical DBMSs, relational data bases are not built with a limited number of logical views or access paths. Their access paths are specified by the user.

The relational approach to a DBMS is increasing in use. Mainframe products, such as IBM's SQL, are based on the relational model. Most microcomputer-based DBMS software, such as the dBase series from Ashton-Tate, Culver City, California, and the R:Base series, from Microrim, Bellevue, Washington, use the relational approach.

The primary strength of a relational DBMS is its simplicity. The concept of tables is familiar to application developers and users and provides for a logical segmentation of data.

The placement of data in tables also provides a large degree of flexibility if requirements change.

Because of the tabular structure of data, users are not limited by the number of access paths to it. This is a significant advantage because users can create multiple views into an organization's data, extending processing capability.

Because the tabular operations of Select, Project, and Join are applied against entire tables, application developers are relieved from a significant amount of procedural coding. The relational DBMS performs comparison and matching functions across tables, which enables an application developer to concentrate on subsequent operations.

The main weakness of a relational DBMS stems from its strengths. There is a potential risk of costly and inefficient accesses. Users may not select the optimal access path, and may not state their data requests in the manner most efficient for the DBMS. This results from the user's lack of awareness of the physical storage of data, which differs from the tables presented.

It is also difficult for a data base designer to optimize the physical representation of data prior to its use. These problems become more readily apparent when large data bases are being maintained.

INVERTED LIST APPROACH

The inverted list is typified by products such as Adabas from Software AG of Reston, Virginia, in which variable-length records are distributed randomly in a disk file and are indexed on one or more data sets known as "associators."

Each associator is an inverted list that consists of the complete set of values for a specified attribute, such as all colors of automobiles for a finite set of automobiles. For each value, such as black, the associator lists the record numbers that have that value for the attribute of color.

Once established, associators can be used to locate data base records quickly that match a stated criterion. Commands such as "Find all black cars" or "List all red Chevrolets" can be executed rapidly because the associators of color and make point directly to records meeting the criteria. Because of the associators, it is unnecessary to step through the entire data base.

The DBMS uses associators whenever a data base record is accessed, requiring at least one associator per data base. There is no theoretical limit to the number of associators that may be established but the greater the number of associators, the poorer the performance of the DBMS.

Each time a data base record is added, deleted or modified, all associators also are updated, which requires multiple input-output activities when a large number of associators are used.

The inverted list is an excellent DBMS for applications requiring query or ad hoc reporting. Natural, English-style query languages can simplify programming efforts and significantly reduce application development time.

A primary drawback is that performance is relatively poor whenever sequential processing is required, such as batch reporting or bulk transaction processing.

Processing will be faster if other types of DBMSs are used, and probably will be faster if even simpler ISAM or VSAM file organizations or access methods are used.

PERFORMANCE OPTIMIZATION

Performance of a DBMS is related directly to the manner in which data are stored, retrieved, and processed. A hierarchical DBMS, as stated, accesses records through a combination of pointers, physical positioning, chains, directories, and bit maps.

An inverted list DBMS uses associators, a type of index, for access. In a relational DBMS, access is based solely on the comparison of field values. Hierarchical and inverted list approaches both use predetermined access paths, but no access paths are predetermined in a relational DBMS.

The impact of access paths on performance is significant. In an environment in which applications are well defined and data access is thoroughly understood, data base designers are able to optimize the performance of the DBMS.

In a hierarchical data structure, the designer can place active segments close to the highest level in the hierarchy. In an inverted list record, the designer can place the fields most likely to be indexed toward the front of the record layout.

The designer of a relational data base does not have as much control over the access to data. Because access paths in a relational data base can be fabricated, modified, or abandoned quickly, the designer has a more difficult time trying to optimize performance.

To some extent, DBMS performance is affected by the type of indexing. Because a relational DBMS uses no indexing, its performance is not hindered by maintaining pointers. On the other hand, a hierarchical DBMS uses a variety of pointers that must be updated whenever a record is added, deleted, or modified substantially.

Likewise, all associators in an inverted list must be updated when the data base changes. The greater the number of associators, the more performance will be hampered. Simpler structures, such as relational tables, will accommodate numerous record changes quickly.

The effect is dramatic when a data base is reorganized or condensed: relational data bases are a snap, but hierarchical and inverted list data bases require substantially greater machine time and resources. In a relatively static environment, the effect is not as noticeable.

FLEXIBILITY

Flexibility is generally the opposite of performance: As flexibility is enhanced, performance degrades. Relational data bases can be modified easily and used in applications that are not well defined or in a state of flux.

Hierarchical data bases are less forgiving. If the data base structure changes, implementing the change can be time-consuming. Application programs, because they contain procedural logic, also may require modification to match the new hierarchy.

Inverted list modifications fall somewhere in between: data base changes have a somewhat greater impact than relational data base changes, but usually are not nearly as far-reaching as hierarchical modifications.

A critical factor in the selection of a DBMS is the application that the DBMS will serve. If an application tends to be a traditional, transaction-driven system featuring a significant amount of sequential batch processing, a hierarchical DBMS is the optimal choice because it is the best sequential processor and the most efficient handler of large transaction volumes.

Applications using the hierarchical DBMS will require substantial amounts of programming, but the application will be able to use the primary advantages of a DBMS: centralized, nonredundant data; standard file descriptions; improved security; transaction logging; and back-up/recovery capabilities.

If an application requires a substantial amount of query or ad hoc reporting and the bulk of processing is real-time, an inverted list or relational DBMS is appropriate.

Both use simplified, English-style command sets that eliminate the need for detailed, procedural instructions. Both also enable significant improvements in the productivity of application developers.

Both the inverted list and relational DBMS also handle the ever-changing data requirements of end users. The primary advantage of these two DBMSs stems from the simplicity of their structures.

The most talked about topics in the data processing field today are microcomputers, local area networks, and sophisticated telecommunication technologies. To a certain extent, emphasis has shifted from the means of storing data efficiently to the means of allowing data access and manipulation by individual, geographically dispersed users.

But the need to develop useful and well-organized data structures persists. No matter how simple or complex an application, data storage and availability are critical to its success. This requires a careful and well-planned data base design that takes advantage of the attributes of specific DBMS technologies.

Reading 3–2

USING THE RELATIONAL DATA BASE

By James F. Smith and Amer Mufti

Data base management systems (DBMS) are widely used today to store and manage diverse kinds of business data. Because the data files in a DBMS are substantially more centralized and integrated than the files in a traditional system, the DBMS is capable of readily combining and presenting data from different files in ways that would be difficult, or perhaps impossible, using traditional filing systems.

For example, maintenance of personnel and payroll records on a common DBMS allows the user to reconcile these two separate files easily to assure that all individuals who are on the payroll are in fact employees. Under a

Published by *Management Accounting*. Copyright 1985 by National Association of Accountants, Montvale, NJ 07645.

traditional system, it would be necessary to write a separate computer program to perform that reconciliation.

To further complicate matters, under a traditional decentralized file-handling system, separate data files often have their own specific naming conventions as well as their own specific definitions for data elements contained in each file. As a result, a reconciliation or integration of the two files may be extremely difficult. Use of a common DBMS alleviates many of these problems inherent in most traditional decentralized systems.

OBSTACLES TO USE OF DBMS

Despite the considerable advantage to be derived from employing a DBMS, its use, until recently, has been greatly limited due to costs associated with large computer memory requirements and increased processing time needed for a DBMS. But in recent years, the technological improvement of computer hardware has reduced acquisition costs and accelerated data processing speeds to a point where the benefits of employing a common DBMS frequently far outweigh any related additional implementation costs. As a result, the common data base has replaced traditional computer file-handling systems for many types of applications, particularly where timely access to information is essential.

Perhaps the most significant obstacles to the widespread acceptance of the DBMS, however, have involved software rather than hardware limitations, as exemplified by the difficulties experienced by many of us who have tried to use this type of system. As recently as the late 1970s the use of most data base management systems required an understanding of complex, often cumbersome software architecture, and a proficiency in computer languages.

One example of such a system is the commonly used "network" type DBMS currently fostered by the Conference on Data Systems Languages (CODASYL) committee, a body which sponsors the development and use of COBOL, which is the single most widely used computer language for business-related programming. Admittedly, the use of the network model is in certain important respects advantageous, particularly in terms of efficiencies in machine usage. However, for all but the simplest of applications, this model has not proven to be readily understandable to persons without specialized training in data processing. As a result, this type of model seems to be best suited for applications which are by their nature recurring and voluminous, such as payroll preparation or maintenance of accounts receivable and accounts payable.

Correspondingly, such data base systems seem to be least suited for applications such as investment or operating analyses, which by their nature tend to be nonrecurring and varied. Such analyses typically require considerable flexibility in data retrieval and manipulation, and, therefore, often require significant user-machine interaction. Because this type of model generally has been found to be unsuitable for direct use by most managers and management accountants, its use has been limited to relatively simple applications. More sophisticated and interesting applications often require the employment of computer specialists, and, unfortunately, such arrangements are all too frequently characterized by problems of communication, coordination, and timely access to information.

In recent years, however, data base researchers have developed a new architecture, known as the "relational" model, which appears to be readily understandable even to users without formal training in data processing. Our purpose here is to introduce the reader to the relational model of a data base, to discuss its basic characteristics, its advantages and disadvantages relative to other models, and its particular suitability to management accounting applications. Finally, we will present some important factors that management accountants should consider when setting up a relational data base.

THE RELATIONAL DATA BASE

A relational data base consists simply of a *set of tables* containing data on any subject of interest. The term *relational* has its theoretical foundation in the area of relational algebra. However, understanding how to use a relational data base will in most circumstances require little if any knowledge of relational algebra. Rather, one can develop a thorough understanding of the concepts and applications of the relational model simply by focusing on the essence of that model, the data table.

A primary reason that nonrelational type data base models (e.g., the network model) are most often not directly used by accountants is that they require the user to employ highly detailed logical frameworks which, although very well suited for programming a digital computer, often prove to be cumbersome and unwieldy for the typical human mental process. However, the relational model is much more consistent with the human mental process, and because most accountants are familiar and comfortable with data presented in a tabular format, it should be particularly well suited for most management accountants.

Figures 1 and 2 provide a comparison of an inventory record as it may typically exist in a common network-type data base (Figure 1) versus a relational type data base (Figure 2). In Figure 1, the upper left-hand corner shows a list of item numbers used to identify various inventory items. For each item the data base contains supporting data regarding the quantity on hand, minimum and maximum quantities allowed, and the item classification (lower left corner). In addition, a list of inventory suppliers is maintained by vendor number (upper right corner) and is supported by data regarding vendor names, addresses, and telephone numbers (lower right corner).

Finally, the center of the figure depicts a table of authorized suppliers for each of the various inventory items. The arrows represent but a few of the many relationships among the various data. For example, the relationships represented by the solid arrows labeled "A1" and "A2" would be used by the

FIGURE 1   Network Data Base Design for Inventory Record

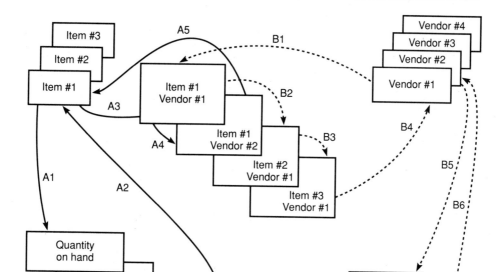

computer to obtain Quantity and Classification data for Inventory Item #1. Similarly, the computer would use the relationships represented by the solid arrows labeled "A3," "A4," and "A5" to determine which vendors are authorized to supply inventory item #1, and the relationships represented by the broken arrows labeled "B1," "B2," "B3," and "B4" to determine those inventory items that Vendor #1 is authorized to supply.

Figure 2 presents the identical inventory record in the tabular format of the relational type data base. Notice how much easier it is to understand the nature of the data being stored in the tabular structure of the relational model. The appeal of the simple tabular structure, however, is only one of the advantages of the relational model. A second major advantage is the user's ease of *direct* access to the data base. With traditional systems, such as the network model, data retrieval requires a facility with computer instructions which is usually possessed only by persons trained in data processing. The software associated with a relational data base management system allows the management accountant to use the data base *directly* with simple, readily understandable instructions.

FIGURE 2   Relational Data Base Design for Inventory Record

a. Inventory item table

Item Number	Quantity on Hand	Minimum Quantity	Maximum Quantity	Item Classification
1	310	20	500	B
2	50	10	200	B
3	200	50	400	F

b. Vendor table

Vendor Number	Name	Address	Telephone
1	Daxon	33 1st Street	351-8080
2	Alphametics	508 Drapers Road	525-3310
3	Green Ridge	334 Chauncey Place	978-1005
4	Bower Supplies	1995 Main Street	555-1000

c. Authorized vendor table

Item Number	Vendor Number
1	1
1	2
1	4
2	1
2	4
3	1
3	2
3	3
3	4

Suppose, for example, that we want to place an order for inventory items within the inventory classification "B," and toward that end we want a printed list of the names and addresses of all vendors authorized to supply these items. To generate such a list using either the network or the relational model requires us to integrate the separate data files on the inventory items, vendors, and the authorized vendor table. To perform such an integration using the network model requires considerable programming skills, including proficiency in a computer language such as COBOL, and a thorough knowledge of the relationships contained in the data base, such as those presented in Figure 1. For most management accountants this process would require the assistance of a computer specialist. However, to generate this printed list of vendors using a relational DBMS would require us to use a keyboard to issue *directly* to the computer a set of simple, readily understandable instructions such as the following:

> PRINT ITEM NUMBER FROM INVENTORY ITEM TABLE
> AND NAME AND ADDRESS FROM VENDOR TABLE
> WHERE ITEM CLASSIFICATION IS B IN INVENTORY ITEM
> TABLE.

Having issued those simple commands, we need only wait while the data base system itself: (1) extracts from the Inventory Item Table (Figure 2a) the item numbers for all inventory items having a "B" classification, (2) uses those item numbers to find in the Authorized Vendor Table (Figure 2c) the Vendor Numbers for all vendors authorized to supply those items, and (3) uses these vendor numbers to retrieve from the Vendor Table (Figure 2b) all of the appropriate vendor names and addresses. Figure 3 is an example of how this retrieved data might be presented on a printed report.

Still another important advantage of a relational DBMS is the ease with which it can be made to integrate data from a large number of separate data tables, providing great flexibility in retrieving data. This capability permits us to create personally tailored reports easily and *directly,* with no dependence on computer specialists. For example, if our inventory record also had included data tables containing information regarding unit prices for inventory items and geographical location of vendors (see Figure 4), we could just as easily have generated a printed list of vendors within a particular geographical region authorized to supply items having a "B" inventory classification,

FIGURE 3 Information from DBMS Based on a User Request

Item Number	Vendor Name	Address
1	Daxon	33 1st Street
1	Alphametics	508 Drapers Road
1	Bower Electronics	1995 Main Street
2	Daxon	33 1st Street
2	Bower	1995 Main Street

FIGURE 4   Relational Data Base Design for Inventory Record

a. Unit price table

Item Number	Vendor Number	Unit Price
1	1	5.35
1	2	5.12
1	4	4.99
2	1	11.25
2	3	9.75
3	1	2.20
3	2	2.48
3	3	2.35
3	4	2.30

b. Vendors by region table

Vendor Number	Geographical Region
1	A
1	C
2	A
3	B
3	C
4	A
4	B
4	C
4	D

or a list of vendors within a particular geographical region which supply inventory item 2 at a unit price no greater than, say, $10.

It should be apparent that a relational DBMS can provide us with direct, easy, and immediate access to a readily understandable data base, and can allow considerable flexibility in generating reports. The essence of a well-designed relational data base is that it can provide us with the particular information that we want, when we want it.

MANAGEMENT ACCOUNTANTS AND THE RELATIONAL DATA BASE

The functions of management accountants include accumulating, classifying, summarizing, interpreting, analyzing, and reporting information to management to facilitate its planning, decision-making, and control activities. A relational DBMS should prove to be a highly valuable tool in any of these functions. The value of any management information system rests in its ability to assist managers to meet their varied responsibilities in an effective, efficient, and timely manner.

The information demands of managers may include cost-volume-profit analyses for new and existing products, present value analyses of capital budgeting proposals, development of current operating budgets or a five-year plan, analyses of cost variances using a standard cost system, and of course numerous others. Management accountants must be able to respond quickly to these highly varied and changing information requirements, and thus should greatly benefit from having direct and immediate access to a base of highly differentiated data. It is this ease, timeliness, and flexibility of data retrieval and data manipulation which characterizes a well-designed relational data base.

FACTORS TO CONSIDER IN DEVELOPING A RELATIONAL DATA BASE

An effective relational DBMS requires that careful consideration be given to both the acquisition of appropriate equipment and software, and the design of the data tables. The process of selecting specific hardware and software requires an expertise beyond the capabilities of most management accountants and is probably best handled through consultation with computer professionals. However, because management accountants can provide valuable insights into a firm's accounting processes, as well as management's decision processes and information preferences, they can and should be directly involved in the function of designing data tables. And, because even the most powerful software package and hardware configuration cannot compensate for a poorly designed data base, it is certainly an important function.

A primary goal in designing data tables is to maximize data retrievability without resulting in significant data redundancy. Moreover, tables should be structured to reflect the logical relationships among data items. To help achieve these goals in designing data tables we should follow two simple but important guidelines:

> Guideline 1: A separate data table should be used for each conceptual relationship of interest (i.e., no table should incorporate more than one conceptual relationship).

In Figure 2, for example, the Inventory Item Table (2a) contains only information about inventory items—the quantity, the minimum and maximum quantities, and the classification of *each inventory item*. Similarly, the Vendor Table (2b) contains only information relating specifically to each vendor (i.e., name, address and telephone number), organized by vendor number. And the Authorized Vendor Table (2c) contains only information specifying which inventory items are supplied by which vendors. Conversely, Figure 5 presents

FIGURE 5 Data Table Containing Two Distinct Concepts

Inventory table								
Item Number	Quantity on Hand	Minimum Quantity	Maximum Quantity	Item Classification	Vendor Number	Vendor Name	Vendor Address	Telephone
1	310	20	500	B	1	Daxon	33 1st Street	351-8080
1	310	20	500	B	2	Alphametics	508 Drapers Road	525-3310
1	310	20	500	B	4	Bower Supplies	1995 Main St.	555-1000
2	50	10	200	B	1	Daxon	33 1st Street	351-8080
2	50	10	200	B	4	Bower Supplies	1995 Main St.	555-1000
3	200	50	400	F	1	Daxon	33 1st Street	351-8080
3	200	50	400	F	2	Alphametics	508 Drapers Road	525-3310
3	200	50	400	F	3	Green Ridge	334 Chauncey Pl.	978-1005
3	200	50	400	F	4	Bower Supplies	1995 Main St.	555-1000

an example of a data table which contains information pertaining to two separate objects of interest: inventory items and vendors. Notice that this table contains the information from two of the data tables in Figure 2 (i.e., 2a and 2b).

A data table of this design has two major weaknesses. The *first* involves data redundancy. Because vendor information is presented for each inventory item, and because each vendor may supply hundreds or even thousands of inventory items, the vendor information may be repeated an inordinate number of times. This redundancy could cause the maintenance of the files to be unnecessarily time-consuming and highly susceptible to errors.

For example, using the well-designed data tables in Figure 2, the addition of the name, address, and telephone number for a new vendor could be accomplished by simply adding a single line to the Vendor Table (2b). But, using the Inventory Table in Figure 5 that one line addendum would have to be repeated for every inventory item supplied by that vendor. This procedure would obviously be time-consuming and could easily result in errors and inconsistencies. Similarly, to change the address and/or telephone number of an existing vendor would require, at most, two simple changes to the Vendor Table in Figure 2b, but conceivably could require hundreds or thousands of changes to the Inventory Table in Figure 5.

The *second* major weakness of the design presented in Figure 5 is that the data on one of the concepts included in the table (e.g., vendor data) is not maintained *independently* of the data on the second concept (e.g., inventory item data). If, for example, a vendor is not currently supplying any inventory items to the firm, its name, address, and telephone number will not be included in the data base, even though we may wish to maintain this vendor information for future reference. Notice that in the appropriately designed tables of Figure 2, the maintenance of vendor data in the Vendor Table (2b) is *independent* of the inventory item data. Thus, the fact that particular vendors are not currently supplying any inventory items to the firm would not result in the loss of basic information on those vendors unless the firm consciously decided to make such a change to the Vendor Table.

Guideline 2: Each table should be designed so that every row in the table is unique.

This can be accomplished by assuring that at least one column, referred to as the *Key* to the table, contains a different value for each row. For example, the *key* to the Inventory Item Table (Figure 2a) is the *Item Number* column. In this instance each item number, which uniquely identifies each item of inventory, also uniquely identifies a row in the table. Thus, each row contains information pertaining to a specific item of inventory. Similarly, the *key* to the Vendor Table (2b) is the *Vendor Number* column. Each vendor number, which uniquely identifies a vendor, also uniquely identifies a row in the table. Notice, however, that on the Authorized Vendor Table (2c) there is no single column that contains unique row values. In this instance the two columns, *taken together*, constitute a key. That is, the combined values in the two columns, which uniquely identify a relationship between inventory items and vendors authorized to supply those items, also uniquely identify each row.

The reason for this rule is quite simple. Each row of a table contains information about a distinct item of interest to the accountant. If each row is not unique, one or more of the distinct items of interest have been duplicated. The human reader faced with such duplicate entries would probably simply ignore those entries that are duplicates. However, unless a computer has been specifically programmed to do so it may not be able to handle the duplicates in the same manner, and errors may result.

As previously indicated, the relational type data base may not be the best choice for certain types of applications. The major disadvantage of using a relational DBMS is that it may be significantly less efficient in terms of machine time usage than a traditional, nonrelational DBMS such as a network type model. Therefore, for high volume, recurring applications the relational data base may offer no significant advantage over traditional systems. In fact, because the format for recurring reports is typically fixed, giving little value to flexibility, and because the high data volume requires careful consideration of cost efficiencies, a traditional DBMS (e.g., the network model) may be more appropriate for this type of application.

It is worth noting, however, that many companies now employ a two-level data base in which a traditional model is used to produce routine, prespecified reports for use at the operating management level, and at regular intervals data from this data base is uploaded (i.e., copied) onto a relational data base

FIGURE 6   Two-Level Data Base

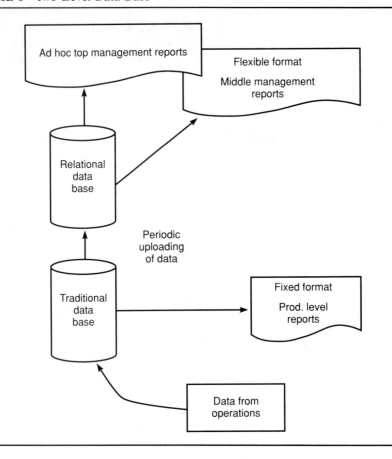

where it is available for higher level managers to use on an ad hoc basis (Figure 6).

The relational data base is a type of data base that we believe represents a major step forward in a continuing management information revolution. The relational data base can place vast data resources literally at the fingertips of accountants and managers. Because dependence on computer specialists is minimized, we are allowed direct and much more timely access to valuable information. In the business environment, having access to a major project analysis *now*, rather than later, can have serious implications for our bottom-line profit and possibly our economic survival.

Reading 3–3

CURRENT TRENDS IN TRANSACTION PROCESSING SYSTEMS

By Vijay Kumar, Ph.D.

A data base is a symbolic representation of the state of a part of the real world in terms of computable objects. The state of the part of the real world is not static, and changes in this state must be reflected in the data base. The part of the real world may be an airline, a banking institution, or a university. In a computer system, the computable objects take the form of interrelated files and are stored, more or less, permanently on disks, magnetic tapes, etc. The collection of these files is called the *physical data base*. The changes in the part of the real world are implanted in the data base by a mechanism called a *transaction*. A user expresses these changes as transactions, which are then accepted and processed by the data base management system (DBMS), and the data base is brought up to date. Transactions in this way establish a link between the organization and its data base. We, therefore, refer to a data base management system also as a *transaction processing system*.

Data base management system technology can be traced back to the late 1950s. Initially it started with a set of generalized routines that operated on a set of files. Since then, a DBMS has become more than just a monolithic file processing system. Today, for users it is a fully conversational, intelligent decision-making system. For vendors it is a very profitable product, and for computer scientists it is a highly complex and challenging area of research.

The transaction processing demands have since increased more rapidly than the power of transaction processing systems. Off-the-shelf systems are unable to handle the volume of transactions generated by organizations. Ordinary transaction processing systems and techniques bottleneck at 50 transactions per second (TPS) and even the high-performance systems can barely manage 200 TPS. Organizations that generate higher TPS have to develop specialized systems to handle this workload. In this article we report the current state of transaction processing technology and describe how well the technology has been able to handle the ever-growing information processing volume. In particular, we explain the problems in designing high-volume transaction processing systems.

Reprinted with permission from *Journal of Systems Management*, January 1990, pp. 33–37.

CURRENT STATE OF DATA BASES AND POTENTIAL USERS OF HIGH-POWER TPS

Since the advent of the data base, its size has grown significantly. The size of present-day commercial data bases is in the range of gigabytes (10^9 bytes) and they are continually increasing. Some data bases are as large as 1,000 giga-bytes. The massive size of data bases is one of the main problems in designing storage structures and installing and operating these systems. A data base may occupy many disks. This creates management problems, since current disk transfer algorithms are unable to provide efficient services. Some schemes, such as disk stripping (in which a file of records is stored on several disks and is read in parallel when required) have been suggested but still I/O remains the bottleneck.

Transaction processing systems that are capable of efficiently managing at least 500 TPS can be defined as high-performance transaction systems. Efficiency can be measured in terms of response time. If a system can deliver a one-second response time to about 95 percent of the transactions, then it can be categorized as a high-performance system.

Airlines are the obvious users of high-performance systems, since their workload consists of millions of small transactions (seat reservation, seat con-firmation, inquiries, etc.). We will use TWA airline to explain some facts.[1,2]

When TWA first implemented its system in 1970, it was basically a name reservation and inventory system. Since then, it has added many functions necessary for providing services to passengers, and has also added facilities to provide services for cargo and travel agencies.

TWA's system has about 50,000 communication terminals in the field worldwide. The size of the data base is about 850 gigabytes and is stored on 340 of 3380s DADS. It is fully duplicated for performance and availability reasons. About 8 percent of 850 gigabytes are occupied by passenger records. A typical daily workload is about 20 million transactions. The peak perform-ance rate is about 800 TPS. The average rate is 552 TPS with a response time of 1.5 seconds. Reliability of these systems is also an important parameter. A partial data base recovery (recovery from transaction or system program fail-ure) takes about two minutes. A cold start (total failure or starting system from scratch) takes about eight hours. In 1972, TWA lost about $2 million and in 1976 about $250,000 due to system unavailability. However, the airline has improved its software reliability and did not have a major system outage for the last two years. Initially, it had a 9083 CPR that ran on a 3083 uniprocessor. Since then, it has gone to multi-processors (3390), four of which are dedicated to on-line processing. TWA can accommodate up to eight processors that might give it adequate power to reach 1,000 TPS.

Many banks have peak transaction rates in excess of 500 TPS. With the advent of electronic funds transfer, automatic teller machines, on-line ac-counting facilities, automatic payment systems and other facilities, the trans-action volume is continuously multiplying. In addition, the transition from cash to plastic will multiply transaction volume. A single direct transaction is equivalent to about five plastic transactions; that is, a single transaction is required to withdraw cash directly from an automatic teller, whereas about five transactions are needed to process a withdrawal on credit cards.

Telecommunication industries are not far behind in this growth. Telecommunication is becoming much more complex. Accounting procedures are changing to include billing by call, by packet, by duration, or even reverse billing. New services such as autocall, teleconferencing, call forwarding and so on are adding to the complexity of the system. The largest switches are generating 200 to 400 TPS. The next generation switches will require higher capacity and more sophisticated call management logic. This will, in turn, further increase the volume of transactions, reaching about 1,000 TPS.

The problem of managing real-time transactions is more complicated. At present there does not exist a commonly acceptable definition of real-time transactions. Informally, it can be defined as an interactive short transaction that must be completed within a defined period. Some areas in which real-time transactions exist are stock exchanges, threat analysis in the air force, arbitrage trading, etc. The stock exchange is a complex process. One type of a set of transactions maintains the accuracy of the data base; in other words, they update the data base to reflect the current state of the market. The other type of a set of transactions asks prices and manages bidding. These transactions have real-time constraints and if they are not processed within the defined time period, many people will have insomnia.

Similar situations exist in arbitrage trading in which the prices of precious metals change within minutes. Queries from the buyers of these metals must be answered within seconds for profitable shopping. Similarly, tracking of an enemy aircraft must be computed within a defined period of time to avoid having to shoot in the dark.

DO WE HAVE SOLUTIONS?

At present we do not have a general satisfactory solution. Organizations generating large TPS apply ad hoc solutions to modify/upgrade their existing system (data base/operating systems) to manage the workloads. Following is a review of the possible solutions and their current status.

Transaction Processing Facility. The airline and travel industries pioneered a high-volume transaction processing system called Transaction Processing Facility (TPF), which is built on the top of the airline operating systems. A TPF is not a data base system, but a system to manage terminals and disks. The tasks of files and other resource management are the responsibilities of the application programmers or application designers. In this way a TPF is not a high-power transaction processing system and must be enhanced to include data base management features. Currently a TPF can manage about 800 TPS with 60K terminals. The Bank of America plans to use TPF as the basis for a high-volume transaction processor front-end using IMS as the back-end system, and is also planning to enhance the power and capability of TPF. In its present form, however, it does not offer a solution to transaction processing problems.

Distributed Data Base Management Systems.   Distribution of the entire workload among multiple computers for processing has been a partially efficient solution. This scheme is called distributed data base management system (DDBMS). Structurally, it is a set of geographically dispersed multiple computers (mainframes, minis, micros, personal computers, etc.) interconnected via a network system. An individual computer in a distributed system is called a node or site. A distributed system can be homogeneous, that is, all of the members of the set are identical computer systems, or they can be heterogeneous, in which members may not be identical systems. The entire data base can be divided into as many parts as there are nodes (partitioned data base), or it can be completely duplicated (i.e., each node has a copy of the entire data base). Distributed systems provide higher transaction processing power, they are reliable, and they seem to be emerging as a viable solution. However, in its present state, it is incapable of providing the required processing power for the following reasons:

Not Easily Manageable Due to Their Enormous Size.   Distributed systems are enormous, since thousands of terminals are likely to be connected to such a system. Data base size is likely to be in the range of several gigabytes. Hundreds of disks may be required to store the data base redundantly to provide improved reliability. Operating such a large system would not be easy. As the number of these peripheral devices (disks, tapes, etc.) increases, so does the probability of partial failure. At least one communication line will be out at any time, making network management a difficult problem. Each day a subset of these peripherals will have some trouble requiring attention. The volume of maintenance will increase in the absence of good development and operational tools, thus affecting system availability.

Communication Overheads.   The proper functioning of distributed systems depends on an efficient message communication facility. Message communication is expensive. The time and equipment cost to transport messages rise and the reliability of message transmission drops by at least an order of magnitude at the degree of distribution (i.e., the number of nodes in the systems). We report here the communication problems in distributed systems whose nodes are not more than 1,000 meters apart (local area network) and systems where the internode distance is greater than 1,000 meters (wide area network). Due to non-technical reasons, it is difficult to put a dollar figure on the cost of message communication, so we compute the time cost (delay).[3]

In a local area network, the cost of sending a message may be anywhere from 25,000 instructions and in the wide area network it may be 12,000 instructions. There are several other factors (we do not consider them here) responsible for creating communication delay.[3] The net result is a message delay of 270 microseconds in local area networks and 31,000 microseconds in wide area networks in sending and receiving a message of 100 bytes. Table 3–3–7 projects the future of message communication capabilities.

To summarize:

a. Local network messages are 10 times more expensive than shared memory messages.

b. Wide area network messages are 100 times more expensive than local area network messages.

c. CPU speed remains the bottleneck in message communication.

Reliability Issues.   Since a data base reflects the part of the real world, at any time it must give the correct picture of the organization. Providing high reliability in distributed systems is difficult. The system must be able to recover quickly from any kind of failure. The effect of system failure in some environments, such as the stock market, army, etc., cannot be eliminated completely, but it can be minimized. A medium-size centralized system takes about 15 minutes to recover from a system failure. This recovery time is regarded as quite good, but with presently available recovery algorithms, it is difficult to complete recovery within this time period in distributed systems. An organization cannot tolerate so much down time without losing money.

Enhancement Problems.   When organizations expand, the data bases representing these organizations grow much faster. It is not an easy task to manage the explosive growth gracefully. To accommodate the growth, more floor space, more hardware (such as disk space and larger memory), more terminals and more communication ports become necessary. To manage extra hardware resources, new software needs to be added. The addition of software increases the software maintenance cost. Computer software is becoming more and more complex, making maintenance even more expensive. Software maintenance cost is the highest in any organization, and there is no sign that it will decline. This disrupts the price/performance metric. Ideally, price would include the cost of ownership, the cost of designing, programming, and operating the entire system, and software maintenance. If we divide this price by the TPS rating of the system, then we get the price/performance measure. Typically the value of this measure ranges from $40K/TPS to $500K/TPS.[3] Obviously, systems that have a lower $/TPS value are

TABLE 3–3–1   Delay to Send and Receive 100 Bytes

	1980	*1990*	*2000*
Local Area Network	2,000 μs	270 μs	36 μs
Wide Area Network	222,000 μs	31,000 μs	11,000 μs

desirable: $60K/TPS is acceptable, but $40K/TPS is preferable. At present, no large system has a good price/performance value.

Main Memory Data Base Systems (MDBS).   Main memory prices have declined rapidly, and are expected to continue this trend. At the present time, memory for a DEC VAX costs approximately $1,500 a megabyte. By 1990, 1 gigabyte will cost about $30,000 to $40,000. With such a downward trend in the price of memory, the idea of memory resident data base systems is rapidly gaining momentum.

In disk-based systems, the entire data base resides on several disks, and desired portions are transferred on demand to a main memory for manipulation. At the end of manipulation, the modified pages are written back to the disk (immediately or at some later time), thus replacing their old versions. A disk-based system in a normal session spends a significant amount of time (roughly one-third of the entire transaction processing session) in managing I/O traffic. In the event of a system failure, the data base is recovered from the disk, thereby further increasing I/O activity. Thus, I/O traffic is one of the main reasons affecting data base performance.

In main memory data base systems, I/O is eliminated by permanently storing the entire data base in the main memory. Under this system, therefore, the place of data manipulation and the place of data storage are "very close" to each other. Transactions do not have to wait for data to be transferred to the memory so, consequently, more transactions can be processed concurrently. This results in improved response time and throughput. The first system to apply some of the main memory features is IBM's IMS Fastpath. IBM Fastpath supports two types of data bases: one is memory resident and the other is disk resident. The memory resident part is regarded as "hot spots" and treated differently from the disk portion of the data base. The memory portion does not require I/O and transactions' updates to this portion are applied in groups (group commit). Log records of these transactions are entered at this time in the data base log and the disk copy of the memory resident data base is updated.

At present, there is no complete (i.e., entire data base is memory resident) main memory system. There are problems with main memory data base systems, and these must be resolved before such a system can be realized. The following is a discussion of management and recovery problems.

RECOVERY IN MAIN MEMORY DATA BASE SYSTEMS (MDBSs)

A data base recovery mechanism guarantees the consistency of data in the event of any kind of failure. Although a system failure may not corrupt the entire memory, it is usually too difficult to determine which parts were actually corrupted by the failure. So one generally assumes the worst and re-initializes the entire main memory.

The recovery algorithms of disk-based data base systems would function correctly for main memory systems, but they would probably not perform satisfactorily. To make them suitable for main memory systems, they must be modified or new recovery algorithms must be developed.

In MDBSs, due to the volatility of main memory, the maintenance of log and checkpointing operations becomes difficult and, therefore, time-consuming. An up-to-date copy of the log must be available to the recovery system at the time of recovery. This means it must be sorted on some stable storage device (usually a disk). A recovery mechanism then must have an efficient logging method and a carefully defined policy for check-pointing frequency that must minimize I/O traffic in maintaining these operations. Recent work on recovery mechanisms for main memory have realized and addressed these issues.

Most of the problems of MDBS will disappear if non-volatile main memory as fast as volatile memory becomes available. There are several non-volatile memory systems on the market, such as BBRAM (Battery Backup RAM)[5,6] Programmable Read-Only Memory (PROM),[6] Electically Erasable PROMS (EEPRPMS) and Shadow RAM.[6,7] but they are slower than volatile memory. Furthermore, their life span is bound by the number of reads/writes performed on them. This number is usually between 10,000 and 100,000 reads/writes.[7] Once this number is reached, the memory must be replaced.

The other alternative is Universal Power Supply (UPS).[7] This system provides back-up power to the entire volatile main memory. Thus, in the case of a power failure, a UPS can keep the memory alive for six to 310 minutes. This system, however, is not satisfactory because it is expensive and its support time is too short to save the entire data base.

In MDBSs the question of initial data base loading is a crucial one. In CDBS the data pages from disk to memory are moved on demand. In MDBSs, a similar approach can be taken, or the whole data base can be loaded at the system initialization. Since a data base is normally very large, the initial loading might use a large amount of I/O resources. For example, in a small system that processes 100 TPS with each transaction writing two log pages, the total number of pages written in an eight-hour day is 5,760,000 (2* 100 * 3600 * 8). With a page size of 1,024 bytes and a transfer rate of three megabytes, it would take about 25 minutes simply to read the log and about an hour to recover the entire data base. Thus, the entire system will remain unavailable for about 60–70 minutes. Organizations that generate large transaction volumes cannot afford to tolerate system downtime of this magnitude.

SUMMARY

We realize that there is a clear need for high-power transaction processing systems. The projects mentioned above may succeed or they may fail. Several groups (Tandem, IBM, etc.) are attempting to evolve current systems to meet this need. Most of these efforts are about three years old and it will require another three to four years to see the fruit of the effort. We believe that at least one of them will succeed in providing a system with an attractive price/performance metric.

References

1. D. Gilford and A. Spector, "The TWA Reservation System," *CACM*, Vol. 27, No. 7, July 1984.
2. N. Buckley, Private Communication, TWA, 1989.
3. J. Gray, et al., "One Thousand Transactions per Second," *Technical Report 85.1*, Tandem Computers, November 1984.
4. K. G. Brill, "Keeping Up Your UPS," *Datamation*, Vol. 33, No. 14, July 1987.
5. T. J. Byers, "How to Make Your Computer's Memory Nonvolatile," *Computer Digest*, August 1984.
6. D. Cormier, "Erasable/Programmable Solid-State Memories," *EDN*, November 1985.
7. I. Dithie, "ROMs to Bubbles: The Selection of Nonvolatile Memories," *Electronics and Power*, Vol. 30, No. 12, December 1984.

CHAPTER 4

Advanced Systems

Many data processing systems combine a host of advanced technologies to form systems with multiple capabilities. These advanced systems typically support on-line real-time (OLRT) applications and rely heavily on data communications, or electronic data interchange (EDI), and on distributed processing and distributed data bases to link together a vast array of computing and information resources. Users are provided with immediate access to a network of system resources, many of which may be geographically distant from the user. These networks allow the immediate transfer of information to all locations within an organization, and can even transfer documents to the computers of other organizations. However, despite the many advantages provided by such systems, harnessing these technologies also creates new risks and concerns for management, accountants, and auditors. This chapter examines these advanced technologies and explores their implications for accountants and auditors.

On-line systems overcome many of the inherent limitations of the simpler (and cheaper) batch systems which they typically replace. Since batch systems update account balances only periodically (daily, weekly, monthly), account balances are never completely current and up to date. Also, the sequential access media (magnetic tape) and simpler file structures used in batch systems cannot support user inquiries regarding the status of particular accounts. Hence, in batch systems, account balance and current activity information is available only at the end of a processing period.

On-line systems are characterized by the immediate updating of account balances and the rapid retrieval of account information. Input for on-line systems is typically made from computer terminals and programs, and data (master) files are stored on direct access devices such as magnetic disks. When the transaction is accepted by the system, all appropriate master files are immediately updated. In addition, on-line systems typically allow users to query the system regarding a specific balance or current activity in the account. Many on-line systems provide a system response in time to guide a user's decision (i.e., in real time) and are referred to as on-line real-time (OLRT) systems. Such a system response, for example, may take the form of an account balance, a credit limit, a price, or an address. Typical OLRT applications include airline reservations, bank automatic teller machines

(ATMs), point-of-sale (POS) terminals, production quality control, inventory control, and credit approval.

The increased speed and flexibility of on-line systems require the use of hardware and software elements which are both more costly and more sophisticated than the simpler (batch) systems. Data is stored in on-line files on direct access storage devices (such as magnetic disks). File organization structures and access methods are no longer sequential but rather are quite complex. File management requires the support of more elaborate software programs. For example, files may be integrated into data bases and accessed through data base management systems.

As both the volume and cost of processing transactions escalate, many firms are turning to electronic data interchange (EDI) to satisfy many of their routine processing needs. EDI involves the electronic transfer of documents between the computers of different organizations or between the various units within a single organization. EDI is being used by many firms to order and pay for goods from suppliers, to arrange transportation with carriers, to receive orders from customers, and to invoice and collect from customers. EDI not only reduces or eliminates the flow of paper documents associated with such transactions, but also allows these communications to be made faster and more reliably. These direct communications within and between companies facilitate better coordination, tighter scheduling, and an overall more efficient use of resources.

Many large business systems integrate numerous mainframe computers, microcomputers, specialized processors, and other computer resources into an integrated network of computing resources. These distributed data processing (DDP) systems are linked together by means of a data communication system and may take many forms. Among the numerous benefits provided by DDP systems are a more optimal sharing of system resources, greater flexibility and responsiveness to user needs, and increased availability and reliability. In addition to geographical dispersion of hardware, advanced systems are now emerging which utilize distributed DBMS. Distributed DBMS involves the partitioning of integrated DBMS and the distribution of the resulting partitions to multiple geographically dispersed locations. Such distribution is transparent to users and provides many potential benefits.

From an audit standpoint, advanced systems pose a far greater problem to the auditor than do simpler batch systems. These systems usually provide much less paper documentation of computer processing steps than do batch systems. Thus, the audit trail in advanced systems may be less adequate, and tracing transactions through the system may be quite difficult. Additional problems may be encountered controlling user access to the system, since access may be gained locally and from numerous remote points.

The first two readings in this chapter focus on EDI. The first of these, "Electronic Data Interchange: A Quiet Revolution," describes the basics of EDI and discusses how EDI can improve the bottom line for national and international firms. The second, "Electronic Systems Enhance JIT Operations," describes the critical role played by EDI in the just-in-time (JIT) inventory management environment. The final reading focuses on distributed data processing (DDP). The article, "The Drive toward DDP: A Management Perspective," examines the technical, operational, and behavioral issues related to DDP from the perspective of management.

CHAPTER 4 READINGS

1. Nicole V. Willenz, "Electronic Data Interchange: A Quiet Revolution," *Price Waterhouse Review*, 1988, No. 3, pp. 33–45.
2. Arjan T. Sadhwani and M. H. Sarhan, "Electronic Systems Enhance JIT Operations," *Management Accounting*, December 1987, pp. 25–30.
3. Harry Mishkin and Dan C. Kneer, "The Drive toward DDP: A Management Perspective," *CMA Magazine*, January/February 1987, pp. 36–41.

CHAPTER 4 QUESTIONS

Article 1

1. Describe the "bottom line" implications of EDI for U.S. multinational firms?
2. Comment on the audit implications of EDI.

Article 2

3. Explain the role of EDI in just-in-time (JIT) inventory management. Would JIT systems be feasible without EDI?
4. In what situations might a company prefer to establish electronic links for EDI via a point-to-point configuration, value-added networks, or third-party networks?

Article 3

5. Discuss the concept of the distributed data processing system (DDP). What is "distributed" in a DDP system?
6. Discuss the primary operational and philosophical issues raised by a change to DDP.

Case 4–1

CROSBY COMPANY

The controller of Crosby Company has been working with the data processing department to revise a part of the company's financial reporting system. A study is under way on how to develop and implement a data entry and data retention system for key computer files used by various departments responsible to the controller. The departments involved and details on their data processing-related activities are as follows.

1. General Accounting

   - Daily processing of journal entries submitted by various departments.
   - Weekly updating of file balances with subsystem data from areas such as payroll, accounts receivable, and accounts payable.
   - Sporadic requests for account balances during the month, with increased activity at month-end.

2. Accounts Receivable

   - Daily processing of receipts for payments on account.
   - Daily processing of sales to customers.
   - Daily checks to be certain that a credit limit of $200,000 (maximum) per customer is not exceeded and that there is identification of orders in excess of $20,000 per customer.
   - Daily requests for customer credit status regarding payments and account balances.
   - Weekly reporting to general accounting file.

3. Accounts Payable

   - Processing of payments to vendors three times a week.
   - Weekly expense distribution reporting to general accounting file.

4. Budget Planning and Control

   - Updating of flexible budgets on a monthly basis.
   - Quarterly rebudgeting based on sales forecast and production schedule changes.
   - Monthly inquiry requests for budget balances.

Crosby's manager of data processing has indicated to the controller that batch processing is the least expensive processing technique and that a rough estimate of the cost of each of the other techniques would be as follows.

Technique	Cost in Relation to Batch
On-line processing	1.5 times
Real-time processing	2.5 times
On-line inquiry	1.5 times

REQUIRED:

1. Define and discuss the major differences among the following data processing approaches:

    a. Batch processing.

    b. On-line processing.

    c. Real-time processing.

2. Identify and explain: (*a*) the type of input technique, and (*b*) the type of inquiry that probably should be employed by Crosby Company for each of the four departments responsible to the controller. Assume that the volume of transactions is not a key variable in the decision.

    a. General accounting.

    b. Accounts receivable.

    c. Accounts payable.

    d. Budget planning and control.

(CMA Adapted)

Reading 4–1

ELECTRONIC DATA INTERCHANGE: A QUIET REVOLUTION

By Nicole V. Willenz

It is early morning on the West Coast and the second shift at a manufacturing plant has packed up and gone home. Only the low hum and blinking lights of computers in the data center indicate that material requirements for the next few weeks of production are being scheduled and ordered. The computer is extracting data and formatting purchase orders and releases for direct mate-

---

Reprinted with permission from *Price Waterhouse Review*, 1988, No. 3 pp. 33–45.

rials into a special computer-to-computer communications language that will be transmitted directly to a major supplier's computer without any human intervention.

In the Midwest, dawn is breaking and computers in another data center are hungrily accepting and processing the purchase orders and shipping schedules from the West Coast. Orders received electronically will be verified against databases containing information on customer profiles, part numbers, and plant locations. Software in the receiving computer will evaluate the data, sort emergency and routine orders, and determine how each will be handled. Some orders may be fed directly into the production system for the first shift of the assembly line that will arrive shortly. Production can begin without any manual processing.

Less urgent orders will be used to drive the purchase of direct materials that the supplier will need to fill customer orders over the next few weeks and to maintain the minimum stock levels required in an electronic environment. At the appropriate point in the business cycle, receiving advice, billing information, and payments will also be exchanged electronically.

Sound a little like science fiction? Well, check *The Wall Street Journal, Business Week,* and *Datamation,* because this is a real-life example of a technological innovation that is steadily changing the way businesses are operating. From the delivery dock to the executive suite, businesses and governments are trumpeting success stories about an information systems technology that has the potential to significantly cut costs and fundamentally change traditionally accepted ways of conducting business.

WHAT IS EDI?

The cause of the stir is a standardized method of electronically transmitting and processing data, called electronic data interchange or, in the industry vernacular, EDI. EDI is a high-speed method of electronic communication that facilitates the exchange and processing of high volumes of business data from one computer to another. Data is presented in a standardized format that provides for generating, revising, and processing information with no human intervention. Although the technology has been available since the 1970s, it has been only in the past two years that industry has begun to recognize the significance of this quiet revolution.

The essence of EDI is the replacement of conventional paper documents, such as purchase orders, invoices, and transportation documents, with computer messages in a nonproprietary, noncopyrightable, publicly accepted format. These messages contain data that can be used to automatically update inventory, issue material releases against open purchase orders, invoice a customer, pay a supplier, and advise a party of a shipment or discrepancy.

Currently, major corporations and numerous industries that have implemented EDI are reporting substantial savings as a result of streamlined operations in automated ordering and material management systems environments such as the one implemented between the West Coast manufacturer and its Midwest supplier. A case in point: The grocery industry, which is a heavy user of this technology for purchasing and direct store delivery, estimates overall savings at $300 million per year through use of EDI.

BOTTOM LINE RESULTS

Chief executive, finance, and operating officers are interested in EDI and electronic funds transfer (a subset of EDI) because of the significant impact they can have on costs, accounts receivable and payable, corporate cash management strategies, and quality and service improvements. In addition, EDI can heavily influence a corporation's ability to reduce overhead, manage the creation and maintenance of the audit trail, enhance materials management, improve inventory controls and forecasts, and maximize the effective use of logistical resources.

Furthermore, tight deadlines in just-in-time operations, shrinking domestic markets, and expanding international opportunities focus even more attention on the need for optimal productivity in an already tight production environment. Across-the-border operations such as offshore sourcing and assembling are fraught with voluminous paperwork required by international regulations. Added time and efficiency pressures make implementing EDI critical to reducing time lags and a vital link in international operations strategies.

Benefits from implementing EDI can add dollars directly to the bottom line through significant savings in the following areas: reduced clerical-intensive activities, allowing labor to be more efficiently utilized in problem solving and other activities that require human judgment; better forecasting and decision support from more accurate information; improved customer service through a heightened ability to detect and resolve problems faster; and increased financial control through enhanced cash management made possible by more exact payment methods and timely, accurate information.

In addition to the fact that businesses are experiencing major savings, battles for market share are intensifying the scramble to improve service and quality as a tool for achieving product differentiation. EDI is proving to be an important strategic weapon when it comes to cutting costs effectively—while at the same time responding to higher customer expectations of better responsiveness and lower prices.

IDENTIFYING SAVINGS

The adoption of EDI can provide significant savings in the following areas:

Less Rekeying and Fewer Errors

A recent industry newsletter quoted James P. Witkins, senior financial officer of Manufacturers Hanover Trust Company, as noting that "today, 70 percent of data in a typical firm's mainframe computer was output from another mainframe, compared to 20 percent five years ago." Eliminating the reentering of that 70 percent, which predictably is rekeyed multiple times for many functional systems, is one of the major benefits of implementing EDI.

In addition, each time an individual reenters data, there is a risk that keystroking errors will occur or that papers will be misplaced or destroyed.

Reduced Overhead

Reduced paperwork processing, decreased postage costs, and diminished clerical activities also yield major savings for EDI implementors. For example, the U.S. Department of the Treasury saved $60 million in postage in 1986 by eliminating the mailing of paper checks and implementing electronic funds transfer.

Several years ago, the automotive industry estimated that shuffling paper around was wasting $2 billion per year. The paper included bills, orders, and information requests that generated approximately $200 of extra cost for each car.

In addition, Douglas Aircraft Company estimates that the manual processing cost of a purchase order was $4–$6, versus an EDI processing cost of less than $1 for the same document. Others have estimated that the per transaction cost in a manual environment could be as high as $50, with a reduction through use of EDI to $3–$12.

Decreased Inventory Levels

An efficient order management and purchasing cycle means manufacturers have a more accurate picture of material and parts requirements. Accurate

---

International Costs More

The paperwork required to conduct international trade costs billions of dollars annually. EDI provides a significant opportunity to deflate these expenses. For example:

- A European EDI trade group estimates that $15 billion a year could be saved worldwide by reducing paperwork required for international trade.

- The First National Bank of Chicago estimates that the United States could save $6.5 billion annually by generating trade documents electronically. FNBC specified that for each of the 23 million shipments out of the United States each year, there are 360 original copies of 46 separate documents.

- In a recent study, Price Waterhouse noted that of the transactions required to conduct international trade, 25 contained duplicate information.

information systems provide EDI messages at frequent intervals with the correct ordering data. This facilitates the ordering of the right supplies, encourages a decline in the need to stock up on parts based on guesswork, and provides an opportunity to expedite unanticipated emergency changes and orders.

This added control can yield significant savings in inventory costs. Navistar International Corporation, for example, reports that EDI made it possible to reduce truck inventories by $167 million in the first year and to decrease premium freight charges by 90 percent. And First National Bank of Chicago saved $500,000 annually by reducing inventory of general business supplies when it implemented EDI with 20 of its top suppliers. The corporation expects to generate an annual savings of $2 million once it gets the top 50 on board.

Evaluated Receipt Settlements

EDI implementors are also maximizing opportunities for cost savings in the financial arena by eliminating the paperwork involved in receiving invoices and reconciling accounts payable and receivables as well as in executing payments.

In the example of the Midwest supplier, when the manufacturing process is completed and the final product rolls off the assembly line ready to be shipped, the freight is loaded onto carriers destined for the customer on the West Coast. As soon as the product is on its way, the supplier transmits an electronic advance shipment notice (ASN) which notifies the customer that the order is on its way and provides specific details on the freight.

When the ASN is received on the West Coast, the data goes directly to the receiving dock supervisor, who now has information that can help him schedule workers and dedicate space on the dock and in the warehouse for the expected material. The ASN can also be used as a request for payment from the supplier and can serve as a trigger for the customer's accounts payable system to generate a payment, once all other conditions are met. This process is called evaluated receipt settlement (ERS).

If the customer is paying the supplier electronically via EFT, authorization to move funds can be transmitted directly to a bank along with the payment remittance details. Funds are then transferred to the supplier's account and a balance, along with the remittance information, is passed on to the supplier.

Electronic Funds Transfer

Using EDI to initiate payment instructions to a bank and provide remittance information to the supplier eliminates the need to produce and mail checks or to handle remittance details. For the supplier, remittance advice in EDI format facilitates automated reconciliation, reducing the time needed for account closing and cash application.

Responding to the need to innovate and streamline its operations, General Motors pioneered an EDI payment system using an eight-bank network. Through this system, GM is currently paying 1,200 of its auto parts suppliers. The ultimate goal is to replace the 300,000 paper checks per month to 5,500 suppliers with electronic payments. To date, electronic payments have reduced overdue bills from 32 percent to 4.7 percent.

Another user of EDI technology is the U.S. Government, which pays 45 percent of federal salaries via electronic funds transfer for a total of 260 million electronic payments every year.

Audit Effectiveness

Implementation of EDI has broad ramifications for all functions that depend heavily on paper. One of the most critical is maintaining an audit trail in the absence of hard copy records. The transfer of data from paper to computer data bases presents a new challenge to those who must reconcile accounts and check for valid controls in the financial system.

In practice, record keeping and controls can be tighter and more accurate when not dependent on human reliability. After all, computers do not forget

---

EDI and the Audit

As paper is replaced with data records, maintaining the integrity of the audit trail deserves significant attention. Some issues that should be considered when establishing an EDI system include:

1. Controls that either duplicate the paper procedure or strengthen it should be put in place in the preliminary stages of EDI implementation.

2. EDP audit requirements and those of current users must be integrated into the EDI system.

3. Legal agreements should be signed by both parties to ensure that responsibilities for lost or distorted data are clearly defined. Because there are currently no legal precedents with regard to specific cases in EDI, companies do not have proven language or rules to follow in setting up the proper legal frameworks. To protect yourself against lost or altered transmissions, you should thoroughly review any new contractual agreement with your legal department. This includes agreements with third parties, which claim to have limited responsibility for the integrity of your data.

4. Access to the system should reflect stronger security precautions than those taken in a paper-based system.

5. Transmission and functional acknowledgment management reports are essential to controlling the EDI environment. Control and transmission totals can be validated faster from a computer data base.

instructions and always perform the same task in the exact same order and manner for each and every transaction.

Improving Customer Service

Adding EDI to a company's capabilities not only provides more information much faster, but also produces greater expectations. Suppliers are expected to be more flexible and responsive to trends as well as to detect and correct problems quicker, with greater ease, and at less expense. The shrinking window of time available between discovering problems and resolving them presents businesses with even greater challenges for enhancing customer service and improving quality and productivity. In international operations, the sense of urgency and the need for effective tools to maintain acceptable levels of customer service become even more critical.

For example, in a five-month test at four J. C. Penney Company stores, sales of one of the retailer's brand suits increased 59 percent after the stores linked electronically with the apparel supplier. The reason for the jump: EDI made it possible to replenish supplies quickly enough to meet the season's demand.

INTEGRATING EDI INTO OPERATIONS

Back at the Midwest supplier's manufacturing plant, previously received purchase orders and releases have been processed and fed into the production schedule that generates the plant's daily material and parts requirements for the assembly line. This data is fed into the manufacturing requirements planning system that automatically debits inventory and generates EDI material releases to replenish parts and material from the appropriate suppliers.

Of course, because the ordering between customer and supplier is taking place electronically, the lead time needed to order direct materials is reduced by eliminating the preparation and mailing of paperwork. With less time needed to order supplies for the assembly line, safety stocks and inventories can be reduced significantly—a high priority for those manufacturers adopting a just-in-time environment. In addition, since the materials requirements have been produced directly from the manufacturing process, the orders should meet the exact needs of the assembly line.

This scenario illustrates how implementing EDI in automated ordering and materials management systems can streamline operations and generate substantial productivity gains. However, in order to electronically feed and process data from one functional area to another, businesses must reexamine the current information flow and address the issue of how to adapt the systems environment to increased and more complex demands.

Although there may be more information generated, and it may be easier to access, the challenge for management is how to effectively deploy those resources. In this search for more productive decision-support tools, EDI can

Key Security Considerations

Adequate security controls are critical in an EDI environment, particularly when multiple parties are communicating across common links and/or mailbox facilities. Here are some points that must be addressed as part of any EDI implementation:

1. Access to the system should require authorization. EDI users must be individually validated by the system. Each EDI user must have a unique ID and password as well as mailboxes and segregated print files.
2. Data from one party cannot be accidentally disclosed to another.
3. Exposure of the data to the EDI third-party vendor should not be allowed.
4. Data should not be vulnerable to manipulation by anyone other than the sender or receiver.
5. Systems must have adequate acknowledgment facilities to ensure that data is not "lost."
6. Acknowledgments should ensure the accuracy and completeness of the data.
7. Access to customer records and browsing of files should be restricted.
8. Authentication and encryption should be used wherever feasible.
9. There should be provision for an auto-callback feature for redialing when a busy signal is reached.

do more than present opportunities for productivity gains and significant improvements in quality and service. It can also serve as a catalyst to shift senior management's attention to the overall management and utilization of information systems in its operation.

Intensified scrutiny of information management often leads to focusing on specific operations and how the information flows from one function to another. This new perspective highlights the inefficiencies of antiquated systems that are incompatible and cannot handle the speed or level of detail needed to respond to today's management demands. Identification of information bottlenecks where data is being printed out and processed manually or information systems are being jerry-built to accomplish vital tasks is the first step in laying the foundation of a truly integrated systems environment.

A typical scenario that demonstrates the internal nonintegrated systems environment at many large corporations would go something like this: Purchase orders are received in EDI format and accepted into a system that prints them out for manual verification and modification. The validated data is then rekeyed into the plant production system. Information is printed out and rekeyed innumerable times throughout the manufacturing process until,

---

Price Waterhouse and EDI

The Price Waterhouse EDI Development and Consulting Practice has international experience in addressing strategic and operations EDI issues such as planning corporate objectives, security, training, implementation support, and project management for major corporations and government. Based in Washington, under the direction of partner Thomas P. Colberg, the team draws on a broad range of hands-on industry experience in standards development, software design, and implementation for a variety of industries. Services include interpreting EDI standards and how changes can impact operations, EDI software evaluation and installation assistance, corporate policy development, diagnostic and security reviews, and the development of methodology to identify costs and benefits as well as track progress.

---

finally, EDI formats replace both paper invoices and telephone calls advising that a shipment has left the dock.

Throughout this information flow, the accuracy of the data has been subject to compromise each time an individual has rekeyed the information, not to mention the time lost by shuffling paper around from one location to another. Each step in the information flow where data has "dropped out" of the system and into a hard copy format represents added cost and should be examined as a candidate for an EDI application.

Eliminating these "paper drops" and establishing a smooth flow of information from one functional system to another are the keys to reaping the maximum benefits from an EDI implementation.

LEARNING FROM EXPERIENCE

The earliest implementations of electronically exchanged information were typically in proprietary formats that large companies developed and installed to use exclusively with their own suppliers and customers. Initially, these systems were successful because they provided a unique service, which included real-time access to the latest information, enhanced customer service, and time and labor savings with each trading partner.

Today, many companies are recognizing the demand for open access and compatibility in networks and telecommunication formats. These enterprises are rapidly abandoning their proprietary formats and adopting the publicly accepted EDI standards. Some of the benefits they are capitalizing on include: easier start-up with less initial education required, greater general acceptance of conducting business electronically, larger population of capable trading partners, and fewer internal resources required for internal standards development and maintenance.

One example of this phenomenon is the American Airlines SABRE system. Initially, the system provided information only on American's flights, thereby locking in travel agents and their customers. Soon, American recognized the market value of opening its network to other reservation systems and charging a fee for the privilege of being listed on a network that was already firmly entrenched in thousands of travel agents' offices around the world. Thus, one of the first third-party networks was born.

The facility to provide for "many to many" communications at a reasonable cost has been essential to the feasibility of widespread EDI implementation. And, as more companies penetrate the third-party network provider community, value-added services such as translation, error reporting, standards compliance checking, transmission acknowledgments, and mailbox services will create distinctive product niches for a wide range of corporations. Maturity in the EDI software market as well as declining prices for hardware and network services are also contributing to the accelerating adoption of EDI as a standard way of conducting business.

A good illustration of the advantages of using third parties and off-the-shelf software can be found in the Midwest supplier's EDI direct materials purchasing project. Initially, the company planned to implement direct EDI connections with its top 200 suppliers. However, after 18 months of battling for internal resources and tackling the difficulties of establishing and maintaining many new direct electronic connections, the company turned to a third-party service that could offer supplier education conferences, technical support, electronic mailbox capabilities, and translation software. After barely one year, 165 suppliers are now receiving electronic material releases.

Impressive results have also been recorded at IBM, which expects to save $60 million over the next five years by connecting 2,000 of its largest suppliers worldwide through use of IBM's EDI network.

GETTING STARTED

There are many important considerations to be addressed as a company embarks on the journey to implement EDI. Here are a few hints:

1. It is critical to have top management commitment at the outset and throughout the process, since EDI will require an ongoing allocation of systems, staff, and financial resources. Also, be sure to avoid unrealistically low cost and time forecasts that can seriously erode top management's confidence in the project.

2. Review the internal situation. Is the pressure to implement EDI coming from the top or bottom? Is there a realistic awareness of the magnitude of EDI applications and the resources required to be successful? Are there particular areas where you are getting pressure (or ultimatums) from a key supplier or customer? Where are your biggest paper and administrative bottlenecks? What are the corporation's priorities?

3. Establish a corporate EDI philosophy and guidelines for adhering to it, including which standards will be used. Give the documents wide distribution among internal staff, suppliers, and customers alike.

4. Concurrently, build an internal team with key people from the user departments and divisions. Internal strategies and activities should be coordinated by one senior manager whose sole responsibility is implementing EDI.

5. Establish clear and consistent lines of communication and responsibility. Due to the technical nature of this activity and the need for heavy user involvement, this step is crucial for successful implementation. Communicate success stories and share lessons learned from failures. Also, document decisions and establish priorities, especially staff and systems requirements.

6. Be sure to obtain any EDI implementation guidelines or conventions for your industry as well as material from standards development groups. These documents are vital to understanding how a particular industry has decided to interpret the EDI standards and should reflect the expectations of your trading partners in that industry.

7. Wherever possible, use available software instead of in-house development. EDI software is currently available for a wide variety of applications at various levels of sophistication and prices. Considering the maturity of the current EDI software market, building an EDI system in-house will cost many times a package price and may not possess the versatility of packaged software.

8. Carefully select EDI trading partner targets. Experienced trading partners already have software and hardware and should require significantly less support than a new player in the EDI field.

9. Review paper procedures to ensure that implementing EDI does not eliminate vital functions without a plan to compensate for the changes. For example, an adequate audit trail must be maintained when the paper trail disappears.

10. Start small. Begin with a pilot project and expand the implementation based on this experience. For example, the Midwest supplier's purchasing project started with only a few selected suppliers. As the various kinks in the system were worked out, the application was expanded to 165 suppliers.

11. Plan for constant maintenance of the EDI environment and budget systems staff and resources for ongoing efforts.

WHO SHOULD LEAD THE EDI EFFORT?

As reality sets in and corporations recognize that EDI will change the very basics of operations, the internal struggle for control of this powerful tool begins. As the EDI strategic plan crystallizes, one of the most frequently asked questions is, "Who should lead the EDI effort in my company?"

First, a few points to remember:

1. EDI is a new way to do business. Therefore, current procedures should not restrict your imagination for implementation approaches.
2. Always remember that, while EDI can improve many processes, it alone cannot cure fundamental flaws in these processes. It is better to reexamine the processes and objectives, correct the fundamental errors, and then implement EDI to better achieve the desired results.
3. Above all, EDI is a method for accomplishing a task and should not stand alone. Therefore, user input for the targeted task is absolutely critical.

With these thoughts in mind, let's consider leadership alternatives. Although the leadership question does not have a simple answer, there are a few typical pitfalls that should be recognized and avoided.

Since the impact of implementing EDI will affect a broad segment of the corporation's population, top level attention and approval are critical. Consider, then, the following two schools of thought:

1. "EDI is a systems issue. Let the MIS department handle it."

In many instances, because EDI is a fairly technical area, it is inviting to hand over the entire process to the MIS department with little or no user participation. Certainly MIS is the group that is most familiar with the systems environment and what is practical to implement as well as what is totally incompatible with available resources and philosophies. MIS professionals understand the intricacies of hardware and software differences and the potential disasters that come from incompatible modems and overloaded communication lines.

However, the danger of neglecting user participation is that, in most cases, the MIS professional has a dominantly technical perspective and does not have a broad appreciation for special operations considerations as well as the unique requirements of different business relationships.

2. "EDI is merely a method of conducting business that just happens to include computer technology—users can handle all the issues."

Users that embark on the EDI voyage without substantial help from MIS risk many false starts, frustration at being unable to resolve and anticipate technical difficulties, and the probability of greater costs in added implementation time and cumbersome procedures.

The solution: Establish a group of users and MIS personnel who will work together as a team. This team should be given direct responsibility by senior management to integrate the system's capabilities with well-defined user requirements.

QUIET BUT STEADY GROWTH

For early pioneers, it may seem that the idea of replacing paper with electronic data has been slow to catch the imagination of the public at large. However, for mainstream corporate America, the world trading community, and governments, the concept that computers can communicate and process information without any human intervention is still extraordinary. In another 10 years, paper piles and in-boxes will be things of the past and EDI will be just another information systems tool. That's revolutionary indeed.

Reading 4–2

ELECTRONIC SYSTEMS ENHANCE JIT OPERATIONS

By Arjan T. Sadhwani and M. H. Sarhan

Management accountants increasingly are required to provide information for monitoring and controlling the acquisition and movement of raw materials, subassemblies, and finished products. To meet the information needs, those companies with just-in-time inventory systems have been establishing systems to incorporate electronic documents into computerized accounting, inventory management, and related reporting subsystems. These systems produce documents such as material releases, advance shipping notices, invoices, purchase orders, and so on, to track the precise status, location, and condition of an order as it moves from the supplier's loading docks to the JIT manufacturer's plant.

The methodology that deals with efficient and cost-effective electronic communication is called electronic data interchange (EDI). A thorough understanding of the elements of electronic data interchange and the benefits available under the EDI environment can help management accountants transcend company boundaries in providing relevant and timely information for decision making. Several illustrations based on our interviews, literature search, and experiences of JIT manufacturers show how EDI is used to achieve these benefits.

Published by *Management Accounting*. Copyright 1987, by National Association of Accountants, Montvale, NJ 07645.

Electronic data interchange is the exchange of documents and transactions by a computer in one company with the computer of another company. The application of EDI involves the conversion of a written document
into a machine readable form so that a computer in one company can communicate directly with the computer of the other company. The bulk of these
documents relate to events that would generate input transactions for accounting systems to be processed into information. Because accounting systems vary across companies, effective electronic communication requires
accountants to understand the following three important elements: standards
and conventions, data dictionary, and transmission protocols.

Standards and Conventions.   EDI standards deal with methods of converting written documents into a common electronic document-messaging
format to facilitate electronic interchange of documents. Conventions describe the procedural format for arranging various data elements in a prescribed format for various accounting transactions such as invoices, material
releases, advance shipment notices, and so on. For example, the convention
for an advance shipping notice transaction may require a list and the arrangement of the contents of the document such as product number, product description, physical characteristics of the goods to be shipped, type of
packaging, special markings, carrier information, and arrangement of goods
within the transportation equipment.

Data Dictionary.   A data dictionary describes the precise meaning of
data elements and some related specifications that are used in structuring a
transaction. It is used to translate some special codes and provide additional
information when necessary.

Transmission Protocols.   Normally, a set of accounting transactions is
packaged in an electronic envelope and transmitted throughout a communication network. Transmission protocols describe rules by which an envelope
is structured and handled by various communication devices. For example,
several electronic transactions such as invoices may be sent together in a
package with appropriate standard separators indicating parts of invoices or
identifying the beginning and ending of the message. Because the envelopes
containing these messages are handled by the various devices in the communication network, it is necessary that standard rules be established for transmission and separators.

BENEFITS OF EDI

Electronic data interchange has numerous benefits. In the traditional paper
exchange environment, even when a company has a computerized inventory
management system, purchase orders and other related documents are prepared and exchanged. Under EDI, however, transactions are machine read-

able and therefore computers can do the bulk of the tedious work without extensive paperwork. Transaction sets are standardized and computer-to-computer exchange is instantaneous.

EDI complements just-in-time inventory management objectives. "EDI has reaped tangible benefits for corporations trying to reduce pre-production inventories using just-in-time inventory methods. . . . Chicago-based Navistar, for instance, has some materials delivered only four hours before they are needed for processing. Navistar's JIT program, which includes electronic links with suppliers, has helped reduce inventories by $80 million in its first year of operations."[1]

In the auto industry where just-in-time inventory management systems are heavily used, all three large automakers are encouraging their suppliers to establish EDI links that can be tied into their computerized systems. Several GM plants support electronic exchange of material releases, purchase orders, and invoices with their suppliers or among their divisions. This year, GM plans to introduce an invoiceless payment system where all invoices will be paid electronically by using EDI and electronic fund transfers (EFT) because several financial institutions are setting up third-party EDI networks.

Ford uses an electronic registered "mailbox" for both inbound and outbound data exchange. Security of transactions is maintained via user codes and customer-controlled passwords. The documents exchanged include invoices for production and nonproduction parts; purchasing documents, such as purchase orders, requests, and response for quotations; advanced forwarding data that has been priced out, such as production and nonproduction parts; and electronic fund transfers.

Chrysler has integrated electronic data interchange with the Dynamic Inventory Analysis System where communication is in an interactive mode. This interesting feature is proving valuable because Chrysler can notify its suppliers at once of discrepancies in input data and year-to-date accumulated figures, as well as overshipped conditions, at a relatively cheaper cost.

As an extension, computer-to-computer communication with suppliers provides an opportunity for a management accountant involved in providing supplier analysis reports to generate relevant cost management reports by scanning the computers of suppliers with the lowest bids and consistent quality. This type of information is becoming a necessity for JIT systems to function smoothly.

EDI streamlines the order/delivery cycle in an inventory management system, lowering overhead costs because of the reduction in paper flow and mailing costs. Transactions and documents are electronic and do not require printing, licking, and opening of envelopes or humans shuffling various documents. According to a recent report on EDI by INPUT, a Mountain View, Calif.-based market research firm, EDI leads to substantial cost savings. Its estimates indicate that in the order/delivery cycle, preparation of manual paper documents to support accounting transactions can cost approximately $50. But, by installing an EDI system, the cost of preparing and sending documents has been reduced to $3 from $12. The report points out that the actual cost of sending and receiving a business document using EDI is usually less than a dollar.[2]

Furthermore, many companies are finding out that storing accounting documents in cartons is more expensive than storing the same information in a computer with EDI capability. For example, in the grocery industry, Kraft, Inc., and Procter & Gamble Co. launched electronic data interchange with supermarkets and other retailers. The estimated savings are $300 million a year.

Many companies are finding out that the real savings from EDI are realized not only by transportation departments, but also by accounting and finance departments. Electronic data interchange eliminates the wasteful data rekeying and significantly reduces errors that normally result in repeated manual data transcription by suppliers, manufacturers, transportation companies, and other related parties in the order/delivery/payment cycle.

Reduction of errors is one of the EDI's biggest selling points. For example, Union Pacific's experience indicates that computer-to-computer handling of information generates a dramatic improvement in quality and consistency. Therefore, lots of problems are eliminated as data go through subsequent processing steps. Auditing of carrier bills, receiving reports, remittance advances, etc. are virtually eliminated when EDI is used to generate and transmit electronic documents. LTV Steel Company of Cleveland uses EDI to exchange nearly 100,000 or about 80 percent of its freight bills with railroad companies. The company has improved the accuracy and timeliness of freight bills flow and has saved between $20,000 and $30,000 per month in clerical costs and overcharges. The company gets electronic documents and pre-audits all the bills against the electronic data base when they are electronically received via the EDI network.

Electronic data interchange systems speed operations in the purchasing/delivery and related information processing cycle. With mail, there is a 7- to 10-day lag from the time a part is ordered until it is received. The use of EDI has reduced this cycle time to less than two days in many companies using EDI with just-in-time inventory management systems.

In addition, productivity is enhanced because of reduction in paper-handling chores such as copying, forwarding, filing, stamping, initializing, matching, verifying, and refiling. Accountants become free to weigh facts and make judgments in performing their functions and related operations. This freedom, in turn, allows JIT manufacturers and their suppliers to reap many indirect benefits.

Production efficiency is enhanced because timely, accurate material requirements schedules and actual receipt of material information are transmitted via the EDI network to various plant locations. The up-to-date information is important for production planning and scheduling. For example, Auto-Con, a Dayton, Ohio-based public warehouse used by GM to handle just-in-time storage of various parts is required to ship parts to GM's assembly plants in strict adherence to JIT production schedules. By using a computerized setup mounted on a forklift, data are transmitted to GM's computer, sending information about arrival of various parts. The forklift operator can electronically communicate with production personnel via GM's computer and get instructions about what to do with the shipment. In some instances, Auto-Con may be required to stage and ship parts within 15 minutes of receiving from suppliers. With these techniques, many JIT manufacturers can generate daily or even hourly shipping schedules efficiently because the facts are accurate and timely for making judgments.

EDI provides an ability to do electronic tracing of material movement and can provide information related to the status of a shipment or other document. As pointed out by Thomas Johnson and Robert S. Kaplan in "The Rise and Fall of Management Accounting," January 1987, "With many production processes under direct control of digital computers, information can be recorded in real time for analysis of operating performance . . . Automated parts recognition and tracking systems combined with Local Area Network technology can provide continual status reports."

Companies using the electronic data interchange network systems are capable of dialing into the EDI network and finding out the status or location of the shipment. Some shippers indicate that the tracing capability of EDI can save a significant amount of time and money. Interamerican, which moves full load freight via piggyback and truck between the United States and Canada, has saved 16 labor-hours a day tracing 5,000 trailers. Using EDI communication, through a third-party network with 15 railroad companies, Interamerican's computers request tracing information every evening and the report is received the next morning. Similarly, EDI-EXPRESS, a third-party network operated by GE Information Services, can provide reports, on request, indicating a list of changes to the status of every document sent or received by a company, status and list of documents not yet received by the receiver, and an error listing when special editing features are used.

METHODS OF ELECTRONIC COMMUNICATION

In order for EDI to function smoothly, both companies must establish the required electronic link to move information. Three methods are used for communication and transfer of information: point-to-point configuration, value-added network, and third-party networks. Management accountants should understand these methods to realize EDI benefits in a cost-effective manner.

Point-to-Point Configuration

Point-to-point configuration links JIT manufacturer's and supplier's computer via a communication network. Both companies must use the same standards and conventions for setting up formats for various transactions and conform to required modem line speeds. Both companies are responsible for developing and monitoring their individual systems. If they have different computers

FIGURE 1   Point-to-Point Configuration

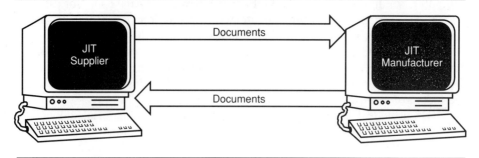

or use different software packages, translation software would be required. The translation software can either be developed in-house or purchased or leased from software companies for their computer systems. Private leased lines or public switched lines (dial-up services) are used for transmission of data. Figure 1 illustrates this method of EDI.

Value-Added Networks

This method provides "mailbox" service for JIT manufacturer and supplier companies. All companies are responsible for developing protocols and for-mat-handling requirements, but contract with a public network such as Tym-net or MCI to act as a communication carrier. The carrier provides mailboxes where electronic documents may be stored for all companies. The mailbox makes it unnecessary for the companies to provide a dedicated computer for the purpose of awaiting incoming calls. It also provides the ability to consol-idate EDI transactions, allowing the user to send information to multiple re-ceivers in a single dial-up session.

Mailbox service arrangements facilitate adaptation by each company to its modem line speed, permits some flexibility in terms of using different pro-tocols because receivers can translate retrieved messages in their format, and permits communication during different times of the day to take advantage of lower rates during off-peak times. Control Data offers a value-added network called REDINET designed especially for just-in-time inventory management systems and related industrial applications. IBM and several transportation companies have developed value-added networks through their EDI services divisions (Figure 2).

Third-Party Networks

Third-party networks serve as electronic data interchange service bureaus in addition to providing "mailbox" service available from value-added networks. The service bureaus would act as an EDI network for JIT manufacturers and

FIGURE 2   Value-Added Network

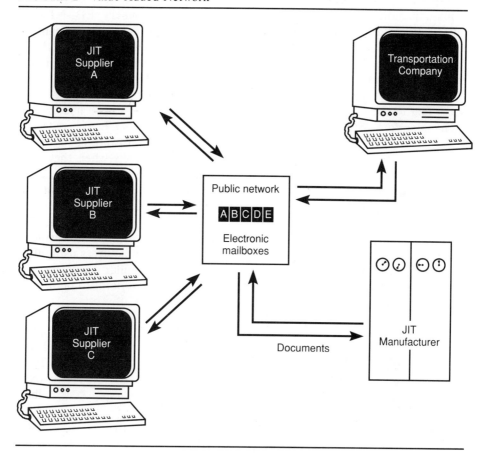

their suppliers, receive transaction sets in any protocol, and translate these transactions according to the JIT manufacturer's protocols. These networks take responsibility for all communication needs. The third-party networks reformat transactions to meet different standards, formats, or conventions, or even provide communication links and transmission of electronic documents to and from various transportation companies.

When suppliers of a JIT manufacturer have many different types of computer setups and use a variety of paperwork procedures, the third-party networks remove the hurdle of incompatibility of computers resulting in the inability of these computers to communicate with each other.

For example, EDI-NET service bureau of McDonnell Douglas allows a user to communicate with 117 different communication protocols. Hewlett-Packard (H-P), a leading JIT manufacturer of computer hardware, uses

EDI-NET services provided by McDonnell Douglas to ensure that its EDI communication documents will be understood by the suppliers. EDI-NET allows H-P to maintain its own computer system but permits the company to input purchase orders for various suppliers into the network. The EDI-NET uses translation software, converts these orders into the supplier's format, and sorts and transmits to the supplier's computer systems.

Suppliers receive the orders in their own format and continue processing according to the "requirements" of their own system.[3] H-P also has started exchanging forecasting data with suppliers through EDI-NET. The data are automatically aggregated and translated, then forwarded to waiting suppliers. Third-party networks also perform more complicated tasks when they provide EDI services (Figure 3).

To select a method for an EDI system, you should consider certain factors. These factors include the distance the data are transported, required delivery time frame, volume of transactions, number of destinations, frequency of transport, compatibility of recording media, cost, and security and reliability. If a company's volume is heavy with JIT manufacturers using similar standards, conventions, and protocols, and sharing similar documents, or if it has a great deal of business with one supplier, then a point-to-point network is a preferable option.

FIGURE 3   Third-Party Network (EDI Service Bureau)

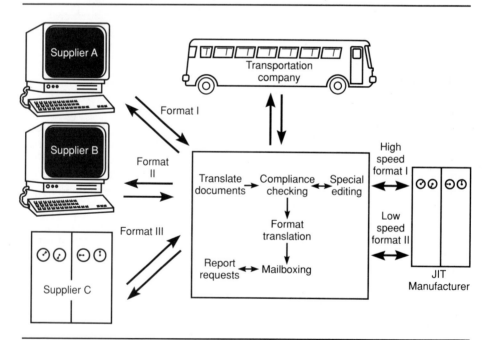

A very simple EDI system requires the supplier to purchase a compatible personal computer (PC), a communication device such as a modem and related communication software, and telephone line hookups. Many software packages are available that will support one or two standards and protocols used by JIT manufacturers in some major industries.[4]

On the other hand, if a company has a low volume of transactions with a large number of JIT manufacturers who use different standards or protocols, then it may be better served by using either a value-added or a third-party network method. Similarly, if the company emphasizes the integration between its EDI system and other existing functional subsystems that have different internal formats from those mandated by standards and protocols, then a value-added or a third-party network method would be appropriate.

This approach would make it possible for a company to communicate with JIT manufacturers or transportation companies even if their computers are not compatible.

A MEGATREND

For JIT manufacturers, EDI has evolved as the preferred method of exchanging documents in the order/delivery/payment cycle. These companies use EDI to electronically send and receive purchase orders, advance shipping notices, invoices, and other documents. EDI is becoming a megatrend in the JIT inventory management environment. It encourages the removal of roadblocks that make the transition to the automated factory difficult and paves the way for establishing cost management systems needed for automated factories.[5] When EDI is properly implemented, users gain speed, accuracy, and automatic acknowledgment.

JIT manufacturers are realizing that electronic data interchange helps in keeping their inventory at the desirable low levels because of quicker communication with suppliers and accurate and timely availability of relevant information. Smaller companies also can realize many of the benefits described. For example, Rebmann Plastic Molding, Redford, Mich., a small manufacturer of a variety of plastic parts for the auto industry, has achieved several benefits by installing an automated inventory management system to meet the automakers' EDI requirements. The company has saved several hours a day that were spent on the phone to trace or call in shipping notices.

In addition, the auto industry's mandate to communicate electronically encouraged Rebmann to computerize other functions such as accounting, shop floor scheduling, and inventory management. Six months after the implementation, Rebmann's inventory was reduced from about $1 million to $355,000.

Our interviews with other companies using electronic data interchange indicate that some of these companies are starting to replace various accounting documents by electronic messages integrated into their accounting and cost management systems. Recent advances in microcomputer technology facilitate development of management accounting systems based on electronic links transcending the boundaries of the company.

Notes

1. Gary Stix, "EDI Standards: A Crucial Juncture," *Computer Decisions,* March 1986, p. 82.
2. Jeffrey A. Chester, "Electronic Data Interchange," *Infosystems,* June 1986, pp. 48–50.
3. Bruce Heydt, "Computers—Hewlett Packard," *Distribution,* February 1986, pp. 50–53.
4. Automotive Industry Action Group and other trade groups maintain lists of approved software packages and their suppliers.
5. For further details, see James A. Brimson, "How Advanced Manufacturing Technologies Are Reshaping Cost Management," *Management Accounting,* March 1986, pp. 25–29.

Reading 4–3

THE DRIVE TOWARD DDP:
A MANAGEMENT PERSPECTIVE

By Harry Mishkin and Dan C. Kneer

Management information systems are in the midst of a radical transformation most immediately evidenced by the proliferation of microcomputers in organizations and the frequent introduction of products enabling these desktop computers to communicate with each other and with mini or mainframe computers.

Rather than being a sudden, unexpected development, the current microcomputer boom can be seen as part of a longer-established trend toward decentralization of computing power, commonly called distributed data processing or DDP. This transition toward decentralization is being driven by a spectrum of forces, including the increased capabilities of mini and microcomputers, the growing availability of network and communications software, greater user knowledge of computers, and user demand for computing power and local processing authority and/or autonomy.

Even as this phenomenon gains momentum, its impact on the organization remains unclear. Businesses have, for years, been acquiring mini and microcomputers to augment or replace their mainframes. Yet the functions of

Reprinted from the January/February 1987 issue of *CMA Magazine,* by permission of The Society of Management Accountants of Canada.

these smaller machines and their architectural relationships to one another (and to the mainframe) bear on the degree to which the functioning of data processing will change along with a change in corporate philosophy.

Whether the transition is a grassroots phenomenon traveling up the organization or a central directive proceeding downward, some key decisions will have to be made about organizational restructuring. Upper management may no longer be oblivious of the computing demands of employees.

FRAMEWORK FOR ORGANIZATIONAL CHANGE

While technical guidelines for DDP are beginning to emerge, a comprehensive framework for making decisions about the implementation of a distributed system does not yet exist. The dimensions of such a framework include:

1. Technical issues: The design alternatives—the basic design parameters for distributed systems (as well as available products).
2. Operational issues: The concerns for the proper functioning of an information system raised by distributed processing.
3. Philosophical issues: The context in which the change is occurring, including:
   a. The motivations for DDP.
   b. Organizational considerations and constraints.
   c. Political implications.

The third item is the "reality check" to counterbalance theoretical indications for design choices. The inclusion of this item is an acknowledgment that design choices are just as likely to be dictated by special vendor relations or a key player's favorite software as by error rates or data integrity.

Defining the organizational consequences of shifting to DDP becomes a more significant consideration, given the lack of consensus about the effect of computerization itself as a point of reference. The stereotypical image of a corporate decision maker inundated with reams of computer printout alludes to the possibility that our ability to create computers has outstripped our ability to use them wisely.

Perhaps the new stereotype is one of a corporate decision maker hunched over a personal computer typing in numbers to a spreadsheet. This manager might or might not know the origin of the numbers or how accurate they are. The reader of a report based on one of these spreadsheets might or might not be aware of the manipulations involved, let alone the accuracy of the data or the validity of the inferences drawn from it.

The potential consequences to an organization of a decrease in the quality of information on which it operates make it imperative to examine at the outset the possible consequences of any major change in the information system.

TECHNICAL ISSUES: DDP AND THE
DESIGN ALTERNATIVES

The organizational information system is going through a transformation characterized by offloading or downloading some aspect of the system from a central computer to other machines.

These other computers might be in the same room, in the same building, or across the country. They might be connected by telephone lines, data communication services, optical fiber or microwave links. They might not be physically connected at all, as in personal computer use. The point is that the machines interact to perform the functions of an information system—a system which controls, distributes, and tracks the resources and results of an organization.

What is DDP?   Distributed data processing might seem to be a self-explanatory term, implying the use of more than one computer to accomplish a data processing task. But current definitions of DDP are far from uniform. They range from tacit acceptance of any system involving multiple computers as DDP, to definitions so restrictive that true DDP is seen to be only a promise.

In the broadest sense, an information system is an organizational function which must be developed, operated, and managed. Taking this frame of reference, an MIT study divides development, operation, and management into subprocesses:

- System development: functional design, detailed specifications, and programming, implementation, maintenance.
- System operations: edit and control, update, process, and report data.
- System management: management control and strategic planning.[1]

Each subprocess is associated with either equipment or personnel resources, or both. For an implementation to be successful, the study maintains, an organization must think of its information system in this broad perspective and decide whether or not to distribute each subprocess.

What Is There to Distribute?   A breakdown by Martin[2] incorporates another range of aspects of an information system:

Application processing. This refers to the complete handling of a transaction, from input to output.

Intelligence. Intelligence refers to the performance of specific functions, as opposed to the complete handling of a transaction. Creation of screen prompts and instructions (dialogues), formatting report output, and editing data input are examples of such functions.

Expectations and Objectives for DDP

- Local autonomy and improved local decision making
- End-user productivity
- Appealing terminal dialogues
- Access to remote resources and data
- Making distance transparent to the end-user
- Availability
- Better information—more timely and specific
- Faster application development
- Closer control of such items as expense and inventory
- Fewer errors due to user responsibility for data entry
- Less cost
- Ease of system growth (extensibility)
- Less drastic consequences of system failure ("failsoft" or "graceful degradation")
- Disaster protection (everything not in one location)

SOURCES: James Martin, *Strategy for Distributed Data Processing* (New Jersey: Prentice Hall, 1982). Philip H. Enslow, "What Is 'Distributed Data Processing System,' " *Computer,* January 1978, pp. 13–21.

I/O. This refers to the actual input and output of data. Input can be via keyboard, computer-readable forms, cards, or tape. Output might simply be a screen display but could also include printed reports or tape.

Network Control. The software that performs the communication function (e.g., routing, error detection) is called network control.

Files. Analogous to the conventional usage of the term, files are the arrangement of data in a computer. They can be a simple collection of records or a more complex arrangement of data items and indexes and pointers to those items (sometimes referred to as a data base).

These system components/tasks can each be located at different points on the centralized–decentralized continuum. Thus, for each component comprising a system—for example, a given piece of software (application processing) or data entry for a given operation (I/O) —the question of *where* to locate the function or *where* the process takes place must be answered.

Distribution. The idea that a DDP system has an "architecture" makes the distribution concept easier to understand. The foundation of a sys-

FIGURE 1 Basic Topologies of Distributed Systems

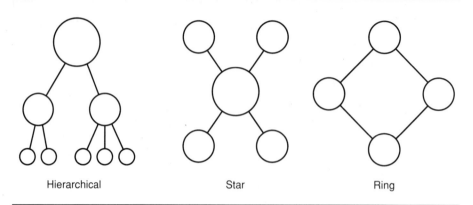

| Hierarchical | Star | Ring |

tem's architecture is its topology or "shape"—the nodes (processing points, work stations, etc.) and their interconnection. A system's topology will consist of one or more of the basic shapes shown in the diagrams (Figure 1).

These diagrams reveal a dimension of architecture beyond shape. Two of the topologies shown have a central node and one does not. At issue is the relationship between the nodes. Can the nodes be thought of as "peers" (as Martin calls them) or is there some degree of dependence or subservience (a master/slave relationship) between them? This question of the interaction between nodes involves technical considerations which won't be gone into here. But whatever direction the technical considerations favor must be weighed against the management considerations.

With data, the location question becomes more complex. Should data be split by geographical considerations, by the type of data, or by the way the data is used? Is the data replicated and, if so, is one copy designated the master copy? Here also, both management and technical implications must be considered.

OPERATIONAL ISSUES IN DDP

The change to DDP raises concerns about the proper functioning of an organization's information system; for example, concern about the loss or alteration of data, either accidentally or intentionally.

The new system would be expected to be predictable—that repeated operations on the same data would yield the same results. Data received at a distant location should be the same as the data that was sent. Inputs should be traceable from the system output, and output should be reproducible from input—the system must be capable of being audited. Such system objectives are no different than those for remote job entry in a standard centralized system. The DDP attitude of autonomy, however, works against standardized teleprocessing.

Beyond the basic concern that the system work properly are considerations of what is expected of the system, considerations relating to resources and to the existing system. But these must be weighed against the critical areas for proper system operation as outlined below. Since guidelines barely exist for DDP design, and since uncertainty is synonymous with risk, these areas of concern can be seen as vulnerabilities of a DDP system.

Security. Much of the concern for control relates to the ability to control access, not only physical access to equipment and data storage, but also to the on-line data and software. With a DDP system, these controls move "out into the network" and the exposure is increased. More people have access to hardware, software, and data. The increased complexity of distributed systems raises the prospect that all possible "loopholes" in control functions (e.g., password and terminal user identification requirements) have not been blocked.

Other Controls. Control in a managerial sense is also an issue. As the pace of microcomputer and software acquisition increases, the ability to "keep the reigns" on the system decreases. As the new corporate computer owners access mainframe data to produce reports that will be distributed to and used by others, the issue of control ties in directly with the issue of quality of information and decision making.

Control also refers to the establishment of standards. In the case of microcomputer hardware and software acquisition, lack of such standards can create a limiting and costly future incompatibility. For example, such a threat is motivating one major corporation to depart from its usually decentralized decision making in favor of centrally mandating hardware and software choices.

Quality of Data. The very nature of distributed processing creates questions about the quality and status of the data anywhere in the system: Is the information accurate and current? Has it arrived at the correct destination? Is the information that arrived the same information that was sent? Has the information arrived at its destination at all?

Routing, error detection, and network software assume paramount importance in DDP. With less standardization of supervision and more system users, the completeness and accuracy of the data become questionable. Although some proponents of DDP predict that errors will decrease because users are responsible for their own data, this has not been proven.

Replicated data greatly increases the concern about consistency of the data: Will any given copy be current? Restart/recovery procedures are complicated by the likelihood that given copies of data will be in different states at the time of a system crash.

Replicated data serves as an example of weighing desired system functioning (data access enhanced by proximity—it is stored where it is being used) against concerns (for unrecoverable loss of data—if only one copy of any data item exists and that item might exist at any given node in the system). Moreover, the additional concern for data integrity posed by data replication can be subjected to this balancing of expectations and concerns. Specifically, a balance must be reached between the desire for data proximity, currency requirements (how up-to-date must the data be for its intended use), frequency of updates, and number of update sources.

Audit Capability. An adverse effect on the audit capability of a corporate information system can be dangerous. A system that can't be audited is out of control since there can be no substantiation of any figures. Most observers agree that DDP can ". . .cause the auditor no end of trouble and humiliation . . ."[3]

Audit concerns center on danger to data in transmission; the increased number of locations of data input, storage, processing, and output; unauthorized program changes; the absence or failure of controls; the lack of audit trails; excessive complexity; data access via the network; system predictability; and adequacy and standardization of restart and recovery procedures should a program fail or system crash.

Another auditing concern relates to an accounting axiom that a separation of duties should exist between asset recording, authority, and custody. Because the staff at a local site is likely smaller than the staff at a centralized site, this separation would probably not be maintainable throughout a distributed system. The user of a system at a local site is often the operator, and the person who created the data is often the one who enters it. Hence, there is a danger of manipulation that does not exist with a central system.

Small staffs, geographical dispersion, and a greater likelihood of lax standards combine to make physical security more difficult in a distributed system. The implications go beyond capability of auditing the system, since illegal access could result in theft or vandalism.

Addressing the problems of auditing DDP systems, Kneer presents a list of controls divided among operations/security, application software, data set, input/output, networking/transmission/distributed intelligence, and common controls.[4]

PHILOSOPHICAL ISSUES: DDP IN THE ORGANIZATIONAL CONTEXT

A system involves people—the people who created it, the people who pay for it, the ones who run it, those who put the data in and those who use the data the system puts out. The opinions and reactions of these individuals influence, or should influence, the design choices for a system as well as its functioning. Their collective opinions and behaviors form the political context for the possibilities, motivations, and dangers thus far noted.

Motivations.   Only some of the expectations about the benefits to be derived from DDP are directly related to problems. Other expectations of those lobbying for DDP are purely political. Line managers, aware of the increasing funds going to the data processing department, might see the opportunities created by the dramatically improved price/performance ratio of smaller computers as a way to gain control over a greater portion of the corporate budget, and over their domain of information. In a less political context, they are motivated by the desire to couple managerial responsibility with authority over resources.

Another study by MIT lists the factors behind the DDP momentum as the rapid deceleration of hardware prices, increased computer literacy, and the growing complexity of the managerial environment. Management's information needs have increased. At the same time, management has become more aware of what is available to meet those needs and more able to afford the new technology.[5]

This new technology is also facilitating a closer fit between the information system and the structure and management style of an organization. In a poll of managers from 25 organizations that had decentralized their data processing function, geographical separation of organizational subunits was the second most frequently mentioned factor in the decision to decentralize.[6] The degree of information system distribution follows corporate structure in two pioneers of DDP—Hewlett-Packard and Texas Instruments.[7] Flexibility is the key word to describe this attractiveness of DDP.

The desire to push decision making down the organizational hierarchy is a recurring theme in modern management. Several authors emphasize this theme as a motivator for DDP. A major objective of the new technology, Martin states, is to "improve and expand the way computers are employed by the end users."[8]

The Problems with Centralized Data Processing.   Interest in DDP is motivated, not only by the increased flexibility it offers, but also by a frequently found frustration with centralized data processing departments. The notion that centralized data processing breeds problems runs through much of the literature. "Centralized data processing is inherently flawed."[9] Users' needs will inevitably conflict in the competition for mainframe time. An increased dependence on a central system breeds increased conflicts.

Martin sees the problem as the "bureaucratization" of the data department inherent in growth. As the department expands, the following effects take place:

- The cost of coordination and control becomes disproportionate.
- Effectiveness decreases.
- Preoccupation with internal departmental problems increases.

- Dependence on experts, isolated from users, increases.
- User alienation increases, along with the perception of the department as elitist or unresponsive.[10]

The workload gets too big for the computer, and response time (the time it takes the computer to perform an action requested by an on-line user) degrades. In the poll cited earlier, the factor mentioned most often in the decision to establish DDP was response time/turnaround time (the time it takes for a report or new application to be delivered).[11]

The desirability of DDP lies in the belief that more machines, and machines located closer to and controlled by the users, will improve this situation. The enlightened data processing department will be able to adapt to these new expectations and initiate DDP projects where appropriate.

Expectations.   Current technical realities and future possibilities of DDP, such as the dramatic increase in microprocessor power and memory storage capacity, provide the catalyst for a growing list of needs and wants of system designers and users. Some of these items can be seen as remedial while others may be viewed as enhancements to the existing system.

An important question may be raised about the feasibility of the listed items. With expectations derived from a rapidly changing technology, some of these expectations might outstrip technical reality.

The diversity of the motivations toward DDP, combined with the lack of standards for DDP, makes these motivations more significant. If a goal is well defined, motivations can decide *whether or not* the goal will be attained. With DDP, motivations help decide *what* will be attained.

Political Context.   If the ability to access and use information is a form of power, the change to DDP can alter the power balances in an organization. Key design questions, such as the location of controls or node autonomy, can become questions of enfranchisement or disenfranchisement, or so they may be seen by the affected parties. The possible reactions to the perceived and actual shifts in power can affect the success of the system and the health of the organization.

Will the new system be seen as a territorial invasion or as the provision of ammunition? Will the new system be resisted? Will its implementation be undermined?

The existing centralized data processing department is the probable focus of such questions. If the department is not the change agent in the move to DDP, departmental personnel will likely feel threatened by the move. Polarization is a possibility.

There are other implications of redistributing the information-handling power base as well. A change to DDP is likely more than a switch of hardware. One possibility is the exposure of mid-level managers who had existed in a "cocoon of ineffective information systems."[12] Another concern is that managers will become so fascinated with their new EDP tools that they are in danger of becoming "highly paid computer operators."[13]

Development and Implementation.   A veteran data processing professional defines a successful development project as one that meets its goals and specifications, satisfies its users, and is on time and within budget.[14] Distributed systems have an advantage over centralized systems when it comes to satisfying user needs. The development tools can be placed closer to the future system users, if not directly in their hands.

This capability, however, weakens DDP's chances for success on the other criteria. If the development process itself is distributed, as the MIT study suggested, the relevant parties could very well be geographically and organizationally dispersed. Communication and coordination would become more difficult. Goal differences might exist within the development team.

CREATE YOUR OWN DDP FRAMEWORK

Any organization contemplating the distribution of part or all of its information system needs a framework for making the decisions fundamental to that change. Such a framework is not currently found in any textbook or trade journal, for it must relate design choices that are just now being recognized to the management style and politics peculiar to an organization.

Technical Considerations.   The first step in creating a framework for decision making is learning what design choices are available. A possible difficulty here is in separating design choices from product choices. Design choices are conceptual in nature and should address the questions of what to distribute, what to leave centralized, and what decision criteria to use. Those responsible for making or recommending product choices must be aware of these criteria and must keep informed of the currently proposed technological remedies to the potential problems of DDP.

This conceptual framework thus enables system designers to know what to ask for from system vendors. Aside from a given product's specifications, questions about future growth and compatibility with existing machines must be answered. System manufacturers are beginning to address these issues. For example, Intel Corporation bases its microcomputer line on what it calls the "open systems concept"—designing ease of future growth into the product.

The issue of locus of control should also bear directly on product choice. One Intel product, "iDIS" (Intel Database Information System), is a microcomputer that can function as an intermediary between multiple users on either terminals or individual computers and the mainframe. Access to data is controlled at the iDIS, thus permitting a balance of power to be established between distributed and centralized functioning.

Operational and Organizational Concerns. In addition to knowing the DDP design alternatives, decision makers must understand why people in their organizations are interested in distributed processing. Wants must be separated from needs in evaluating any request for decentralization or in evaluating each design choice (which might or might not relate to one of these requests).

Design choices thus need to be evaluated in the following contexts:

1. Level of (or existence of) need.
2. System objectives.
3. Potential for system degradation, including loss of data, slack in control, data errors, loss of auditing capability, and hardware or software incompatibility.
4. Political implications.
5. Technical feasibility and product availability.
6. Resource availability, including money and expertise.

The "spirit" of DDP is decentralization and user autonomy. Many DDP implementations are user driven, with product choices being based on local need. The potential benefits from the initiative and motivation inherent in this phenomenon need to be continually weighed against potential hardware or software incompatibility. This vigilance must be the responsibility of a chief decision maker, one most removed from localized, vested interests.

Future Considerations. The concept of power in relation to information systems is new. An attempt to clarify or elaborate upon the concept can help to put awareness of the "players' " motivations in the development of that system into perspective for the key decision makers.

Questions arise in this endeavor: Is location synonymous with ownership and is ownership synonymous with control? For instance, does the decision to place certain files on a minicomputer at a local site give the site manager ownership of that data? Or control over such data? What exactly is the definition of control? Is control the authority to define the format of the data, the responsibility for data I/O, programming power, access authority, lockout capabilities, or specification of the distribution list for the output of the data? These are probably only some of the issues that bear on control as well as power.

The design alternatives for a distributed system must be evaluated with a clear insight into the objectives for the new system and with concern for its potential improvements and weaknesses. If this decision-making process occurs with full awareness of the organizational context in which it is occurring, chances for successful system design, development, and implementation will be enhanced.

Notes

1. John F. Rockart, Christine V. Bullen, and Joav Leventer, "Centralization vs. Decentralization" (Cambridge, MA: M.I.T.—Center for Information System Research, 1981), pp. 16–22. Transparency categories posed by Jim Gray of IBM.
2. James Martin, *Design and Strategy for Distributed Data Processing* (Englewood Cliffs, N.J.: Prentice Hall, 1981), pp. 92–101.
3. Robert L. Patric (commentary), *The EDP Audit, Control and Security Newsletter,* August 1980, p. 1.
4. Dan Kneer, *Internal Control in Distributed Data Processing,* doctoral dissertation, University of Missouri, 1981, pp. 146–186.
5. John F. Rockart, Christine V. Bullen, and John N. Kogan, "The Management of Distributed Processing" (Cambridge, MA: M.I.T.—Center for Information System Research, 1978), p. 13.
6. Rockart et al., "Centralization versus Decentralization," p.5.
7. Conversation with Bill Kinzie, of Intel Corporation, who was involved in a survey of Hewlett-Packard and Texas Instruments in 1983.
8. Martin, p. 14.
9. Paula Klein, "DDP Gains Major Beachhead at Corporate Sites," *Information Systems News,* October 10, 1983, pp. 49–50.
10. Martin, p. 230.
11. Rockart et al., p. 44.
12. Ann Dooley, moderator; "Office Automation Roundtable—What's Next in OA," *Computerworld,* December 7, 1983, p. 15 (from participant Will Zachman).
13. Kenneth M. Sullivan, "Decentralization? Or Reinventing the Wheel," *Computerworld,* December 7, 1983, pp. 84–90.
14. Robert Block, *The Politics of Projects* (New York: Yourdon Press, 1983), pp. 1–8.

CHAPTER 5

Computer Crime and Security

As computer usage has increased over the last two decades, computer crime has become a major threat to the business community, to governments at all levels, and to private citizens. Almost daily we hear of new reports of computer crime involving losses of money, inventories, or other resources. The magnitude of computer crime in our society is unknown. However, investigators estimate that annual losses are in the billions of dollars. More frightening is the fact that experts fear that only a small fraction of all incidents are detected, and that only a small portion of these are reported. Thus, the incidents we know about may reflect "only the tip of a giant iceberg."

Computer crime (also referred to as computer abuse or computer fraud) may be broadly defined as an illegal and intentional act to defraud which is performed in a computer environment. As defined, computer crime may or may not involve sophisticated computer knowledge or even the direct use of computers. In fact, most incidents of computer crime are not dependent on intricate programming schemes, such as trap doors, viruses, or logic bombs—most involve simple and nontechnical ploys such as the manipulation of input data. Known incidents of computer crime are usually perpetrated by one of the following tactics: entering fictitious or altered transactions into a system; deleting legitimate transactions; direct modification or destruction of computer files or records; making unauthorized changes to programs; theft of or unauthorized use of computer equipment; theft or illegal copying of computer software or records; and illegally accessing computer resources (even if there is no theft).

While the actual magnitude of losses from computer crime is unknown, reported incidents reveal several alarming trends. The FBI has estimated that the average dollar impact (or loss to victims) from reported computer crimes is in excess of $600,000. This exceeds the average loss from noncomputer crimes, approximately $23,000 per reported incident. Experts believe the total annual loss from computer fraud in the United States ranges from $3 billion to $5 billion. These experts also agree that both the incidence and the magnitude of such losses are increasing.

Several factors contribute to the anticipated future increase in computer crime. A computer (or any other) crime occurs when a perpetrator has the motivation, the requisite knowledge, and the opportunity to commit the illegal act. All three of these key ingredients are likely to become more common in the 1990s. Motivation for computer crime is provided by the rapidly increasing number of computer files and data bases currently being developed and maintained by businesses, governmental units, and other organizations. These data bases often contain valuable and sensitive information, the loss or alteration of which may be extremely damaging to the owner and/or valuable to the perpetrator. Examples of this information include bank records, credit records, confidential payroll information, inventory records, business transactions, and trade secrets. These computer data bases are attractive targets which may motivate computer criminals to act more frequently.

Computer knowledge and opportunity are also becoming more readily attainable. Without question, the general level of computer literacy is increasing around the world. Children are exposed to microcomputers as early as kindergarten, and their knowledge often surpasses that of their parents. Colleges, universities, and technical schools offer and require far more computer training in their curricula than ever before. In short, computers have permeated almost every aspect of our lives so that a minimum level of computer knowledge is becoming a necessity for most people to function in their jobs. A major impetus for this heightened level of computer knowledge has been and continues to be the microcomputer revolution.

In addition to expanding computer literacy, microcomputers also provide new opportunities for computer fraud. Microcomputers with modem connections are capable of acting as remote terminals and can link to mainframe computers or computer networks which have telephone dial-in capabilities. Thus, microcomputers may be used to illegally penetrate inadequately secured proprietary (nonpublic) systems. To guard against such penetrations, a system of security controls must be in place which can distinguish "phantom" terminals from legitimate terminals, and which can successfully block access to system resources by intruders (or "hackers"). The increasing use of electronic data interchange (EDI) by the business community also provides new opportunities for computer fraud. As more transactions become paperless, electronic transmissions which are inadequately secured become easy prey and potential primary targets for intruders.

An awareness of the methodology, targets, and internal control implications of computer crime is essential for both accountants and auditors. The two readings included with this chapter further discuss the growing threat of computer crime and suggest strategies for reducing its risk. A common theme in each article is the paramount importance of strong internal controls to an organization's overall efforts to safeguard its computer resources. The first article, "Preventing Computer Fraud," identifies four critical high-exposure areas for most businesses and suggests specific control measures for defending each. The second article, "Preventing Computer Fraud—A Message for Management," outlines the steps management may take in reducing the risk of computer fraud, and suggests ways CPAs might provide assistance to management in these efforts.

CHAPTER 5 READINGS

1. Earl Chrysler and Donald E. Keller, "Preventing Computer Fraud," *Management Accounting,* April 1988, pp. 28–32.
2. Stephen M. Paroby and William J. Barrett, "Preventing Computer Fraud—A Message for Management," *The CPA Journal,* November 1987, pp. 36–48.

CHAPTER 5 QUESTIONS

Article 1

1. Describe a "logic bomb." What can be done to prevent it?
2. Discuss control measures which may be taken to avoid the compromising of valid passwords.

Article 2

3. Discuss the special control concerns which are present in an EDP setting which may contribute to computer fraud.
4. Describe the assistance CPAs may provide to management in their efforts to combat computer crime.

Reading 5–1

PREVENTING COMPUTER FRAUD

By Earl Chrysler and Donald E. Keller

As computerization of accounting records has increased over the past years, so has the opportunity for computer crime. Ernst & Whinney estimates computer fraud losses at more than $3 billion a year.

Some cases involving bankruptcies or enormous sums of money have been widely publicized. But experts say that they are only the tip of the iceberg. Most companies don't like to admit they were outfoxed by a computer hacker and so do not report frauds.

In the notorious Equity Funding fraud, nonexistent insurance policy records were added to the customer master file of the organization. This was

Published by *Management Accounting,* copyright 1988, by National Association of Accountants, Montvale, NJ 07645.

allegedly accomplished by performing what could be categorized as *unscheduled file updating* which occurred outside the mainstream of normal data processing operations.

The incident when *Pacific Telephone* had its purchasing system penetrated was another of the well-known computer crimes. In this instance, the person responsible for the crime was able to manipulate the system by exploiting the following organizational weaknesses:

1. Computer-related purchasing procedures were available to persons in positions where there was no need to know the procedures.
2. Account numbers and passwords appearing on printouts were not properly controlled or destroyed.
3. The system allowed equipment to be shipped to destinations that were not among those normally used by this particular company.

The national press also gave significant coverage to the discovery that Penn Central Railroad had "misplaced" nearly 400 railcars. Upon investigation, it was found that the computerized system had been modified so that missing railcars would not be noticed.

The on-line systems of the State of Colorado and the University of Southern California both were used to modify records of individuals. In Colorado, the driving records of persons were changed by removing the information regarding violation convictions. The changes reportedly were made to improve the insurability of the persons whose records were altered. In the case of the University of Southern California, the type of alteration performed is what one would predict—revision of course grades of persons to improve their academic standing.

It is noteworthy that in both of these cases the modification of data was not performed by the individuals whose records were changed but by authorized operators.

Accounting managers and/or management accountants, who should be involved in designing procedures to prevent a computerized fraud, or detect one in progress, should consider including additional procedures to be followed during the design, programming, and review of computerized systems. The areas that need careful attention are program logic, system execution variance analysis, system access control, and system access variance analysis. A discussion of each of these areas follows.

PROGRAM LOGIC

Within the program logic area, the following types of controls should be present:

Verification of Critical Data. There are certain data items which can be readily identified as "critical." By "critical" we mean that if a fraud is to occur it will most likely involve one of these data items. Some examples of critical items and the tests that should be performed in specific types of applications are:

- If the program is used for ordering merchandise, the vendor name or identification number should be checked against a file of approved vendors for the item or class of item being ordered.
- If the program is used to pay an invoice, the payee identification number or name should be checked against a file of approved suppliers of goods and services.
- If the program is used to develop an order for merchandise, the "ship to" address should be checked against a file of acceptable "ship to" addresses for the item or class of item being ordered.
- If the program is used to place an order for merchandise, the requesting buyer should be checked against a file of approved buyers for the item or class of item being ordered.

Confirmation Reporting. The primary focus of this area is that of implicit control through review. In many systems, both manual and computerized, a person will submit an order for merchandise or a bill for payment and assume the desired action will take place.

The use of confirmation reporting provides feedback to the one who requested action. Confirmation reporting fulfills two purposes. It assures the person that the requested material was ordered or the invoice was paid. If person A submits a request for action using the name or identification code of person B, the fact that the action was requested in person B's name will be reported to person B. If the action was not requested by person B, an investigation can be initiated by person B to resolve the discrepancy.

Record Counting and Reconciling of File Sizes. During processing, the program should develop counts for the various types of records read, accepted, rejected, processed, and written. When a run has been completed, the program should print the list of counters on a report to be provided to the data control group. This group should confirm, for example, that the number of old master records read from a sequential file on this run is equal to the number of new master records written during the previous run.

It is also advisable to have the program print the file header information on the above report. In this manner the data control group could detect if the continuity of the generation/version sequence had been broken, whether accidentally or intentionally.

Key Field Comparisons. A "key field" is typically the field on which a file is sequenced. More important, it is the unique field which identifies a specific member of a file. Examples of key fields for different types of applications are illustrated in Table 1.

The reason the key field is important for control purposes is that each transaction record contains the key field of the master file record to which the transaction data should be posted. A program which posts transactions

TABLE 1   Key Fields

Key Field	Application
Social security number	Payroll/personnel
Vendor identification number	Purchasing/accounts payable
Customer identification number	Sales/accounts receivable
Part identification number	Inventory control
Accountant number	General ledger

to a master file reads a transaction record and attempts to locate a master file record which has the same key field value. Therefore there should never be program logic that compares the key field value of a transaction record to a preset, fixed value.

Program logic should be reviewed to assure that a fixed value for a record key comparison is not present. If a program is looking for a transaction for a specific customer or vendor, the implication is that some unusual processing is going to occur when a match is found. The fixed value may reside in working storage disguised as a variable, as demonstrated in this COBOL statement:

WS-TEST-KEY-FIELD   PICTURE IS X(6)   VALUE IS "017934"

or be readily apparent as a literal in the Procedure Division or its equivalent where the comparison is performed, for example:

IF TRAN-KEY-FIELD IS EQUAL TO "017934"

THEN PERFORM ALTERNATE-EDIT-ROUTINE.

If this type of condition is found, you must pursue the processing of the matching record. The types of processing you might expect to find upon following the nonstandard processing to its conclusion include:

- The record with the matching key is allowed to circumvent various edits. For example, a customer with a specific identification number is allowed to purchase items on open account even though the credit limit will be exceeded.

- Items are shipped to the customer, but the amount of the transaction is not posted to the customer's account.

- Regardless of the amount of payment received from a customer, the program sets the customer balance due to zero.

- In a financial institution, for example, the amount added to a customer's account balance is significantly greater than the deposit transaction amount and/or the amount subtracted from the customer's account balance is significantly less than the withdrawal transaction amount.

While the above are indicative of the types of processing which could occur when a matching key field value was found, some undesirable effects could be produced by a program with logic designed to detect when a key field was *not* found while processing records in, say, a payroll file. In this instance, the program uses the concept of a "flag" or "switch." A "flag" or "switch" is a memory location that is initialized with a value such as 1, 0, Y, or N. If a specific condition occurs during processing, the value of the field is changed. Each time a master file key is read, it is compared to a predefined value, once again either hidden in working storage with a variable name or appearing in the Procedure Division as a literal value as stated previously. If a matching key is found, the value of the flag is changed. No other unusual processing occurs at this point in the program.

When the program concludes all the normal processing for the run, it then tests the value of the flag. If the flag was unchanged, the program performs additional processing which should not occur. If the file processed was the payroll master for the organization, the program, if written by a vindictive person, could methodically destroy one or more files currently on line. If the organization were a financial institution and the program was developed by a person interested in personal financial gain, the program might post a large deposit to a predetermined account number. A group of instructions that accomplishes this type of processing is what is known as a "logic bomb," in a program. Logic bombs of this type are designed to perform their processing after the programmer is no longer with the firm.

Run-Time Parameter and Transaction Code Processing.   Some programs require that data be provided at the start of processing. One example could be a command code which the program uses to determine which of several optional modes is appropriate for processing data during this specific run. Programs also use fields referred to as *transaction codes* during mainline processing. These codes direct the program to the appropriate routine for processing each different type of input record.

A "logic bomb" that is triggered by the program detecting a matching run option code or transaction code is more difficult to discover than one precipitated by a matching or missing key value. In the instance where option codes or transaction codes are concerned, the clue of a predefined key value is absent. As a consequence, one must confirm that no option code or transaction code will direct the program to instructions which cause processing that is not defined for this code in the program specifications.

Data Modification Control.   A system must provide the capability of revising the value of almost all fields in a master file record, regardless of the sensitivity of the field. For example, in a business environment the credit limit field of a customer record must be revisable. Similarly, the pay rate for an employee must be subject to change.

A program that provides the user with the ability to modify a critical field value, however, should require that the identification code of the person approving the change be provided. The program should then confirm that the identification code supplied is among those in a file of those authorized to approve the type of change requested.

In this type of situation, there should be not only confirmation reporting, but a procedure for notification of invalid attempts as well.

If the authorization code is valid, all the data found on the input transaction, plus the before and after images of the affected record, should be written to a file. These data then should be sorted by approver identification code and a list of relevant changes distributed to those who allegedly approved the changes.

If the authorization code is invalid, all available information regarding the invalid attempt should be printed and delivered to the person responsible for the system.

SYSTEM EXECUTION VARIANCE

It is vital that controls be installed so that you can confirm, by physical evidence, that all programs were executed in the appropriate sequence using the correct version of each file.

Using system documentation, typically in flowchart form, one can develop the sequence of jobs that should appear on the job schedules for the computer center. Although there will occasionally be special request runs of unscheduled jobs, the workload of the computer center should be quite predictable.

During processing the operating system generates a system log. This log documents which files were used as input to each job, which files were created as output by each job, and the sequence in which the jobs were executed, among other information. One of the basic accounting control concepts is to use prenumbered documents so that no gaps in transaction history can escape detection. Because the system log is essentially the continuous record of all jobs processed, a key control is to assure that all log pages be retained. In this manner, the events that occurred in computerized systems can be reconstructed. By comparing the computer center work schedule with the system log, you also can develop a type of variance analysis approach so that differences between planned and actual program executions can be identified and analyzed.

SYSTEM ACCESS CONTROL

Some years ago, the computer and all its peripheral devices were contained within a "computer room" where access was strictly controlled. Also, most applications used tape master files which were not accessible except by production programs.

Within the past few years, however, many organizations have installed computer systems that allow persons to access the system from remote locations. An organization which allows such access must install controls to protect its information. The following procedures should be in place to control access to the financial information of an organization.

Automatic Password Obsolescence. Users can and should be required to modify their passwords on a random, short-time cycle basis. This procedure can be programmed into the system so that when a user whose password has not been changed for a specified period of time accesses the system, the security software will not allow the user to proceed, or log off, until the user changes passwords.

Co-Validation of User, Terminal and Access Time. The terminal or terminals regularly used by a person to access the system, the days of the week, and times of the day a person normally accesses the system are predictable. As a consequence, the security software should assure that all three conditions—valid user, valid terminal for this user, and valid day of week and time of day for this user—are met before allowing access to sensitive information.

Test for Duplicate Simultaneous Access by User or Terminal. There is always the possibility that a password will become compromised. If a user is authorized to access the system from multiple terminals, it is possible the person who attempts to use the password illegally will attempt to access the system when the legitimate user of the password is also using the system. To prevent this violation, the security software should test to see if one who is attempting access is apparently already using the system. Ideally, the security system should notify a security representative on a system monitor of what is occurring and the location of the two terminals involved. For control purposes, however, immediate disconnection of both users is desired.

Unfortunately, some computer "hackers" can cause a microcomputer or terminal to imitate another terminal and respond to the security system in a manner whereby the security system believes the microcomputer or terminal is a valid access device. The best control mechanism in this situation is, once more, a test for a duplicate access attempt. In this case, however, each time a user attempts to access the system, the security system would test to see if an access device with the identification code of the one attempting access is already using the system. Because the system cannot know who the legitimate user is, immediate disconnection of both users is the most prudent action.

System Access Variance Analysis. One should not construct a set of controls that is so strict that they are an undue hindrance to legitimate users. As a consequence, the controls in terms of access time for a user could be relatively lax, allowing the user a relatively wide "window." The use of variance analysis is a method of monitoring access to guard against questionable processing.

Users and their superiors could develop an estimated number of accesses per day and average duration of session per access. The security software access logs could then be used to construct reports which compare expected versus actual number of accesses and duration of sessions for each user. If a variance exceeds some predefined value, the user should be contacted to determine the reasons for the variance.

TABLE 2 Examples of Fraud Techniques and Related EDP Control Measures

Fraud Technique	General Control Measure	Specific Control Measure
Overpayment to specific vendor	Review of program logic	Matching key analysis
Purchase of merchandise or service from unauthorized source	Review of program logic Confirmation reporting	Validation to authorized vendor file Not applicable
Create fictitious transaction	Review of program logic	Missing key analysis Transaction code analysis
Data modification by unauthorized user	Access control	Automatic password obsolescence Password, terminal and time validation Duplicate password rejection Duplicate terminal rejection

The proliferation of microcomputers has led to many instances of systems being subverted for illegal purposes. Experience has shown that most crimes committed with a computer were accomplished because system controls were not adequate.

These findings imply that current controls should be tightened and new areas must have controls installed. The areas that need added controls are those which have been found vulnerable in the past and, consequently, represent the most likely targets of those bent on computer fraud. Examples of fraud techniques and related control measures are listed in Table 2.

While the potential for computer fraud requires management accountants to become more knowledgeable about computer systems, the philosophy of the control mechanisms is fundamentally the same as those associated with manual systems: if possible, stop the fraud from occurring; if it does occur, attempt to document who committed the crime; and in the worst possible scenario, at least document how the crime was accomplished.

Reading 5-2

PREVENTING COMPUTER FRAUD—A MESSAGE FOR MANAGEMENT*

By Stephen M. Paroby, CPA, and William J. Barrett, CPA

Corporate managers in all industries are aware of the application—indeed the necessity—for computers in many aspects of their activities. And they are learning to make increasing use of this equipment.

The business world is also learning that there are security risks connected with computers and these risks are increasing. While the status of the computer field has been difficult to measure, a survey taken by Ernst & Whinney at the November 1986 Computer Security Institute Conference indicates computer security concerns are prevalent in all sectors of business.

Organizations recognize that security risks have substantially increased within the past five years, and over half of the respondents reported financial losses through their computer systems. Fifteen percent of the respondents said their losses were greater than $50,000, and 3 percent said their losses were greater than $1 million.

The increased use of computer networks, the need for security over data and information, and easy access to microcomputers are cited as top-priority security issues organizations are facing. Networking and easy access to microcomputers have caused hardware, software, and stored information to become increasingly vulnerable to security risks, including fraud.

In a survey conducted by the American Bar Association, respondents ranked the following as requirements to prevent and detect computer crime:

- More comprehensive and effective self-protection by private business.
- More education of users concerning vulnerabilities of computer usage.
- More severe penalties for fraud perpetrators.
- Greater education of the public about computer crime.

CONDITIONS FOR FRAUD

Donn Parker,[1] a well-known expert on computer fraud, has stated at least three conditions are necessary to enable a would-be perpetrator to commit computer fraud—knowledge, access, and resources. Historically, few people

---

have had all three. However, because of recent changes in technology and in the way computers are used in business today, there is an increase in the number of people who have the knowledge and capabilities to access an organization's computerized resources to perpetrate fraud.

Knowledge

Mainly because of proliferation in microcomputer use, the number of people with the necessary knowledge—a knowledge about computers, including their strengths and weaknesses—is increasing.

Access

Today's computer environment provides increased capability to access computerized data. A movement toward decentralized processing has increased the use of networks, telecommunications, and remote job entry, including the linking of microcomputers to mainframe computers and the use of on-line systems. This, coupled with the increasing number of microcomputers in the workplace and at home, has resulted in an increase in the means for entry into many computer systems. With the appropriate knowledge, one would have little difficulty using a personal microcomputer and telecommunication equipment to gain access to an inadequately protected system.

Resources

The number of knowledgeable people and the means for entry have increased, along with dependence on computerized resources to store vast quantities of data. Computerized resources are being used more and more to process and store confidential, sensitive and important data—data that, in the hands of the wrong party, can be misused and can threaten the existence of a business enterprise.

NEED FOR ACTION

Management has a critical stake in the accurate processing of computerized data. Management clearly is responsible for maintaining (1) an internal control system that minimizes risk of loss from errors and irregularities, (2) confidentiality of information, and (3) continuity of operations.

Management, internal auditors, and the public accounting profession have reacted to the rapid technological advances in electronic data processing, but technology is constantly changing—often faster than organizations can control it.

REASONS FOR COMPUTER FRAUD

Increased Opportunities

The increasing number of knowledgeable users—and the increased capability to access computerized data resulting from use of decentralized processing, networks, telecommunications, and remote job entry—have provided more opportunities for fraud in an inadequately controlled computerized data processing environment.

Difficult Detection

Computer fraud is difficult to detect. The vast quantities of data and information stored in a computer system make concealing a theft easier. The perpetrator seldom leaves a trail to follow, but merely alters the bits and bytes used to store magnetically coded data. As a result, numbers are changed and investors and creditors are deceived.

Lucrative Payoff

Computerized systems offer the fraud perpetrator a lucrative payoff. The vast quantities of information stored on a system, coupled with the processing speed of the computer, have magnified the payoff from computer fraud. The average dollar amount in reported computer frauds is estimated by the FBI to be $600,000, significantly more than the $23,000 average for the perpetrator using manual methods.

PREVENTING, DETECTING, AND LIMITING COMPUTER FRAUD

Control over its data processing environment should be part of an organization's system of internal controls designed to safeguard assets, check the accuracy and reliability of financial records, minimize risk of loss from errors and irregularities, maintain the confidentiality and integrity of information, and maintain continuity of operations.

Many of the discovered computer frauds could have been prevented or detected sooner (thereby limiting the loss) had certain control procedures been implemented. A fraudulent financial reporting scheme at Saxon Industries was able to continue over a 13-year period because of a lack of segregation of duties between data processing and financial department personnel. If Saxon Industries had complied with a system of internal controls that included proper segregation of duties among the chief executive officer, the finance group, and the data processing department, the fraud would not have been so easy to commit. A lack of appropriate segregation of duties at Equity Funding also enabled perpetration of a significant fraud scheme.

A \$21.3 million fraud at Wells Fargo Bank was accomplished because of weaknesses in controls over their interbranch transaction-processing system. An adequate system of transaction logging, requiring regular reviews by appropriate personnel, should have revealed the unusual activity—resulting in earlier detection of the fraud and reducing the loss.

Stronger controls over passwords and access codes would have made a theft of communication supplies from Pacific Telephone Company more difficult. These controls could have prevented the perpetrator from accessing the inventory budget data, economic order quantities, and the equipment-ordering system.

OBJECTIVE OF COMPUTER CONTROLS

In designing an adequate system of controls for computerized accounting systems, management should realize that the consistency, speed, and flexibility of the computer pose additional control concerns:

- The effects of errors may be compounded. For example, the computer may prepare sales invoices by taking the quantity input and extending it by a price from the sales price master file. If the program is malfunctioning (e.g., selecting incorrect prices, performing extensions improperly), all sales invoices may be incorrect.
- The reduction in manual involvement in the accounting system may lead to inadequate segregation of duties.
- Audit trails may be reduced, eliminated, or exist only for a short time in computer-readable form.
- Changes to data and programs may be made by individuals lacking sufficient understanding of internal controls and accounting policies, or such changes may be made without adequate testing or without the consent of management.
- More individuals may have access to data—a critical corporate resource.

So while a computer's involvement in the accounting system often has a positive impact, it does not necessarily mean the data generated are correct. To ensure data are accurate and complete, an organization must implement computer controls.

The two major objectives of an organization's controls over its data processing environment are to provide reasonable assurance that:

- Development of and changes to programs are authorized, tested, and approved prior to being placed into production.
- Access to data files is appropriately restricted to authorized users and programs.

These objectives are referred to as general computer control objectives because they affect all or many computerized accounting activities, and impact numerous accounts or classes of transactions.

Development of and Changes to Programs

Controls over development of and changes to programs are important to ensure that programs used to process an organization's accounting data are accurate and based upon management's understanding and intent. New applications and program changes should be authorized, tested, and approved before being used. Weak or nonexistent controls over program development and changes to programs can lead to the use of unauthorized programs to perpetrate fraud.

Data File Access

Controls over access to data files are important to help ensure the integrity of an organization's data. Controls should provide reasonable assurance that the correct files are used in an application, data files are restricted to authorized users, and data is not changed without proper authorization. Moreover, the execution of programs that access data files should be authorized and executed as planned. If controls over access to data files are weak, the organization will be susceptible to unauthorized access and manipulation of these files.

Passwords have been used to control access to data and programs. However, password systems have proved difficult to manage and can be easy to penetrate because passwords are frequently written down, overheard, or simply noticed by casual observers. In addition, passwords are sometimes shared between people.

In response to this concern, more sophisticated identification schemes are being created to better authenticate a user. A computer can authenticate a user by something the user knows (e.g., passwords), by something the user holds (e.g., "smart" cards, programmed electronic keys), or by personal characteristics of the user (e.g., fingerprints, voice scans). Security would be increased through more use of these sophisticated identification schemes.

Segregation of Duties

To achieve the two general computer control objectives, segregation of duties must be adequate. Although not considered a key control in and of itself, segregation of duties is considered an environmental factor that must exist for the controls to function. Duties should be segregated within the data processing department and between the data processing and user departments.

The objective of segregation of duties is to have different people responsible for recordkeeping, physical custody of assets, and general supervision and authorization of transactions. The data processing department should be organized to segregate responsibility for recording transactions and handling assets. The department should provide for separation of duties among three basic functions—operations, application development and maintenance, and data control.

Segregation of duties between the data processing and user departments also is important. Data processing personnel should be independent from users. If an employee can initiate a transaction within a user department and handle its processing within data processing, control is diminished.

Continuity of Operation

Controls that ensure continuity of operations (disaster recovery and contingency planning) also are important because they address the effect of a potential disaster. Although these controls have no direct bearing on an organization's historical financial statements, they are among an organization's main concerns. These controls include:

- Physical security measures to prevent, detect, and limit the effect of fire, flooding, and other hazards.
- A well-documented, well-tested contingency plan communicated to appropriate personnel.
- An alternate processing site in the event of a disaster or extended hardware failure.
- Up-to-date backup of data files, application programs, data base and systems documentation.
- Adequate insurance coverage for equipment, files, and other EDP-related losses.

ROLE OF CORPORATE MANAGEMENT

The Foreign Corrupt Practices Act of 1977 amended the Securities Exchange Act of 1934 to require publicly held companies to "devise and maintain a system of internal accounting controls sufficient to provide reasonable assurance that:

- "Transactions are executed in accordance with management's general or specific authorization.
- "Transactions are recorded as necessary (*a*) to permit preparation of financial statements in conformity with generally accepted accounting principles or any other criteria applicable to such statements, and (*b*) to maintain accountability for assets.
- "Access to assets is permitted only in accordance with management's general or specific authorization.

- "The recorded accountability for assets is compared with the existing assets at reasonable intervals, and appropriate action is taken with respect to any differences."

To fulfill this requirement, a publicly held company that uses a computer to process significant accounting applications should ensure that adequate computer controls exist, or manual user department controls adequately compensate for any weaknesses in the computer controls.

Although an effective internal control system is required for publicly held companies, all organizations should have an effective system of internal controls. Management should recognize that internal controls are essential to safeguard its assets, ensure the accuracy and reliability of financial records, minimize risk of loss from errors and irregularities, maintain confidentiality and integrity of information, and maintain continuity of operations.

However, many organizations neglect adequate controls and safeguards. This can be attributed to one or more factors:

- Lack of understanding of the magnitude of the problem.
- An attitude that fraud cannot or will not happen to an organization.
- Lack of expertise necessary to understand and address the controls over the computerized data processing environment.
- Reluctance to allocate the resources necessary to secure the computer system properly.

The potential for an organization to be victimized by computer fraud grows daily. The attitude that fraud cannot and will not happen within an organization must be changed. All organizations are potential victims of fraud. Only through adequate internal controls can an organization prevent, detect, and limit the occurrences of fraud.

The lack of knowledge necessary to adequately understand a computer environment has resulted in a reluctance by management to deal with the security and control concerns at hand. To make better-informed decisions regarding computer security, management personnel not primarily involved in computer-related activities should understand fundamental data processing concepts.

A management team with a high level of understanding of computer systems will be able to make better decisions about the required level of security and take measures to prevent, detect, and limit the potential for fraud. To obtain this level of understanding will require increased training and a continuous effort. A detailed description of the fundamental data processing concepts that help provide this increased level of computer literacy is discussed in the Appendix.

As with all other internal control procedures, allocating the necessary resources involves cost. And there is a point beyond which the cost associated with controls exceeds the benefit that would be derived. Identifying this point is no easy task, and requires the judgment of a knowledgeable management team that understands the magnitude of the concern and recognizes the vulnerabilities the organization faces. Furthermore, despite management's best efforts and due diligence, there can never be absolute assurance that computer fraud will not occur.

Corporate Ethics

Management is responsible for directing and controlling an organization's operations and for establishing, communicating, and monitoring policies and procedures. Management characteristics are a significant factor in the internal environment of an organization. They help to establish the level of "control consciousness," which is the basis for the control environment—the framework in which the accounting system operates. Formal code of conduct and ethics policies contribute to a disciplined control environment. All organizations should adopt formal codes of conduct that include conduct related to computer resources. For example, an organization may require all employees to periodically sign a formal code of conduct that stipulates computer resources are to be used only for appropriate business purposes, and any fraud or abuse will be prosecuted.

ASSISTANCE FROM INDEPENDENT AUDITORS

An organization's independent auditor, following GAAS, does not necessarily perform an in-depth study and evaluation of the system of internal accounting controls of an organization, including controls over its computerized data processing system, to render an opinion on the organization's financial statements. GAAS require the independent auditor to perform a review of the accounting system to (1) obtain sufficient knowledge and understanding to make a determination of whether there may be internal accounting control procedures that may provide a basis for reliance thereon in determining the nature, extent, and timing of audit tests, or (2) aid the auditor in designing audit tests in the absence of such reliance. The extent of the review of internal accounting controls varies widely, depending on the audit approach the independent auditor decides to take.

The independent auditor is required to perform a preliminary review (preliminary assessment) to obtain an understanding of the control environment and the flow of transactions through the accounting system. Obtaining an understanding of the control environment includes gaining a general knowledge of such matters as the organizational structure, the methods used by the business to communicate responsibility and authority, and the methods used by management to supervise the system. This understanding helps the auditor to evaluate the potential for errors and irregularities, including fraud.

In connection with the assessment of the overall control environment, the independent auditor should assess the control environment in the computerized data processing area whenever significant accounting applications are processed by a computer.

Obtaining an understanding of the flow of transactions through the accounting system provides the auditor with a general knowledge of the various classes of transactions and the methods by which each significant class of transactions is authorized, executed, recorded, and subsequently processed. The preliminary review does not provide the auditor with an in-depth understanding of the system of internal accounting controls. Its primary focus is on the accounting system and the environment in which the system operates. As part of this understanding, the auditor should obtain information about (1) the computer installation, (2) the computerized accounting applications, and (3) the procedures relating to program changes and data file access. This work of the independent auditor can be of great help to management in their evaluation of the computer operations.

CURTAILING COMPUTER FRAUD, USING COMPUTER TECHNOLOGY

Current technology, which in many respects has resulted in increased vulnerability to fraud, also has provided a means to reduce fraudulent reporting. The speed and power of the computer can be used by an auditor to test more transactions and calculations than would be possible using conventional means. The use of computer-assisted audit techniques, including audit software, integrated test facilities, and microcomputer applications, provides the means for performing more effective and more efficient audit procedures.

Some of the most effective fraud detective measures involve the use of the computer itself—effective because the perpetrator usually does not know that the detective measures are in place. Through the use of access control software, transaction logging, and embedded audit modules, the computer can produce valuable reports of unauthorized access attempts, unusual transactions, or deviations from normal processing. Use of these reports by management and internal auditors can be a very effective means of detecting computer fraud.

The use of microcomputers by management and auditors also can help in detecting fraudulent financial reporting. With the current capabilities of transferring information from an organization's mainframe computer system to a microcomputer, auditors can examine, test, and review more data and transactions than possible under conventional methods. This also contributes to a more effective and efficient audit.

In considering this serious matter of computer fraud, management should give careful attention to the following factors, some of which have been mentioned and discussed in previous sections of this article. The CPA, with his knowledge of internal controls and of computer operations, can furnish clients with a valuable service in emphasizing these points to clients having significant computer operations.

Corporate management should carefully consider the following:

- Computer security is an issue of increasing concern.
- Security concerns are prevalent in all sectors of business, public and private.
- All organizations, regardless of their size, are currently facing security issues.
- Security risks have increased in recent years, and businesses are suffering financial loss because of security problems.
- Networking, security over data and information, and microcomputer security, are the top-priority security issues.
- Many organizations are just beginning to recognize the importance of adequate security. Security officers need help with establishing credibility for their security recommendations.

Control Procedures

There are three lines of defense against computer fraud:

1. *Prevention* restricts the access of potential perpetrators to the computer facility, computer terminals, data files, programs, and reports.
2. *Detection* discovers the fraud in the event a perpetrator slips past established prevention mechanisms.
3. *Limitation* restricts losses if a well-planned and well-executed fraud should occur despite prevention and detection defenses.

The three lines of defense—prevention, detection, and limitation of computer fraud—can be accomplished by three types of control procedures.

1. *Administrative Controls* are internal control policies that establish standard operating procedures for the computer installation.
2. *Physical Controls* regulate the physical environment of the computer facility, as well as physical computer input and output.
3. *Technical Controls* employ the processing facilities of the computer itself to restrict user access to data files and programs.

Control procedures designed to prevent, detect, and limit computer fraud are as follows:

Prevention

Administrative.   Security checks on personnel prior to hiring may reveal criminal activity in their backgrounds.

Proper segregation of duties among data processing employees and between data processing and user departments avoids potential fraud situations.

Program authorization procedures ensure no changes are made to programs without the authorization of the user department.

Physical.   An inconspicuous location helps protect the computer facility from intruders.

Controlled access to the facility by use of keys or magnetic cards physically restricts unauthorized users from computer terminals, significantly reducing the opportunities for fraud.

Technical.   Encoding is the conversion of data from one system of communication to another. A perpetrator must "crack the code" before he or she can fraudulently manipulate the data.

Access control software and passwords allow a user access to a terminal, data file, program, or utility only after entering the correct password for that resource.

Detection

Administrative.   Access and execution logs reveal, by time and terminal, those who have accessed the system and executed programs. Regular reviews of these logs may detect fraudulent activity.

Program testing may be conducted after a program has been modified to ensure no fraudulent processes have been introduced.

Physical.   A computer-room guard assigned full-time, or maintaining frequent but irregular checks of the facility, may reveal unauthorized system users, particularly during off-hours.

A computer room entry log, which individuals must sign on entering the computer facility, may help identify unauthorized individuals.

Technical.   Transaction logging produces reports that may detect both accidental and fraudulent data errors.

Running totals of dollar or amount fields in files, and hash totals of non-amount fields, such as department or part numbers, are effective in detecting both accidental and fraudulent data errors.

Source code comparisons are accomplished by computer programs that compare one source code version of a program to another, indicating whether the programs are exact matches or have been altered.

Limitation

Administrative.   Rotation of duties in data processing can limit fraud losses, since an individual would be able to perpetrate a fraud for only a limited period of time.

Transaction limits are administrative ceilings on specified transactions that limit possible fraud losses.

Physical.   Preprinted limits on documents, particularly asset-value documents like checks, may limit fraud losses.

Data backup limits potential losses by facilitating the restoration of destroyed data.

Technical. Range checks ensure entered data fall within a range of permissible values and limit the losses that may occur from sizable unauthorized transactions.

Reasonableness checks determine whether an input is one that might be expected in normal circumstances by comparing amounts to established standards.

APPENDIX

Management, internal auditors, and independent auditors should understand fundamental EDP concepts to enable them to (1) assess the adequacy of controls in a computer installation, (2) evaluate whether data is properly protected, (3) decide whether proper procedures are used to develop and maintain programs, (4) understand controls needed to prove adequate backup and recovery for computers and software, and (5) communicate effectively with EDP personnel. This understanding will enable them to address the control concerns in a computerized data processing environment and thereby limit the risk of fraud perpetrated through the computer.

A fundamental understanding of EDP concepts should include a knowledge and understanding of:

Access Control and Security

- Importance of physical computer security.
- Conditions that indicate deficiencies in the physical controls that could lead to errors or irregularities.
- Reasons for controlling computer room access.
- Methods of restricting access to a computer room.
- Controls to prevent unauthorized use of data.
- Characteristics of password control systems.
- Control techniques for restricting access to programs.
- Consequences of weak access controls.
- Controls over utilities that can change data.
- Control concerns of on-line systems.
- Procedures to determine which terminals and users can access an on-line system.
- Access control software packages.
- Objectives of a good contingency plan.
- Major steps in contingency planning.

Data Processing Personnel

- Functions of an EDP manager, systems analyst, applications programmer, operations manager, computer operator, tape/disk librarian, data base administrator, systems programmer, and EDP internal auditor.
- Internal auditor's functions that might be useful to the external auditor performing a review of computer controls.
- Combinations of functions having a neutral or negative effect on the department's segregation of duties.

The System Development Life Cycle

- Proper sequence of the system development life cycle steps.
- Purpose of a system development life cycle.
- Programming techniques.
- Causes of system failure during the system development life cycle.
- Controls during the system development life cycle that help prevent system failure.
- Purpose of systems, user, and program documentation.

Programs and Languages

- Purpose of programs.
- Functions of operating systems.
- Major types of programs.
- Difference between source code and object code.
- Purpose and function of the linkage editor.
- Functions of service/utility programs.
- Purpose of data base management systems.
- Characteristics of good data base management systems.
- Types of programmed controls and their functions.
- Advantages and disadvantages of purchasing software rather than developing it.
- Purposes of general audit software.
- Differences between centralized and decentralized processing.
- Types of on-line processing.
- Differences between on-line and batch processing.
- Differences between real-time and on-line processing.

Data and Data Processing

- Differences between data and information.
- Differences between fields, records, and files.
- Differences between physical and logical records.
- Differences between transaction files and master files, and between their functions.
- Characteristics and benefits of labels.
- Purpose and characteristics of access methods.
- Types of data manipulation and their function.
- Procedures in any data processing operation.

Computers and Their Components

- Primary purpose of the CPU.
- Functions of the CPU components.
- Major types of computer memory (storage).
- Advantages and disadvantages of direct-access devices and sequential storage devices.
- Purpose of input/output devices.
- Functions of peripheral devices such as the CRT, intelligent terminal, POS terminal, flexible diskettes, MICR, OCR, and COM.
- Hardware elements of a data processing system.

Notes

* Adapted from *Computer Fraud, A Report Presented to the National Commission on Fraudulent Financial Reporting* (The Treadway Commission), Ernst & Whinney.
1. Senior management systems consultant at SRI International.

CHAPTER 6

Can We Audit and Control the New Technology?

An effective control structure is a critical component of a successful business. The importance of control is emphasized in the standards followed by the public accounting profession. In addition, government legislation, specifically the Foreign Corrupt Practices Act of 1977 (FCPA), mandates that an adequate system of controls be maintained by all companies which come under its jurisdiction. The American Institute of CPAs (AICPA) has categorized control structure into two parts, accounting control and administrative control. Accounting and administrative controls are defined as follows:

> Administrative control includes, but is not limited to, the plan of organization and the procedures and records that are concerned with the decision processes leading to management's authorization of transactions. Such authorization is a management function directly associated with the responsibility for achieving the objectives of the organization and is the starting point for establishing accounting control of transactions.
>
> Accounting control comprises the plan of organization and the procedures and records that are concerned with the safeguarding of assets and the reliability of financial records and consequently are designed to provide reasonable assurance that
>
> a. Transactions are executed in accordance with management's general or specific authorization.
>
> b. Transactions are recorded as necessary (1) to permit preparation of financial statements in conformity with generally accepted accounting principles or any other criteria applicable to such statements and (2) to maintain accountability for assets.
>
> c. Access to assets is permitted only in accordance with management's authorization.
>
> d. The recorded accountability for assets is compared with the existing assets at reasonable intervals and appropriate action is taken with respect to any differences.

The independent auditor (CPA) is concerned primarily with accounting controls. However, many specific controls in a business firm could be properly categorized as both accounting and administrative controls, that is, the control procedure fulfills objectives of both types of controls.

The FCPA applies to all publicly owned corporations subject to the Securities Exchange Act of 1934. Thus, a company does not have to be involved in foreign trade to be subject to the provisions of the FCPA. The primary intent of the FCPA is to prevent corrupt practices such as bribes. However, the Act's biggest impact on the business community has been its requirement that every corporation maintain a good system of accounting control. Specifically the FCPA states that all corporations must:

(A) Make and keep books, records, and accounts, which in reasonable detail, accurately and fairly reflect the transactions and dispositions of the assets of the issuer; and (B) devise and maintain a system of internal accounting controls sufficient to provide reasonable assurances that

i. Transactions are executed in accordance with management's general or specific authorization.

ii. Transactions are recorded as necessary

I. to permit preparation of financial statements in conformity with generally accepted accounting principles or any other criteria applicable to such statements, and

II. to maintain accountability for assets.

iii. Access to assets is permitted only in accordance with management's general or specific authorization.

iv. The recorded accountability for assets is compared with the existing assets at reasonable intervals and appropriate action is taken with respect to any differences.

The control structure may be designed to: (1) prevent errors and irregularities (intentional errors) from occurring; and (2) identify errors and irregularities after they occur so that corrective action may be taken. Thus, controls can be referred to as preventive controls or feedback controls. Both types of controls are essential in a company's control structure.

The separation of related organizational functions (or separation of duties) is an example of a preventive or accounting control. Typically, this control involves assigning the tasks related to a particular transaction among two or more employees. In particular, the physical custody of an asset should be kept separate from the recordkeeping function. For example, the person who is responsible for writing checks for disbursements should not be assigned the task of reconciling the bank account. Other preventive controls include: (1) hiring competent and ethical employees; (2) written policies and procedures; (3) physical security of firm assets; (4) adequate management supervision; and (5) adequate documents and records.

Feedback control systems are effective only if they include the following characteristics: (1) benefits exceed costs of operating the controls; (2) deviations from the benchmarks (e.g., budget or standards) are reported on a timely basis; (3) relevant and understandable information is provided; and (4) the manager on a timely basis takes action. Examples of feedback or administrative accounting systems include credit control, production control, and internal audit.

A well-designed control structure is essential to the success of any organization. Since management is responsible for meeting a company's goals and objectives, it is responsible for the adequacy of the company's control structure. The independent auditor, on the other hand, has a responsibility to evaluate these controls and to report any material weaknesses noted to management.

Effective on January 1, 1990, Statement on Auditing Standards No. 55, *Consideration of the Internal Control Structure in a Financial Statement Audit,* requires the auditor to obtain greater knowledge about the client's internal control structure than was previously required. SAS No. 55 is one of several "expectation gap" standards issued by the Auditing Standards Board in 1988. A principal objective of SAS No. 55 is to improve audit effectiveness by better audit planning and more precise assessment of control risk. The standard establishes and discusses the relationship between internal control structure and assessing control risk and financial statement assertions.

Auditors must document their understanding of the control environment, accounting system, and control procedures. Prior to SAS No. 55, documentation of control procedures was required only when the auditor planned to rely on them; previously there was no requirement to document the control environment or accounting system.

The accounting information system and its control structure are the foundation on which financial information is gathered, verified, and disseminated. The independent auditor must develop a thorough understanding of the client's control structure and system. Understanding, testing, and evaluating accounting information systems has become more difficult due to the general complexity of systems as well as to their increasing computerization. Auditors must possess a clear understanding of the impact of electronic data processing on the audit process. Statement on Auditing Standards (SAS) No. 48 states:

> The auditor should consider the methods the entity uses to process accounting information in planning the audit because such methods influence the design of the accounting system and the nature of the internal accounting control procedures. The extent to which computer processing is used in significant accounting applications, as well as the complexity of that processing, may also influence the nature, timing and extent of audit procedures.

Various approaches have been developed to assist auditors in evaluating the control structure that has been incorporated in a computer processing system. Three example approaches are:

1. *Test data.* The test data approach allows the independent auditor to obtain information concerning the operation of programs and related controls.

Basically, the auditor creates a set of fictitious transactions which contain various errors (e.g., invalid account numbers). This test data is then processed, using the client's programs to determine whether controls exist to detect the errors. The auditor examines the processing results to determine if the errors contained in the test data were identified by the processing controls (e.g., a check digit test to identify invalid account numbers).

2. *Parallel simulation.* In this approach, the auditor prepares or obtains a computer program to process the client's actual data. The auditor then compares the output from his or her program with output from the client's program.

3. *Integrated test facility (ITF).* Under this approach, fictitious test transactions are entered into the client's processing system during the processing of the client's actual transactions. ITF is well-suited for auditing on-line systems. It tests client programs as they are actually processing and client personnel are unaware of the specific programs being tested.

For a number of years, auditors have had specialized computer programs available to assist them in the examination of computerized systems. These programs are referred to as generalized audit software programs and are used to perform various audit procedures, including routine audit tests (e.g., footing and cross-footing), selecting statistical samples, performing statistical tests (e.g., discriminant analysis to determine a client's going concern probability), and generating audit workpaper schedules.

Compared to manual systems, computerized accounting information systems have several inherent advantages. The advantages include: (1) reducing human error caused by fatigue or carelessness; (2) processing transactions in a consistent fashion; and (3) no dishonest or disloyal motivations on the part of the computer. Computer systems have certain disadvantages, however, such as: (1) lack of judgment; (2) some users' assumption that computers are always correct; (3) less segregation of duties and functions; (4) audit trail being more difficult to follow because it is hidden or fragmented; (5) greater potential for tampering with data to cause unauthorized actions; (6) easier access to information concentrated in computerized files; and (7) easier loss of information electronically (a few keystrokes can erase whole files).

The auditor must be aware of these advantages and disadvantages when planning the examination of a computerized (EDP) accounting system. Guidance is provided in SAS No. 48.

Six articles concerned with auditing and the control structure are included in this chapter. The initial article deals with ethical issues associated with the new technology. Unethical behavior (e.g., planting computer viruses) can result in major computer problems. The author makes a strong case for teaching ethics in computer classes. The second article examines the external auditor's responsibility to assess the internal control structure under SAS No. 55. The third article presents a computerized simulation tool that may be used to evaluate the reliability of control structure. The fourth article presents control considerations in a microcomputer environment. The fifth reading discusses how to develop a system of internal control for microcomputers. The final reading discusses how generalized audit software packages for microcomputers can greatly assist the auditor with audits of small and medium-sized clients.

CHAPTER 6 READINGS

1. Leslie S. Chalmers, "A Question of Ethics," *Journal of Accounting and EDP,* Summer 1989, pp. 50–53.
2. Charles W. Stanley and C. William Thomas, "Assessing the MIS Internal Control Structure in a Financial Statement Audit under SAS No. 55," *Journal of Accounting and EDP,* Winter 1990, pp. 19–24.
3. Casper E. Wiggins, Jr., and L. Murphy Smith, "A Generalized Audit Simulation Tool for Evaluating the Reliability of Internal Controls," *Contemporary Accounting Research,* Spring 1987, pp. 316–337.
4. Christopher Wolfe and Casper E. Wiggins, Jr., "Internal Control in the Microcomputer Environment," *The Internal Auditor,* December 1986, pp. 54–60.
5. Alan I. Blankley; Tarek S. Amer; and Craig E. Bain, "Developing a System of Internal Control for Microcomputers," *Financial and Accounting Systems,* Summer 1990, pp. 40–45.
6. Scott D. Jacobson and Christopher Wolfe, "Auditing with Your Microcomputer," *Journal of Accountancy,* February 1990, pp. 70–80.

CHAPTER 6 QUESTIONS

Article 1

1. Computer "hackers" often do not see the harm of planting code (e.g., viruses) in other people's computers. Why?
2. What can you do to help discourage unethical computer behavior?

Article 2

3. Describe the purpose of Statement on Auditing Standards No. 55, "Consideration of the Internal Control Structure in a Financial Statement Audit."
4. Differentiate general controls and application controls.

Article 3

5. Why is the auditor's review of internal control so important?
6. What are the general requirements of the auditor's study and evaluation of internal controls?

Article 4

7. What are some special risks associated with microcomputers?

Article 5

8. List the three sources of risks associated with computerized accounting systems. Discuss each of these sources of risks.

Article 6

9. Describe generalized audit software.

Case 6–1

BAGGINS PIPE COMPANY

Baggins Pipe Company, a direct-mail merchandising business with annual sales of approximately $1,000,000, maintains an inventory consisting of about 1,000 for-sale items. In addition, it carries an inventory of packaging materials including boxes, wrapping paper, tape, string, and markers which are used to prepare orders for mailing. The for-sale inventory is carefully controlled and stored in a special area of the plant. The control structure includes the use of locked bins and the employment of only a few issuing supervisors who release only a sufficient quantity of items to meet the day's orders. The packaging materials, which are stored on open shelves at several locations in the plant, are easily accessible to all employees.

The manager of the Internal Audit Department, Mavis Creech, is concerned with the control of these packaging materials. Ms. Creech has determined that the monthly losses of packaging materials approach $50. Horrified at the thought of employees stealing from the company, she suggests redesigning the plant layout so that the packaging materials can be more easily controlled in the same way as are the other inventories. She suggested that two supervisors be hired to issue the materials for the day's orders. Mavis feels that this procedure would be an effective preventive control. Should the management of Baggins Pipe accept this suggestion? Are there other more efficient preventive controls that could be used to prevent the theft or misappropriation of these materials?

Case 6–2

TEXAS AGGIE UNIVERSITY

The Records Department of the Texas Aggie University at Aggieland, U.S.A. employs an office supervisor, 8 senior-level clerks, 10 junior-level clerks and 30 student workers. The supervisor and the clerks are full-time employees. The students work whenever they can. Once a week each employee completes a time card similar to the one shown below. The supervisor collects the time cards, checks each card for reasonableness and initials the total hours.

a. List the control weaknesses in this system.

b. What type of errors could result?

c. How could this system be improved?

```
                         —TIME CARD—
   NAME _____ SS# _____ DEPT# _____
      TIME           LUNCH   TIME   REGULAR    OT HOURS    TOTAL
      IN ____ OUT ____ IN ____OUT____HOURS____ _____  _____



      M_____
      T_____
      W_____
      T_____
      F_____

      SIGNATURE _____ GRAND TOTAL: _____
```

Case 6–3

WILLIE BARFOOT, CPA

Willie Barfoot, CPA, is examining the financial statements of his client, the Creech Sales Corporation. The Company recently installed an off-line electronic computer. The following comments have been extracted from Mr. Barfoot's notes on his client's computer operations, the processing and control of shipping notices, and customers' invoices.

To minimize inconvenience, Creech converted its prior data processing system, which utilized tabulating equipment, to the new system which uses magnetic tape drives. A computer company supervised the conversion and provided training to all of Creech's computer department employees (except keypunch operators) in systems design, operations, and programming.

Each computer run is assigned to a specific employee, who is responsible for making all program changes, running the program, and responding to any questions. This procedure has the advantage of eliminating the need for records of computer operations because each employee is responsible for his or her own computer runs.

At least one computer department employee remains in the computer room during office hours, and only computer department employees have keys to the computer room.

System documentation consists of materials furnished by the computer company—a set of record formats and program listings. These records and the tape library are kept in a corner of the computer department office.

The company considered the desirability of installing programmed controls but decided to retain the manual controls used in its existing system.

Company products are shipped directly from public warehouses. The warehouses forward shipping notices to general accounting. In general accounting, a billing clerk enters the price of the item and accounts for the numerical sequence of all shipping notices from each warehouse. The billing clerk also prepares daily adding-machine tapes ("control tapes") of the units shipped and the unit prices.

Shipping notices and control tapes are forwarded to the computer department for keypunching and processing. All extensions are made on the computer. Output consists of invoices (in six copies) and a daily sales register. The daily sales register shows the aggregate totals of units shipped and unit prices, which the computer operator compares with the control tapes.

All copies of the invoices are returned to the billing clerk. The clerk mails three copies to the customer, forwards one copy to the warehouse, maintains one copy in a numerical file, and retains one copy in an open invoice file that serves as a detailed accounts-receivable record.

REQUIRED:

1. Describe weaknesses in the control over information and data flows and the procedures for processing shipping notices and customer invoices.

2. Recommend improvements in these controls and processing procedures.

3. Organize your response as follows:

Weaknesses   *Recommended Improvements*

Reading 6–1

A QUESTION OF ETHICS

By Leslie S. Chalmers

The need for new computer ethics seems to concern many people these days. Not long ago, I read three different communications in one week about the problem. In November 1988, when I was a panelist at a seminar for people in the insurance field, a member of the audience asked whether I saw a need for computer ethics classes in light of recent problems with computer viruses and hackers. Given this recent interest in the subject, it is time to address computer ethics in this column.

Perhaps the most interesting and encouraging communication I read was a recent article by Gardner, Samuels, Render, and Coffinberger. The authors surveyed three groups: FBI agents, undergraduate business majors, and business and government managers, asking each group to judge seven cases of questionable computer use and to state whether the actions described were ethical, unethical, or criminal.

It was encouraging to note that in a couple of cases, the students were as stern as or sterner in their judgments than the other two groups (I may be getting very cynical from my years in the security field, but I wish this survey had included a group of computer science majors; I might not feel quite so encouraged with the results). In four of the seven cases, there was almost total agreement that the behavior described was at least unethical if not criminal. These cases involved an employee breaking a security code and using it to read the company's payroll records; a bank teller manipulating money in a client's account for personal gain and then replacing it without causing the client to lose any money; and an authorized student giving an unauthorized student a password to use a university computer. (The last case counts twice because the survey participants were asked to judge the behavior of both students.)

What is not encouraging about the survey results are the cases in which many of the participants condoned what should be considered unethical behavior. Forty-nine percent of the students thought it ethical for a computer operator to run a program for a friend on his employer's computer when it was not being used for other purposes (compared with 18% of the managers and 6% of the FBI agents). Twenty-four percent of the managers considered it ethical for a programmer to intentionally generate false information for distribution to company stockholders if threatened with job loss for not complying (compared with 14% of the students and none of the agents).

I occasionally monitor an electronic forum that deals with the risks of high technology. (A forum is an electronic bulletin board where people leave messages discussing a particular topic.) Many of the participants in this forum are computer security professionals and almost all are data processing professionals who are concerned about computer security. Even in this group, however, opinions vary as to what is acceptable behavior. Some even believe that people who attack computers are providing a useful service by finding security holes and drawing attention to them.

Clearly, our society has not come to grips with the technological changes that are presenting us with new behavioral possibilities. Each new action involves a choice; too often, we are unable to agree on which of these choices should be rejected as unethical.

Consider the following situations and the resulting choices and ask yourself whether you believe society as a whole would agree that a particular behavior is required:

- Your teenage son wants to borrow a friend's copy of the latest hit album so he can copy it for his own use. Do you ignore this, lecture your son but let him do it anyway, or forbid it?

- Your bank's ATM misfeeds and gives you an extra $20. Do you report this to the bank?

- Your daughter tells you about her friend who has figured out how to break into the XYZ company's computer. The friend is using the computer to learn more about the system for a computer science course, and your daughter believes she is not touching the company's files. Do you violate your daughter's confidence by reporting the incident?

- Would your response to the preceding problem be different if the XYZ company had laid you off three years ago, causing you to collect unemployment for five months?

- You have paid for basic cable TV service, but by mistake you are also getting the movie channel, which you did not pay for. Do you inform the cable company?

None of these ethical choices existed 30 or 40 years ago because the technologies didn't exist. As we develop new technologies, we create an enormous number of dilemmas like these for which there may not be clear solutions. In the past, people looked to spiritual or moral leaders and religious writings for guidance on how to live moral lives. Unfortunately, there is nothing in the sacred scriptures that discusses the issues of photocopying copyrighted publications or breaking into computer systems.

DEFINITION OF TERMS

One source of the problem may be the language we use to describe new behavior. Earlier, I referred to "breaking into computer systems," thus drawing an analogy to the actions of a burglar or vandal who breaks into a house. A high school student who indulges in such behavior may refer to it as hacking, thus equating it to the joyful playing around with computers that went on in the early days of personal computing when thousands of users delighted in trying everything they could to see what their computers could do. Part of the joy came from being able to impress others with their technical wizardry.

Some of these pioneers grew up to start companies that made PC hardware or software, and a few became millionaires before they were 30. One such person even endowed a college scholarship at a large university for students who show great talent for hacking. His purpose was to encourage young people to engage in the kind of creative messing around that gave him so much fun many years ago and, incidentally, made him wealthy.

Since many of the young people who have broken into computer systems have described themselves as hackers, computer security folks have taken to equating hacking with breaking in. Old-time hackers, however, do not make that connection; for them, there is no pejorative connotation associated with the word. In the interest of better communication, perhaps computer security people should give the word back to the hackers. Certainly if we could all agree that logging on to someone else's computer system without permission is breaking in and that being wildly creative and experimenting with the capabilities of your own system is hacking, we would be much closer to establishing universal agreement that the former is not ethical.

There are subtle problems with our language that are introduced by these new technologies. Think about the word *steal*—what does it mean? If you think stealing means to take away someone's property without permission, you may find it hard to think that copying copyrighted software is stealing because the person who owns the package has not lost anything by your action. However, if you think stealing is depriving others of what is rightfully theirs, it is easy to make the case that the person doing the copying is stealing—not from the person who purchased the software but from the person who owns the rights to it. By making a copy, the copier is failing to pay the real owners the fee to which they are entitled. Depending on how you define *steal*, copying copyrighted software is or is not ethical. Of course, it is illegal, regardless of how you define it.

LEGAL ISSUES

I do not necessarily equate ethical behavior with legal behavior. Some problems posed in the survey and in the situations I list are covered by state or federal laws that clearly state that a certain choice is illegal. But so was drinking during Prohibition. So were many actions of civil rights activists in the 1960s. So is driving over 55 miles per hour on most of the nation's highways. Just because an action is illegal does not mean that society as a whole disapproves of it. Until society condemns a certain behavior, that behavior is likely to continue.

I believe there is a need for strong computer crime laws. If it is not a crime to break into my computer system, I am that much more vulnerable to such invasions. The more people see that there are no adverse consequences to such activities, the more likely some people are to engage in this behavior. We need to establish and enforce legal penalties for behavior that is not in the best interests of society. But more than that, we need to work on changing the public's attitudes.

TEACHING ETHICS

There is a particular need to educate our young people about what is and is not acceptable behavior; this must begin at a very early age. By the time students reach high school, they have learned that hitting people, breaking others' possessions, stealing, and lying are not ethical. Shouldn't we also teach youngsters that property is a concept that extends to ideas and information? Shouldn't a child who is taught how to use a computer also be taught that one can "steal" or "break" information and that such behavior is as wrong as stealing or breaking physical objects?

I expect most readers will agree with this. But can we agree on what is to be taught? My recent reading suggests that we probably can, but not in every subject.

Then there is the problem of how to teach what we decide should be taught. The forum on high technology risks I referred to had an interesting message on it the other day. A professor had written that he is considering setting up a computer ethics course for his university and invited comments from the forum readers. This would be a project I would find worthy of praise except for one part of the message which shocked me—the course would not meet as a class except for the first and last sessions. Rather, students would participate by means of an electronic bulletin board on the school's main computer.

If we have learned anything about the kinds of kids who get involved in the computer break-ins, it is that they are, on average, very poorly socialized. They become obsessively involved with their computers and the friendships they form by exchanging electronic mail with other computer users, but they often have few friends who they know face-to-face. Working from the isolation of their homes, they end up with a poorly formed understanding of the social skills and concerns that underlie much of our sense of civilization. The last thing in the world we should do is to try to teach these kids about ethics by sending them impersonal computer messages!

PERSONALIZING COMPUTER ETHICS

Impersonal is the key word here. As children, we learn that certain behaviors are unacceptable because we are taught to respect the feelings of others. As youngsters, we are rewarded when we make others happy and punished when we make them unhappy. This gives us a firm basis for testing out new situations and deciding for ourselves what is good or ethical behavior. An adult corrected our first missteps, but we are able to correct ourselves after a while if we observe the consequences of our behavior. If we break Susie's wagon and Susie cries, we know we have done wrong because that is how we judge something to be wrong. As we grow older, we learn to judge our unethical actions by more subtle signs of discomfort in the people around us.

The problem with high technology misdeeds is that there is rarely direct contact between the perpetrator and the victim. When the victim is an institution or a company, the connection between certain behavior and resulting unhappiness becomes even more tenuous.

Consider the situations I discussed previously. Who are the victims of these questionable behaviors? A recording company (and its musicians), a bank, the XYZ company, and a cable television service. Can you imagine getting worked up about the fate of any of them? Would you ever lie awake feeling guilty about having done one of them wrong? Maybe you could but, believe me, very few people would join you.

Yet behind the record company, bank, and cable service, there are people who are made unhappy in very real ways by the actions of others. Granted that many of these people may feel very little direct pain as a consequence of a single person's unethical behavior, but the cumulative effect can still be great. The record company may charge $2 more per record than it would otherwise to make up lost revenue due to pirated copies and may employ fewer people to produce and distribute its products. The bank may tack on a 25¢-per-transaction service charge to ATM transactions to cover the losses caused by hardware problems. The cable company may raise the cost of either the basic service or the movie channel or both. Someone has to pay for a company's losses, and that someone is usually the client.

Data processing professionals waste much valuable time cleaning up unnecessary messes. in November 1988, the ARPANET, a network that links thousands of government and university computers, was hit by a computer virus. It was estimated that more than 100 worker-years had been expended on the cleanup effort. Many people lost a lot of sleep over that incident. When long hours, often at night and on weekends, are required to find and fix unnecessary problems, an employee's health, family life, or quality of life may suffer. Employers must suffer the cost of the time their employees had to devote to finding the problem rather than doing the work they are paid to do.

The worst suffering may be that of individuals whose personal information is stored in a system that is under attack. Their bank accounts may become inaccessible, they may be denied essential services, or they may be given the wrong medical treatment.

When computer whizzes plant codes that get passed to thousands of other computers, they probably don't have any sense of harming other people. The fact that thousands of people will have to spend thousands of hours finding and eliminating a code is not a reality to the perpetrators, because they will never meet most of the victims. People who use stolen credit card numbers do not have to confront the owners of those credit cards and see the anxiety and pain they experience as they try to get the charges eliminated without damaging their credit rating.

The answer to the question of how to teach computer ethics is simple: we must personalize the problem. We must teach by focusing on the suffering that results when people have to clean up or pay for the messes made by the irresponsible acts of others. We have to show how the price of a product or service increased because the company had to pay its people for performing the cleanup and had to add new security measures to prevent a recurrence. We have to demonstrate how dangerous it can be for a patient if the medical center's computer records are damaged or become inaccessible. We have to tie the destruction of a government file of welfare recipients to the people who go hungry when their checks don't arrive. Just because one does not see the victims does not mean they do not exist.

CONCLUSION

Perhaps most important in this age of connectivity, we must make computer users understand that they cannot foresee all consequences of their behavior. What is intended as a prank on one local system may spread to other systems and cause unexpected damage, which must be paid for. We must impress on the public that they are the ultimate victims of computer misbehavior; when the consequences of an action cannot be predicted, the behavior is to be avoided. To do otherwise creates unacceptable risks for society as a whole.

Do I think computer ethics classes are needed in light of recent problems with viruses and hackers? I sure do! But this is not a trivial matter. We are going to have to create a new, expanded set of ethics, and we are going to have to find effective ways to teach them. We must get started immediately because these things take time.

What can you as an individual do? If you are a parent, contact the schools your children attend and find out if they are teaching students about the ethical use of computers. If they are not, apply some pressure to get them to do so. If you don't have school-age children, urge your local school board to include ethics in all computer classes. If you have the time and expertise, volunteer to teach—a one-hour lecture is better than none, and a good teacher will follow up with class discussions or homework to reinforce the points you make.

If you read an article in a newspaper or magazine that treats an incident of unethical behavior as if it were not a problem, write a letter to the editor. If a television show presents an unethical situation as glamorous or amusing, call the station. As long as the media do not label unethical behavior for what it is, certain people will be drawn to commit such acts. After all, they might just make the six o'clock news.

If the professional technical community doesn't start to take stands and make clear to the less technical population that certain behaviors are unethical, the problems will continue to grow. It is in your best interest to stop unethical behavior. The next system to be disrupted could be yours.

Notes

1. E. P. Garnder et al., "The Importance of Ethical and Legal Standards in End-User Computing," *Data Security Management Series* (New York: Auerbach Publishers, November–December, 1988).

Reading 6–2

ASSESSING THE MIS INTERNAL CONTROL STRUCTURE IN A FINANCIAL STATEMENT AUDIT UNDER SAS NO. 55

By Charles W. Stanley and C. William Thomas

In 1988, the AICPA's Auditing Standards Board issued Statement on Auditing Standards No. 55, "Consideration of the Internal Control Structure in a Financial Statement Audit." The purpose of this statement is to provide guidance to auditors in reviewing a company's internal control structure in conjunction with a financial statement audit. In addition, the elements of the control structure of a typical audit have been redefined and a more detailed requirement has been imposed for considering the control structure in planning and performing an audit. This article discusses the need for understanding the MIS internal control structure and suggests an approach that can be followed to meet the new standard when significant MIS operations exist.

The auditing approach outlined here is an adaptation of the one previously suggested by SAS No.3, "The Auditor's Study and Evaluation of Internal Control in EDP Systems," which was superseded by SAS No. 55. Like the method suggested in SAS No. 3, this process consists of a preliminary review phase, a detailed review phase, and a tests-of-controls phase, This article discusses each phase in detail and provides suggestions as to which areas might require more auditing time and consideration for EDP audits.

UNDERSTANDING THE MIS INTERNAL CONTROL STRUCTURE

Although computers are ideally suited for accounting transactions because of their capacity for handling voluminous routine transactions quickly and accurately, recent technological advances, particularly those involving the microcomputer, have increased audit risk and the vulnerability to fraud for both large and small businesses. In addition, such factors as the concentrated nature of EDP activities, the vulnerability of data to unauthorized changes, the fragmentation of the audit trail, and the added complexity of automated systems have contributed to the increased audit risk and the likelihood of material losses due to computer fraud.

Losses due to computer fraud are estimated to be between $3 billion and $5 billion annually for U.S. businesses alone.[1] It has also been reported that undetected frauds continue to exist, although their number and magnitude are uncertain, and that only 5 percent to 20 percent of committed frauds are ever reported. This means that total losses due to computer fraud could be as much as $100 billion annually. This increase in the incidence of fraud is due primarily to increasing automation. The computer is particularly vulnerable to this type of fraud because of increased opportunities due to more knowledgeable users coupled with an improved access capability, the difficulty in trying to detect fraud because of the volume of data and the lack of a visible audit trail, and the existing opportunity to obtain a lucrative payoff that is nearly 30 times greater in an automated system than in a manual system. In addition, it has become difficult to determine the impact of such frauds on financial reporting. Therefore, it is critical for auditors to obtain a sufficient understanding of the MIS internal control structure through a specified approach that is designed to help auditors meet the new auditing standards.

THE PRELIMINARY REVIEW PHASE

In the preliminary phase of the review of the MIS internal control structure, the auditor should obtain an understanding of the design of relevant MIS policies and procedures and whether they have been placed in operation in the entity. The knowledge obtained from this understanding should be used to plan the audit. Specifically, the auditor should identify potential material misstatements, consider factors that affect the risk of material misstatements, and design substantive tests accordingly. In addition, the auditor should develop an initial understanding of the three elements that constitute the control structure: the control environment, the accounting system, and control procedures.

The Control Environment

The EDP auditor must develop an understanding of management's attitudes, awareness, and actions concerning all of the issues that can have an impact on the control environment.

Management's Philosophy.   To understand the control environment, the auditor must thoroughly examine management and director attitudes and actions concerning computer operations. For example, the auditor should develop an understanding of management's philosophy and operating style, including management's approach to taking risks, attitudes and actions toward financial reporting, and the emphasis placed on meeting goals. This understanding is especially critical in an MIS setting because, with automation, significant data processing activities are concentrated in a central point and traditional segregation of duties may be lost. If management is prone to taking excessive risks, there may be greater pressure on MIS activities to deliberately misstate the financial statements. The auditor must be aware that management may place an unusually strong emphasis on meeting budget, profits, or other financial goals, and the centralized nature of MIS may be conducive to employees' deliberately misstating financial documents by circumventing established control procedures.

Organizational Structure.   Another important aspect of the control environment that provides the overall framework for planning, directing, and controlling MIS operations is the organizational structure. An effective organizational structure helps provide reasonable assurance that transactions are properly authorized and executed. On the other hand, if an ineffective organizational structure exists, authority and responsibility may not be assigned in an appropriate manner, thus increasing the likelihood that material errors may go undetected. These conditions should be noted, along with the presence of any mitigating controls (e.g., the use of computer logs that are reconciled regularly by a separate control group).

Responsibility Divisions.   In conjunction with the organizational structure, the auditor should also understand the methods of assigning authority and responsibility through the use of job descriptions and systems documentation. Employee job descriptions, if adequate, should delineate specific duties, reporting relationships, and constraints on employees. Most employees like to know exactly what their duties are and what is expected of them in the performance of those duties. This knowledge helps employees to perform their jobs efficiently, which should help to decrease the likelihood that material errors may occur or go undetected. Systems documentation indicates the procedures for authorizing transactions and approving system changes. Again, if an employee knows that procedures are clearly written and that the lines of authority and responsibility have been clearly drawn, errors and irregularities should be kept to a minimum.

The Internal Audit Function.   The internal audit function is critical to the auditor reviewing an information system. The internal audit function can compensate for weaknesses in other areas of the control environment. For example, if weaknesses exist in the organizational structure, the internal audit department can be used to help monitor and review the system of MIS internal accounting controls. Functions might include periodic unannounced visits to operating units and staff offices to test the effectiveness of the accounting controls in the systems. Similarly, the internal audit department can take an active role in the development, monitoring, coordination, and implementation of new systems and changes to existing systems. Internal auditors typically are well versed in MIS operations and know a great deal about their company's system. In addition, an effective internal audit team can test MIS controls more thoroughly than an independent auditor can and usually plays an active role in systems documentation.

Personnel Policies.   Along with the internal audit function, effective personnel policies and practices can have a significant impact on the control environment. These include hiring and promotion practices as well as initial and ongoing company training policies. In addition, the potential loss exposure is much greater with an automated system than with a manual system. Therefore, a company that does not hire and train competent personnel may experience a diminished ability to accomplish goals and objectives. In the preparation of financial statements, incompetence increases the likelihood that material errors will occur and thereby increases control risk. MIS candidates should be subjected to extensive testing in such areas as programming and operator skills. Competency tests should be taken regularly by all MIS personnel. Such tests may be developed internally or provided by hardware and software manufacturers.

The Accounting System

To obtain a sufficient understanding of the company's accounting system, the EDP auditor must investigate the company's flow of transactions as well as the methods used to process and report those transactions.

Transaction Flow.   In understanding the accounting system, the auditor should obtain a sufficient working knowledge concerning the classes of transactions that exist in the company as well as the flow of charges and credits into and out of the accounts. In particular, the auditor must determine that transactions are properly initiated in the respective user departments. The auditor also needs to understand what accounting records are processed by the computer, how the accounting information is provided to the MIS department and subsequently converted to machine-readable form, how the computer is used to process accounting data, and the financial reporting process used to prepare the company's financial statements.

Records, Documents, and Accounts.   In obtaining an understanding of the control environment and the accounting system, the auditor also obtains some knowledge of the specific control procedures that are used in conjunction with certain documents, records, and processing steps. The auditor should consider such knowledge in light of the understanding obtained about the control environment and the accounting system and decide whether it is necessary to devote additional time to the understanding of control procedures. Knowledge of many of the control procedures can be obtained from such documentation as systems flowcharts, program flowcharts, and procedures manuals.

Control Procedures

In this section of the preliminary phase, EDP auditors must first consider the knowledge obtained about the control environment and the accounting system. The auditor should then ensure that the understanding of the control procedures that have been developed is sufficient to begin planning.

PLANNING ASSESSMENT OF CONTROL RISK

The auditor should make a preliminary assessment of control risk on the basis of the results of the preliminary review of the internal control structure. The assessment should focus on whether there is sufficient evidence of strength in the control structure to justify lowering the control risk below the maximum level. If it is not possible to lower the assessment of control risk through further review and testing, the auditor should not perform further review of the internal control structure. Instead, the auditor may review, test, and evaluate user controls if it is believed that some reliance can be placed on those controls. These controls include the establishment of such user control totals as record counts, hash totals, and financial totals.

If no reliance can be placed on user controls, the auditor should document that the assessed level of control risk is the maximum, and complete the design of the substantive audit tests. if the auditor's preliminary assessment of control risk is that it could be cost-effectively lowered by performing further tests, additional evidence should be obtained to support the lower level. In this case, the auditor proceeds to the detailed phase of the review. On the other hand, the auditor can decide to leave the assessed level of control risk at the maximum level because he or she may believe that it is more effective or efficient to do so. That is, the additional costs or time involved in attempting to justify potential reduction in the assessed level of control risk may exceed any benefit to be derived by a reduction in control risk.

THE DETAILED REVIEW PHASE

The detailed review is conducted in two stages. In the first stage, the general controls for the system are reviewed, and in the second stage, the application controls for significant accounting applications are reviewed.

General Controls

In reviewing a system's general controls, the auditor should identify those general controls on which reliance can be justified to support reduction in the assessed level of control risk. The auditor should also determine how these controls operate and how they relate to some of management's financial statement assertions (existence or occurrence, completeness, valuation, rights or obligations, presentation, and disclosure).

Completeness.   The auditor should be particularly concerned with the general controls that affect completeness. The completeness assertion states that all properly authorized transactions that should be included in the financial statements have been included and that no unauthorized transactions have been improperly included. Given the centralized nature of data processing and the vulnerability of the data files to change or possible destruction, it is vital that controls ensure that all transactions are properly authorized and correctly processed. For example, the auditor should ensure that transactions are authorized and initiated by the user departments and not by the MIS department. Changes to master files and transactions files, changes to existing systems, and the adoption of new systems should all be initiated by the user departments.

Valuation and Allocation.   A valuation assertion is important because the computer is used to record transactions, calculate such amounts as total sales and interest, and handle all processing that involves summarizing the accounting data. Therefore, the auditor should look for proper documentation of forms and procedures in the various user and system manuals. Changes to existing systems or the development of new systems should be properly authorized and tested before implementation and should be documented through the use of program change forms. Access to programs and files should be adequately controlled to prevent unauthorized changes in the programs that perform many of the accounting and mathematical calculations.

Statement Presentation and Disclosure.   The statement presentation and disclosure assertion is included here because most companies that use the computer for processing accounting data also use the computer to prepare financial statements. Auditors should determine that existing access controls prevent unauthorized persons from penetrating the data or program files and performing changes that would cause the financial statements to be misstated. Transactions should be submitted to manual or machine review in the user departments before being submitted to the MIS department. Disclosures should be initiated and approved by the various user departments and never by MIS. The other two assertions of existence and ownership are also important in the EDP audit because the computer can affect whether the information that supports the existence or ownership assertions can be accessed. However, because the computer's primary function is to process the data that supports existence or ownership, the assertions of completeness and valuation are critical. For example, such an asset as inventory exists or it does not exist; data processing does not affect the inventory's existence. Similarly, the computer does not affect the ownership of the inventory. Yet, if the completeness assertion does not have proper support controls, the documentation and the information that support the inventory's existence and ownership could be incomplete or improperly documented.

Application Controls

Once the review of general controls is completed, the auditor should review application controls. These consist of input controls, processing controls, and output controls. The auditor should identify those application controls on which reliance can be justified to support reduction of control risk. Again, the auditor should determine how the controls operate and the effect they have on the financial statement assertions of management. Although the same assertions apply here that were suggested for the general controls, the emphasis is different with application controls since they are highly detailed. Specifically, controls should be reviewed for each significant accounting application on which justification for reducing control risk exists. Therefore, the auditor might review the cash receipts application program but not the inventory application program.

Whereas general controls are concerned with the completeness of all accounting data, application controls are concerned with the completeness of a particular class of transactions (e.g., cash receipts) or a specific account balance (e.g., accounts receivable or inventory). In this context, the auditor determines how the application controls over cash receipts affect the financial statement assertions. For example, such controls as the establishment of record counts to determine how many records are to be processed could affect completeness, and the establishment of financial totals could affect valuation. Similarly, such controls as limit checks, reasonableness tests, validity checks, sign tests, and field checks can affect valuation and statement presentation and disclosure.

In addition to the identification of application controls, the auditor should consider tests of controls that may be performed as well as the potential effect of identified strengths and weaknesses on those tests of controls. For each significant accounting application, the auditor should consider the errors of irregularities that could occur, determine the accounting control procedures that prevent or detect such errors or irregularities, and assess the effectiveness of MIS and non-MIS accounting controls.

In performing the review of application controls, the auditor should use the same evidence-gathering techniques as discussed previously. A detailed examination of documentation should be conducted for each application. Such documentation should include systems flowcharts, charts of accounts, procedure manuals, organizational charts, and systems, program, operations, and user manuals. The documentation also includes forms for input, program change, and output as well as distribution routes. The auditor should interview company personnel, particularly internal auditors who concentrate on EDP audits, MIS personnel, and user department personnel. Finally, auditors should observe the operation of the various general and application controls.

DETAILED ASSESSMENT OF CONTROL RISK

On completion of the detailed review, the auditor should conduct another assessment of control risk. Again, the auditor must ask whether there is a basis for reliance on the general controls and application controls to justify a further reduction of the assessed level of control risk. However, the consideration is more detailed at this stage than it is at the preliminary stage. As before, if the auditor believes that the controls are too weak to merit any reduction in the control risk, the internal control structure review has been completed (assuming that documentation is proper and complete), and the auditor should complete the design of the substantive tests.

THE TESTS-OF-CONTROLS PHASE

If the auditor believes that the controls are strong enough to merit further reduction in the assessed level of control risk, tests of controls should be performed. Tests of controls are directed toward either the effectiveness of the design or the operation of MIS policies and procedures. They are intended to help the auditor to determine if the necessary control procedures that have been prescribed by the company are being followed and are functioning properly. The auditor should document when, how, and by whom controls are provided.

The tests that the auditor performs in this phase are a function of the approach that the auditor takes. If the general approach is to audit around the computer, then the tests of controls consist primarily of extensive use of error listings or error logs to verify the existence and function of control procedures. For example, if the error listing shows that a particular transaction has not been processed because the credit limit field exceeded the limit allowed, the auditor would then have evidence that the limit test existed and was functioning. The auditor must also trace transactions from the source documents to their final recording in the accounting records. If the auditor chooses to audit through the computer, then the tests of controls performed by the auditor can follow such approaches as use of test data, an integrated test facility, controlled processing and reprocessing tests, and other well-known methods.

CONTROL EVALUATION

After the auditor has completed tests of controls, a final evaluation should be made of the MIS control structure and the auditor should determine the extent of reliance that is to be placed on the MIS accounting controls that may justify lowering the control risk below the maximum level. The auditor should have previously determined the errors or irregularities that could have occurred with the system and the accounting control procedures that could prevent or detect such errors and irregularities. Such consideration of these items should be done again after completion of the tests of controls. It is possible that the results of the tests of controls could cause the auditor to change or reassess potential errors and irregularities, depending on the status of the prescribed controls. For each weakness determined to exist as a result of the tests of controls, the auditor should assess the effect of the weakness on the preliminary assessment of control risk discussed previously.

In addition to an assessment of the MIS controls, the auditor must review, test, and evaluate user controls to the extent possible. However, the auditor needs to review only those user controls on which any reliance can be justified to support the reduction of control risk. The review and evaluation of user controls is typically performed as a part of the review of the general and application controls. In addition, since many of the user controls are in the manual part of the system, much of the review and evaluation of user controls is performed with the usual internal control structure review procedures. Finally, once the auditor has completed the tests of controls and has considered the effect user controls could have on the assessed level of control risk, the auditor should complete the design of substantive audit tests.

CONCLUSION

SAS No. 55 represents a significant departure from the traditional ways in which auditors evaluate internal controls. As the profession moves toward more risk-analysis approaches in the auditing process, auditors should be aware of the problems that can arise as a result of widespread business automation. This article has adapted the superseded model of SAS No. 3 to include the more contemporary terminology and methodology of SAS No. 55.

Thus, it can be used to help auditors understand their responsibility for assessment of the MIS control structure.

Notes

1. Ernst & Whinney, *Computer Fraud: A Report Presented to the National Commission on Fraudulent Financial Reporting*, pp. 5–10.

Reading 6–3

A GENERALIZED AUDIT SIMULATION TOOL FOR EVALUATING THE RELIABILITY OF INTERNAL CONTROLS

By Casper E. Wiggins, Jr., and L. Murphy Smith

Abstract. The study and evaluation of internal control requires an auditor to analyze all key controls and control relationships included in each major transaction cycle. Gaining the requisite level of understanding can become a formidable task where complex systems with intricate control relationships, computer-based accounting systems, or systems with suspected collusion are involved. This study describes an audit simulation model which is designed to assist auditors in evaluating and documenting the reliability of complex internal control systems. The proposed simulation extends previous ones in two primary respects. First, dependencies between error and control processes can be modeled, which allows an auditor to investigate the effects of collusion on system reliability and final balance error amounts. Second, the simulation is an interactive computer model which can be tailored to different client applications without the need for programming knowledge. An application of the simulation approach in a typical payroll cycle is described.

INTRODUCTION

A careful review of a client's internal control system is an integral part of the auditing process. Recent developments, which include the U.S. Foreign Corrupt Practices Act of 1977, the recommendations of the Commission on Au-

Reprinted with permission from *Contemporary Accounting Research*, Spring 1987, pp. 316–337.

ditors' Responsibilities, a number of recently issued professional standards, and the spiraling cost of performing audit procedures, have caused auditors to attach increased importance to this audit step. The auditor's study and evaluation of internal control is conducted for each major transaction cycle or application area and draws substantially upon the auditor's professional judgment. The internal control conclusions derived are a major determinant of the extent of audit procedure to be performed and, hence, of overall audit costs.

The study and evaluation of internal control requires the auditor to analyze all key controls and control relationships included in each major transaction cycle and application area. For example, the auditor must understand the sensitivity of final account balance errors to small changes in failure rates for related controls. Achieving this level of understanding for simple systems normally presents little difficulty to auditors. However, gaining the requisite understanding can become a formidable task where numerous processing and control steps and intricate control relationships are involved. The task becomes even more difficult for computer-based accounting systems and for systems in which systematic errors or collusion are suspected. Objective decision aids are needed to assist auditors in making these audit judgments in complex control environments.

This paper describes a simulation approach for the design and evaluation of complex internal control systems. The simulation tool proposed (henceforth, referred to as SIM) allows an auditor to model a client's internal control system and to use this model to investigate important system reliability characteristics, and the resulting magnitude of errors in a related final account balance. Unlike previous approaches, SIM is a generalized modeling tool which can be tailored to specific client applications and does not require knowledge of computer programming languages to employ. SIM has been implemented on a mainframe computer and is currently being developed for microcomputer applications.[1]

Typical Applications of SIM

SIM can assist both internal and external auditors in the design and analysis of internal control systems. Internal auditors might use the simulation tool to design control elements for new systems, and to evaluate the need for additional controls in existing systems. Sensitivity analyses can be performed with SIM to explore the reliability of alternative configurations for specific control systems. Both internal and external auditors might use SIM to explore the effect of varying assumptions regarding error rates, error amounts, and control failure rates upon the magnitude of error amounts in the final balance for a related account. For external auditors, SIM can be used to identify key internal controls and to plan compliance and substantive testing strategies. An example of how SIM can assist auditors in determining tolerable error rates for compliance testing procedures is presented in a later section of this paper. Management consultants might also utilize SIM for evaluating alternative system designs.

Among the audit questions which can be explored with the model are:

1. What is the overall reliability of the system with respect to particular errors?

2. How sensitive is the system reliability to changes in failure rates for key controls?

3. What is the expected magnitude of the dollar amount of errors in the final account balance(s) under examination?

4. How sensitive are these final balance error amounts to changes in assumed failure rates for key controls?

In short, the simulation tool (SIM) provides a risk-free environment in which sensitivity analyses of important internal control relationships can be performed. Thus, the impacts of various assumptions regarding error rates, control failure rates, and error amount distributions upon system reliability and upon expected final balance error amounts can be explored before audit resources are committed.

Prior Research

Objective decision aids for the design and evaluation of internal control systems previously offered have been primarily mathematical models (see Yu and Neter, 1973; Cushing, 1974; Hamlen, 1980; Grimlund, 1982; and Ahituv, 1985), or simulation models (see Burns and Loebbecke, 1975; Stratton, 1981; and Knechel, 1985a and 1985b). Other modeling approaches include the TICOM model (see Bailey et al., 1985). The current research extends the earlier simulation approaches by addressing two practical limitations which they share.[2] The first major weakness of previous approaches addressed by this research relates to the perceived complexity of the mathematical formulations and/or the degree of computer expertise or other technical knowledge required for use of the models. A second major difficulty addressed by the current research concerns the statistical independence of operating elements which reliability theory assumes, an assumption which effectively rules out the possibility of collusion in the internal control environment. Since collusion embodies a major threat to internal control systems (Carmichael, 1970, p. 238), this assumption of previous approaches may pose an unrealistic simplification.

Simulation avoids the mathematical complexity and many of the restrictive assumptions associated with quantitative models. However, a primary disadvantage of previous simulation approaches is that the simulation must be reprogrammed for each client application, a task which may require considerable programming expertise. The usefulness of a simulation decision aid similar to that offered by Burns and Loebbecke is supported by Weber (1978)

who found that auditors using the simulation (1) made more accurate decisions, (2) had more confidence in their decisions, and (3) required less time to
make decisions. Weber also noted that development of the simulation aid required extensive computer programming and that, consequently, a generalized
audit simulation language was needed.

The simulation approach proposed herein addresses this need by providing a generalized audit simulation tool which can be tailored to different client
applications without reprogramming by the auditor. Use of SIM does not
require knowledge of either general-purpose programming languages (such
as Fortran or Cobol) or of simulation languages (such as SLAM or
SIMSCRIPT), as do previous simulation approaches. The level of computer
literacy necessary to use SIM is comparable to that of the generalized audit
software packages which are widely used by public accounting firms today. In
essence, SIM provides a set of simple building blocks which can be used to
model and evaluate internal control relationships. In addition to demonstrat-
ing the feasibility of a generalized simulation approach, SIM extends previous
approaches by allowing the representation and analysis of systems in which
collusion between system elements and/or systematic (nonrandom) errors or
control failures may exist. Thus, the implications of fraudulent acts having
irregular occurrence patterns can be investigated.

Knechel (1985a) also addresses this need by proposing an events-based
simulation model of an accounting system. This model differs from that of the
present research principally in the level of analysis for which the respective
models are intended. The Knechel model utilizes simulation building blocks
which are best suited for analysis at macrosystem (i.e., transaction cycle or
major subcycle) levels. Each of the modules or routines in Knechel's model
may represent many individual processing and control tasks which are intended to be representative of most accounting systems. In contrast, the simulation approach proposed in the current paper (SIM) is designed for the
detailed analysis of error and control relationships at a microsystem level.
Thus, SIM provides simulation building blocks which are generalized at a
much lower level so that individual processing and control tasks can be modeled in detail. In this regard, the level of analysis assumed in the present
study is similar to that employed by Cushing (1974). For example, Knechel's
building blocks are specific subsystems (such as shipping, billing, or accounts
receivable posting) for which typical errors and controls are predefined.
SIM's building blocks are far more generic and consist of just three step types
(processing, control, and branch steps) which can be easily tailored to diverse
client applications.

A second major distinction in the two models is that programming knowledge (SIMSCRIPT) is required in order to tailor Knechel's model to the details of specific client applications. The simulation model proposed in the
present study is an interactive tool and requires no programming knowledge
to utilize. In summary, the Knechel model attempts to model a larger segment
of an internal control system than the model proposed in the present study,

and is necessarily less flexible and less capable of capturing detailed relationships. On the other hand, SIM attempts to model a much smaller portion of an internal control system and is more flexible and more capable of capturing detailed internal control relationships. In fact, the two models might be used in a complementary fashion; SIM for analyzing detailed internal control relationships within subcycles, the results of which could be used as input for the Knechel model which provides a broader internal control evaluation. Thus, an appropriate application for SIM would be the determination of probable error parameters for the various component modules comprising the Knechel model.

In a second study by Knechel (1985b), a simulation approach is employed to test the bias introduced by two simplifying assumptions regarding error behavior which are common to prior reliability models. In this study the simulation model was used to estimate "actual" error rates which were compared to analytically determined error rates. Knechel concluded that simplifying assumptions regarding the independence and mutual exclusivity of error processes do not introduce significant bias unless error rates are high. It should be noted that the simulation approach proposed in the current study does not require the simplifying assumptions tested by Knechel. As noted earlier, a primary advantage of SIM is that dependencies between error processes and/or controls can be modeled. Furthermore, the Knechel study demonstrates the advantages of simulation models over analytical reliability models for the analysis of internal control systems.

One principal advantage that simulation offers is the linking of assumptions regarding error rates and control failure rates to the resulting error amounts generated in a related final account balance. This mapping of system reliability characteristics to final balance dollar errors is extremely critical both to audit efficiency and effectiveness, and is traditionally accomplished subjectively. A major advantage of simulation approaches (including the current study) is that this linkage can be explored, thus providing valuable decision support to the auditor. This linkage is not feasible in analytical reliability models (see Knechel, 1985b, p. 201).

A major focus within the auditing community is the potential auditing role of artificial intelligence (AI) and specifically of expert systems. The simulation approach proposed in the current research is designed to provide decision support to auditors in their efforts to evaluate internal control system reliability. It does not integrate a conventional knowledge base and, therefore, would not technically be categorized as an expert system. However, the proposed simulation approach shares many of the decision support features often associated with expert systems and can play an important role in the development of rule systems for future expert systems. For example, SIM can be used to determine the probability that a given system configuration will produce material errors in a final account balance; a probability which might be incorporated into a specific rule within a knowledge base. In addition, quantitative results from a simulation model such as SIM can be used to complement findings from a nonquantitative model such as TICOM (Bailey et al., 1985), which is principally designed for the analysis of organizational segregation of duties in an internal control system. Thus, simulation can play a critical support role in the development of expert systems in auditing.

DESCRIPTION OF SIM

This section describes the principal features of SIM. The overall steps involved in the use of SIM are summarized first, followed by a more detailed discussion of SIM's basic features. It is assumed that a preliminary evaluation of the internal control system (a cycle, subcycle, or application system) has been performed. Thus, the auditor has considered the errors and irregularities that could occur in the system and has identified key controls that may tentatively be relied upon to prevent or detect these errors. Additionally, a flowchart of the cycle's internal control system has already been developed.

The auditor begins the simulation by communicating the characteristics of the internal control system to SIM. These internal control system specifications are developed in a straightforward manner from the system flowchart, and are in terms of the simple building blocks which are described later. After input to SIM, these building block specifications define all relevant aspects of the internal control system in terms that SIM can recognize. At this point SIM accepts the input specifications and uses them to construct a computer model of the internal control system. SIM then causes a number of simulated transactions to be processed through this computer model. This simulated transaction activity is monitored by SIM, and the processing results are used to develop SIM's output. This output consists of reliability statistics for the various elements of the internal control system and error characteristics for related final account balances.

System Overview

SIM requires that the auditor view the internal control system as a transaction processing system. This system view is depicted in Figure 1. Inputs to the system are source documents, such as customer invoices, purchase orders, time cards, or employee record change authorizations. Each transaction passes through a number of processing stages which involve such tasks as transcription, journalizing, posting, verification, and review. Outputs of the transaction processing system are the basic financial statements for external users and various internal reports for use by management. At certain steps in the processing for a given transaction, errors may occur, which may or may not be detected and corrected by control elements in the system. Errors which occur and are not detected by the system will appear in the final balance of one or more general ledger accounts, and thus will contaminate the statements or reports produced by the system. The auditor's primary concern is that the aggregate errors remaining in one or more account balances are material in amount.

FIGURE 1   Overview of System Perspective

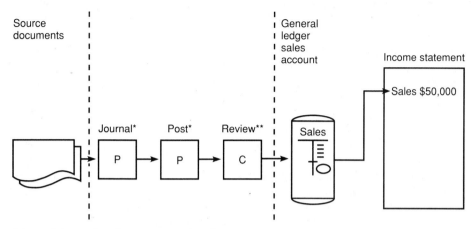

* Journalizing and posting are processing steps.
** Review is a control step.

SIM allows the auditor to represent the operating elements of the internal control systems in terms of three types of system entities. These basic building units are: processing steps, control steps, and branch steps. Processing steps are operating elements in the system which have the ability to introduce errors into a stream of transactions. Examples of processing steps are journalizing, posting, coding, and keypunching activities. Control steps are operating elements in the system which are capable of detecting one or more specific errors which have occurred previously in the system. Examples of control steps are preparation of a trial balance, reconciliation of subsidiary and control account balances, key verification, and batch control totals. Branch steps represent decision points in the system which allow branching to occur in the processing sequence for particular transactions. Branching is typically needed after a control step to direct a transaction to the appropriate processing step for correction of a detected error. Thus, the auditor defines the internal control system for SIM as a network of processing steps, control steps, and branch steps. These different step types are examined in the next section.

Transaction Processing

As noted above, SIM uses auditor specifications to develop a computer model of the internal control system. SIM then creates a number of simulated transactions and causes them to be processed through this system model. This simulated transaction activity represents the actual processing activity for an accounting period, and is monitored by SIM to develop the reliability statistics and final balance profile which are produced by SIM.

Each transaction generated by SIM is completely processed through the internal control system network. The operating statistics for the transaction are then collected by SIM, and the transaction is terminated. A new transaction is then generated by SIM and processed through the network in the same fashion. Thus, only one transaction (the current transaction) is in the system at any one time. The transaction processing for an individual transaction proceeds as follows. When a transaction passes through a processing step, SIM randomly determines whether an error will occur, using an error probability assigned by the auditor. The error rate (probability) assigned to SIM will be based on the auditor's judgment. Methods which might be used by an auditor to estimate these and other parameters are discussed in a later section of this paper.

In addition to unintentional mistakes, auditors may also encounter intentional or fraudulent errors. Unlike the simulation approaches discussed earlier, SIM provides for analyzing these intentional errors or irregularities. For irregularities, SIM allows the auditor to specify systematic error patterns (such as every tenth or fiftieth transaction), or the auditor can specify that an irregularity is to occur whenever an error in one or more designated colluding steps has occurred for the current transaction. When an error or irregularity occurs for a given transaction, SIM randomly determines the error amount based on distributional parameters specified by the auditor.

Control steps are operating elements in the system which are capable of detecting one or more specific errors which have occurred previously for the current transaction. When the current transaction enters a control step, SIM determines whether the control will detect the specific error(s) which may be associated with the current transaction. SIM allows control failures to occur either randomly at an auditor specified rate, or with collusion. With collusion a control will fail at a higher specified rate whenever an error has occurred in a designated colluding step. If an error is detected by a control, the control activates the appropriate branch step, which will cause the transaction to be routed to a processing step for correction. Thus, errors may be detected by a control but not corrected by the system. SIM logs all control failures and error detections made by each control, including the dollar amount of detected errors.

Branch steps operate in conjunction with control steps and are the means by which transactions may be diverted from the normal processing path. Each branch step can be activated by a related control step. When the current transaction reaches an activated branch step, the transaction will be routed directly to a predetermined destination (usually a processing step for correction of an error). No branching will occur if the branch step has not been activated.

Figure 2 suggests how an auditor might characterize a typical payroll subcycle as a network of processing steps, control steps, and branch steps. As shown, control C1 serves as a control for errors generated by step P1, and control C2 controls for errors introduced by step P6. Thus, if an error is

FIGURE 2   Simulation Model of Payroll Subcycle

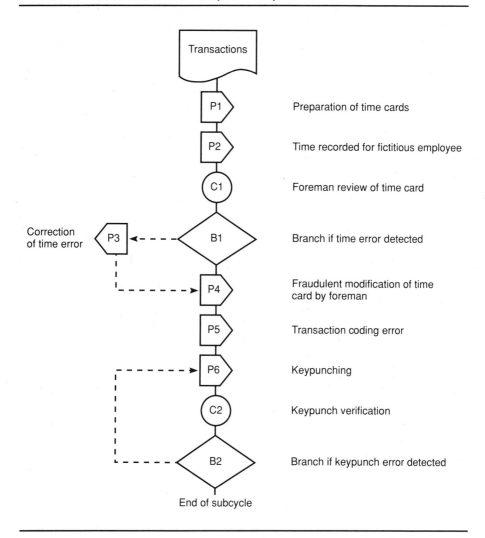

detected by C1, control C1 activates branch step B1, and C2 similarly activates B2. The Appendix at the end of this reading provides a detailed illustration of how SIM performs transaction processing.

Results for SIM

The simulation monitors the simulated processing of a number of transactions through the internal control system and uses the processing results to generate reliability data for the various system elements. As a transaction is processed through the internal control system, various errors, irregularities, and control exceptions may become associated with the transaction. Likewise, if certain of these deviations are detected and corrected by the system, they are disassociated from the transaction. Of course, only deviations associated with the transaction at the completion of processing have an impact on the final balance under examination. The simulation maintains a system of counters to record the processing history of each transaction and to characterize the activity of each processing and control step. Simulation results are then generated based on the final activity counts for each step and then averaged over all runs to obtain the overall results for the simulation experiment.

Figure 3 illustrates the simulation results produced for a typical processing step (Processing Step 2—Transaction Coding error) and a typical control step (Control Step 1—Foreman Review of Time Cards). This sample output is provided at this point to merely acquaint the reader with the nature of the system reliability statistics which are produced by SIM. For this run, processing step 2 exhibited an actual error rate of 10.19 percent and a final balance reliability of 97.59 percent. The final balance reliability implies that less than 3 percent of all transactions in the final balance had an error in step

FIGURE 3   Typical Processing and Control Step Results

RESULTS FOR PROCESSING STEP 2—TRANSACTION CODING ERROR
TOTAL ACTIVITY = 500   ERROR RATE = 10.19%
ERRORS OCCURRED = 51   ERRORS DETECTED BY SYSTEM = 39
ERRORS IN FINAL BALANCE = 12
TOTAL ERROR AMOUNT = $2,646.90
TOTAL ERROR AMOUNT IN FINAL BALANCE = $636.37
PERCENTAGE OF ERRORS DETECTED BY SYSTEM = 76.47%
FINAL BALANCE RELIABILITY = 97.59%

RESULTS FOR CONTROL STEP 1—FOREMAN REVIEW OF TIME CARDS
NO. OF EXCEPTIONS = 65   FAILURE RATE = 13.00%
TOTAL AMOUNT OF UNDETECTED ERRORS = $881.13

THIS CONTROL DETECTED 20 OF 21 OCCURRENCES OF ERROR #1
ERROR NAME = INVALID EMPLOYEE
ERROR AMOUNT DETECTED = $10,222.08
PERCENT OF TOTAL ERROR AMOUNT FOR ERROR #1 = 94.85%

THIS CONTROL DETECTED 65 OF 77 OCCURRENCES OF ERROR #2
ERROR NAME = ERROR IN HOURS RECORDED
ERROR AMOUNT DETECTED = $1,845.61
PERCENT OF TOTAL ERROR AMOUNT FOR ERROR #2 = 84.97%

---

2 associated with it (i.e., 97 percent had no errors for step 2). Furthermore, 51 errors for step 2 occurred for a total error amount of $2,646.90, of which 39 were corrected by system controls. The total error amount in the final balance for this step was $636.37 and was due to 12 undetected error occurrences. Overall, 76.47 percent of errors which occurred for this step was detected and corrected by the system. The reliability of the final balance with respect to this error was 97.59 per cent (i.e., 97.59 percent of the transactions in the final balance had no errors from step 2).

The results for control step 1 (Figure 3) indicate that 65 exceptions (or failures) occurred for the control, producing a failure rate of 13 percent. This control failure rate resulted in a total of $881.13 of undetected errors for the two errors (errors in step no. 1 and step no. 2) the control can detect. This control detected 20 of 21 occurrences of the errors in step no. 1 (invalid employee). The total error amount detected was $10,222.08, or 94.85 percent of the total error amount for the step. Control step 3 also detected 65 of the 77 occurrences of the errors in step no. 2, representing a total detected error amount of $1,845.61 (or 84.97 percent of the total error amount for step no. 2). These control results provide a measure of (1) the audit exposure (dollar amount of undetected errors) of control failures for the control, and (2) the benefits (error amounts detected) derived from inclusion of the control in the internal control system design.

Thus, the simulation results provide audit information useful for appraising the reliability of the system with respect to each error type, the effectiveness of each control type, and the probable audit exposure (in dollars) from the particular audit cycle. Use of the simulation tool should involve an iterative strategy in which the auditor observes the sensitivity of final balance reliabilities and audit exposure amounts over a number of simulation experiments (computer runs), where each experiment reflects different error and exception rate assumptions for key processing and control steps.

Input Requirements

SIM requires two categories of auditor specifications. These specifications are needed to define:

1. The characteristics of the internal control system to be simulated.
2. The scope of the simulated transaction activity to be performed.

The initial category of specifications represents the internal control system to SIM in terms of processing, control, and branch steps. Figure 4 delineates the auditor specifications needed for each of the three step types. These specifications may be entered interactively from a computer terminal and are immediately edited by SIM for syntax errors. The simulation flags syntax errors by displaying a diagnostic error message. After all auditor specifications are

FIGURE 4   Auditor Specifications for Internal Control System

---

For each processing step:
1 Step number and descriptive name
2 Estimated error occurrence rate
3 Cyclic pattern (if irregularity is present)
4 Error amount distribution type and parameters
5 Step numbers this step can correct (if a reprocessing step)
6 Step number of next step

For each control step:
1 Step number and descriptive name
2 Estimated exception rate
3 Colluding step and collusion exception rate (if collusion is present)
4 Step numbers of processing steps controlled by this step
5 Next step if no errors in controlled steps are detected
6 Branch step to be activated if error is detected

For each branch step:
1 Step number and descriptive name
2 Next step if branch occurs
3 Next step if no branch occurs

---

completed, the simulation displays these inputs for the auditor to review and provides an opportunity for the auditor to correct erroneous entries.

The specifications for transaction error rates are based on the auditor's judgment. There are several methods by which the auditor may estimate the error rate, including (1) taking a sample of the current period's transactions or (2) evaluating error rates and error types from previous audit workpapers. Prior academic research, which may be helpful to the auditor in estimating error rates and error distributions, include: Johnson, Leitch, and Neter (1981); Ramage, Krieger, and Spero (1979); Leslie (1977); and Neter and Loebbecke (1975).[3]

As Figure 4 reveals, SIM requires the auditor to specify the error occurrence rate and the distributional characteristics of error amounts. For example, if the error is believed to be distributed randomly throughout the transaction population, then the auditor can specify the mean probability of the error occurring (e.g., 5 percent) and the standard deviation (e.g., 1 percent). If the error can be measured in dollar amounts, then the distributional parameters of the error amount might be given (e.g., normal distribution, mean = $100, standard deviation = $10). Other error amount distribution types (e.g., uniform or poisson) may be specified in the model as well.

The second category of specifications defines the scope of the simulated transaction activity to be performed. An overall simulation experiment consists of a number of simulation runs. Each simulation run, in turn, involves the processing of numerous transactions through the network of processing, control, and branch steps. Consequently, the auditor must describe the simulated transaction activity to be performed by specifying:

1. The number of simulation runs to be performed.
2. The number of transactions to be processed in each run.

A PAYROLL APPLICATION

An application of the simulation model in a typical payroll cycle is now described and illustrated. Although the simulation tool is useful in analyzing, and capable of accommodating, systems which are considerably more complex, the example used will focus upon a subcycle within the overall payroll cycle for simplicity of illustration. The subcycle examined involves data capture and batch preparation in the computerized batch-oriented payroll cycle of a small manufacturing concern. A flowchart of the major processing and control activities (denoted by numbered arrows) comprising the subcycle is presented in Figure 5. In addition, a preliminary review of internal control strengths and weaknesses has been performed by the auditor.

During this preliminary review, the auditor identifies the major errors and irregularities that could occur in the subcycle, and key controls that might prevent or detect these errors and irregularities. These preliminary review findings are summarized in Table 1. On an overall basis, the auditor is satisfied with the system of internal controls in the payroll cycle and plans to place reliance on certain key controls in order to reduce the extent of substantive testing to be performed. Of course, this planned reliance is contingent upon satisfactory compliance results.

Role of Simulation

The next step in the audit process involves the development of a tentative audit strategy for the subcycle. The simulation tool will be used to assist the auditor in making decisions regarding two specific aspects of this task:

1. The auditor has determined that compliance tests are necessary to assess the reliability of the foreman review control. The simulation tool will be used to assist the auditor in determining the tolerable error rate for this control, a critical judgment in determining the appropriate sample size for compliance testing.
2. The simulation tool will be used to investigate the audit exposure that might result from collusive activity between the foreman and the individual responsible for transaction coding.

FIGURE 5   Flowchart of Payroll Subcycle

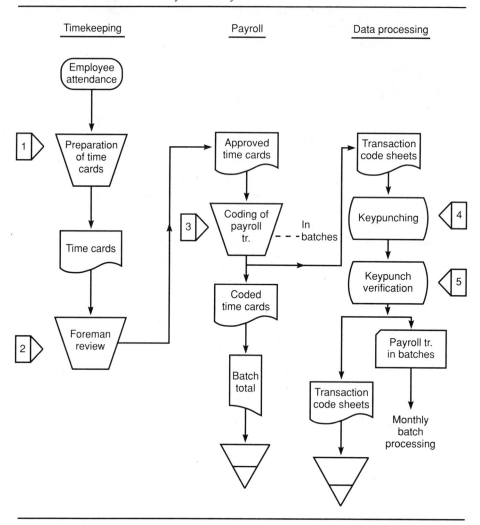

Internal Control Model Specifications

The initial task to be accomplished in using the simulation tool is to develop input specifications to model the internal control system. Based on the sub-cycle flowchart presented in Figure 5 and the preliminary review finding summarized in Table 1, the auditor configured a conceptual model of the system consisting of six processing steps, two control steps, and two branch steps. This conceptual model is diagrammed in Figure 2 and represents the major processing steps and control steps performed in the subcycle for each em-

TABLE 1 Summary of Errors and Controls

Activity No.	Error Code	Description of Error or Irregularity	Identified Controls	Activity No.	Control Code	Errors Controlled	Control Description
1	E1	Incorrect hours recorded on time card	C1	2	C1	E1, E2	Foreman review of time cards
	E2	Time recorded for fictitious employee	C2	5	C2	E5	Keypunch verification
2	E3	Fraudulent modification of time cards by foreman	NONE*				
3	E4	Transaction coding error	NONE*				
4	E5	Keypunch error	C2				

* No controls identified in this subcycle.

ployee during a given payroll period. Many of the processing steps (labeled P1—P6) and control steps (labeled C1—C2) correspond directly with symbols on the system flowchart.

Input specifications were then formulated to define (1) the attributes of the 10 internal control model steps depicted in Figure 2, and (2) the scope of the simulation activity to be performed. Auditor judgment was involved in several aspects of this formulation process. The necessary auditor judgments were made by consulting previous payroll cycle working papers and preliminary evidence already gathered in the current examination. For example, based on a simple analysis of payroll account activity for the current year, the auditor approximated payroll transaction activity to be a normal distribution with a mean of $500, a standard deviation of $50, a minimum value of $300, and a maximum value of $700. Error and exception (deviation) occurrence rates were estimated from compliance testing results documented in payroll working papers of the previous year. Similarly, error amount distribution types and parameters were estimated based on compliance error analysis results of the previous year. The input specifications developed by the auditor for the initial five model steps are illustrated in Table 2.

The input specifications appearing in Table 2 are interpreted as follows. Processing step P1 produces the error E1. The expected occurrence rate of E1 is 10 percent. The dollar amount of exposure from E1 occurrence is assumed to be normally distributed with a mean of $50 and a standard deviation of $30. Similarly, processing step P2 produces error E2 with an estimated occurrence rate of 1 percent. The dollar amount of exposure from an E2 occurrence is uniformly distributed between $5 and $40. Control step C1 is capable of detecting E1 and E2 occurrences and activates branch step B1 when a detection is made. If C1 fails to detect an existing occurrence of E1 or E2 in a given transaction, the control deviation X1 occurs. The occurrence

TABLE 2 Typical Input Specifications

Step	Functions	Potential Deviation	Estimated Occurrence Rate Deviation	Error Amount Distribution and Parameters
P1	Processing step	E1	10%	N (50, 30)
P2	Processing step	E2	1%	U (5–40)
C1	Control step for E1 and E2	X1	6%	—
B1	Branch step—branch to P3 activated by C1	—	—	—
P3	Corrects for E1 and E2	—	5%	—

rate of X1 is estimated to be 6 percent. If an occurrence of E1 or E2 is detected by C1 in a given transaction, branch step B1 will cause the transaction to be directed to P3 for error correction.

Simulation Experiments

Two sets of simulation experiments were conducted. Each set of experiments involved an iterative strategy in which the auditor observed the sensitivity of final balance reliabilities for key processing and control steps over different error and exception rate settings. The initial set of simulation experiments was performed to assist the auditor in establishing the maximum acceptable "tolerable rate of errors" for the foreman review control (C2). The results of these simulation experiments are presented in Table 3.

The strategy employed by the auditor in conducting these experiments was to observe the sensitivity of the final balance error amounts of E1 and E2 errors (both detectable by C1), while the specified failure rate for C1 was allowed to vary from 6 percent to 16 percent. All other error and exception rate settings were unchanged during these six simulation experiments. The auditor has established a materiality threshold for errors E1 and E2 of $2,500. Table 3 is interpreted as follows. When the auditor specified the failure rate for control C1 to be 6 percent, the resulting final balance error amounts for errors E1 and E2 totaled only $100 ($50 and $50), which is far below the stated materiality threshold for these errors. The highest allowable failure rate resulting in combined E1 and E2 error amounts less than the $2,500 threshold is 12 percent, which produces $2,390 of E1 and E2 errors. Based on these simulation results and given a materiality threshold for these error types of $2,500, the auditor concluded that the maximum tolerable rate of

TABLE 3   Simulation Results without Collusion

Results for Control Step C1—Foreman Review		
	Resulting Final Balance Error Amount	
Control Failure Rate	E1	E2
6%	$ 50	$ 50
8	250	60
10	1,250	75
*12	2,300	90
14	3,100	120
16	3,900	130

* Denotes maximum "tolerable rate of errors," given materiality assumptions for E1 and E2 errors.

errors for this control would be established as 12 percent. Hence, a tolerable rate of errors of 12 percent was employed in determining the appropriate sample size for compliance testing of this key control.

The second set of simulation experiments included collusion between the foreman and the transaction coder. The collusive activity under investigation involved the initiation and approval of a time card for a fictitious employee by the foreman, for which the transaction coder had caused a fraudulent master file employee number to be entered. Modeling this collusive activity required two input specification changes. First, the one percent occurrence rate for processing step P2 (time recorded for fictitious employee) was modified to include a systematic 50th transaction as well as randomly at the originally specified rate (one percent). Second, control step C1 (Foreman review) was altered to include collusion with the modified step P2 occurring at a rate of 30 percent. Thus, X1 exceptions would occur 30 percent of the time the current transaction has an E2 error, as well as randomly at the originally specified rate (six percent). A collusion rate of 30 percent was selected to represent a rate sufficiently high to generate a material embezzlement amount, yet low enough to avoid direct implication of the conspirators, should the fraud be discovered.

With these system modifications, a second set of simulation experiments was performed. The simulation results indicated that the presence of collusion significantly reduced the probable final balance reliability of step P2 (time recorded for fictitious employee) and produced an increased exposure due to E2 errors of approximately $8,500. Because this exposure was considered material and no compensating controls were identified, the auditor concluded that if foreman verification was to be relied upon, then the tentative audit plan must be modified to include more stringent compliance testing for this key control.

Summary

A possible use of the simulation model in a typical payroll audit situation was described. The simulation was employed by the auditor to investigate the sensitivity of expected final balance error amounts for two error types to varying reliability assumptions for a key control in the subcycle. These sensitivity analysis results were used by the auditor to establish the maximum "tolerable rate of errors" for the specific control, given a dollar materiality threshold for the cycle. Without the simulation tool, the auditor would have been required to make this determination based entirely upon professional judgment.

The simulation tool was also used by the auditor to explore the potential audit exposure that might result from a specific collusion possibility observed in the payroll cycle. The simulation model was modified for this purpose by simply altering the original input specifications for two model steps. Thus, the simulation model provides a means of investigating the probable audit exposure from numerous fraudulent schemes that might occur. For complex systems, such schemes might be difficult, if not impossible, to appraise subjectively.

IMPLEMENTATION CONSIDERATIONS AND EXTENSIONS

The decision aid offered here, as well as all other objective approaches to internal control evaluation, attempts to model the characteristics of real world systems. These models are capable of abstracting only those elements which leave a documentary audit trail. Other control elements, such as segregation of duties, are assumed to influence the auditor's assignment of potential error rates and control failure rates, and are not directly modeled.

Another consideration regards the assignment of error rates and control failure rates. It is anticipated that initial assignments for these parameters can be made based upon data available in the prior year's working papers for most clients. For example, attribute sampling results from prior years could be used for many of these parameters. Note that it is not necessary that these assignments be precise because a primary utility of using SIM is to better acquaint the auditor with system relationships by providing a facility to perform sensitivity analyses for approximating tolerable rates for these parameters.

Although the simulation approach proposed here does not require computer programming expertise, it does require a moderate degree of modeling skill. Given the analytical nature of the audit process itself, it is anticipated that most auditors would have little difficulty in characterizing internal control systems as networks of processing, control, and branch steps.

The simulation model described here may be viewed as a prototype and can be extended in several respects. First, other types of processing steps (such as a merge step) can be implemented to provide added modeling flexibility. Second, more detailed final account balance error profiles might be produced. Errors affecting multiple account balances might be allowed. Finally, the model might be expanded to incorporate errors and control failures which are nonmonetary and do not have a direct final account balance impact.

CONCLUSION

This paper proposes an audit simulation model designed to assist an auditor in evaluating the reliability of complex internal control systems. The simulation model is readily adaptable to different audit applications. The audit model provides a risk-free environment in which an auditor can explore numerous internal control relationships before audit resources are committed. The increased understanding of system reliability gained through use of the simulation model can produce efficient and effective audit strategies for the evaluation of internal controls.

The simulation model is unique in that the effect of collusion between internal control system elements can be quantitatively measured. Unlike previous approaches, system elements are not assumed to be independent and may be interdependent. In addition, systematic error patterns, which are often associated with irregularities, can be incorporated in the model as appropriate. Thus, the simulation allows the auditor to conveniently model and evaluate the audit consequences of numerous potential collusion/irregularity possibilities.

Finally, the simulation model generates objective evidence which can help support the auditor's final conclusions regarding internal control. This important documentation can assist auditors in meeting documentation requirements. It is important to note that this simulation is not a substitute for the professional judgment of the auditor. Rather, it is a unique tool which provides quantitative objective evidence; thus enabling the auditor to exercise judgment in a manner that is more efficient, effective, and defensible.

APPENDIX

Illustration of Transaction Processing and Auditor Specifications

Figure A presents a simple system configuration which will be used to illustrate this simulated processing activity. This simple system consists of four processing steps (one a reprocessing step), two control steps, and two branch steps and exhibits all primary features of the simulation. Typical auditor specifications for each step are presented in Figure B. Assuming that a flowchart (see Figure 5) and a summary of errors and key controls (see Table 1) have already been developed, it is estimated that a SIM model for this application could be developed by an auditor in approximately one hour. The computer processing time required for each simulation experiment is very small and interactive response time on a mainframe computer is measured in seconds. Memory requirements and other related computer costs are negligible.

The auditor specifications necessary to represent this system appear in Figure B and are interpreted as follows. Processing step #1 (PS #1) produces the deviation Error #1. The estimated occurrence rate for Error #1 is 10 percent. The dollar amount of Error #1 is assumed to be normally distributed with a mean of $50 and a standard deviation of $30. Similarly, processing Step #2 (PS #2) produces Error #2. The estimated occurrence rate for Error #2 is 8 percent. However, a dependence (collusion) exists between PS #2 and PS #1, so that if an Error #1 is present in the current transaction, the occurrence rate for Error #2 increases to 30 percent. The dollar amount of Error #2 is uniformly distributed between $5 and $40. Control step #1 (CS #1) is capable of detecting Error #1 and activates branch step #1 (BS #1)

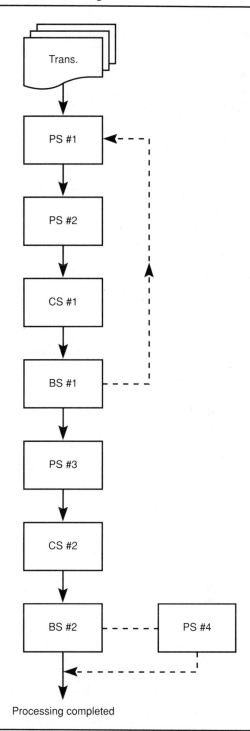

FIGURE B   Typical Step Specifications

Step	Function	Potential deviation	Estimated occurrence rate or pattern	Error amount distribution and parameters
PS #1	Processing step	Error #1	10%	N (50, 30)
PS #2	Processing step	Error #2	8% (30% if Error #1 present)	U (5,40)
CS #1	Control step for Error #1	Exc #1	5%	—
BS #1	Branch step—branch to PS #1 activated by CS #1	—	—	—
CS #2	Control step for Error #2	Exc #2	6% (20% if Exc #1 present)	—
PS #3	Processing step	Error #3	Cyclic pattern of every 25th transaction	N (25, 50)
BS #2	Branch step—branch to PS #1 activated by CS #2	—	—	—
PS #4	Reprocessing step—corrects for Error #2	Error #4	20%	—

when a detection is made. If CS #1 fails to detect an existing Error #1 in the current transaction, the deviation (Exc #1) occurs. Exc #1 has an estimated occurrence rate of 5 percent. The remaining steps are interpreted in a similar fashion. Note that Error #3 (deviation produced by PS #3) occurs on every 25th transaction, that a dependency exists between CS #2 and CS #1, and that PS #4 is a reprocessing step capable of correcting Error #2.

In order to demonstrate the transaction processing steps performed by the simulation, a walk-through of the processing for a typical transaction through the system depicted in Figure A will be presented. Transaction #1, representing the first economic event affecting the account balance under examination, enters the system and proceeds to step PS #1. The simulation randomly determines that no error occurs at this step for the transaction. Processing for the transaction then continues at PS #2, where the simulation randomly determines that an Error #2 of $35 occurs and becomes associated with the transaction. Next, the transaction proceeds to CS #1 where the simulation determines that no exception occurs. Note that an Exc #1 (with no dollar impact on the final balance) could have occurred for this transaction, even though an Error #1 was not present. Since BS #1 was not activated by CS #1, no branching occurs at BS #1 and the transaction proceeds to PS #3, where the simulation determines that Error #3 does not occur.

Processing for the transaction continues at CS #2, which detects (Exc #2 does not occur) the Error #2 already associated with the transaction, and activates BS #2. The now-activated BS #2 then causes a branch to PS #4. Finally, the simulation determines that an Error #4 occurs at PS #4 (i.e., Error #2 is not corrected). This completes processing for the transaction. In summary, the only deviation that occurred for this transaction was Error #2. Since this deviation, although detected by CS #2, was not corrected by PS #4, an Error #2 of $35 will appear in the final balance for the account. Note that if an Error #1 had occurred and been detected by CS #1, the transaction would have been routed to PS #1 for additional processing. In this case, upon leaving PS #1, the transaction would again be processed sequentially by PS #2, CS #1, BS #1, etc.

Notes

1. SIM was developed using the PASCAL programming language.
2. Bodnar (1975) identifies a number of behavioral problems related to the application of reliability theory to internal control systems which involve human elements. These limitations relate to all objective decision approaches, including the present study.
3. For example, the Johnson, Leitch, and Neter study, which was based on data from one Big Eight CPA firm (analysis of errors found in 55 accounts receivable audits and 26 inventory audits), indicated the following:
    a. There is great variability in error rates for different types of audits; specifically, error rates in inventory audits tend to be substantially higher than for accounts receivable audits.
    b. Error rates in inventory and receivables audits may be higher for larger accounts and for accounts with larger line items than for other accounts.
    c. Most errors in receivables audits are overstatement errors; while in inventory audits, overstatement and understatement errors are more balanced.

References

Ahituv, Niv; J. Halpern; and H. Will. "Audit Planning: An Algorithmic Approach." *Contemporary Accounting Research*, Fall 1985, pp. 95–110.

Bailey, A. D., Jr.; G. L. Duke; J. Gerlach; C. Ko; R. Meservy; and A. B. Whinston. "TICOM and the Analysis of Internal Controls." *The Accounting Review*, April 1985, pp. 186–201.

Bodnar, G. "Reliability Modeling of Internal Control Systems." *The Accounting Review*, October 1975, pp. 747–757.

Burns, D. C., and J. K. Loebbecke. "Internal Control Evaluation: How the Computer Can Help." *Journal of Accountancy*, August 1975, pp. 60–70.

Carmichael, D. R. "Behavioral Hypotheses of Internal Control." *The Accounting Review*, April 1970, pp. 235–245.

Cushing, B. E. "A Mathematical Approach to the Analysis and Design of Internal Control Systems." *The Accounting Review*, January 1974, pp. 24–41.

Grimlund, R. A. "An Integration of Internal Control System and Account Balance Evidence." *Journal of Accounting Research*, Autumn 1982, pp. 316–342.

Hamlen, S. "A Chance-Constrained Mixed Integer Programming Model for Internal Control Design." *The Accounting Review*, October 1980, pp. 578–593.

Johnson, J. R.; R. A. Leitch; and J. Neter. "Characteristics of Errors in Accounts Receivable and Inventory Audits." *The Accounting Review*, April 1981, pp. 270–293.

Knechel, W. R. "A Simulation Model for Evaluating Accounting System Reliability." *Auditing: A Journal of Practice and Theory*, Spring 1985a, pp. 38–62.

———. "An Analysis of Alternative Error Assumptions in Modeling the Reliability of Accounting Systems." *Journal of Accounting Research*, Spring 1985b, pp. 194–212.

Leslie, D. A. "Discussant's Response to 'Computing Upper Error Limits in Dollar Unit Sampling,' " in B. E. Cushing and J. L. Krogstad (eds.), *Frontiers of Auditing Research*, Studies in Accounting No. 7, The University of Texas at Austin, 1977, pp. 183–194.

Neter, J. and J. K. Loebbecke. *Behavior of Major Statistical Estimators in Sampling Accounting Populations—An Empirical Study* (AICPA, 1975).

Ramage, J. G.; A. M. Krieger; and L. L. Spero. "An Empirical Study of Error Characteristics in Audit Populations." *Studies on Auditing: Selections from Research Opportunities in Auditing Program*, supplement to the *Journal of Accounting Research*, 1979, pp. 72–102.

Stratton, W. O. "Accounting Systems: The Reliability Approach to Internal Control Evaluation." *Decision Sciences*, January 1981, pp. 51–67.

Weber, R. "Auditor Decision Making on Overall System Reliability: Accuracy, Concensus, and the Usefulness of a Simulation Decision Aid." *Journal of Accounting Research*, Autumn 1978, pp. 368–388.

Yu, S., and J. Neter. "A Stochastic Model of the Internal Control System." *Journal of Accounting Research*, Autumn 1973, pp. 273–295.

Reading 6–4

INTERNAL CONTROL IN THE MICROCOMPUTER ENVIRONMENT

By Christopher Wolfe and Casper E. Wiggins, Jr.

As the internal auditor walked into the accounting department of one of his firm's eastern subsidiaries, he immediately noticed the widespread use of microcomputers. He also noticed some of the machines had modems, which allowed the users to access the firm's mainframe computer. Numerous floppy disks were lying about in disarray.

Curious about the importance of the data or programs the disks might contain, the auditor questioned one of the staff accountants who was at that moment working on a microcomputer. The staffer told the auditor the depart-

---

This article was reprinted with permission from the December 1986 issue of *Internal Auditor*, published by The Institute of Internal Auditors, Inc.

ment was using microcomputers for many of their processing needs. But the really beautiful part, the staffer explained, was the ability to download data from the mainframe into the microcomputer. This circumvented the need to manually type data files.

The auditor then asked if most of the disks lying around contained financial data from the company's computer files. The staff accountant replied, "Of course, this is the accounting department." (This story is based on a real incident which has essentially the same set of facts.)

Clearly, most firms would not willingly permit just anyone to browse through its computer files. In fact, firms with large central computers, or mainframes, go to great lengths to guard their data by using fireproof vaults and strict procedures for their file library.

Microcomputers, however, are a different animal. In the opening story, the firm had distributed data and processing power but had no effective control over either. This may have occurred because management viewed microcomputers as autonomous calculators meant to save the accountants from mundane calculations. The microcomputers were not autonomous, however. They had become an important part of the company's data processing system and needed to be controlled just as other elements of the system were controlled. Although there are risks present in a microcomputer system, there are also microcomputer controls which can be relied on to reduce these risks.

MICROSYSTEM RISKS

Most firms with mainframe computers realized long ago the unique risks associated with automated information systems. This has led to the development and implementation of sophisticated controls for mainframe systems. Microcomputer systems, however, generate risks similar not only to those in a mainframe environment, but also to those specific to a microsystem. Firms with no mainframe experience may not recognize the basic control risks in a newly acquired microsystem. Firms with mainframe computers, on the other hand, may not realize the unique risks inherent in their expanding use of microcomputers.

General Risks. The general risks and exposures which arise when a manual system is upgraded to a computerized system typically result from the nature of the computer itself. The computer's ability to act on large amounts of data and to follow instructions precisely, all in a "black-box" environment, are characteristics unique to an automated system. The control matrix (see box) outlines the general computer risks discussed below and suggests controls which reduce the risks.

Recurring Errors. In manual systems, an error is usually caught before that same error is repeated hundreds of times. This often is not the case in a computerized environment. A computer is a consistent machine, and, if it is instructed incorrectly, it will perform a series of incorrect steps repetitively,

Control Matrix for General Computer Risks

Controls / Risk	Recurring Errors	Concentration of Data	Functional Concentration	Input Risks	Output Risks	Processing Risks
Documentation	✓			✓	✓	✓
Testing	✓					
Separation of duties		✓	✓			
Audit trail						✓
Control totals				✓		✓
Record counts				✓		
Reasonableness check					✓	
Cross-footings						✓
Limit test				✓		✓
Check digits				✓		✓
File labels				✓		
Supervision			✓			

causing a proliferation of errors. Similarly, if errors occur in a subsystem, they will affect all subsequent subsystems which depend upon the initial error-ridden subsystem for data. Again, this is a risk a manual system might circumvent simply because a manual analysis would probably occur at each subsystem entry point.

Concentration of Data. Computerized systems allow large amounts of data to be saved on compact storage mediums such as tapes and disks. This concentrates information, triggering several risks: data duplication, destruction, and theft. Data which is stored in a computer or on some magnetic storage medium can usually be duplicated very easily. Files can be misappropriated or misused without proper controls. Data concentration also increases the risks of physical destruction since a small mishap can quickly destroy a large amount of information. In a manual system, files are typically stored in the departments which use the information, and individual items are retained on separate paper documents. This control, inherent in a manual situation, is lost in a computerized system.

Functional Concentration. Just as data is concentrated in a computerized system, so are system duties. Procedures performed by an entire department in a manual system may become the responsibility of one computer program, possibly controlled by one person. This can result in a critical loss of traditional separation of duties. Separation of duties, the most fundamental internal control device, takes on an entirely different complexion in a computerized environment.

Input, Processing, Output. Every accounting information system, whether manual or computerized, goes through the steps of input, processing, and output. A computerized system, however, varies radically from a manual system at every step. Data must always be put into machine-readable form for an automated system to function. This conversion process can create errors which may not be detected by the system. Computer processing takes place in a "black box" that is invisible to the human eye. Embedded data errors or incorrect programs can generate results which appear correct but may, in fact, be false.

Output in a computerized environment occurs at the end of the processing cycle, whereas in a manual system output may occur throughout the processing cycle. This means output, in an understandable form, must be distributed to all parties who need the information. Any breakdown in the clarity or distribution of output negates much of the value of an automated processing system.

Special Risks. These risks represent items often overlooked in a microsystem. They are more critical in a microcomputer environment than in either a mainframe or minicomputer environment because of the size, cost, and psychology surrounding microcomputers.

Technology. All computer systems must deal with advancing technology. Questions regarding hardware and software features and compatibility must always be addressed. The low cost of microcomputers makes them easy to purchase, and this often precludes the answering of fundamental preacquisition questions. Authorization to spend $2,000 on a microcomputer is a low-level decision which may have high-level ramifications.

System Access. Mainframe systems may be controlled by the data processing department, but microcomputers are controlled by their users. Very few micros have software which requires users to enter a password. Anyone who can physically gain access to the computer can usually get into it. Since control over an organization's micros is not embodied in one department, how they are used, who uses them, and what they are used for vary not only between departments but within departments.

System Failure. Physical hardware backup and file recovery methods are a common aspect of most mainframe systems. Microsystems rarely have backup hardware. This, of course, can be crucial in a small business which depends on its microcomputers for the handling of routine accounting transactions. Backup hardware is also necessary in large firms where dependence on microcomputers virtually negates manual backup procedures.

A system of data recovery is also necessary with a microsystem. Most firms have no specific file backup requirements for microcomputer files. System failure in the microcomputer environment is just as likely or even more so than in the mainframe environment. The results are just as devastating.

Templates. Much of the work done on microcomputers revolves around proprietary software packages designed to handle general business needs. These software packages often allow customization or template building so that standard problems can be solved without reentering program parameters for each problem occurrence. Templates then are, in effect, software. Consequently, templates should be tested, controlled, and documented as software. The risk of not treating templates as software is the generation of output which appears correct but is not.

INTERNAL CONTROL

Microsystems clearly need internal controls, but too much control may stifle the unique microcomputer operating environment. A major contribution of microcomputers is putting processing power in the hands of the information user. By too tightly controlling microcomputers, users may become reluctant to use microsystems to their fullest. This is not to suggest microsystems should be characterized by weak or ineffective controls, but that the control procedures should attempt to ensure data and system integrity without suffocating the system. Of course, microsystems vary from firm to firm and even within firms, but the control design must account for the specific needs of each microsystem.

The most important controls in an automated system are accounting controls. Accounting controls operate to safeguard assets and to ensure the reliability of data. These controls are categorized as general controls and application controls. General controls transcend application boundaries and apply to all computer applications. Application controls, on the other hand, relate to specific applications and are usually concerned with the input, processing, and output of a specific job. Both general and application controls should exist in a system in a complementary fashion.

General Controls.   These relate to the microsystem as a whole, and provide for the protection of the system and the general reliability of the data it produces. General controls form the basis of a microsystem's control structure.

Physical.   Microcomputers are small, and they do not have to be placed in special rooms with false floors and constant air conditioning. In fact, the positioning of most microcomputers is one based purely on convenience. Poor physical positioning of microcomputers can trigger two risks: system access and system failure. If microcomputer hardware is left unprotected, it is extremely difficult to control who uses the system. Also, the proper positioning of microcomputers can reduce exposure to physical hazards such as water, fire, or theft. Finally, elements such as dust and static electricity should be controlled as they too affect system performance.

Probably the best physical control for a microsystem is a designated microcomputer room. To reduce the risk of water damage, this room should not have a sprinkler system. The microcomputer room should not be carpeted to minimize static electricity problems, and special cleaning precautions should be used to reduce dust. Access to the computer room can be controlled if the firm desires. However, movement of the microcomputers from this room should be forbidden. The use of a separate computer room allows data files and application programs to be more tightly controlled since their use occurs in only one location. The centralized control of a specific computer room for microcomputers reduces both system access risks and system failure risks.

The computer room solution, although effective, may not be a realistic solution for all firms. If this is the case, alternative measures must be taken to protect the system. The risk of water damage can be reduced by plastic covers. These covers can also reduce dust damage if used whenever the machine is not in operation. Software requiring passwords can be used. Physically fastening microcomputer components to large objects, such as a desk, can help prevent theft. Library procedures can be implemented so that data and programs are more tightly controlled. The personal nature of the microcomputer does not have to be destroyed in order to control it.

Separation of Duties.   Separation of duties is an old accounting control used by most firms in one form or another. Microsystems often have the effect of combining duties in one program or a group of programs used or controlled by one person. This concentration of duties increases the potential for fraud and reduces the likelihood of detecting recurring errors.

The standard separation of recording assets and controlling assets, of course, continues to be important. However, in an automated environment this may be even more significant than in a manual system. It is generally agreed that an expert programmer can modify a program in a virtually undetectable manner. The only thing stopping the programmer, then, is gaining access to the assets once the records have been modified.

A person need not be an expert programmer to modify data files or a program, especially in the user friendly environment of a microcomputer. As such, duties must be separated in a microsystem to prevent asset misappropriation. This may require increased employee training on the microcomputers, but effective separation of critical functions can prove invaluable.

Separation of duties can be achieved in a microcomputer environment by separating the functions which surround the processing of data. For instance, data input and output analysis should be performed by different parties or individuals. In a microsystem, this may mean that output from one subsystem is checked for reasonableness before it becomes input into another subsystem.

Functions such as library file procedures, programming, and actual system use can be separated to increase internal control in the microcomputer environment. Separation of duties is an effective means of reducing the risks inherent in functional concentration and data concentration.

Backup. Record reconstruction is something relatively unique to computerized systems. Since all data is stored on either magnetic tape or disk, the propensity to lose that data is far greater in an automated environment. A system of backing up data files is necessary. In a microsystem, floppy disks can be backed up by making duplicate disks, while hard disks typically use a tape backup. The backup process in a microcomputer system is neither complex nor expensive, but it is necessary. The most important facets of data backup are a formal policy and compliance.

Backup hardware facilities may not seem pertinent for a microsystem. However, if a firm depends on their microcomputers for payroll, accounts receivable, or any accounting subsystem, the loss of their microcomputer can mean chaos. Backup facilities can be as simple as a personal microcomputer at the owner's home or as structured as a formal agreement with a local computer dealer. The sudden loss of a firm's microsystem need not have disastrous consequences.

Documentation. System documentation is recognized as an important aspect of mainframe computer control. Documentation is also important in a microsystem. Unfortunately, this is one of the most overlooked areas in microcomputer control. In most instances, documentation consists of nothing more than program manuals purchased with software or user guides which accompany hardware. This documentation is often inadequate since generic software is usually modified for specific uses. Templates, built with generic spreadsheet packages, need documentation. Software developed internally should include a formalized documentation phase.

Run manuals for system hardware, internally produced, can greatly facilitate computer use. Microsystem documentation reduces errors, communicates system standards, and generally makes the computer easier to use.

Application Controls. These are job specific. Because application controls relate to specific functions, they vary between functions. As was previously mentioned, application controls usually relate to the input, processing, and output of specific applications. They do not take the place of general controls. In fact, strong general controls can make up for weaker application controls; however, the converse is not usually true. The need for application controls depends upon each unique situation and must be so implemented.

Audit Trail. The development of an audit trail is a basic necessity. In a computerized system the audit trail can become disjointed due to internal processing by the computer. Common audit trail problems in a computerized environment include:

- Source documents are not generated or are discarded after initial input.
- Journals are not generated by the system. Entries are made directly into the ledger.
- Computer files and data bases are not visible and do not allow for a clear tracing of transactions through all parts of a system.
- Sequencing and processing cannot be observed since they occur inside the computer.

The problem of a disjointed audit trail must be overcome by system design. The audit trail must be consciously built into the processing cycle. Building the audit trail may require a program to take steps or generate output only for audit trail determination. Audit trail provisions may degrade system performance, but a good audit trail is an essential control element.

Input, Output. Input controls attempt to ensure accuracy. Microsystems can benefit from several simple input control procedures such as control totals, record counts, and manual editing. Control totals can be used to verify input. Typically, an adding machine tape is run on some aspect of the input prior to processing. The computer calculates a similar control total internally. These totals are compared and any discrepancy investigated.

Control totals can be dollar figures or they can be meaningless figures, such as the summation of a series of invoice numbers. A record count is another simple input control. This can be a manual count compared to a computer count of input documents or a check of serial numbers related to the input documents. Manual editing of input data can also be performed to ensure input accuracy. Some form of input control should be used for each application program.

Output controls have similar purposes, and may offset some input controls. Probably the most needed control in the microcomputer application environment, as far as output is concerned, is a reasonableness check. Simply because something comes out of a computer is no indication it is correct. Output should be scrutinized for correctness.

Processing. Mainframes often have complex processing controls because of the large volume of transactions processed. Microcomputers, on the other hand, do not usually have extensive processing controls. Depending on the importance of the application program, microcomputers need some controls which check the processing function.

Cross-footing is a simple yet effective processing control that works just as well in a computerized system as in a manual system. Check digits are also a good processing control designed to validate data which has been input. Check digits involve adding a digit to the end of a number string. The digit is a mathematical result of some formula into which the number string is entered. If the number string entered generates a check digit different than the one entered, then the number string has probably been entered incorrectly.

Other input validation processing controls are a limit test and valid-character set test. A limit test checks certain fields to determine if their amounts have exceeded a preset limit. This is particularly useful in payroll applications where limits might be set on employee pay. A valid-character set check simply ensures that there are numbers, not letters or other symbols, where numbers are supposed to be.

Finally, the use of both internal file labels and external file labels is extremely important. In the microcomputer environment data files are often stored on floppy disks. These disks should be appropriately labeled on the outside, and the first record in each file should also identify the file. This simple control can ensure that the proper data is being processed. Microcomputer processing controls should be used to ensure the accuracy of the data being processed.

CONCLUSION

Microcomputer technology is new, and many firms are just beginning to experience the vast productivity gains possible with a microsystem or a group of microcomputer subsystems. In this rush to put microcomputers to work, control factors surrounding the use of microcomputers are often forsaken, but an effective control system can guard assets, assure data integrity, and produce reliable outputs. The tenets of internal control apply as strongly to microcomputer systems as they do to any other system. The long-term effectiveness of microcomputers depends on management's ability to control them.

Reading 6–5

DEVELOPING A SYSTEM OF INTERNAL CONTROL FOR MICROCOMPUTERS

By Alan I. Blankley, Tarek S. Amer, and Craig E. Bain

The Foreign Corrupt Practices Act of 1977 inspired managers to vigorously pursue cost-effective systems of internal control. Although many accounting organizations had an effective system of internal controls on manual accounting systems, technology ushered in computerized mainframe accounting systems. Then, just as management found cost-effective controls over mainframe systems, microcomputers became more powerful, useful, and popular. The technological advances evident in computer systems have changed the nature of internal accounting control, and managers are struggling to keep up.

Just how serious this problem is has been documented in a survey conducted by Ernst & Whinney (now Ernst & Young) during a Computer Security Institute Conference. The survey revealed that many organizations' security risks had risen substantially during the previous five years. More than half of the respondents reported financial losses through their computer systems, with 15 percent having losses greater than $50,000 and 3 percent having losses greater that $1 million. Although computers have dramatically improved the speed and efficiency of most accounting functions, they have also increased opportunities for errors and fraud.

What is particularly noticeable about the issue of internal accounting control is not how computers have changed it but how the microcomputer has changed it yet again. Because they are easy to use, powerful, and often portable and because data and audit trails in this kind of environment are difficult to control, microcomputers have created additional security concerns for managers.

Although mainframe security controls alone are inadequate protection for microcomputers, it is important to recognize that many similarities exist between the micro and mainframe environments and that many of the internal accounting controls used for mainframes apply equally well to microcomputers. By using as many of the established controls as possible, a firm can lower its security risks and minimize its costs. It is equally important, however, to recognize the unique risks associated with micros. This article first discusses the risks and controls similar to both mainframe and microcomputing environments, then addresses the risks and controls unique to microcomputers.

RISKS SIMILAR TO BOTH MAINFRAMES AND MICROS

Most risks associated with computerized accounting systems usually stem from one of three sources: errors, fraud, or general security threats. These risks are not unique to computerized accounting, but they are exaggerated by the lack of a paper audit trail and by the nature of the computer itself.

Errors.   Because the computer acts logically and can process thousands of bits of information per second, there is a common risk of errors appearing consistently throughout accounting information. If an instruction in a program is incorrect, the computer will process accurate information incorrectly, spreading errors as it goes. The same holds true if any information is incorrectly entered; in both cases, errors spread instantly through the data. The risk of errors threatening the integrity of the accounting information results from either input errors or programming errors, which in turn result in processing errors, and is as likely to occur in the micro environment as in the mainframe environment.

Fraud.   Lindsay Mercer identifies two types of fraud. The smash-and-grab perpetrator commits only one or two fraudulent acts, each one of a large monetary value, and then absconds with the proceeds before the act is discovered. The second type is the drip perpetrator, who commits many separate fraudulent acts over a long period of time, each of relatively little value but whose sum is large. For example, the computer programmer instructs the computer to enter all rounding values from interest-bearing accounts past the third digit into his own account. Fraud does not necessarily have to be so dramatic. Any attempt to manipulate data or disrupt accounting controls is fraudulent activity. The FBI estimates that the average payoff for reported computer fraud is approximately $600,000. With networks, communications packages, and the terminal emulation capabilities of microcomputers, the risk of fraud is as real for micros as it is for mainframes.

General Threats to Security.   These threats are common to both mainframe and microcomputer environments. Such risks as a reduced or eliminated audit trail, computer viruses, system failure, unauthorized program changes, lack of separation of duties, and unauthorized system access all present general threats to an organization's assets and information.

CONTROLS APPLICABLE TO BOTH MAINFRAMES AND MICROS

The controls useful for reducing the preceding risks can be divided into general controls and application controls. General controls are intended to protect the entire system and do not focus on any one specific function, as in controlling input functions. Although they are necessary, application controls are weaker than general controls. Strong application controls will not compensate for weak general controls, but strong general controls can usually compensate for weak application controls.

Personnel Control.   An important general control is for management to hire competent, trustworthy people and then adequately train them. An organization is only as strong as its employees. By checking references, by asking probing questions during interviews, by concerning themselves with a potential employee's character and integrity, managers can help ensure a reasonably secure environment. A security indoctrination program should be provided for new employees. It is important to stress the relevance of internal control and the necessity of adhering to the established system. By enlisting the cooperation of employees, an organization can protect itself from security breaches.

Segregation of Duties.   Segregating high-risk duties (e.g., controlling and recording assets) is a vital general control. Segregating duties in a computerized environment, however, becomes more difficult than in a manual environment because computers tend to combine duties into one program and data into one place. This situation makes separating duties even more important. Several computer functions should be kept apart: for example, those who write computer programs should not be allowed access to records; those responsible for data input should not be responsible for analyzing the output, and output should be checked against any source document available for accuracy before it is used in another part of the system; and those responsible for handling inventories and shipping orders should not have access to customer records.

Rotation of Duties.   Like separating duties, rotating duties helps overcome the concentration of functions and data inherent in computerized accounting systems. Requiring periodic vacations or rotating workstations can discourage fraudulent activity and reveal attempts at fraud.

Access Controls.   It is necessary to create an environment in which damage, system failure, and theft are unlikely, and it is necessary to restrict access to computers and data to authorized personnel only. Both mainframes and microcomputers need a congenial environment. Although micros do not require the false floors or constant air conditioning that many mainframes do, both types of computers should be kept free of dust, static electricity, and food or drink, and should have some sort of electrical surge protection device. In addition, an alternate power supply should be available to protect data.

More important, however, is the necessity of restricting access to the computing system to authorized users only. Varying degrees in controlling access to the system exist. In situations in which the data is vital to the security and survival of the firm, the computer should be kept in a separate, locked, and perhaps even guarded room, allowing access only to persons with appropriate authorization. In situations in which data is less sensitive, it may be sufficient to keep the computer in a highly visible part of the office so that managers can see who is using it or, in the case of micros, have the equipment at the desks of authorized personnel only.

Access to the data must be protected. Although passwords are the most common tool employed to restrict access to data, they are far from infallible. Passwords are predictable, forgotten, and, if written down, can be found by someone else. Nevertheless, passwords offer limited effectiveness and should be used in most situations. In situations in which data is extremely sensitive, some sort of electronic scanning device should be used, instead of a password, to restrict access to data. For mainframes, such methods as signature verification, fingerprint scan, hand geometry, and voice print should be available; for micros, a coder-card system has been developed. This is a hardware device connected to the micro through a standard RS232 port. Authorized users are given a plastic card that identifies them to the computer and allows access.

As a corollary to access controls, managers can also employ such techniques as transaction logging, a software program that keeps a log of who uses the system, when, and for how long. This technique allows managers to periodically check for unauthorized use or any other sort of suspicious activity.

Data Control.   Data controls are general-purpose controls that allow managers to protect data and software. Such techniques as backup procedures and source code comparisons are the most common general-purpose controls. Unlike mainframes, with which backing up data is commonplace, microcomputer data is rarely backed up adequately. Although it is often bothersome to back data up, a single episode of lost data will serve as strong incentive to back up important information. A small batch file containing a backup routine run at least once a day is an inexpensive way to protect vital data. Once backed up, the tape or diskette should be stored in a safe place. The portability of diskettes in a microcomputing environment allows for easy off-site storage of backup copies.

Source code comparisons are detective in nature and are useful in determining whether a program has been modified. A copy of the original program's source code can be compared with another copy of the program to determine whether modifications have been made.

Application Controls

Application controls are aimed at specific functions of the system and cannot compensate for weak general controls. Application controls are usually unique to each situation and have to do with the input, processing, and output of a system. Most controls are written into the software.

Input. These controls are designed to restrict input and prevent input errors. For example, a template designed to ask certain questions and wait for specific answers will restrict the information that can be entered. Turnaround documents, or output documents from one part of the system serving as the input to another part, are another form of input control. Programmed controls that check for valid numbers, amounts, fields, and reasonable values are another form.

Processing. Processing controls should produce a clear audit trail. These controls require that a printout of all transactions run during the day be produced and that each transaction be cross-referenced to the general ledger accounts and source documents from which the information was drawn. This allows an auditor to trace from the general ledger through the processing step back to the source documents.

Output. Consistent reviews of the system output is the most effective output control. Exception and summary reports should be produced, reviewed for errors, and checked against any control totals produced earlier.

RISKS UNIQUE TO MICROCOMPUTERS

General and application controls can apply equally well to either a mainframe or microcomputer environment to safeguard accounting information and computer systems from the risks common to both types of environments. Because many of the risks are the same, the use of common controls is an efficient and inexpensive way to control such risks. These controls are, by themselves, not enough to safeguard assets in a microcomputer environment because the micro has unique risks.

Many controls used to secure a mainframe environment would either stifle the unique advantages that micros offer or would not be cost beneficial. Therefore, managers find themselves in a dilemma. With the increasing prevalence of computer crime and the fact that microcomputers make such crime easier to commit, it has become essential to implement effective internal control over microcomputers, yet often the best controls cost more than the assets they protect. By using cost-effective common controls, however, and employing several inexpensive hardware and software controls, a manager can protect the microcomputer and information assets efficiently and effectively.

Microcomputers present special control risks over and above their mainframe counterparts in two basic areas:

- Hardware—Because microcomputers are portable, they or any part of their peripheral equipment can easily be stolen or destroyed. It is difficult to restrict access to microcomputer equipment; it is simple to remove a hardware card from a unit or take a monitor home. With laptop computers the problem is compounded because many powerful laptops can now be hidden inside a briefcase.

- Data—Data and software are easy to access, modify, copy, or destroy and thus are very difficult to control. Anyone with enough computer know-how and access to a microcomputer can access all the information and software on the machine. Therefore, there is a danger that an employee might access unauthorized records and manipulate the data, or that a disgruntled employee might decide to reformat the machine's hard disk, destroying all software and data it contained,

CONTROLS UNIQUE TO THE MICROCOMPUTER ENVIRONMENT

Because microcomputers are relatively inexpensive, costing, on average, less than $5,000, it is not in the organization's best interest to go to elaborate lengths to protect the equipment. Creating a separate computing area with security personnel restricting access is like paying $10 to protect $5. What is needed is an inexpensive yet effective way to secure the equipment.

Locks can protect most of the microcomputer system. Keyboard locks are either built into the CPU and activated with a key, as on the IBM AT-style shell, or a cover that is placed over the keyboard. Either alternative is useful in discouraging unwanted entry to the system. Locks are available that prevent accidentally turning off the system and that secure the backplate or cover, preventing tampering inside the CPU. Although no security measure will prove effective against the most determined thieves, locks can deter most theft attempts because they make stealing difficult.

Locks are cost effective as well. Columbia University has used them in its public-access computer laboratory at a minimal expense. Managers should insist that employees lock keyboards when they finish work or put the laptop into a locked cabinet before they leave at night. Security over equipment is improved when employees get used to established procedures.

To discourage outright theft of the whole system, many businesses bolt the machine in place or attach monitors to desks with strong adhesives. The Houghton Mifflin publishing company has secured its new IBM PC ATs to steel carts to keep the machines portable. Physical system security and adequate application of locking mechanisms effectively reduce the risk of system theft.

Protecting data through software protection schemes for micros (including password programs, encryption programs, user definition software, and systems manager software) can make it difficult for unauthorized personnel to read sensitive data but cannot prevent someone from erasing a file. As a result, many firms advocate hardware data security products that combine several protection mechanisms because hardware is more difficult to violate than software.

Chips can contain algorithms, which encrypt data and prevent a hacker from tampering with it; passwords, if tampered with, will cause the machine to shut down. Boards are available that will authenticate or identify users on the basis of a password program: if the correct password is entered, the board will release control to the operating system; if not, the board shuts the machine down. When an employee is terminated, that person's access code should be removed from the system immediately.

Many hardware devices store a record of attempted entries. In addition, some boards will allow access but restrict the users to a predetermined directory or file. Depending on the sensitivity of the data on the microcomputers, these devices are worth the cost ($300 to $700).

Finally, there are several commonsense approaches to protecting data that cost virtually nothing. Such approaches may not stop a determined malcontent but are useful for preventing errors and removing the temptation from the average employee. When dealing with very sensitive data, the file can be copied from the hard disk to diskette. The diskettes can then be secured behind locked doors and the file on the hard disk erased. Simply using the **DEL** command in DOS would not do, however, because the data is still on the disk. Using such utilities programs as Norton's Wipe File will remove the file completely. If this is inconvenient, a less effective but usable approach might be to hide files under layers of directories and give them unusual names. In addition, removing any prompt signal and clearing the screen through the **AUTOEXEC** file when the machine is booted will make it difficult for unauthorized persons not familiar with the machine and directories to know exactly where they are in relation to the information they may be seeking. Finally, doors to offices containing microcomputing equipment should be closed and locked when authorized personnel leave.

THE ROLE OF THE MANAGEMENT INFORMATION SYSTEMS DEPARTMENT

As computing within the firm becomes increasingly decentralized, the role of the management information systems (MIS) department changes significantly. This change should be managed to facilitate the effective control over microcomputing resources and data. MIS should support microcomputer users and encourage increased productivity while coordinating activities and reducing risks to the firm. This can be accomplished by implementing support levels.

Support levels are formal divisions of computing responsibility and activity between MIS microcomputer end users. These divisions are based on a set of specific criteria, which are agreed on by both parties and are established for hardware, software, and data. For example, a hardware support level could be established with criteria that all hardware should be compatible and registered with MIS. If the hardware meets these criteria, MIS will provide technical support for the users. If the criteria are not met, the user cannot expect to receive support from MIS. Only authorized software should be permitted to access organizational data to reduce the risk of data contamination.

The advantages of establishing support levels include the provision of:

- Clearly specified responsibilities
- Structured design and delivery of MIS support services.
- A means for MIS to monitor and coordinate computing.
- Incentives for microcomputer users to improve their computing practices while reducing the risks to the organization.

CONCLUSION

Establishing effective internal control over the computer system is an important part of overall internal accounting control. Although managers have been learning to control mainframe systems, microcomputer systems have grown in usefulness and popularity, thereby presenting additional security concerns. To establish the most cost-effective control over a micro system, managers should understand the risks and controls common to both mainframes and micros and employ those common controls over their microcomputer systems. In addition, managers must know the risks unique to microcomputers and be familiar with the controls for those risks. Recognizing the changing role of MIS in managing this change will facilitate the effective use of microcomputer resources while minimizing the risks to the accounting organization.

Reading 6–6

AUDITING WITH YOUR MICROCOMPUTER

By Scott D. Jacobson and Christopher Wolfe

Computer-assisted techniques are a mandatory part of auditing large clients with voluminous transaction files. Computer assistance can also add efficiency and effectiveness to audits of medium-sized and smaller clients. Today, readily available software and low-cost microcomputer hardware make it feasible to use computer-assisted auditing with clients of any size.

This article focuses on generalized audit software for microcomputers. It is referred to as generalized because it is designed to facilitate the audit of any client, regardless of type of organization or industry. The ultimate goal of using such software is to automate audit functions while reducing dependence on clients' staff and systems.

GENERALIZED AUDIT SOFTWARE

A generalized audit software program consists of integrated applications that can be useful in virtually any audit setting. Historically, such software was used only on large mainframe systems. Auditors would run their software on the client's mainframe, directly accessing client files for analysis. While this is still an effective process, acquiring and using audit software designed for a mainframe computer is expensive and technically complex.

The alternative is using microcomputer-based audit software. Clearly, this is ineffective when client files are so large they would inundate a microcomputer. However, for medium-sized and smaller applications, microcomputer-based audit software represents an inexpensive and readily usable auditing tool.

As with all software, the key facets of microcomputer-based audit software are input, processing, and output. That is, the auditor is concerned with getting client data into the microcomputer, manipulating the data, and producing output that documents the audit.

Input. Manually keying in data is slow, expensive, and error-prone. If generalized audit software is to be effective, data must be downloaded from the client's system into the auditor's computer. Access to client data typically occurs via magnetic tape, floppy disk, or a telephone connection between computers. Regardless of the method to access client data, however, the format of the data and the type of file are the critical factors in reading the data.

Format refers to the internal scheme used to represent a character in a particular system. An IBM mainframe or minicomputer format that internally represents the letter "a" would be different from an IBM microcomputer format. Therefore, data have to be converted to the appropriate format before unlike systems can share data. The two most common data formats are EBCDIC, the IBM large system standard, and ASCII, the microcomputer standard. Numbers in the EBCDIC format are often stored in a condensed fashion, referred to as packed. Generalized audit software must translate and "unpack" EBCDIC files before a microcomputer can read the data.

Even when data are in the same format, different file types exist among programs. Therefore, generalized audit software must be able to either read multiple file types or translate foreign files into readable files. The three most common types of microcomputer files dealt with in an audit are native ASCII files, delimited files, and Lotus 1-2-3 files. Natives ASCII files contain only data. Delimited files separate individual pieces of data with a comma and surround nonnumeric data with quotes; microcomputer data base and general ledger packages commonly produce delimited files. Lotus files are spreadsheet files that contain not only the data in the spreadsheet but also directions for the Lotus application software on how to build the spreadsheet. Additionally, other data base application files are often used.

Given the mixed formats and file types among client systems, the first task generalized audit software must perform is converting client files into files the audit software can read and manipulate. The more flexible a software package is in accessing files of varying format and type, the more useful it will be in auditing diverse client systems.

Processing. Once data are made readable by audit software, the next step is data manipulation. Such capabilities are designed to perform general procedures inherent in all audits. In addition to complete mathematical manipulation of a data file, common functions include

- *Sample selection*—calculating different types of statistical samples.
- *Extract*—the ability to query a data file and remove data that meet the auditor's specified criterion.
- *Index*—giving each data item in a file a specific reference so the data can be quickly searched and sorted.
- *Join*—taking two independent files that have at least one data item in common and combining them by matching the common data item.
- *Stratify*—segmenting the data into subgroups that are based on auditor specified criteria.
- *Date arithmetic*—counting the number of days since a specific date, so that determining elapsed time between dates is simple addition and subtraction (for example, aging of accounts receivable is easily done if the current date can be subtracted from the invoice date). Exhibits 1 and 2 outline some of the features of generalized audit software currently available for the microcomputer.

EXHIBIT 1 Generalized Audit Software Features

	ACL Plus	Applaud	Easytrieve	IDEA
General				
Price	$1,995	$495	*	$695
Microprocessor	8088 & up	8088 & up	8088 & up	8088 & up
Memory needed	256k	640k	512k	640k
Hard disk space				
needed	None	2.5Mb	3.0Mb	2.5Mb
User features				
Menu driven	Optional†	Yes	Yes	Yes
Programmable	Yes	Yes	Yes	No
Input				
Formats read:				
ASCII	Yes	Yes	Yes	Yes
EBCDIC	Yes	Yes	Yes	Yes
Packed	Yes	Yes	Yes	Yes
File types read:				
Delimited	Yes	Yes	Yes	Yes
Lotus	No	No	Yes	Yes
Nine-track tape:				
Read directly	Yes	No	No	No
Dump to disk	Yes	Yes	Yes	Yes
On-screen record				
layout	No	Yes	No	Yes
Processing				
Sampling	Yes	Yes	Program††	Yes
Data extraction	Yes	Yes	Yes	Yes
Indexing	Yes	Yes	Yes	Yes
Joining files	Yes	Yes	Yes	No
Stratification	Yes	Program††	Program††	No
Date arithmetic	Yes	Yes	Yes	Yes
Output				
Custom reports	Yes	Yes	Yes	No
Transfer files:				
ASCII	Yes	Yes	Yes	Yes
Lotus	No	No	Yes	Yes
Delimited	Yes	No	Yes	Yes
Logging				
documentation	Yes	Yes	No	No

*Easytrieve for the microcomputer is not priced separately, because it is bundled with the mainframe version of the program. However, a stand-alone version of Easytrieve was made available in 1990.

†ACL offers both a command-line interface and a menu-driven interface.

††The function can be accomplished only through user programming.

Generalized audit software gives the auditor the tools to manipulate a data set. It does not suggest or design audit programs.

Processing features differ among the generalized audit software products. ACL and Applaud allow a broad range of custom data manipulation to any set of data files. Easytrieve, on the other hand, is less structured and highly flexible but requires some technical expertise. IDEA is menu-driven, which means the auditor simply selects a manipulation task from the menu; however, if the task is not included in the menu, it cannot be done.

The features and functions a package has are listed in Exhibit 1. In our use, it appears that the speed differs substantially among generalized audit software programs when carrying out these functions. Individual auditors must decide what levels of technical complexity, speed, and flexibility/functionality are appropriate for their practices.

Output. Output can take three forms: standard reports, custom reports, and transferring output to another microcomputer application. In addition, the standard report can be a user log, which monitors files used, functions used, and elapsed times of work sessions on the microcomputer—effective workpaper documentation for tracking the exact microcomputer audit functions performed.

At A Glance

- There is an increasing need to audit with computers. The sheer volume of data requires computer processing both to ensure transactions are properly recorded and to aid in data analysis. In addition, the auditor can spend less time performing mechanical operations and more time on issues requiring judgment.

- Auditing on a microcomputer requires taking data from a client's computer and converting it to a format the microcomputer can read. The auditor then can easily perform such procedures as selecting statistical samples and extracting, indexing, or stratifying selected data.

- Generalized audit software for microcomputers consists of related and integrated applications melded into one program designed to be useful in virtually any audit setting. The features of ACL Plus, Applaud, Easytrieve, and IDEA—four currently available generalized audit software programs—and how they will assist in an audit are discussed here.

- Computer-assisted auditing of accounts receivables is used to illustrate some applications of generalized audit software. The microcomputer is used to select and print confirmations to test for existence, produce an aging of receivables to help analyze collectibility, and extract a schedule of invoices for testing. Thus, the confirmation, bad debt review, and invoice selection processes are automated.

EXHIBIT 2   Generalized Audit Software Buyer Information

ACL Plus
ACL Services Ltd.
400-1190 Melville Street
Vancouver,
British Columbia
Canada V6E3W1
(604) 669-4225

ACL is a sophisticated audit program offering speed and features that puts it in a class by itself. This functionality necessarily leads to complexity, and ACL's menus do tend to overwhelm the user. However, the documentation supplied is good, and technical telephone support is available for $300 a year.

Applaud
Premier International
1660 North LaSalle
Chicago, Illinois 60614
(800) 426-0428
(312) 280-4600

Applaud offers a menu-driven method of programming that simplifies the process to some extent. Other notable features include extensive report generation capabilities, a strong on-screen record layout feature, and a print preview for easy output production. Applaud offers powerful data base manipulation capabilities in a relatively easy-to-use package.

Easytrieve Plus/PC
Pansophic Systems, Inc.
2400 Cabot Drive
Lisle, Illinois 60532
(800) 323-7335
(708) 954-2822

Easytrieve has an English-like language for programming that allows the product to be customized extensively. The microcomputer version of Easytrieve is designed to be used in conjunction with mainframe Easytrieve. If a client uses the mainframe Easytrieve, teaming the microcomputer version with it is a powerful solution to integrating the PC in the audit function.

IDEA
American Institute of CPAs
1211 Avenue of the Americas
New York, New York 10036
(212) 575-6200

IDEA is the only package of the four that does not offer customization through programming or report generation. While this is certainly limiting, it reduces complexity. IDEA is easy to use. It is also relatively complete, making it powerful even without programming. This may be an ideal package for the auditor who wants to use generalized audit software but who is concerned about his or her lack of the technical skills necessary to use such software.

Standard report printouts are common to all generalized audit software products. However, custom reports require report generators, which are included in three of the packages. The report format can be saved so it can be used over again with different data. Generating custom output is often necessary, since standard reports may not conform sufficiently to a firm's workpaper style.

Workpaper preparation is also facilitated with a software program often referred to as workpaper software. See Exhibit 3 for a discussion and listings of this type of software.

The final option, transferring output to another program, is desirable for two reasons:

- Data can be further processed in other microcomputer applications, such as spreadsheets or data bases.
- Generalized audit software does not produce elegant output, but numerous microcomputer programs can create impressive printed documents.

AN EXAMPLE: ACCOUNTS RECEIVABLE

Auditing on a microcomputer basically involves taking data from the client's computer, converting them to a format the auditor's computer can read, processing the client data, and finally producing printed output. An example is used to illustrate steps taken in the implementation of computer-assisted auditing. This simple accounts-receivable example is not meant to extend generalized audit software to its limit. Rather, the example illustrates the variety of potential audit applications. The following phases are discussed:

- Planning the application.
- Converting the data.
- Processing the data.

Planning the Application. Planning the audit is always important, and particularly so when computer processing is involved. A written plan guides implementation and provides audit documentation. The plan starts with the audit objectives and defines the data input and processes necessary to perform the required analyses. If there is any question about using the microcomputer in the audit, an investigation of its feasibility should be performed immediately, particularly if the plan involves audit steps that cannot achieve the intended results in an alternative noncomputerized way.

The primary audit objectives for accounts receivable are existence and valuation. The computer is used to select and print confirmations to test for existence. It also is used to produce an aging of receivables and special reports to help the auditor analyze collectibility. Finally, a schedule of invoices is extracted for auditor testing. Thus, the entire confirmation, bad debt re-

EXHIBIT 3   Automated Workpaper Software

Programs known as workpaper, or trial balance, software are probably used more often by accountants who audit with microcomputers than are generalized audit software programs. Workpaper software simplifies the preparation of financial statements by integrating the audit workpapers, schedules, and trial balances. When the auditor enters adjustments and reclassifications, related schedules and financial statements are updated automatically. These programs are valuable time-saving tools since they streamline some of the tedious work of preparing financial statements.

A number of stand-alone and template packages (used in conjunction with a spreadsheet) are available. Following are some popular programs. Prices are generally for site licenses, which vary with the number of users. In some cases, a single-user price is also available.

Accountant's Trial Balance $950
  American Institue of CPAs
  1211 Avenue of the Americas
  New York, New York 10036
  (212) 575-5412

AuditCube $1,750
  Blackman, Kallick & Co.
  300 South Riverside Plaza
  Chicago, Illinois 60606
  (312) 207-1040

Express Workpapers $550
  Litton Shafer Computer
    Services, Inc.
  2 West Second Street
  Frederick, Maryland 21701
  (800) 638-2220

FAST! Financial $1,995
  Prentice Hall Professional
    Software
  P.O. Box 723597
  Atlanta, Georgia 30339
  (800) 241-3306

FAST/CPA $2,225
  McGladrey, Hendrickson & Pullen
  1300 Midwest Plaza East
  800 Marquette Avenue
  Minneapolis, Minnesota 55402
  (612) 332-4300

focus: ABC $495
  Hemming Morse, Inc.   (template)
  160 Bovet Road
  San Mateo, California 94402
  (415) 574-1900

Pre-Audit $3,600
  Coopers & Lybrand
  1251 Avenue of the Americas
  New York, New York 10020
  (800) 223-0535

view, and invoice selection processes are automated, and the auditor is left with more time to concentrate on factors requiring judgment such as the valuation of doubtful accounts.

Converting the Data. After the application has been defined in general audit terms, the auditor should look at the client's data files. These will need to be downloaded so they can be processed by the generalized audit software.

Typically, the client's data processing department assists in this request. Because of the setup and size of mainframe files, it is often necessary for the client to produce an extract file—a special file containing only audit-related data items—for the auditor. Although producing extract files is straightforward, all data requests should be placed early to avoid timing conflicts with the data processing department. In our example, we would request a file with records consisting of the following fields: customer name, account number, balance, address, city, state, and ZIP Code. Additionally, we would request individual invoice data for aging and analysis. With these data we can select and print confirmations, print a negative balance report, print a customer report sorted by balance size, perform an aging of accounts receivable, and select a group of invoice records to trace to the original source documents.

The size of the extract file should be estimated before the data request to ensure the data fit on the microcomputer's hard disk. Technical knowledge of field sizes and "bytes" is needed, but the client's data processing staff should be able to assist. In our example, an accounts-receivable file with 5,000 customers, their balances, names, and addresses occupies between one and two megabytes of disk space (that is, 10 percent of a small microcomputer hard disk). However, processing requires additional disk space. The amount of space needed depends on the type of software used, but two to three times the size of the data file is a good rule of thumb for estimating disk space needed.

The extract file must be loaded into the auditor's microcomputer by electronic transfer or magnetic tape. Electronic transfer can take place using a modem (that is, a piece of telephone communications hardware connected to the microcomputer) or may be accomplished directly if the client's system supports electronic transfer between the mainframe and microcomputers.

The auditor also should request the data be saved on magnetic tape. Mainframe and minicomputers use nine-track tape. Microcomputers with an attached tape drive can either read this tape directly or dump its contents to the microcomputer's hard disk. In the absence of a tape drive, nine-track tape can be converted to a microcomputer file format and saved to floppy disks by a service bureau.

When the client data have been loaded into the auditor's microcomputer, generalized audit software can perform an on-screen record layout of the extract file, which allows on-screen viewing of the data definitions before converting any formats or file types. If the data are correct, the conversion functions in the generalized audit software package transform the extract file so it can be processed by the auditor's microcomputer.

Processing the Data.   The extract file can be queried based on the auditor's criteria; in this case, we will use dollar unit sampling. The output from the sample calculations are used as the basis for determining which receivables to confirm. Personalized confirmations are printed for each customer by the audit software, and the accounts selected for confirmation are saved to a file for analyzing returned responses. The only manual step involves adding a signature to the confirmations.

The negative balance report is easily prepared by extracting all receivables with balances less than zero, and a sort on receivable balances is the basis for a customer balance report. From the invoice file, the date arithmetic function allows an aging of accounts receivable, and the extract function creates a file containing records that will be traced to original invoices. Output from these procedures involves sending the appropriate files and the aging schedule to a printer.

The only caveat is: If a data file is of significant size, the processing should be tested on a small sample first. This will allow the "bugs" to be worked out quickly in a risk-free setting.

ADDITIONAL SERVICES

The added flexibility and speed of using microcomputer-based generalized audit software to assist in audits do not come without costs. Initial start-up costs, employee training, microcomputer hardware, and software purchase and maintenance are the major outlays required. A generalized auditing system is probably not cost effective for a one-time application, but it may be so for a single client if the audit is repeated; it certainly *is* cost-effective if multiple clients can be processed with the same auditing system. While the initial costs may be more easily quantified than the initial benefits, the long-term potential of microcomputer-assisted auditing should be considered in the decision to implement this technology.

Other than costs, the size of files is the most common limiting physical factor in microcomputer-assisted auditing. However, if the auditor is careful to make data requests for only the necessary data fields for auditing, a surprisingly large amount of information can be processed efficiently on the microcomputer.

Performing an effective audit at a lower overall cost is indeed possible with a smooth-running microcomputer system using generalized audit software. Additionally, the client may be so impressed with the auditor's computerized reports that it may request additional services from the auditor. Reduced audit costs, increased audit quality, and expanded client services are the rationale for using microcomputer-based generalized audit software.

CHAPTER 7

AIS Subsystems—Specific Applications

The accounting information system (AIS) is intended to provide all of the financial-related information needed by management for effective decision making. The AIS is a financial subsystem of the management information system (MIS). The MIS provides all of the information needed by management, financial and nonfinancial. In addition to the accounting subsystem, the MIS includes marketing, personnel, production, and so forth.

The AIS must interface with other subsystems to provide appropriate financial information for each of the managers of the various subsystems. Several reports that the AIS might prepare for use by other subsystems are as follows:

Subsystem	Report	Use
Marketing	Sales by product type	Evaluating product sales performance
	Sales by salesperson	Evaluating employee performance
Production	Cost-benefit analysis of acquiring a new machine	Determining effect on profitability
Personnel	Agency fund reports and filings	Ensuring that payments such as federal income tax and FICA are properly filed.

In this chapter are five articles concerned with specific AIS applications. The initial paper deals with the production process. Specifically, it presents the steps used in an actual systems development project in which an integrated job cost accounting system was implemented. The second article is based on a case from audit practice regarding the application of regression analysis in estimating a retail store's inventories and gross profits. The third article concerns the development of a computerized accounts payable system. The fourth article presents a firm's experience with automating its financial reporting process using an application software package called CONTROL.

The fifth and last article presents internal auditing considerations associated with church accounting systems. Church accounting systems provide a good example of the types of control issues prevalent in not-for-profit organizations. The article presents several internal control considerations found in biblical passages as well as various characteristics of modern church accounting systems.

CHAPTER 7 READINGS

1. James A. Sena and L. Murphy Smith, "Designing and Implementing an Integrated Job Cost Accounting System," *Journal of Information Systems*, Fall 1986, pp. 102–112.
2. Frank Koster, "A Case from Practice: Regression Analysis Prototype—Retail Store Inventories," *The Auditor's Report*, Summer 1984, pp. 7–9.
3. Michael J. Deeb and Eugene A. Brown, "Automating Accounts Payable at AMSCO," *Management Accounting*, January 1990, pp. 28–30.
4. Mitchell A. Levy, "Sun Microsystems Automates Financial Reporting," *Management Accounting*, January 1990, pp. 24–27.
5. L. Murphy Smith and Jeffrey R. Miller, "An Internal Audit of a Church," *Internal Auditing*, Summer 1989, pp. 34–42.

CHAPTER 7 QUESTIONS

Article 1

1. What is an integrated job cost accounting system? Should such a system be on-line or should it be batch oriented?

Article 2

2. Describe how regression analysis can be used by auditors.

Article 3

3. What were some of the objectives of the computerized accounts-payable system?
4. Besides cost savings, what other advantages occurred as a result of the new computerized accounts-payable system?

Article 4

5. List the requirements of the firm's new financial reporting system.

Article 5

6. What are the five general guidelines for operational audits?

7. What are three reasons that churches should establish adequate internal controls?

8. Briefly discuss a biblical example of an internal control policy.

Case 7–1

KIPYN COMPANY

Kipyn Company manufactures a complete line of walnut office products. Kipyn executives estimate that the annual demand for the double walnut letter tray, one of the company's products, is 6,000 units. This letter tray sells at a price of $80 per unit. The costs related to the letter tray are as follows:

a. Standard manufacturing cost per letter tray: $50.

b. Costs to initiate a production run: $300.

c. Annual cost of carrying the letter tray in inventory: 20 percent of the standard manufacturing cost.

In prior years, Kipyn Company has scheduled the production of the letter tray in two equal production runs. The company is aware that the economic order quantity (EOQ) model can be employed to determine the optimum size of production runs. The EOQ formula as it applies to inventories for determining the optimum order quantity is:

$$EOQ = \sqrt{\frac{2(\text{Annual demand})(\text{Cost per order})}{(\text{Cost per unit})(\text{Carrying cost})}}$$

REQUIRED:

Calculate the expected annual cost savings Kipyn Company could experience if it employed the economic order quantity model to determine the number of production runs which should be initiated during the year for the manufacture of the double walnut letter trays. (AICPA adapted).

Case 7–2

CHRISRAY MANUFACTURING

In connection with her examination of the financial statements of the Chrisray Manufacturing Company, Tracy Smith CPA, is reviewing the procedures used by her client for accumulating direct labor hours. She learns that all production is by job order and that all employees are paid hourly wages, with time-and-a-half for overtime.

Chrisray's direct labor-hour input process for payroll and job-cost determination is summarized in the flowchart shown below. Steps A and C are performed in timekeeping, step B in the factory operating departments, step D in payroll audit and control, step E in data preparation (keypunch), and step F in computer operations.

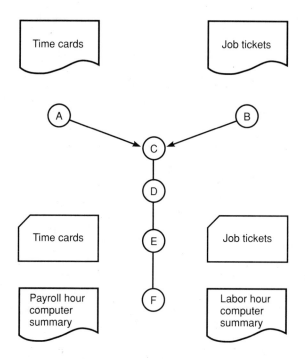

REQUIRED:

1. Redraw and diagram, using standard document flowcharting symbols.

2. For each input processing step, cite possible errors or discrepancies that might arise, and identify the corresponding control procedure that should be in effect for each error or discrepancy. Use the following table organization:

Possible Errors or Disrepancies	Control Procedures

(AICPA Adapted)

Reading 7–1

DESIGNING AND IMPLEMENTING AN INTEGRATED JOB COST ACCOUNTING SYSTEM

By James A. Sena and L. Murphy Smith

Abstract. Incorporating an integrated job cost system into the overall accounting system is a difficult task. Some of the usual guidelines for sound data base design, for instance, cannot be followed. This article describes steps that, if followed, will lead to an integrated cost accounting system that meets the needs of a wide variety of users.

INTRODUCTION

An integrated job cost accounting system operates under some form of data base or file management system. The basic financial elements (material, labor, overhead, etc.) are linked together to provide support for decision making and control of business functions. To ensure that these provisions are fulfilled, the system needs to operate in an on-line fashion with a batch processing background component.

The techniques described in this article were implemented for a group of energy-related companies in the southwest United States. Each company was connected to one central computer facility. Some were connected direct-line, while others were connected by telecommunication lines. The computer system consisted of a large minicomputer (INFO 1000) having a relational data base management system. The relational data base environment permits efficient program development as well as external usage of query and report generation by user personnel.

Prior to the job cost system implementation, an integrated accounting software package had been installed. Significant tailoring of various software components was necessary. The original general ledger system was virtually rewritten.

INTEGRATED ACCOUNTING SYSTEM—WHAT IS IT?

An accounting system generally comprises several subsystems, such as accounts receivable, accounts payable, purchasing, payroll, sales, inventory management, and general ledger.

Reprinted with permission from *Journal of Information Systems*, Fall 1986, pp. 102–112.

Each of these subsystems functions relatively independent of the other subsystems. However, certain interfaces (or data links) between subsystems need to be established to ensure that query and reporting requirements are met. All of these subsystems affect the general ledger, the heart of the accounting system. Using the ledger detail transactions, a flow of activity (audit trail) can be established for the entire organization or for a functional area. A path to the originating transaction and subsystem can be obtained.

Figure 1 presents the format of a typical general ledger transaction. The transaction is posted to a summary master file based on the account number. Once posted, the record is stored in a detail transaction file for inquiry and demand detail processing. The summary master file or general ledger master file is used for trial balances and financial statement reporting. Since the data base system used did not provide for automatic inter-file linking, a cross-reference file was created to facilitate inter-file and sub-file linkages. Figure 2 illustrates the posting and linkage system required for inquiry and random processing. Note the use of the cross-reference file to establish the linkage structure.

The general ledger master file provides immediate account inquiry and facilitates summary reporting for trial balances and financial reporting. The (ledger detail) transaction file provides detailed information, when required, for both inquiry and reporting. The cross-reference file supports the selected detail inquiry or reporting through the establishment of appropriate file cross-references. The system is responsive to inquiry or reporting on either query

FIGURE 1 Format of General Ledger Transaction Record

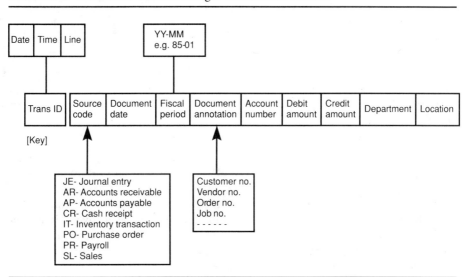

FIGURE 2 General Ledger Posting and Linkage System

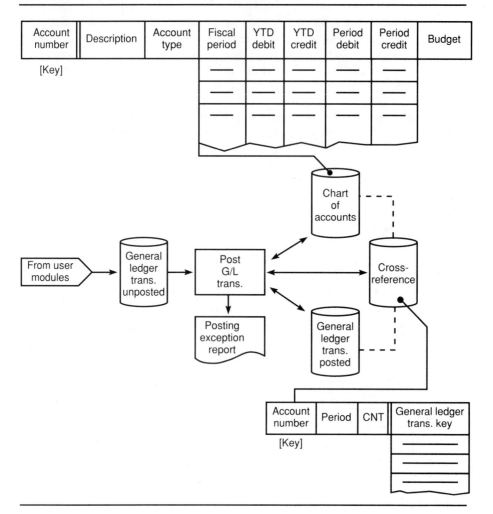

language or programmed basis. An important feature in an on-line, multiuser, multicompany system is response time. A user should be able to quickly retrieve summary information or selected transaction detail. Several factors affect the response time, including the number of users at a given time. The number of users cannot be controlled, but the number of secondary disk storage accesses can be limited or reduced. Figure 3 shows the three levels of general ledger query. Each level increases the number of disk accesses required.

FIGURE 3 The Job Cost Menu System

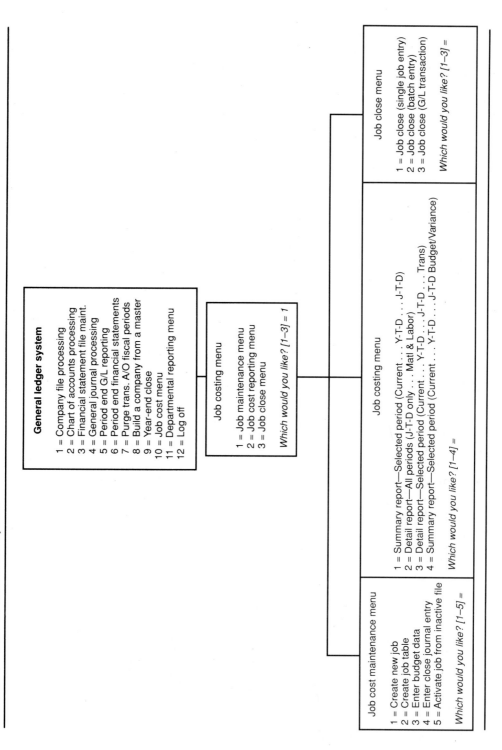

Given a selected account or group of accounts, the system user can examine the general ledger detailed transactions for a selected period or range of periods. The user can then request the originating transactions from the various accounting subsystems. All of these actions are accomplished through the use of either the query language or programs. The programs usually will be more efficient and require less system resources.

WHY AN INTEGRATED JOB COST SYSTEM?

An integrated job cost system collects, stores, and presents information to financial, manufacturing, and sales management concerning every job or product being produced in the organization. The financial status of each job is available on demand, so that progress and performance can be monitored. Typical elements monitored in a job cost system include materials, outside purchase of materials, labor, overhead, outside services, and other.

Without an integrated system for job costing, extensive selection and sorting are required to provide job summary and detail reporting. This situation can be time-consuming and inefficient. Using a query language to establish such reports usually presents the report to the user in a crude form.

An integrated job cost system operates in a manner similar to a typical general ledger system. Transactions originating from various source subsystems are associated with a particular cost account and job. Reporting and queries provide summary and detailed information. One difference between the general ledger and job cost systems is that a job can span an indefinite period of time, whereas the general ledger has an annual cutoff for the retention of detail transaction records. At the end of each year, the detail information from the general ledger is generally stored off-line in archival form. Some of these data will still be needed for job cost reporting.

Many commercial packages have purported integrated job cost modules as part of their accounting systems. However, these modules usually do not have the same status, from a processing perspective, as that of the general ledger. Reporting and inquiries are not handled on a demand basis. Instead, monthly or periodic reports are generated.

A job cost system usually assumes that an organization produces unique products on a special-order basis rather than a recurring production-line basis. The products vary from oil rigs to sailboats to buildings. In certain cases, the product is subdivided into subproducts. For example, in the construction of a building for a government contract, the products or jobs may be defined to conform to the required Project Control System. An adequate integrated job cost system needs to permit such groupings of jobs or products.

Most organizations have common accounting system requirements. However, the job cost system can differ significantly from company to company, depending on the product being produced. The approach described in the following sections has been simplified to facilitate presentation.

THE ELEMENTS OF AN INTEGRATED JOB COST SYSTEM

From a logical viewpoint, the steps to implement a job cost system within an accounting system framework are similar to the creation of the general ledger system. If the general ledger system has already been implemented, much of the groundwork will have been accomplished.

The elements of an integrated job cost system would include four groups: (1) an update component, (2) maintenance, (3) reporting, and (4) closing. Figure 4 illustrates the access of these groups within the job cost system.

In the update component, the appropriate general ledger transactions are posted to the job cost or work-in-progress file. The update program or subprograms are embedded within the general ledger posting program. These programs and procedures are evident to the user. After the general ledger is posted, the job cost summary records are subsequently posted. The maintenance provision gives the user the ability to correct the job cost file, given that there is inadvertent deletion or noninclusion of a job. Other special features, such as budget entry, are included in the maintenance group. Budget data are used for performance measurement. Reports can be presented in either print or display modes. Summary or detail information can be obtained for a specific job, group of jobs, or all jobs.

Closing is a crucial issue in a job cost system. Once a job is completed, the job needs to be moved to inactive status (by the entry: debit Finished Goods, credit Work-in-Process), and the general ledger needs to be adjusted to reflect the account changes. In closing a job, the job cost system generates detail transactions to be posted in the general ledger master file. Depending on the company, intermediate closes may take place. As part of the work will have been completed, charges for services need to be posted.

Within the accounting system, the unit of measurement is monetary units. The job cost system is also concerned with hour and pound units. Since jobs are typically bid based on labor and material requirements, monitoring these elements can aid management in future job proposals. These units provide additional, often required, information to the production manager and the customer.

The general ledger system does not typically capture hour and pound data. To secure these data elements at a summary level would require selection and manipulation within the specific subsystem. This selection could require multiple accesses of on-line files, a very time-consuming and inefficient procedure.

IMPLEMENTING THE INTEGRATED JOB COST SYSTEM

Several false starts were made in implementing the system. At first, the job cost system was modeled directly like the general ledger by including a job cost update program employed during the general ledger posting process. The

FIGURE 4 Flow of Transactions to General Ledger

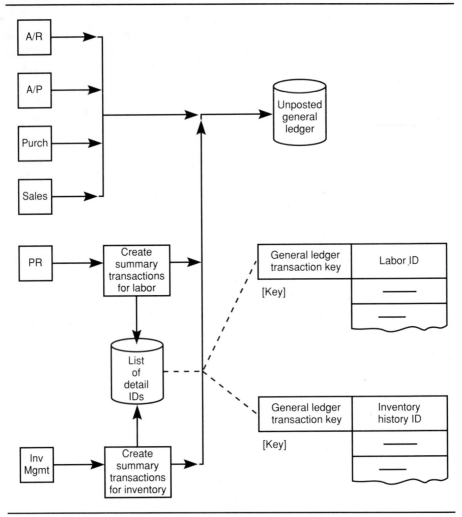

general ledger system had previously been modified to carry summary detail transactions for the payroll and inventory systems. The reason for this change was to prevent simple labor and inventory transactions from inundating the general ledger. In a given day, an employee could charge time against several different jobs. In addition, a job is typically composed of many different parts in a given day. The detail transactions originating from these systems consist of the total labor or inventory amount for a single day and particular job. To provide a link back to the originating source transactions, a supporting file similar to the cross-reference file was created. This file uses the same primary key as the ledger detail transaction. Figure 4 illustrates the process of updating the general ledger file from the source file.

The structure of the job cost or work-in-process record is fairly sophisticated. To provide fast response for query and reporting purposes, period and cumulative data were stored in summary form in the master file. This eliminated or reduced numerous processing runs to accumulate summary figures; however, this approach causes significant redundancy in data content. On the other hand, the time required to process through multiple periods of the various cost categories (to compute year-to-date and job-to-date figures) could become a factor for concern. Figure 5 presents a schematic of the structure for the job cost record.

Initially in the implementation of the job cost system, the additional elements of hours and pounds were captured in the update program by (1) going through the general ledger system to the payroll and inventory originating transactions, and (2) using a saved list of subsystem detail record keys. This process was feasible from an update standpoint but not always accurate due to the sheer volume of transaction activity. In practice, query and reporting time were prohibitive. The resources of the system were strained during peak operations. Usually in a general ledger system, the detail is tied to the account of interest in a direct hierarchical fashion. (Figure 6 illustrates this process.)

In a job cost system, detailed reporting does not use the same hierarchical presentation as a general ledger system. The manager wants to know the detail, grouped by department for labor and by part number for material. Under the first implementation (Figure 7), simple inquiries for a selected job or a detailed report for all jobs were both cumbersome and error-prone. The originating detail for labor or material had to be collected from all transactions into a work area and rearranged.

Generating a detailed report required access of large on-line archival files. Assuming that these files are well organized, access is still slower than access to a dedicated job detail file. An additional factor is retirement of the archival data. Since a given job can span several years, the labor and inventory history, as well as general ledger detail, would have to be retained indefinitely. This quickly became an on-line storage problem.

With general ledger system use, other problems became apparent. One of the companies experienced such a volume in general ledger transactions that retrieval for a specific period became too slow. The file needed to be reorganized on a consistent basis. The solution was to go to monthly files, since the majority of general ledger reporting was periodic. This presented another problem for the integrated job cost system. The need to have a continual increase in the number of monthly files for accessing, either to update or to generate reports, constituted a serious problem. This problem was addressed

FIGURE 5 The Structure of the Job Cost Record

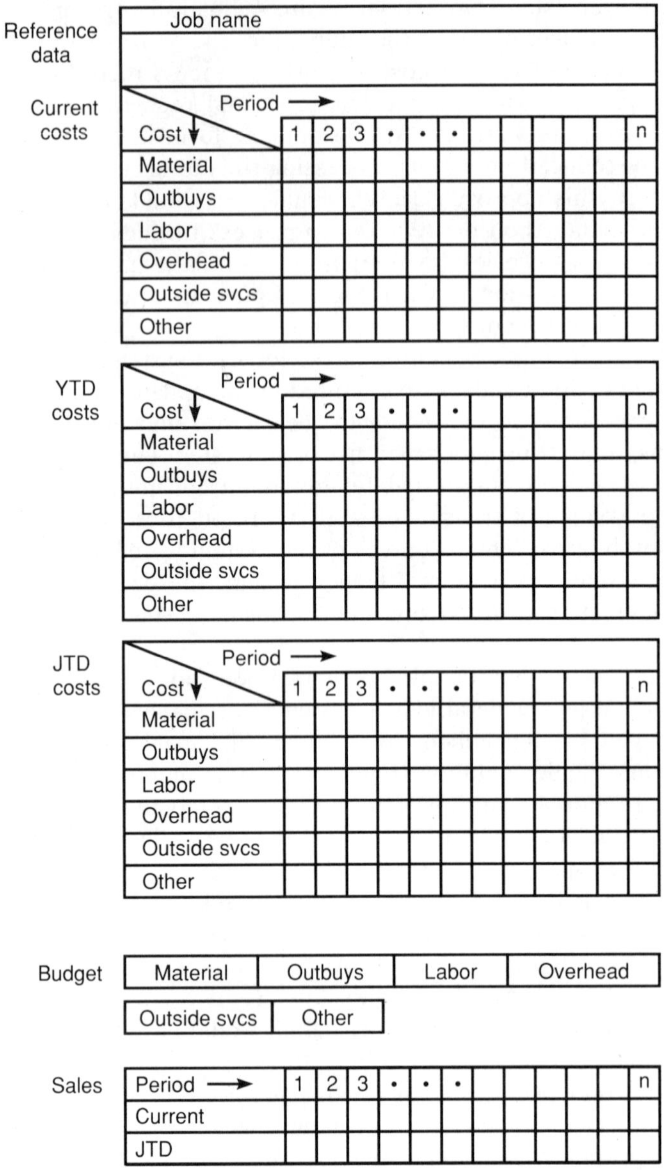

Reference data	Job name

Current costs

Period →												
Cost ↓	1	2	3	•	•	•						n
Material												
Outbuys												
Labor												
Overhead												
Outside svcs												
Other												

YTD costs

Period →												
Cost ↓	1	2	3	•	•	•						n
Material												
Outbuys												
Labor												
Overhead												
Outside svcs												
Other												

JTD costs

Period →												
Cost ↓	1	2	3	•	•	•						n
Material												
Outbuys												
Labor												
Overhead												
Outside svcs												
Other												

Budget

Material	Outbuys	Labor	Overhead
Outside svcs	Other		

Sales

Period →	1	2	3	•	•	•						n
Current												
JTD												

FIGURE 6   Hierarchy of General Ledger Data Access

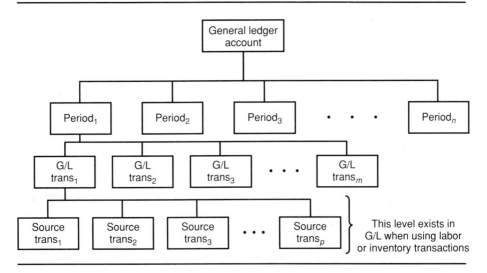

FIGURE 7   Creation of Detail Job Cost Report—Initial Implementation

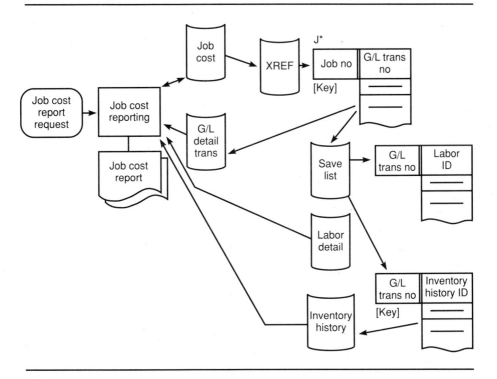

by creating a separate general ledger file containing only job cost-related transactions.

Several changes made to overcome the above problems were:

1. Removing the hourly and weight computations from the update program and placing their computation at the source entry to the general ledger file (e.g., inventory issues and receipts file).
2. Creating three separate job detail files: general ledger detail related to jobs, labor extract data related to jobs, and material extract data related to jobs.
3. Providing for final closing of jobs and retiring both detailed and summary data to an inactive file.

By placing the hour and weight computation and posting responsibility in the source subsystem, both the retrieval time and the error rate were reduced. Reconciliation of hours and pounds to dollar transactions was facilitated. There was no time lag differentiation between labor or material transactions posted to the general ledger and hours and pounds posted to the job cost file. Both of these operations were done in batch, directly following the general ledger and job cost posting.

To accommodate the need for job detail data spanning an indefinite period of time, the detail data required for general ledger transactions, labor detail, and material detail were stored in three separate extract files. This practice generated redundant data. However, only directly relevant information was carried in these extract files. The labor and material transaction data consisted only of selected, directly used fields. The general ledger detail job file consisted only of job-related transactions. With these special relational files, the response time for query and reporting was reduced. Reconciliation against the general ledger file was enhanced.

During final closing, detail data could be removed from the active job file without having an impact on the general ledger system. Hence, the job detail and summary files would contain only the active jobs that are used in answering queries and reporting.

Figure 8 shows the new arrangement. Although this method introduced redundant data at the summary and detail levels, the benefits include:

1. Providing faster response to inquiries.
2. Reducing overall system resources for reporting.
3. Reducing long-term on-line storage requirements.

CONCLUSIONS

The new integrated job cost system focuses on dedicated files. The records contain only data that are directly related to the job cost system. The update process is smoother, since the hour and pound data are posted to the job cost record at the same time the summary general ledger transaction is created.

FIGURE 8   Creating a Detailed Job Cost Report—Revised Implementation

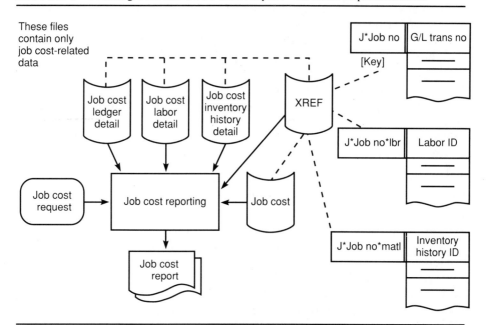

Response times have been shortened. Using this framework, other companies can establish an integrated job cost system with a minimum of tailoring.

Reading 7–2

A CASE FROM PRACTICE: REGRESSION ANALYSIS PROTOTYPE—RETAIL STORE INVENTORIES

By Frank Koster

Much has been written about the theoretical potential of regression analysis in auditing, but little of it deals with real-life situations. This case study, however, concerns an actual prototype application that our firm used to test the store inventory and gross profit of a large retail chain.

Reprinted with permission from *The Auditor's Report,* Summer 1984, pp. 7–9.

Regression analysis utilizes statistical techniques to measure the correlation between a given, or "dependent," variable (such as a store's current gross profit percentage) and other, "independent" variables (such as historical gross profit, turnover and product mix). If a sufficient historical correlation exists, it is possible to construct a regression model that can predict—within reasonable limits—the current value of the dependent variable based on the values of the other variables.

After reviewing this case study, you will be asked to answer several questions about the regression application and to suggest how it might be improved in the future.

PREVIOUS AUDIT APPROACH

The client operates several hundred retail stores in a seven-state area. The operations and product lines of all the stores are similar, and the accounting system has proven to be reliable in prior years. Each store's monthly gross profit and inventory are estimated based on reported purchases, sales, and related activity, with the store's inventory being physically counted only once each year. Because the counts are rotated among the stores on a cycle basis during the year, at year-end about half the chain's inventory has not been counted in over six months. Although we have never encountered a significant misstatement, there always is a risk that errors in the inventory and gross profit estimates might aggregate to a material amount, and we have had to do extensive work to reduce this risk to an acceptable level.

In previous audits our work in this area included, among other things, (1) observation of the count procedures at several randomly selected stores, (2) tests of the related count records, book-to-physical adjustments and gross margins, and (3) analytical review of the inventories and gross margins of all the stores for the year. This work required a substantial amount of audit time, even though we tested only a very small portion of the detail records.

REVISED AUDIT APPROACH

In 1983, a regression model was constructed for testing some of the stores that had not taken recent physicals. The objective was to predict each store's gross profit percentage for the period since its last count; the percentage would be multiplied by the appropriate sales volume to predict the store's gross profit and inventory. This would enable us to:

- Quantify the potential misstatement of gross profit and inventory for the tested stores.
- Identify—and investigate—"problem" stores (i.e., those whose predicted and recorded results were significantly different).
- Reduce the extent of detailed testing of physical inventories.
- Concentrate more on reviewing the related internal control procedures.

CONSTRUCTION OF THE REGRESSION MODEL

We identified a number of potential independent variables that we believed would have a bearing on gross profit margins. These were screened on an "ordinary least squares" time-sharing program by calculating their historical correlations with gross profit. Of these, we chose the following five predictive variables for the regression model, listed in order of significance with the direction of the relationship noted in parentheses: (1) historical gross profit (+), (2) change in "book" inventory (+), (3) inventory shrinkage (−), (4) volume of direct store purchases (merchandise that the stores purchased directly from vendors typically had lower margins than did warehouse issues) (−), and (5) inventory turnover (+).

The model was constructed using pooled time-series and cross-sectional data for the most recent three years (1981–1983) for 40 stores. Its results indicated we should be able to obtain reasonably accurate predictions for other stores for the audit year (1983).

RESULTS OF THE APPLICATION

The new model was applied to 1983 data for 40 stores that had not taken recent physical counts. At a 90 percent confidence level, several stores had predicted gross profits that varied more than one percentage point from their actual (recorded) results. After further investigation, we were satisfied that the actual results were not misstated. The principal cause of the variations was a change in marketing policies at certain stores, which had increased the volume of promotional items with relatively low gross profit margins.

Overall, we considered the regression application successful and were able to change our audit approach as planned.

QUESTION #1:

What other advantages might the use of this regression model have?

Solution:

- Applying the model at interim dates (e.g., quarterly reviews) might help detect trends, potential errors, and problems as they arise. This also would help us shift some of our workload from final closing to an earlier date.
- When all the stores are eventually added to the model, it could be used to predict overall gross profit and inventory for the entire chain.
- The study of the business relationships underlying the model can yield a better understanding of the company. This can lead to suggestions for improving operations and profitability.

- The model draws on known relationships to define an "expected" value that is compared with the current year's results. This is an advantage over the traditional analytical review procedures, which simply compare this year's to last year's results in the hope of spotting unusual conditions.
- The setting of a confidence level provides an objective assessment of the reliance that can be placed on the model's results. The reliance placed on other analytical review procedures must, of course, be measured on a purely subjective basis.

QUESTION #2:

What conditions favored the use of regression analysis in this case study?

Solution:

- The application involved a major risk area (inventory and gross profits). The time and expense of developing the model were justified because it had the potential to substantially improve the quality of the audit. That is, it could provide additional "comfort" about two significant balances that were difficult to test efficiently by other means.
- The balances being tested had a relatively high degree of predictability. Their relationship with the independent variables was straightforward and therefore could be reflected in a regression equation. Many accounts, such as receivables and liabilities, result from more varied and complex relationships and typically are much harder to predict. Also, amounts subject to discretionary management policy (e.g., advertising, repairs and maintenance expenses, and reserve balances) particularly are subject to model shifts and therefore may not be likely candidates for time-series regression analysis.
- Data for a number of potential independent variables were available for at least three years. The data could be obtained quickly, were reliable (e.g., no monthly cutoff problems) and did not require adjustment for seasonality or lag times.
- The company's operations were homogeneous (a single line of business in one country) and reasonably stable: there were no obvious technological changes or other unstabilizing factors that would alter the regression correlations between years.
- The model combined "cross-sectional" analysis (store-to-store comparisons) with "time-series" analysis (period-to-period comparisons for each store). Thus, the population had enough individual observations or data points to establish a valid model. Plotting all stores for a three-

year period eventually should create a very large—and presumably reliable—data base. (Pure time-series models, such as those that predict annual results from corresponding monthly data, typically are based on a three-year period, which provides a maximum of only 36 historical observations. Using a longer period yields a larger base, but the older data may be less meaningful for current predictions.)

- The variable interrelationships were understood and the direction of each coefficient was as expected: a direct or positive sign for historical gross profit, change in "book" inventory, and turnover and an inverse or negative sign for inventory shrinkage and direct store purchases. These are intuitively appealing; for example, as shrinkage increases, gross profit would be expected to decrease.

QUESTION #3:

What other kinds of predictive variables might improve the model's predictive ability?

Solution:

A better model might result if one or two external variables (data originating outside the company) were substituted for one or two of the existing variables, which are all internal ones. This is true because, like most account balances, gross profit is influenced by events both within and outside of the business. External variables have an additional advantage: the data usually needs less testing than internally generated data. Possible external variables might be found in local demographic and economic data for store areas (number of households, population density, average personal income, employment levels, etc.), or by reference to industry trends and changes in competition.

QUESTION #4:

What disadvantages do external variables have?

Solution:

- Current economic and demographic data often are not published quickly enough to be used in an audit.
- The data may be based on too large a geographical area to be an accurate predictor for any given store.
- Industry data may be misleading if the company being tested represents a significant percentage of the industry.

- Many variables involving economic data are closely correlated. This creates the problem of "multicollinearity," which affects the stability of the regression coefficients. (The techniques for dealing with multi-collinearity are complex and need further refinement.)

QUESTION #5:

Assume you applied a "stepwise" technique to screen several potential new predictive variables and found one that was significantly correlated with gross margin. Aside from the issues of the accuracy and availability of the data, what condition must the new variable meet before it can be added to the model?

Solution:

- It must be **relevant.** There should be a logical explanation of why it would influence gross margin. A variable should not be used solely on the strength of mathematical correlations. Some correlations might be largely coincidental, or they might be caused by other, unknown factors. A plausible hypothesis should be developed about the cause-and-effect relationship between each independent variable and the dependent variable. The relationship should make good business sense and should be defensible even to individuals who do not have statistical expertise.

QUESTION #6:

What do you think was the greatest potential weakness in this application?

Solution:

The results showed that a change in the company's marketing strategy altered the model's accuracy. The auditors must be on guard for such events and, if possible, reflect them in the model, such as by adding "dummy" variables or adjusting the input data for the affected stores.

QUESTION #7:

How much knowledge do those who use the model next year need of regression analysis and of the model's underlying assumptions:

Solution:

Regression models usually need frequent updating for changes in the environment, or at least confirmation that they are still appropriate. Any revisions certainly would involve the joint efforts of an expert in mathematics and regression techniques and individuals knowledgeable about the company and its industry. A user of regression analysis need not know how to calculate regression models but must understand the basic approach and how to interpret the results. Even if the model is not changed, there must be enough continuity in the audit team to ensure that someone, such as the engagement manager, has a general understanding of the model and can recognize whether changes in the client's operations or environment might affect the model's validity. Otherwise, there is a danger that the model would become a "black box" and its users would misunderstand its capabilities.

Reading 7–3

AUTOMATING ACCOUNTS PAYABLE AT AMSCO

By Michael J. Deeb and Eugene A. Brown

The accounts-payable staff at your company may wake up at night screaming from nightmares of being drowned in paper—that is, if your company has a manual system. The staff probably is so busy with numeric manipulations, checking for duplications, and shuffling papers looking for the answers to vendor queries that they have very little time for cash control or planning.

At the American Sterilizer Company (AMSCO) we developed our own computerized accounts-payable system, which has reduced the probability of mathematical errors found in manual systems. The system differs from the usual accounts-payable system in that it does a great deal of matching and checking as it operates. This system has enhanced the speed in processing vouchers—month-end closing takes five days less—and reduced operating costs within the department. Management now receives more timely and accurate reports to improve the company's cash flow.

The system operates on a PC network at our three manufacturing locations in Erie, Pa., Montgomery, Ala., and Apex, N.C. AMSCO is a diversified company with operations, licensees, and distribution in 60 countries. It produces equipment, devices, supplies, and systems for the professional

---

Published by *Management Accounting*, copyright 1990, by National Association of Accountants, Montvale, NJ 07645.

health-care, laboratory, and industrial fields and is the leading manufacturer of sterilizing equipment and surgical tables and lights in the United States. We have dealings with a large number of vendors.

GUIDELINES FOR PLANNING A PROFITABLE SYSTEM

In preparing our feasibility study for the new system, we first defined accounts payable. It is a method used to pay invoices within certain time limits and correctly distribute the amounts to the general ledger accounts. The process of controlling and issuing checks is only one link in the total payables process, however. Many functional departments or divisions use information from our payables system or supply it with data.

Our second step was to define objectives for our conversion. The following is a partial list:

1. Get 90 percent of the invoices ready for payment within two days of receipt in house.
2. Improve control over accounts payable.
3. Reduce operating costs sufficiently to achieve payback within one year.
4. Produce more timely and accurate information.
5. Reduce the number of duplicate and overpayments.
6. Improve cash flow.

We specifically chose the following areas in which to implement improved controls and provide more accurate and timely reporting.

- Automatic matching of invoices, which would prevent duplicate payments, simplify entries to the general ledger, and establish actual obligations.
- Check writing.
- Recording vendor history and responding to vendor inquiries.
- Simplifying management reporting.
- Automating recurring transactions.

AUTOMATIC MATCHING OF INVOICES

Our first stated objective was to get 90 percent of all invoices ready for payment within two days of receipt. We started the matching process through the invoice/packing slip matching screen. All information is entered from the vendor invoice—the AMSCO voucher number, the purchase order number, the invoice date, item amount, discount percent, and payment days. When the information is processed, the system checks the on-line purchasing file, verifying the purchase order number and checking the cash discount to maximize profits.

We decided to make our system automatically select and calculate the advantageous term option for payment. Many terms commonly used in United States and foreign markets offer more than one way to pay an invoice. For example, $1/10$ net 30 lets you pay the invoice within 10 days and deduct 1 percent of the invoice amount or pay within the tenth to thirtieth days and take no discount.

What is the vendor really offering? He is saying: pay the bill 20 days early and I will pay you 18 percent per annum interest for the use of your money. Eighteen percent is the annualized interest rate when 1 percent is equal to 20 days ($20/360 = 18 \times 1 = 18$). Which of these two options is more advantageous? It depends upon the cost of the money your company is using currently.

The next screen appears automatically, showing the voucher number, purchase order number, payee vendor number, name, address, and the calculated pay date with the cash discount. Other features displayed on this screen are the AMSCO buyer's number, the tax status on the purchase order, and the voucher year and month.

The next step is to enter the following information on this screen: vendor invoice number in the reference field, the gross dollar amount of the invoice, and freight, tax, or miscellaneous amounts. At this point, the system will edit and cross check all data entered to prevent duplicate payments and eliminate mathematical errors. The matching system includes internal controls to prevent fraud, such as having one division authorize or receive purchases and another make the payments.

A second control feature is that an invoice must match an authorizing packing slip record exactly before a check can be written. If a purchase order price is different from an invoice price, the invoice cannot be paid.

The third control compares all invoices to be paid with previously approved invoices, searching for possible duplicates. This process takes place when each invoice is selected and matched with a packing slip for payment. If a duplicate is located, the system will reject the voucher from the system.

When the user puts an X next to the packing slip number, another screen appears, showing the invoice item amount and the packing slip's extended value. Depending upon whether the two are equal, the user indicates acceptance or rejection.

SIMPLIFY ENTRIES TO THE GENERAL LEDGER

Matching invoices automatically simplifies entries to the general ledger by reducing time at month-end formerly spent correcting invalid account numbers and verifying batch totals during the month. In addition, the staff used to spend numerous hours correcting cost data relating to the inventory quantities of raw materials received and purchase price variance being generated from the manual vouchering system. Now with an automated accounts-payable system these journal entries can be created automatically, either during the period or at month-end. Also, if desired, journal vouchers can be summarized by accounting distribution to cut down on the number of detail transactions that must be entered into the general ledger.

The system verifies the account distribution against the general ledger file for each transaction to reduce the number of errors related to incorrect account numbers, part numbers, vendor numbers, and unit of measure.

ESTABLISH ACTUAL OBLIGATION AND CASH COMMITMENTS

With our manual system, the only forecasting we could perform was reviewing the open balance report generated after the books were closed for the particular month. We needed to be able to project our cash requirements into the future to match them with available cash resources and avoid overdrawing bank accounts.

Cash requirements can be determined easily in an automated system for any number of days into the future (see Table 1). Management can review current obligations and make timely decisions regarding the payments to vendors or can acquire additional capital.

CHECK WRITING

By automating the accounts-payable function, checks and all the necessary supporting detail (invoice and credit memos) can be written automatically. All automated systems also must provide for entering and controlling off-line (manual) checks. In this case, post-audit always should occur to ensure correctness and proper authorization. No checks should be issued without these controls, and those that get post-audit should be held to the bare minimum.

Another important step, which should come before the actual check writing, is to search for possible duplications. This process should include the following procedures?

- Establish a storage period for all approved invoices, based on your business and the normal purchase term.
- Determine the duplicate match criteria; we used invoice number, dollar amount, and vendor number.
- Print the duplicate payment possibility list.

CAPTURING VENDOR HISTORY

It is very difficult to gather historical vendor information in a manual system, particularly with a large number of vendors. It is also difficult to obtain current detailed information regarding outstanding obligations and items that have been paid recently so as to answer vendor inquiries.

TABLE 1 AMSCO—Accounts Payable Outstanding Voucher control

Pay Date	Vouchered Gross Amount	Vouchered Discounts	Vouchered Net Amount	Unvouchered Gross Amount	Unvouchered Discounts	Unvouchered Net Amounts	Total Gross Amount	Total Discount	Total Net
00–00–00	80,271.29	29.77	80,301.06	.00	.00	.00	80,271.29	29.77	80,301.06
10–12–88	905,592.53	3,566.37	902,386.16	.00	.00	.00	905,952.53	3,566.37	902,386.16
10–14–88	1,127,328.34	714.45	1,126,613.89	86,519.80	81.86	86,437.94	1,213,848.14	796.31	1,213,051.83
10–19–88	82,586.95	10.09	82,576.86	950.00	.54	949.46	83,536.95	10.63	83,526.32
TOTAL	2,035,596.53	4,320.68	2,031,275.85	87,369.80	82.40	87,387.40	2,123,066.33	4,403.08	2,118,663.25

This automated system quickly captures and retains historical information by vendor, showing invoice numbers, amount paid, date paid, voucher date, check number, and voucher month. The system also displays individual vouchers, showing the general ledger account number charged and if freight, sales tax, or a cash discount was applied to that voucher. This automated system can display information by vendor number, check number, or purchase order number.

SIMPLIFYING MANAGEMENT REPORTING

Running a manual accounts payable system is a labor-intensive process, so the number of reports often is limited to a basic few—those that enable management to keep its head above water. Once the payables function has been automated, with a report writer, management can expand requests for information.

Possible reports are:

- *Control reports:*
    Daily voucher control
    Detail receiving reports
    Vendor audit log
    Problem purchase orders
    Accounts-payable audit log
    Unbalanced vouchers

- *Management reports:*
    Packing slip detail report
    Accounts-payable default report
    Disbursement analysis
    Check register control totals
    Accounts-payable check register
    1099 reports
    Preliminary report
    Voucher register

AUTOMATING RECURRING TRANSACTIONS

There are generally two types of recurring transactions. The first are expense transactions with the same amount each period, such as lease payments, insurance premiums, and rentals. At the beginning of the year each approved voucher, complete with general ledger distribution, is entered on the system for each accounting month.

The second type of transactions, such as utility bills, has a different amount each period. These bills usually are approved by an appropriate authorizing party, although they rarely are checked as to accuracy unless the amount is very different from a normal bill. They can be automated, except that the purchase order should contain an acceptable amount, and a missing packing slip should be placed on the receiver file for the automatic matching.

Since installing the new matching system, AMSCO has reduced operating costs and duplicate payments, improved cash control through forecasting commitments to actual matched invoice forecasts, and improved internal reporting.

In addition to the cost savings, the morale of the accounts-payable staff has improved greatly. The added reports and quick, easy access to vendor information have reduced frustration in dealing with our vendors. If your firm does not have a computerized accounts-payable matching system, we highly recommend this very useful tool.

Reading 7–4

SUN MICROSYSTEMS AUTOMATES FINANCIAL REPORTING

By Mitchell A. Levy

Imagine starting a company and making the Fortune 500 after six years of operation, then, after seven years, moving to the 327th spot.

Imagine being the nation's fastest-growing major computer company for the second year in a row and, overall, being the third-fastest growing major firm in the nation. Imagine experiencing this growth while trying to provide a consistent mechanism for consolidated financial reporting.

Sun Microsystems did just that. We were founded February 1982. As of June 30, 1989, we had 10,200 employees and had shipped 170,000 units. We made the Fortune 500 in 1987, ranked at No. 463 with $500 million in sales. In 1988, we were ranked No. 327 with $1 billion in sales. For the fiscal year ending June 30, 1989, Sun's revenues had increased to $1.76 billion.

As in many start-up companies, Sun's consolidated financial reporting was generated both from our general ledger (G/L) and from a series of electronic spreadsheets. Our G/L report writer is cumbersome and requires MIS support. Therefore, specific one-time management reports were created from spreadsheets. To produce a management reporting package showing our operating results versus plan (budget) and outlook (forecast), we used a series of spreadsheets.

As we grew, this spreadsheet-based system became more and more complex. Two years ago, we were combining 64 spreadsheets of input to produce 37 spreadsheets of output. The process took one to two hours and had to be

Published by *Management Accounting,* copyright 1990, by National Association of Accountants, Montvale, NJ 07645.

rerun whenever something changed. The financial reporting workload doubled with our reorganization in July 1988, requiring us to consolidate 128 spreadsheets to produce 74 as output. A large amount of data had to be input by hand into the spreadsheets each month, consuming days of financial analysts' effort on clerical tasks.

Sun's current reporting structure is composed of more than 1,000 departments, which roll up to more than a dozen divisions/groups. They, in turn, contain numerous legal entities (geographies) and approximately 200 products: hardware, software, and customer service. With approximately 100 percent growth per year, we found it necessary to reorganize at least every 12 to 18 months, each reorganization straining our consolidated financial reporting system.

We desperately needed a system to streamline our consolidation process. To meet our financial reporting requirements, the system had to:

- Adapt quickly to new organizational structures.
- Consolidate data consistently by company, group, division, department, geography, and product.
- Compare actual operating results easily with plan and outlook.
- Provide standard reports automatically and allow users to build custom reports easily.
- Combine a number of standard and custom reports efficiently into a push-button reporting package.
- Replace the inquiry function of the G/L with a more user-oriented on-line query package.
- Eliminate the need for global distribution of reports and replace with user-generated reports.

After looking at many packages, we chose CONTROL, a product from Kay Consulting of Manhattan Beach, Calif. Today, 70 users from corporate, divisional, and geographical (sales) finance organizations, in U.S., European and intercontinental operations, are using this solution. In addition to streamlining the effort involved with reorganizations, we have saved more than three labor/months per month and more than 500 hours per year with push-button versus intensive data-gathering tasks. The bottom line is that we spend more time analyzing the data and less time gathering it.

THE CHOSEN SOFTWARE

The difference between CONTROL and other packages we looked at is that CONTROL is an application, not a tool. A tool would be a product such as a spreadsheet, in which the user must define the functionality of the system and set up the reporting capabilities. The developers at Kay Consulting have defined the general characteristics of financial analysis in broad terms and have incorporated them in CONTROL. The financial functionality and standard reporting capability are part of the package.

CONTROL allows the user to develop "tasks" (data bases) with financial functionality built in. Each task has four dimensions: time, rows, organizations, and datatypes. This contrasts with a spreadsheet, which has two dimensions, typically rows and time.

The first step in developing a task is to define both the row names (revenue, bookings, and so on) and row logic (defining which rows sum to total operating expenses, for example). The second step is to define the organizational names and their roll-up relationships. Once rows and organizations have been defined, CONTROL automatically produces the two dimensions of time (typically months) and data types (actuals, two different plans, 14 outlooks, and eight test cases).

Once the task is set up and data are loaded, 23 different standard reports can be used to extract information.

Using CONTROL, we set up a financial reporting system called CORONA (Corporate Reporting On Anything). Data for CORONA are fed from a number of different sources (as illustrated in Figure 1).

With CONTROL, data either can be entered by hand or fed through a file. For above-the-line outlook and plan information (revenues and cost of goods sold), the divisional or geographical financial analyst chooses how to input data. For departmental budgeting information (departmental operating expenses), we have an in-house system with a direct feed to CORONA. For actual operating results, there is an automatic feed for G/L data.

REORGANIZATIONS MADE EASY

The automatic feed from the G/L to CONTROL is run every night during close week. We refresh data for the entire month while storing historical data for two years. We also store quarterly data since inception. Using CONTROL utilities, we have set up the feed so that most changes that occur to the G/L will be reflected in CORONA. Whenever a new organization or account is added to the G/L, it is added automatically to CORONA. Only when information is merged in the G/L, do we need to merge it manually in CORONA.

We are currently in the middle of the first user-driven test of CORONA's reorganizational capabilities. Sun has separated our U.S. field organization into three areas: east, central, and west. These three areas will have P&L responsibility, and it was requested that CORONA provide the appropriate P&L reports.

The first step was to get our order entry (O/E) and G/L systems to recognize the three additional geographic areas. Then the O/E system must pass these data to the G/L. Once the additional accounts and data are in the G/L, the CONTROL utilities will add the new organizational structure automati-

FIGURE 1 CORONA Environment Corporate Reporting on Anything

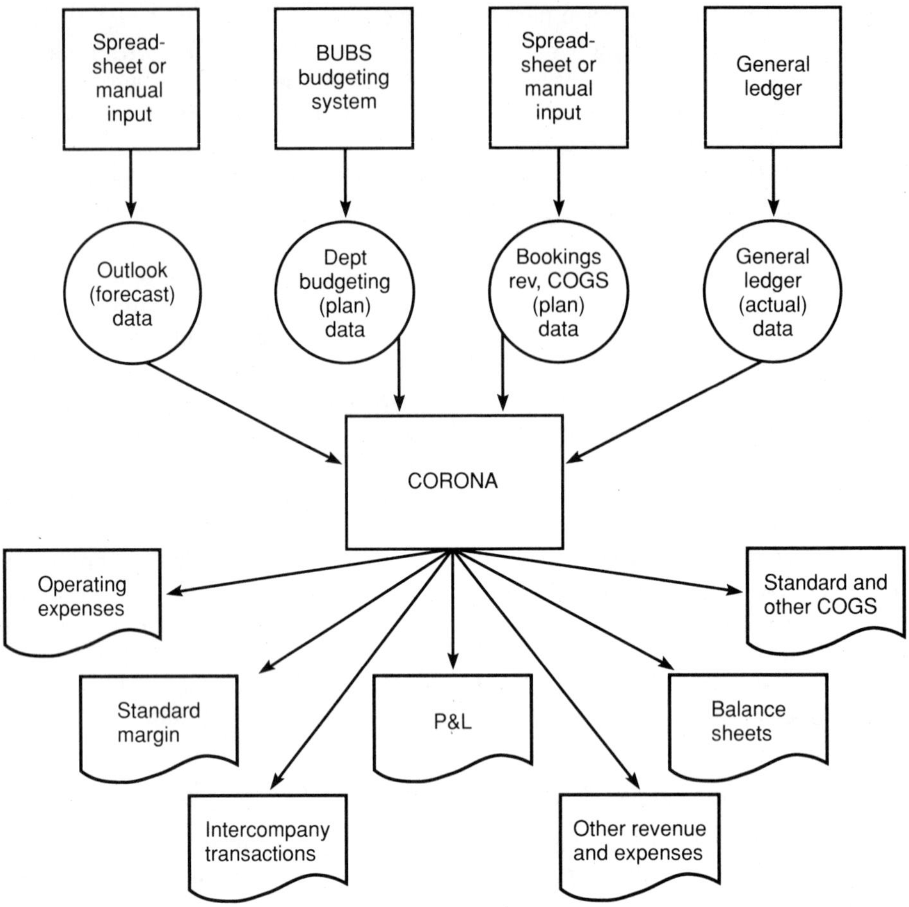

cally. The entire reporting package will reflect this change immediately. Other than taking an advisory role, we do not have to work with CORONA to make this happen.

HARDWARE ENVIRONMENT

CONTROL runs on a number of hardware environments but not on a Sun workstation. Therefore, we rented CONTROL to run on our mainframe computer. Using Sun connectivity tools, users can access the mainframe through their Sun workstation, so that the mainframe terminal becomes just another window on their workstation. With different windows, they can cut text from one window (CONTROL) and paste it to another, such as a spreadsheet, electronic mail, a graphics package, or a host of other applications.

Having access to the mainframe through the network means that all users connected to the network have password-controlled access to this system. There was no additional work so that our European operations could access CORONA. By using our network, any Sun European location can gain access to the computer in our Milpitas data center.

SECURITY IN THREE DIMENSIONS

With CONTROL, we can set up security on three of the four dimensions: rows, organizations, and datatypes. We actually have more flexibility with CONTROL than with our G/L to allow password-controlled access to information. For example, CONTROL has the capability of giving the CFO the opportunity to review all information for SUN, while limiting a divisional financial analyst to access information for his specific division only.

BENEFITS

CONTROL was delivered and installed at the end of November 1988. On February 1, 1989, the first phase of CORONA was released. This phase allowed a few users access to monthly information since the beginning of our fiscal year (July). Mid-February was our first load of month-end close G/L data and the kickoff of the first reporting package. The second phase started March 1, 1989. At that time, it allowed a larger number of users to access operating results but allowed only a limited number of users to input outlook data.

We have found that CORONA can grow with Sun's ever-changing organizational structure. For example, we are able to implement the new U.S. sales organizational structure effortlessly and to add many new products to our product line. Since the first reporting period and the start of the second phase of CORONA, we have passed several important milestones, including:

- Actuals package—monthly management reporting package issued to the board of directors and vice president, detailing our operating results. It includes a detailed and summary P&L by group and geography, a by-product revenue and gross margin analysis, and an extensive review of operating expenses by division and geography, among others. CORONA produces 95 percent of the reports for this package in 30 minutes. Prior to implementing CORONA, this package required 72 labor-hours of effort.

- Close package—monthly package issued to divisional controllers during the close conference, detailing our operating performance. CORONA produces 90 percent of the reports for this package in 30 minutes, versus 60 labor-hours.

- Product margin analysis—monthly package issued by one of our product groups. It includes a product margin analysis, detailing units, revenue, discount and discount percentage, standard margin, and standard margin percentage, among others. CORONA produces 100 percent of the reports for this package in 20 minutes, versus 40 labor-hours.

- Financial planning—our corporate financial planning people used CONTROL to write a model for the 1990 fiscal plan. We have saved more than 200 labor-hours consolidating with CONTROL versus a set of spreadsheets.

- MIS resources—we've freed up a large amount of resources in this MIS area that supported G/L reports and loaded plan data into the G/L. This year, plan data will reside in CORONA, not in the G/L. Last year, more than 300 hours of MIS time were spent with the financial planning people loading plan data into the G/L. This year, none of that resource is being used. Because the data will not reside in the G/L, we will discontinue the production run of any actual-versus-plan reports, also freeing up resources. Instead, users can get these reports in the format they want, when they want to get them, from CORONA.

Table 1 shows some statistics about our implementation of CONTROL.

FROM WISH LIST TO REALITY

Most important, CONTROL gives us a tremendous amount of flexibility. With this system in place, we've been able to develop our management reporting packages sooner with greater accuracy and consistency. We've also been able to produce reports that were on the wish list in the past. CONTROL has made reorganization easy from a management reporting viewpoint and has

TABLE 1   Implementing Control

Time to implement:	3 months
Manpower for CONTROL work	1 person—3 person-months
Manpower for other system work	3 persons—1 person-month
Number of people trained	150
Users today/projected	70\150
Inquiry response time	10–30 seconds versus 3–10 minutes for G/L on-line inquiries
Report turnaround time	10–30 seconds to 1 day (user-written) versus 2–4 months (MIS-written) using G/L report writer

made new ways of dividing our business effortless. Overall, this tool has given us the ability to keep pace with the dynamic growth that Sun has made in the past and will continue to make in the future.

Reading 7-5

AN INTERNAL AUDIT OF A CHURCH

By L. Murphy Smith and Jeffrey R. Miller

"Religious Reporting: Is It the Gospel Truth?" was the eyecatching title of a recent *Management Accounting* article. The authors concluded that, while religious (financial) reporting is making strides, religious organizations need assistance from accounting professionals if the efforts are to succeed.[1]

Church accounting systems operate in a unique environment and have specialized accounting and auditing problems. Most churches are small and thus have limited resources, while only larger churches can afford a full-time financial or business administrator.[2] Consequently, professional accountants are often asked to volunteer their financial expertise in administering church accounting systems. This article addresses how accountants can contribute to the internal audit function of a local church.

Professional accountants working in industry, public accounting, and government who are members of local churches can contribute toward the efficient financial operations of their church. The accountant may serve in an official capacity as the church treasurer, as a member of the finance committee, or as a member of any committee making a financial-related decision (e.g., equipment acquisition or land purchase). Even if the accountant is not in a special office, he or she can contribute as a regular member of the congregation by offering his or her input during the budget process.

Professionals are generally expected to participate in community activities, such as churches and other civic organizations. In an article in the *Journal of Accountancy*, this concept was stated as follows.[3]

> For the profession to fulfill its civic role in a changing society, more CPAs will have to enlist in public service activities. The concept of providing service *pro*

---

bono publico—for the public good—should be accepted, as it has by other professions, by the majority of accountants as a standard of professional behavior.

The AICPA specifically addresses this professional responsibility in the following statement from the AICPA bulletin on *Economics of Accounting Practice:* "The financial resources available to the professional man from his practice must be sufficient to enable him . . . to render the public services which the community may ask him. . . ."[4] This participation could include involvement in churches that are often a focal point of community activity and perhaps affect more people than any other civic or community organization.

Unfortunately, accounting professionals have not always fulfilled this public service responsibility. In a survey of upper-income individuals by one state society of CPAs, it was found that CPAs and the services they offer have a high level of respect. However, this respect did not carry over into the area of volunteer activities. When compared to bankers, attorneys, teachers, and doctors, CPAs were rated "dead last" in volunteer activities.[5]

Accountants can make valuable contributions to their churches by offering their knowledge and skills acquired through work experience in public accounting, government, and industry. Whether their motive is professional in nature, strictly humanitarian, or perhaps some combination of both, there is a need for involvement by professional accountants in church accounting activities.

THE INTERNAL AUDIT FUNCTION

Although a local church would likely not have a full-time accountant, let alone an internal auditor, the church's financial custodians could benefit from the information provided by an internal audit. Persons who could benefit from and carry out the internal audit include the church treasurer, finance committee, and board of deacons.

The origin of auditing can be traced back to ancient Egypt where two records of the fiscal receipts were kept by two officials.[6] The Bible explicitly mentions the importance of monitoring agents in Jesus's parable of the "dishonest accountant" in Luke 16:1-13.[7]

> A rich man hired an accountant to handle his affairs, but soon a rumor went around that the accountant was thoroughly dishonest. So his employer called him in and said, 'What's this I hear about your stealing from me? Get your report in order, for you are to be dismissed.'

An annual internal audit can be used as a "monitoring agent" in the church accounting system. This internal audit could be the responsibility of a special audit committee (perhaps, a subcommittee of the finance/budget committee).

Major objectives of a church audit were given by Loudell Ellis in his *Church Treasurer Handbook,* as follows.[8]

1. To determine that adequate internal control procedures exist and that such procedures are being followed.

2. To determine that all donations to the church were deposited and recorded correctly.

3. To determine that securities were safeguarded and that related revenue was collected and recorded.

4. To determine that disbursements were properly authorized (i.e., that the budget was followed or that changes were approved) and that authorized members approved payment of invoices.

5. To determine that payments to vendors at year-end were not delayed because of overspending the budget.

6. To determine that records were maintained on plant and equipment items and that adequate insurance was obtained.

7. To determine compliance with federal and state regulations, including properly and timely paid employment taxes and income taxes, if applicable.

8. To recommend improved procedures and practices.

Internal auditing involves the evaluation of efficiency and effectiveness of financial and nonfinancial operations. Some specific items that could be evaluated are discussed in the following sections.

The first area involves assessment of financial performance. Since churches are nonprofit organizations, this evaluation would focus on a church's financial goals, which, of course, do not normally include profit maximization. One item that could be evaluated, for example, is whether total church receipts (tithes and offerings) were as much or more than church expenditures.

Other financial goals that could be evaluated include the following: (1) to use a certain percentage of funds for specific projects (a goal might be to use 10 percent of all funds for foreign missions), (2) to reduce debt, and (3) to increase the building fund. The internal audit would determine whether these financial objectives were being achieved. The internal auditors would then report their findings to the whole church membership, board of deacons, church financial committee, or other appropriate party.

Jesus stated the major objective of the church as follows: "[G]o into all the world and preach the Good News to everyone, everywhere."[9] In accomplishing this overall objective, individual churches provide a wide variety of ministries to church members and nonmembers. While providing these ministries, churches should strive to make the most efficient use of resources, while avoiding waste and mismanagement. The objectives of church accounting systems have been defined as follows.[10]

1. To produce complete and accurate accounting information as the basis for the handling of the financial affairs of the church in a businesslike manner.
2. To secure a sound financial foundation.
3. To keep members accurately informed on current financial matters and encourage their more active support.

The second area of internal auditing involves evaluation of nonfinancial operations. For churches, nonfinancial goals might include items such as attendance rates, new memberships, and special community projects (e.g., aid to disaster victims and food pantry services). Again, the internal auditors would report on these items to the appropriate party.

A third area of internal auditing involves compliance with laws, contracts, and directives from the church's governing body (e.g., board of deacons or elders). Compliance and operational auditing are discussed in the next two sections. Then the remainder of the article focuses on aspects of the church accounting system.

COMPLIANCE AUDITING

Compliance with laws, contracts (e.g., loan agreements), and directives from the organization's governing body are extremely important to the financial welfare of a church. Reputation and integrity are important to any business organization, but they are probably even more important to most religious organizations. The downfall of many religious organizations may be traced to instances where its leadership has been accused of failing in meeting its fiduciary responsibilities. Some religious leaders, for example, have been recently indicted for diverting millions of dollars of contributions for personal use.[11] An internal audit may not be only a deterrent but also act as a guard against false accusations.

The Internal Revenue Service has been more aggressive lately in auditing large religious organizations.[12] Favorable tax laws have been established for the benefit of religious organizations and their ministers. However, along with the tax benefits, certain administrative procedures are required. For example, part of a minister's salary may be excluded from taxable income as a housing allowance. A specific amount for the housing allowance, though, should be included in the minutes of the meetings of the church's governing board.

OPERATIONAL AUDITING

While the steps of a financial (external) audit are guided by generally accepted auditing standards (GAAS), internal auditing standards are provided in *Standards for the Professional Practice of Internal Auditing*. These offer guidance in areas of independence, professional proficiency, scope and performance of work, and management of the internal audit department. Although most churches probably do not have an official internal audit department, many churches have an annual audit (internal or external) to evaluate their operations. Internal audits should be based on the guidelines provided by these internal auditing standards.

For operational audits, some general guidelines have been provided as follows.[13]

1. Plan the work to be performed, including the establishment of standards by which the audited operation is to be evaluated.
2. Gather evidence with which to measure the performance of the operation.
3. Analyze and investigate deviations from the standards.
4. Determine corrective action, where needed.
5. Report the results to the appropriate level of management.

In planning the audit, a meeting should be made between the auditors and the supervisors of the operation being audited. The auditor should seek the cooperation of the church's personnel at this time.

Cooperation is essential for the efficient completion of the audit. At the planning meeting, the auditor may ask questions like the following.[14]

1. Do you receive the reports and other information necessary to conduct the operation?
2. What use do you make of each report?
3. What operating problems are you experiencing?
4. Describe your training programs.
5. How do you set priorities for the operation?

For the sake of efficiency if not success, the persons performing the audit will need the cooperation of church personnel. The church's financial-related personnel are discussed below.

CHURCH FINANCIAL POSITIONS

There are many alternative ways to organize the church accounting system. One recommended system would require at least three components or positions: (1) controller, (2) financial secretary, and (3) finance/budget committee. These positions or similar positions are discussed in guidelines for setting up church accounting systems.[15]

The *controller* has a crucial role within the structure of the church accounting system. This person is responsible for supervising the accounting function, preparing the financial reports for the church board and congregation, reviewing all checks following treasurer's signature and completing government forms (e.g., payroll). In many churches, the controller also serves as the treasurer and thus signs checks. However, a better internal control arrangement would provide for both a treasurer position and a controller position.

FIGURE 1   Percentage Distribution of Church Financial Positions

	Denomination		
	Overall	*Catholic*	*Protestant*
Position	*(n = 274)*	*(n = 114)*	*(n = 160)*
Controller	27.7	35.1	22.5
Financial secretary	66.1	45.6	80.6
Finance/budget committee	77.0	73.7	79.4

SOURCE: Adapted from Smith & McDaniel, "Church Accounting Systems: Current Practices and Recommended Procedures," *Business Insights*, Fall 1985, pp. 18–23.

The *financial secretary* is customarily charged with maintaining official accounting records, preparing supporting documents for disbursements, and preparing checks for the treasurer's signature. Following signature, the checks would be forwarded to the controller for review.

The *finance/budget committee* is assigned the job of preparing the budget for its various approvals. Additionally, the finance/budget committee will typically appoint an audit committee. The audit committee (which may be a subcommittee of the finance/budget committee) is delegated responsibility for the annual audit of the church accounting records. In larger churches, the committee may engage a CPA to perform an annual independent audit. Other duties of the audit committee may include reconciling the bank account and confirming that the church's contribution records agree with church members' personal records (i.e., that the contribution record maintained by the financial secretary agrees with the actual contribution of the members).

Figure 1 shows the percentage of churches with each of these positions. A breakdown by Protestant and Catholic churches is included.

RECORDING THE TRANSACTIONS

Considering that most ministers and even various other officers in the church may not have accounting backgrounds, church accounting systems should be designed in an easy to understand straightforward manner. Application of the double-entry system to a church situation requires that a chart of accounts be devised in which appropriate accounts are described in an easy-to-understand fashion. Accounts should be maintained in a general ledger where increases, decreases, and account balances are shown. Generally, transactions should be initially recorded in a journal, then periodically (e.g., daily or weekly) posted/recorded in the ledger from the journal. Every month or so, reports should be provided to the church's governing board (e.g., board of deacons) and/or congregation.

In the church financial statement shown in Figure 2, Part 1 summarizes the activity in all the church funds, and Part 2 provides detailed information about an individual fund.

FIGURE 2 Church Financial Reports

PART 1
Cash-Basis Statement of Inflows and Outflows

Fund	*Beginning Balance (Date)*	*Inflows*	*Outflows*	*Ending Balance (Date)*
General	$ x	$ x	$ x	$ x
Building	x	x	x	x
Debt retirement	x	x	x	x
Foreign missions	x	x	x	x
Total	$xx	$xx	$xx	$xx

PART 2
Fund Activity

	(Date)	*(Date)*
Beginning fund balance	$ xx	$ xx
Inflows		
Plate collections	x	x
Sunday school offerings	x	x
Special collections	x	x
Interest earned	x	x
Miscellaneous	x	x
Total gross inflows	xx	xx
Outflows—operating		
Salaries	x	x
Rent	x	x
Utilities	x	x
Supplies	x	x
Telephone	x	x
Insurance	x	x
Total operating outflows	(xx)	(xx)
Net of operations	$ xx	$ xx
Capital disbursements	(x)	(x)
Debt retirement	(x)	(x)
Transfers	(x)	(x)
Net increase (decrease)	x	x
Ending fund balance	$ xx	$ xx

BUDGETING AND FINANCIAL REPORTING

Budgeting is a paramount planning device for any organization. Churches are no exception. An obvious requirement would be that all disbursements be included in the budget. A church budget should be approved by the membership or by special action of the governing board (e.g., the board of the deacons).

The Bible explicitly mentions the importance of participation in budgeting in Proverbs 15:22: "Plans go wrong with too few counselors; many counselors bring success."[16] Generally, the church's tentative budget is prepared by the finance/budget committee and is later approved by the congregation and/or governing board. Many churches make use of pledge cards which encourage contributions from members, but which also help in the budgeting process. In addition, churches generally provide special contribution envelopes to members.

Periodically, such as monthly, quarterly, and/or yearly, a report should be prepared and distributed to the congregation, indicating amounts collected and disbursed. The actual collections and disbursements can be compared to the budgeted amounts. Consequently, church members can derive more confidence from the church's ability to handle its financial affairs while being assured that their offerings are being used in the manner intended. In some cases, this has been shown to result in greater contributions.[17]

In addition to the periodic churchwide (aggregate) report, members should be provided with their personal (individual) contribution records on a periodic basis. This report will assist members in reporting contributions on their tax returns as well as confirming that their contributions were received and accurately recorded by their church.

The percentage of churches using budget/finance reports is shown in Figure 3. The percentage of churches using other accounting procedures (e.g., an envelope system) is provided in Figure 4.

FIGURE 3   Percentage Distribution of Budget/Finance Reporting Frequency

	Demonination		
Frequency	Overall (n = 274)	Catholic (n = 114)	Protestant (n = 160)
Monthly	65.3	41.2	82.5
Quarterly	33.6	74.6	39.4
Annually	78.1	82.5	75.0

SOURCE: Adapted from Smith & McDaniel, "Church Accounting Systems: Current Practices and Recommended Procedures," *Business Insights,* Fall 1985, pp. 18–23.

FIGURE 4 Percentage Distribution of Church Accounting Procedures

	Denomination		
Procedure	Overall (n = 274)	Catholic (n = 114)	Protestant (n = 160)
Envelope system	91.2	93.9	89.4
Contribution information	81.4	78.9	83.1
Pledge cards	50.3	34.2	63.8
Annual audit	60.9	47.4	70.6

SOURCE: Adapted from Smith & McDaniel, "Church Accounting Systems: Current Practices and Recommended Procedures," *Business Insights*, Fall 1985, pp. 18–23.

THE IMPORTANCE OF INTERNAL CONTROL

The concept of internal control is as relevant to churches as it is to other types of organizations. A primary motive for a well-designed set of internal controls in a church is to support the fiscal management capabilities of the church's officers and employees. Inadequate internal controls can severely hinder the fiscal management capabilities of church officers and employees and place them in a position where they may be unduly tempted to become engaged in questionable activities and accounting practices. To subject well-intentioned officers and employees to this temptation runs against the ideals embraced by the church. Therefore, one of the most beneficial services that a professional accountant can perform for a church is to explain the importance of controls to his or her fellow church members. This will often not be an easy task.

Some members may feel that the concept of internal control is irrelevant to the church. Members embracing this false belief need to be reminded of the following points:

1. Assuming that church officers and employees are honest, strong controls should be provided to guard them from suspicion and false accusations.

2. The church should not permit honest individuals to serve in positions that create strong temptations to commit questionable acts.

3. Chaotic accounting and fiscal management conditions resulting from inadequate controls place officers and employees under unnecessary conditions of stress. This can be expected to impair their mental well-being and task effectiveness.

One important internal control policy in church accounting is to assign joint custody of assets to two or more individuals. The Bible itself addresses this control policy in 2 Corinthians 8:18-22. In this passage, a gift from the church in Corinth to Jerusalem is being delivered by Paul and three others. Paul says[18]:

> By traveling together we will guard against any suspicion, for we are anxious that no one should find fault with the way we are handling this large gift. God knows we are honest but I want everyone else to know it, too. That is why we have made this arrangement.

In this passage, Paul identified the importance of the control policy involving joint custody of assets. Not only does the control reduce the temptation for embezzlement (by removing the opportunity and possible temptation), but it also reduces the suspicions of other people that embezzlement might occur.

CONCLUSION

In addition to possible intrinsic personal rewards received by the accountant from service to his or her church, such service may well enhance the image of the accounting profession as a whole. For a church to achieve its financial and nonfinancial operating objectives, an internal audit might be essential. An internal audit could provide useful information to the governing board or congregation of the church. As shown in Figure 4, only 60.9 percent of all churches have an annual audit. Thus, many churches are not taking advantage of this useful evaluation tool. This article has described a number of financial and nonfinancial items that may be evaluated by an internal audit.

Professional accountants are encouraged to assist churches in carefully evaluating their church accounting systems. Efforts should be made to maintain the most effective system possible by incorporating well-designed internal controls. As this effort is undertaken by accounting professionals, churches will be better equipped to fulfill their responsibilities as good stewards of the money entrusted to them by members of their congregations.

Notes

1. Harper & Harper, "Religious Reporting: Is It the Gospel Truth?" *Management Accounting,* February 1988, pp. 34–39.
2. Boyce, "Accounting for Churches," *Journal of Accountancy,* February 1984, pp. 96–102.
3. Weinstein & Smith, "Public Service and the Profession," *Journal of Accountancy,* May 1985, pp. 114–120.
4. AICPA Bulletin No. 3, "The Different Art of Setting Fees, Economics of Accounting Practice" (New York: AICPA, 1957), p. 5.
5. Flesher, "Letters to the Editor: Public Service and the Profession," *Journal of Accountancy,* July 1985, p. 39.
6. R. Brown, *A History of Accounting and Accounts, New Impression* (London: Frank Cass & Co., 1968).
7. *The Living Bible* (Wheaton, IL: Tyndale House Publishers, 1971). *The Living Bible* is a modern-day paraphrase of the Bible.

8. L. O. Ellis, *Church Treasurer Handbook* (Valley Forge, PA: Judson Press, 1978).

9. *The Living Bible*, p. 777.

10. B. A. Woodward, "Churches," *Encyclopedia of Accounting Systems* (Englewood Cliffs, NJ: Prentice Hall, Inc., 1975).

11. "Ex-PTL Chief Bakker, Aide Dortch Indicted," *Houston Chronicle*, December 6, 1988, at 1A, 14A.

12. Stepp, "IRS Launches Sweeping Probe of TV Preachers," *Houston Chronicle*, December 6, 1988, at 1A, 16A.

13. D. H. Taylor and G. W. Glezen, *Auditing: Integrated Concepts and Procedures*, 3d ed. (New York: John Wiley & Sons, 1985), pp. 41–42.

14. *Ibid.*, p. 43.

15. See, e.g., King, "Constructing a Parish Information System," *Journal of Information Systems Management*, October 1983, pp. 34–39; Cunningham & Reemsnyder II, "Church Accounting: The Other Side of Stewardship," *Management Accounting*, August 1983, pp. 58–62; Prentice, "Church Accounting," *The Woman CPA*, April 1981, pp. 8–14; and Floyd, "Management Accounting for Churches," *Management Accounting*, February 1969, pp. 56–59.

16. *The Living Bible*, p. 511.

17. Cunningham & Reemsnyder II.

18. *The Living Bible*, p. 936.

CHAPTER 8

The New Office Technology— LANs and Desktop Publishing

At a relatively low cost, a local area network (LAN) provides both small and medium-sized firms with the ability to effectively communicate, share equipment, and share data among two to several hundred microcomputers. Conceptually, a LAN achieves the MIS objectives of centralized data and distributed processing. A LAN provides for the allocation of appropriate information to users in the organization who presently require it or may need it in the future. The use of LANs has increased dramatically among all types of organizations, including CPA firms.

The first two articles included with this chapter discuss LANs. "The Network Decision" provides an introduction to local area networks and their use. "Networking Microcomputers in CPA Firms" focuses on LAN applications in firms of independent accountants. As mentioned in this article, even if a practitioner does not presently need a LAN, it is probable that several of the practitioner's clients will be able to effectively use one in the near future. Consequently, practitioners may have consulting opportunities if they can provide their clients with current information on LANs.

Desktop publishing has spread rapidly since its introduction in late 1984. Many persons who initially thought little of desktop publishing soon discovered that they could produce professional quality documents after investing only limited time learning the required technology. Consequently, a variety of customer and trade publications have been developed as a direct consequence of desktop publishing technology. Any publisher, including CPA firms, can create documents at a personal computer without incurring the cost of hiring production artists or designers.

Two articles pertaining to desktop publishing are provided. The first, "Electronic Publishing: The Next Great Office Revolution," provides basic information regarding initial setup, choosing software, and avoiding mistakes. The second paper, "Desktop Publishing: Professional-Looking Documents from the Office Micro," examines basic information and lists a number of full-featured and lower-level desktop publishing software packages.

CHAPTER 8 READINGS

1. D. Scott Hagen and D'arcy Elliot, "The Network Decision," *CMA Magazine,* September/October 1987, pp. 49–53.
2. Michael K. Shaub, "Networking Microcomputers in a CPA Firm," *Today's CPA,* July/August 1987, pp. 31–35.
3. William M. Winsor, "Electronic Publishing: The Next Great Office Revolution" (The Practitioner & The Computer), *The CPA Journal,* February 1988, pp. 90–91.
4. Christopher Wolfe and Kent T. Fields, "Desktop Publishing: Professional-Looking Documents from the Office Micro," *Journal of Accountancy,* March 1988, pp. 81–82, 84–87.

CHAPTER 8 QUESTIONS

Article 1

1. Describe a local area network (LAN).
2. What type of computer usually serves as a LAN "traffic cop"?
3. Describe how a firm can benefit from a LAN.

Article 2

4. Discuss three general categories of LAN applications.
5. Describe three basic LAN configurations.

Article 3

6. Discuss some uses of desktop publishing.
7. Comment on the controversy over industry standards associated with desktop publishing.

Article 4

8. Give examples of and describe the printed materials that may be produced by typical CPA firms.
9. Discuss the distinguishing characteristic of "true" desktop publishing software. What is WYSIWYG?

Reading 8–1

THE NETWORK DECISION

By D. Scott Hagen and D'arcy Elliot

At an astonishingly low cost, the local area network makes it possible for small and medium-sized businesses to bring isolated pockets of productivity into the mainstream of corporation information. The challenge of microcomputer technology has been met head on in the workplace and, from all outward appearances, met successfully. Financial professionals, in particular, have been at the forefront of the revolution. Nowhere is the acceptance of micros more evident than in the accounting departments of business and government offices of all sizes.

But the real challenge has only begun. While microcomputers have often led to astonishing productivity growth, modern managers are frustrated with the inherent duplication and inaccessibility of corporate data on the desks of their peers and subordinates. The goal of satisfying the integrated MIS needs of business is apparently being thwarted by the existence of remote and effectively inaccessible pockets of productivity which arose from the first wave of computer technology.

As society and business become more information-intensive, executives are coming to realize that information is a valuable corporate resource and a powerful competitive tool. They are therefore moving to give the management of corporate data the time and attention it requires.

For many businesses, the solution is a local area network (LAN). With rapid side-by-side development of communications and microcomputer technology, it is now possible to address the higher level MIS needs of an organization without abandoning the investment already made in microcomputers and user training. And this at a cost which is astonishingly low by traditional standards.

WHAT IS A LOCAL AREA NETWORK?

As we use the expression, a local area network is a collection of from three to several hundred microcomputers tied together physically in such a way as to facilitate high-speed communication and information and resource sharing.

A dedicated high-speed microcomputer called a file server, equipped with a high-capacity, high-speed fixed disk drive, is used for storage of all

Reprinted from the September-October 1987 issue of *CMA Magazine*, by permission of the Society of Management Accountants of Canada.

data. This computer acts as a "traffic cop" for workstations accessing the data. A high-speed tape backup unit for regular, reliable backup of corporate data is normally connected to this computer or to one of the network workstations.

Workstations take the form of microcomputers connected by twisted-pair wire or coaxial cable to the file server. The network operates by downloading programs and data required by the workstations, which then operate like stand-alone micros. When finished, the workstations write the revised or updated data back to the fixed disk on the file server. Modern networks are transparent, in the sense that users are unlikely to notice anything other than a dramatic improvement in the speed of load and save operations when interacting with the file server.

Conceptually, a LAN is the physical realization of the MIS objective of centralized data and distributed processing. It implies a recognition of information as a corporate, rather than an individual or departmental, resource, and reflects the importance of information to the management of the modern corporation. It facilitates the distribution of appropriate information to those in the organization who require it, now or in the future.

LAN technology provides an opportunity to eliminate duplication, to maintain currency, and to develop new applications more easily and with greater cohesion. It also enables an organization to progress with relative ease and familiarity to larger-scale, fully integrated MIS development when the need arises and as resources become available.

WHY SHOULD YOU CONSIDER NETWORKING?

Even if full-scale MIS development work is not on your immediate horizon, there are a number of compelling reasons to consider LAN technology.

1. Security.   Modern LAN software makes extensive provision for security. Users normally "log on" to the network with a password, and may be assigned security in a highly selective manner on a file-by-file directory or application basis.

For example, a secretary may only have access to word processing software and documents on which she is presently working, while her superior may be granted access to the secretary's directory, accounting information, spreadsheet software, and an electronic mail function.

Nothing, of course, is totally protected in today's computer world, but security in current LAN packages is extremely tight.

2. Modularity.   Like modern component stereo systems, a network is a modular system. With the right combination of components, the whole becomes much more than the sum of the parts. Flexibility is created to put serious computing power where it is needed, and to shift resources as required.

It is possible to address the "weakest link" when attempting to enhance system performance, and to better plan and budget for development of the system. It becomes relatively easy to standardize workstations and software, and to negotiate and coordinate purchase arrangements.

It is also far less costly to make a mistake on the purchase of LAN software or a peripheral module than to make a corresponding mistake in a microcomputer or mainframe situation.

3. Speed. Networking in a properly planned layout provides an immediate and appreciable increase in speed for most software, as the central disk drive is almost invariably (and certainly should be) much faster than those found in stand-alone microcomputers.

4. Resource Sharing. There is an opportunity to share expensive hardware resources such as high-speed disk drives and tape units, laser printers, plotters, or optical disk readers. There is a further opportunity to standardize software, allowing cost sharing and achievement of considerable depth in applications development.

5. Communications. Electronic mail is a feature of most modern network software. LANs make it easier to communicate with those who are in and out of the office, or frequently on the go.

Many LAN vendors are now introducing products which allow for flexible "off-net" communications as well. A "communications server" allows network users to share a pool of modems, and can dramatically reduce costs associated with purchase of modems and rental of single business telephone lines. A number of practical alternatives are also available for LAN-to-minicomputer, LAN-to-mainframe, and offsite-to-LAN connections where these are required.

6. Data Integrity. You may have encountered a situation where your sales report advised you that total sales for the month were $98B,@!6, and several days' time and outside help were required to sort out the mess.

Network software is now available which provides various levels of fault-tolerance to protect against such horrors. The mechanisms range from dynamic monitoring and maintenance of bad blocks on the fixed disk with read-after-write verification, to complete duplication of file servers with "mirroring" of all disk write operations.

As your business comes to rely more and more on microcomputers, particularly where accounting or financial planning is involved, do not underestimate the value of network software capable of protecting your corporate data from hardware failures.

7. Backup and Secure Backup Storage. Centralized tape backup and secure storage of tapes, both in fireproof magnetic media safes and offsite, ensure that the corporate data is safely put to bed each night, and relieve users of the backup chore they all too often tend to resist.

8. Transactions Capability. There is an immediate opportunity for increased transactions capability, particularly for integrated accounting and data base software. For example, one clerk may be entering receivables at one workstation, another may be working with accounts payable, and still another with the general ledger—all at the same time, and with single copies of accounting software and data.

9. *User Friendliness/Ease of Expansion.* The potential for better communication between those with programming and development responsibilities and users is a natural feature of LANs. In addition, programming expertise can be spread effectively in several key user areas of the organization. Sharing of programming expertise makes it possible to develop applications which are user-friendly, are similar in design and operation, and are more closely aligned to each user's true needs.

Standardization of screens and routines in the various application programs is readily accomplished with current microcomputer software and can dramatically reduce, and often eliminate, the per employee cost of training.

10. *Potential for Formal MIS Development.* A LAN provides a powerful tool for those involved in or contemplating formal MIS development along data base lines. The implementation of a LAN ensures that the first requirement of MIS development—that corporate data exists in one place, and is centrally administered—is satisfied.

Over the longer term, the MIS potential of the corporation can be developed by organizing data according to formal data base design principles, and by overseeing planned and cohesive development and integration of applications.

WHO IS MOST LIKELY TO REALIZE THE BENEFITS?

Generally speaking, small to medium-sized businesses or smaller divisions of large corporations with low to moderate transaction volumes may look favorably to stand-alone microcomputer LAN solutions. This would include most businesses with 10 to 200 employees and 3 to 50 microcomputers.

The greatest benefit will accrue to those firms with multiple users of common data (customer files, sales or employee information) or applications (word processing, accounting, spreadsheet, data base). Those experiencing very rapid growth in number of computers or employees are likely to benefit from the resource-sharing side of LAN technology. Those struggling with the location or form of corporate information and wishing to adopt a more controlled and planned approach will find a local area network a valuable tool on the road to MIS development.

A moderate amount of microcomputer exposure and expertise is necessary to implement a LAN. A successful LAN installation requires, at a minimum, a degree of familiarity with common microcomputer operating systems and applications software.

WHAT IS THE COST?

The costs of a LAN will be both direct and hidden.

1. *Direct Costs.* At present, in Canada, a network file server with fixed disk and tape backup unit will run from $15,000 to $40,000. A new microcomputer workstation will range from $2,500 to $10,000, and existing micros may be added at an incremental cost of about $700. A central laser printer, virtually indispensable for professional word processing, will run from $3,500 to $15,000 or more.

LAN versions of popular software range from $700 to $2,500, often with an additional per user charge of $100 to $500. The network operating software cost will be approximately $2,500. An annual service contract to support the system hardware will range from 7 percent to 15 percent of the total capital outlay involved.

Thus, a small LAN, consisting of two point-of-sale terminals, a file server, and a computer for analysis, could require a capital outlay of about $30,000, while a network of 50 or more workstations and multiple file servers will involve some several hundred thousand dollars.

2. Hidden Costs.   It is important, indeed essential, that one person in the organization have responsibility and authority for system management. The level of technical expertise associated with operating a LAN is relatively high, and "network supervision" can easily become a full-time position for even a small network.

Additionally, introduction of a LAN, particularly in a primarily manual environment, requires a senior-level managerial commitment within the organization.

There is often a tendency to underestimate the rate of LAN expansion, particularly in rapidly growing organizations. LAN technology makes it easier and more cost effective to expand computer usage rapidly, but capital outlays, training, and support expenditures tend to rise rapidly as well.

Conceptual failures are also costly. Any business tying together 10 or more computers should invest in the process of learning about formal MIS design principles and begin planning for data base implementation.

HOW TO GET STARTED

The following is an implementation framework for small to medium-sized businesses considering LAN technology. Large companies with formal systems staff groups may have different requirements, but the general concepts will still apply.

First, appoint a lead person in your firm who understands the business to investigate LAN technology. This individual should be experienced in working with computers, but need not be an expert. It is most important that he or she understands the nature of your business, and be capable of communicating thoroughly with your present and future micro users.

The next order of business is to conduct an inventory of existing microcomputer usage: Which applications are in use, what data is being utilized, and who is using it? This is the single best opportunity to rationalize existing usage and to lay the foundation for effective, efficient LAN design. It should be ascertained which areas are most in need of automation—those where manual workloads are high, where duplicate copies of data can be consolidated and shared, and where new data structures are required to provide information which is needed but not readily accessible in the required format.

For the next step, assess the level of technical sophistication available and define the requirements for improvement where necessary. It is far less expensive in the long term, and safer as well, to invest in developing in-house expertise than to rely too much on outside support. While outside support is almost always necessary for a start-up, it is important that internal staff participate closely and assume responsibility for ongoing operations and development as quickly as possible.

Major headaches can be eliminated simply by talking to experienced vendors. Become familiar with the major types of LANs and their respective advantages and disadvantages. Identify those vendors who can provide **prompt** technical support for LANs, eliminating those who cannot. Establish whether or not the software currently in use is available for the LAN hardware under consideration, and at what cost. Be sure to obtain and thoroughly check out vendor references of existing LAN and LAN application software users, and visit an installation or two if possible. Ask how the installation went, what problems were encountered, how they were resolved, and what the service experience has been.

Only then will you be in a position to conduct a cost-benefit analysis on the two or three LAN alternatives which seem best suited to your needs. Identify clerical positions which can be eliminated or expected future positions which may no longer be required. Identify bottlenecks or areas of duplication which will be eliminated, and areas where information will be available or shareable where it previously was not. Compare cost per workstation for the LAN versus non-LAN solution. Test the sensitivity of doubling or tripling your estimates for network support and user training, as these are often underestimated.

Now choose your system and prepare for implementation. Order the system, arrange for uploading of selected applications, and appoint the network supervisor. This person should be a relatively advanced micro user with a good knowledge of the corporation and its data processing activities. As the network supervisor has effective control over computerized corporate data, he or she **must** be both organized and trustworthy, and be able to devote from 20 percent to all of his or her time to the task, depending on the number of workstations, the expertise of the supervisor, and the complexity of applications.

Finally, implement and maintain the system. Initial installation will require several days and should start small, phasing in if a large number of workstations are ultimately required. Connect only three or four identical or highly similar workstations at first, and operate only your standard, proven applications. Ensure that backup systems are operational, and allow the network supervisor time to learn the network software. You may gradually begin to add on more workstations and applications after about a month. Generally, you should start at the transaction-processing level, and work your way up the organization.

Post implementation considerations are equally important. Make sure controls are in place to prevent uncontrolled and dysfunctional growth. En-

sure that the network supervisor is properly supported, both in terms of resources and in ongoing commitment and support by senior management.
Always maintain an up-to-date succession plan to minimize the impact of the
inevitable staff turnover. Remember that a LAN not only improves the potential of your business, but also increases the potential and mobility of the employees who administer it.

RISE TO THE CHALLENGE

We have attempted to provide you with an outline of current LAN technology, to identify the situations where LAN implementation will have the greatest impact, and to provide a rough road map for you to follow.

   While the implementation, operation and ongoing development of a LAN
may seem daunting, we feel that LAN technology can be a potent competitive
tool in the right situation, and is ignored at considerable peril. The new wave
of computer technology has landed on the beach, and financial professionals
and other corporate executives must once again rise to the challenge.

Reading 8–2

NETWORKING MICROCOMPUTERS IN A CPA FIRM

By Michael K. Shaub, CPA

Many CPAs in public practice—about to embark on their first use of microcomputers—will soon breathe a sigh of relief. They soon will appreciate the
advantages of major efficiencies effected by the use of this young technology.

   Other practitioners have enjoyed this benefit for some time. In fact, public accounting firms have invested millions of dollars in microcomputers designed to make their operations more efficient. These stand-alone units have
been integrated into the practice through the development or purchase of audit, tax, management consulting, and administrative software.

   Recently, a number of local area networks (LANs) have been developed
that allow multiple microcomputers to access the same data, software, and
peripheral equipment simultaneously, as well as to communicate with each

---

Reprinted with permission from *Today's CPA*, July/August 1987, pp. 31–35.

other. Whether your firm has two micros or 100, these LANs may hold the key to increased efficiency in your practice.

THE PUBLIC ACCOUNTING ENVIRONMENT

Because of the proliferation of microcomputers in CPA firms, workpapers and critical client data are stored on scores of floppy diskettes scattered among the desks of secretaries and professional accountants—or perhaps on several hard disks in each department. Stored information includes out-of-date and incorrect data that inadvertently may be used by the firm for analyses and disclosures.

As staff auditors are trained in the use of microcomputers, it is not uncommon to have two or more micros at a major client location to perform the audit efficiently. Often only one is connected to a printer, so auditors wanting to print out schedules or memos must wait until that printer is available, exit from the program on their machine, log on to the other micro, and then print out the required information. This inefficiency is expensive for both the CPA firm and the client.

Tax staff accountants working on the same client may prepare the corporate return, related subsidiary or partnership returns, and officers' individual returns, among others. These accounts may be accessing the same information for several different returns, resulting in regular trading of diskettes that, sometimes, are unknowingly updated or altered. The printer problem noted above would likely be encountered in this situation also.

Administrative functions recently have been automated in many CPA firms. There has been the proliferation of word processing software used by secretaries. Spreadsheet and data base packages have been adapted to meet office administrators' needs in maintaining client job control and in creating departmental performance reports. Providing centralized access to reports and correspondence can be a valuable time-saver for secretaries and administrative personnel, allowing for a more effective workload distribution.

WHAT IS A NETWORK?

Understanding the potential of LANs will help practitioners unleash the full potential of their microcomputers. A network is a means for sharing files, hard disks, peripherals, and communications among microcomputers. This sharing can be implemented using a combination of hardware and software.

The heart of most traditional networks is the computer that acts as a "server." The server's function is similar to that of an air traffic controller, with the commands of the various computers in the network representing the airplanes. A dedicated server is a microcomputer with a hard disk that is used only to control the flow of traffic on the network. Although a nondedicated server can be used as a workstation at the same time it is controlling traffic, it slows the performance of the network (Figure 1).[1]

FIGURE 1 Relationship of Server to PCs and Peripherals in a Star Network

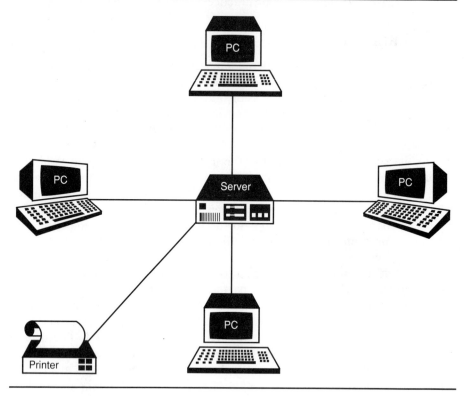

SOURCE: M. K. Guttman, "Strategies for Sharing Resources," *PC World*, February 1985, pp. 44–45.

BENEFITS OF A LAN FOR A CPA FIRM

Many CPA firms will find networks to be valuable cost and time savers in all areas of practice. The applications fall into three general categories:

- Data sharing.
- Peripheral equipment sharing.
- Communications.

Data Sharing. In the initial stages of microcomputer use, stand-alone machines using individual software and data diskettes are sufficient. After all, if someone else needs the program or some data, all they need to do is walk down the hall and ask for the diskette. But the information stored on floppy disks is constantly being updated, and typically there are two or three versions of the same information. Who takes responsibility for updating files and notifying file users of changes? Further, with the advent of high-speed hard disk micros, much more information is being stored on the hard disk—and that information is not available to any user except the current one.

By maintaining one version of the file on a central server accessible by any microcomputer in the network, the firm eliminates both the problems of multiple versions and limited access. There is no unnecessary waiting for access to files, and the information used is the most current available. Thus, the traditional drawback to purchasing the much faster hard disk PCs no longer exists.

What if two users want to access the same information simultaneously? This is an important consideration in deciding on the package to purchase. Depending on the networking software acquired, several things may happen. At a minimum, the package the firm purchases should have a "file locking" procedure that prevents two users from updating the same file at the same time, and, perhaps, destroying data in the process. More sophisticated packages provide for "record locking," in which two users can access the same file, but cannot update the same record simultaneously.

Peripheral Equipment Sharing. A significant part of an accounting firm's investment in microcomputers is in the peripheral equipment, such as printers and plotters. These make the system complete and allow for translation of information on the screen into permanent form. Many firms print reports in-house through the use of sophisticated laser printers. However, laser printers are very expensive, and most can be linked to only one microcomputer. However, if that micro is a server for a network, every PC on that network has effective access to the laser printer—even if it is in another part of the building.

Dollars spent on a LAN can minimize the firm's cost. There no longer exists the need to purchase additional microcomputers because of several people needing to access a printer at one time. Networks allow the firm to acquire only printers, plotters, and other peripherals based on actual workload on the equipment.

Communications.   One noted industry observer stated:

> Locally networked PCs are appropriate for smaller work groups, where personal productivity software carries most of the load, with electronic mail and occasional file transfer as secondary requirements.[2]

This accurately describes the microcomputer environment of most CPA firms, with extensive use of spreadsheet, tax return, word processing, and graphics software, and limited needs for communicating between micros. Still, the ability to use electronic mail to communicate with other employees can be useful, especially in coordinating work done for a client. This feature is generally secondary in the public accounting environment, however, and rarely will be a major factor in selecting a network.

ARE LANs THE WAVE OF THE FUTURE?

LAN sales are increasing dramatically (Figure 2). If it is not the time for an individual firm to purchase a LAN, it is certainly time to become informed about them. By the end of 1986 virtually all major software companies were developing products for the LAN market.[3] The number of PCs on PC-only networks is expected to increase over 750 percent from 1984 to 1988 (Figure 3).

LAN technology is in an important developmental stage, especially in light of IBM's and AT&T's new entries into the market. Their new products seem to confirm the permanence of the technology and offer hope of establishing an industry standard in the near future. Many accounting firms will choose to wait 6 to 12 months or longer to acquire a LAN. Because of the rapid developments of the last year, this may prove to be a wise decision. By mid-to-late 1987, some of the fog will have cleared from the industry, and a more accurate evaluation of a particular network's performance capabilities and compatibility with a firm's needs will be possible.

TELLING THE NETWORKS APART

To select a network, it is helpful to understand some basic differences in the designs of various LANs that are available, and the advantages and limita-

FIGURE 2   Local Area Network Sales: Actual 1984 and Projected 1985–1986

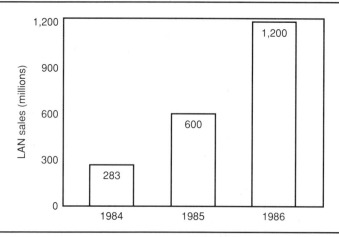

SOURCE: Jocelyn Young of Future Computing, as quoted in Steven Cook, "Net Results," *PC World,* December 1985, p. 270.

FIGURE 3 Growth in Networked PCs

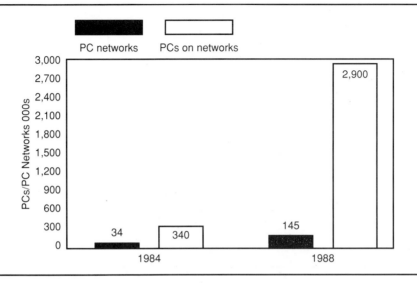

SOURCE: The Yankee Group.

tions that these designs bring. The three basic configurations used are the star, bus, and ring arrangements. Figure 4 illustrates the designs of the various systems. Table 1 compares some of the important features in the star, ring, and bus networks.

Technical differences in these networks are not addressed. The basic differences that may affect your decision in selecting a LAN are presented.

Network Configurations.   The star topology was the first architecture developed for LANs. It consists of a dominant central node with other terminals branching off from it in a starlike pattern. Star LANs are limited in the distance that terminals can be from the central node. Also, if the central node goes down, the entire system is down.

Bus LANs allow for data to be moved over long distances because they consist of a long central cable off of which individual or multistation connections branch. The failure of a node does not halt the system. Expanding the network is relatively simple. However, the network has no central controller, and thus requires a complicated access design when it is installed to determine priorities in information transfer.

A ring LAN is essentially a "closed bus." It can be designed to cover a greater distance than a bus LAN. However, unless a scheme to bypass nodes is designed into the system, the failure of one node can bring down the whole system. No central controller is necessary in a ring network.

FIGURE 4 Network Architectures

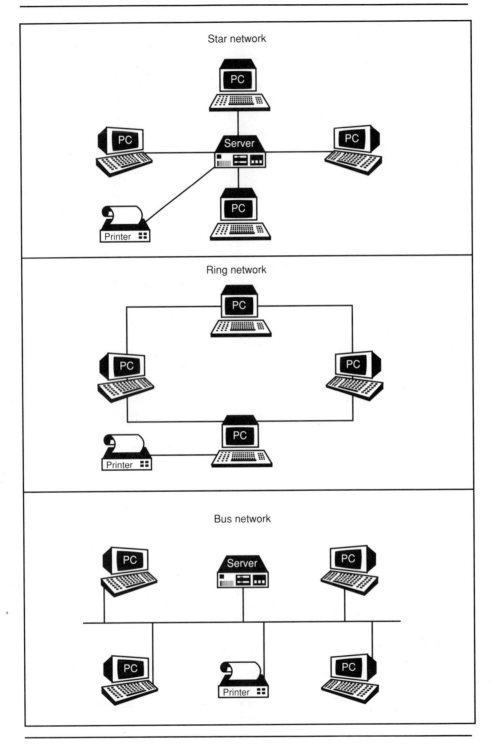

SOURCE: M. K. Guttman, "Strategies for Sharing Resources," *PC World*, February 1985, pp. 44–45.

TABLE 1   LAN Topology—Alternatives and Relative Performance

	Bus	*Ring*	*Star*
Information throughput	Decreases with each added node	Decreases with each added node	Dependent on capacity of central node
Flexibility	High	Moderate	Low
Expandability	High	Moderate	Dependent on capacity of central node
Connectivity	High	Low	Initially high, incrementally low
Reliability	High	Low	Moderate

SOURCE: Martin Pyykkonen, "Handicapping LANs," *Datamation,* March 31, 1985, p. 98.

Other Considerations.   Individual CPA firm needs will control the final selection of a network. For example, most accounting firms will not need their network to link terminals over a mile of cable, so length limitations will not be a major factor in deciding on a LAN. However, some networks only allow for terminals to be connected over a few hundred feet—which can be a major limitation.

Further, do not believe all of the claims of the companies marketing LANs. Some claim that hundreds of PCs can be linked to their system. The firm relying on this claim views its purchase as being expandable to meet its needs for several years. But such systems prove to be inordinately slow if more than 10 microcomputers are linked to the network. The best way to avoid this problem is to ask for references of installed systems that are functioning in accordance with the salesman's claims.

As noted earlier, the development of IBM and AT&T products should be observed closely before a network is purchased. IBM's PC Network has met with mixed reviews; some have seen it as simply a stopgap measure until its Token-Ring Network hits the market. Regardless, IBM is using a familiar strategy introducing its new ring LAN. Just as IBM marketed the IBM Personal Computer—using an open architecture that encouraged software developers to become IBM compatible—"Big Blue" is now distributing the specifications for the Token-Ring Network to third-party hardware and software vendors. IBM hopes that those vendors will interface their application software, peripherals, and computers to the Token-Ring Network.

Anyone who made a major microcomputer purchase prior to the decision of most third-party suppliers to develop IBM-compatible software will be wary of buying a LAN that cannot run IBM-compatible software. Since multiuser software is in the early stages of its development, this caution is well advised.

Software vendors are still trying to develop pricing schemes for their products; many are undecided whether to market their products on a "per server" or "per user" basis. Most software vendors tend to overprice products when they are first released. Waiting 6 to 12 months for prices to flatten out is warranted. This wait also should result in the firm acquiring more sophisticated software.

A CPA firm should be careful in selecting a project manager for the LAN implementation as well. Most partners cannot be expected to invest much time in this type of project. The decision usually will come down to a choice between the office manager and the professional staff person, if any, who pushed for the LAN acquisition. A recent article suggests that selection of a project manager should be based on:

- Who will be the primary LAN users.
- Who has the most experience with personal computers.
- Who has most genuine interest in the success of the project.[4]

CONCLUSION

Most technological developments come as the result of a perceived need. Now that they have passed through the first formative stages, businesses are beginning to see the multiple applications available for LANs.

Many practitioners would benefit from installing a LAN, but not all public accounting firms may need one today. However, if a firm does not need a LAN, it is likely that several of the firm's clients will be in the market for one in the near future. By remaining informed about future LAN developments, CPAs can help their clients' transitions from stand-alone microcomputers to effective information processing networks.

Many established packages that have not been discussed in this article already can provide all the networking services a client may need. Less expensive and more effective networks are being developed continually. In all the confusion, two things are increasingly clear: local area networks are here to stay and they can be major contributors to firm efficiency. Just ask the accounting firms and their clients who are using them—and ask IBM and AT&T.

Notes

1. Art Wilcox, "Untangling Networks," *PC World,* February 1985, p. 234.
2. Omri Serlin: "Departmental Computing: A Choice of Strategies," *Datamation,* May 31, 1985, p. 86.

3. Steven Cook, "Net Results," *PC World,* December 1985, p. 273.
4. Henry Fersko-Weiss, "Who Manages the Network?" *Personal Computing,* March 1987, p. 113.

References

Appleman, David L. "Ho-Hummers Missed AT&T, IBM Impact on LAN Technology." *PC Week,* September 4, 1984, p. 35.

Bernstein, Amy. "On Common Ground." *Business Computer Systems,* December 1985, pp. 19–20.

Catchings, Bill. "PC Networking Wang-Style." *PC Magazine,* October 15, 1985, pp. 173–177.

Cook, Steven. "Net Results." *PC World,* December 1985, pp. 270–277.

Derfler, Jr., Frank J. "The Network News." *PC Week,* October 29, 1985, pp. 69–82.

———. "Zero-Slot LANs: A Low-Cost Solution." *PC Magazine,* November 26, 1985, pp. 169–176.

Fersko-Weiss, Henry. "Who Manages the Network?" *Personal Computing,* March 1987, pp. 107–115.

Geisler, Charles H. "Some Ideas to Consider in Seeking a Local Area Network." *Office,* February 1984, pp. 75–76.

Gruhn, Marty. "Battle of the LANs." *Office Administration and Automation,* March 1984, pp. 26–30, 92.

Guttman, Michael K. "Strategies for Sharing Resources." *PC World,* February 1985, pp. 42–50.

Horwitt, Elisabeth. "IBM's LANslide." *Business Computer Systems,* December 1985, pp. 10–14.

Kramer, Matt. "IBM Seen Ready to Announce Details of Token-Passing LAN." *PC Week,* August 20, 1985, pp. 1, 6.

———. "Software, Not Hardware, Key to LAN Performance." *PC Week,* January 15, 1985, p. 5.

———. "Three Vie to Link Multivendor Office Micro Products." *PC Week,* December 11, 1984, p. 10.

Lemley, Brad. "All the President's PCs." *PC Magazine,* May 29, 1984, pp. 139–144.

Levert, Virginia M. "Application of Local Area Networks of Microcomputers." *Information Technology and Libraries,* March 14, 1985, pp. 9–18.

Lilly, Susan. "IBM LAN Software May Inspire Development." *PC Week,* May 14, 1985, p. 91.

Luhn, Robert, ed. "The Organization LAN." *PC World,* February 1985, pp. 72–80.

Mace, Scott. "Key Application Packages Still Missing." *Infoworld,* June 10, 1985, pp. 30–36.

McCusker, Tom. "Out of Thin Air." *Datamation,* January 31, 1985, pp. 36, 38.

Pallatto, John. "Travel Guide to PC LANs." *PC Week,* June 19, 1984, pp. 45–53.

Porter, Martin. "PC Network Good News for LANs." *PC Magazine,* October 30, 1984, p. 56.

Pyykkonen, Martin. "Handicapping LANs." *Datamation,* March 31, 1985, pp. 96–102.

Sachs, Jonathan. "Six Leading LANs." *PC World,* February 1985, pp. 108–127.

Sandberg-Diment, Erik. "Bridging the Gap in Networks." *New York Times*, December 22, 1985, Section 3, p. 14, col. 1–5.

_____. Serlin, Omri. "Departmental Computing: A Choice of Strategies." *Datamation*, May 31, 1985, pp. 86–96.

Whitmore, Sam. "Cooperative Processing Gives Mainframe Services to PCs." *PC Week*, September 17, 1985, p. 6.

Wilcox, Art. "Untangling Networks." *PC World*, February 1985, pp. 232–241.

Zarley, Craig. "Captains of Video." *PC Week*, September 10, 1985, pp. 53–56.

Reading 8–3

ELECTRONIC PUBLISHING: THE NEXT GREAT OFFICE REVOLUTION

By William M. Winsor

Desktop publishing may be the greatest productivity tool in a modern office environment since the introduction of spreadsheet software in the 1970s. Spreadsheet software was the catalyst that brought the microcomputer into the office environment because office workers embraced it with such enthusiasm.

Desktop publishing hasn't quite reached that plateau, but the writing is on the wall. The total desktop publishing market was approximately $453 million in 1986. Not bad, considering desktop publishing really didn't exist until late 1984. By 1990, the total market should reach $4.9 billion, an increase of more than 1,000 percent in just four years! Clearly, desktop publishing has a bright future for a number of reasons:

- Desktop publishing enables people and businesses to develop their own brochures, newsletters, and other documents at a fraction of the cost and time expended sending the work out to a professional graphics studio.

- Desktop publishing doesn't require a great deal of artistic skill, although the ability to conceptualize is helpful.

• Desktop publishing is opening doors to people who never had the ability to produce documents before.

People who had no interest in publishing suddenly discovered they could produce documents after spending a short time learning the technology. For instance, a church secretary can develop the Sunday bulletin in an afternoon, business executives can quickly generate product documentation at the office and marketing specialists can produce a product brochure in a fraction of the time previously required.

There also has been an emergence of new customer and trade publications that use desktop publishing technology. A publisher can now put together an entire magazine at a personal computer without incurring the cost of hiring production artists or designers. All the publisher has to do is print out the pages, leave empty "knockout windows" for the printer to insert photos and take the pages to the printer. The printer then adds the photos and prints the pages. Instant magazine!

LOGICAL EVOLUTION

Desktop publishing is the result of a logical evolution in publishing. It started with ancient scribes laboriously copying books by hand and evolved into the printing press revolution. Things heated up with computer-generated "cold" type which debuted in the 1950s.

With this process, type was set by computer, pasted on an art board by a layout person, photographed by a printer and transferred to a sheet on the printed press. That concept is moved forward several generations by desktop publishing.

Now an individual can assemble an entire page on a personal computer and produce a finished document. Text is first developed on a word processor and transferred to the screen, then graphics, photos and other art can either be added or developed through several graphics-generating peripherals, such as light pens.

Dot-matrix and laser printers produce a sharp document that is easily reproduced through a photocopy machine. If a large press run is needed, the print-out can be taken to a commercial printer who reproduces the document in quantity. The latter technique is also useful when photographs are used in the document.

STANDARDS NEEDED

From a base of virtually zero just three years ago, nearly every major hardware and software developer is now involved with desktop publishing. As a result, the same controversy over computer industry standards that have been discussed for years is now associated with desktop publishing.

The main alternatives are the Apple MacIntosh and MS/DOS machines, which include IBM personal computers and a host of clones. Apple pioneered desktop publishing and currently enjoys an edge, but the corporate world is populated by MS/DOS.

Manufacturers recognize the standards issue and are making efforts to overcome compatibility problems so that different machines can "talk" with one another. This is challenging, however, since most MS/DOS machines were not designed to handle the high-resolution graphics and page descriptor languages necessary to utilize desktop publishing technology.

SETTING UP

No matter which system is selected, the basics are the same. Hardware requirements should include a personal computer with at least 512K of RAM (random access memory), a high resolution monitor, a "mouse" and a dot-matrix or laser printer. The printer is especially important because it determines the final product's quality.

A dot-matrix printer has a 100 dpi (dots-per-inch) resolution, which is adequate for simple projects, such as newsletters. More sophisticated projects, such as brochures, magazines and documentation, require a laser printer that produces 300 dpi text, which is still less than the 1,000 dpi-and-up resolution provided by professional printers.

As you would expect, there's a price for performance. Dot-matrix printers can be purchased for about $500, while laser printers go for at least four times that much. In either case, the long-term savings are significant compared with outside typesetting charges of $50 to $100 per page.

Virtually every desktop publishing system relies on a hand-held "mouse" as the principal tool for developing a layout. The mouse is a movable device which is connected to the computer by a small cable. It can be pointed in different directions to select menus and options on the computer screen and build a document.

A mouse is especially helpful when selecting "clip" art and electronically assembling a page. (The term "clip" art originates from the newspaper practice of keeping clip sheets containing drawings that were clipped with scissors and pasted on the page.)

The clip art can be selected from a software program and electronically "pasted" onto a page. Because the range of clip art is somewhat limited, an optical scanner enables more complex art to be used.

An optical scanner is a necessary option if photos or other previously produced art are used in the final product. The scanner reads the image and transfers it on to the page. Many scanners are able to read various tones which provide texture to the art. Scanners don't come cheap, however, costing $3,000 to $5,000, which is still considerably less than their $30,000 price tag three years ago.

A light-emitting pen is another option that enables graphics to be hand-drawn on the screen. This art can be original and crisp and works best if the user is an accomplished graphic artist or has access to one. Drawing on a computer requires some of the same skills as drawing on paper, so artistic talent is a definite plus.

CHOOSING SOFTWARE

As with any computer system, the software determines how desktop publishing can be used. A basic piece of desktop publishing software will enable a person to lay out the text and art on the page but requires the manual reformatting of text to accommodate graphics. A second-generation desktop publishing software program will automatically reformat the text to accommodate graphics.

The availability of font designs in software is another factor. Fonts are the type styles available for printing, such as Gothic, Courier, Helvetica, or Old English. Each style has a certain look and it is up to the individual taste of the person designing the document to determine which font is appropriate. Obviously, the more fonts available, the more flexibility the user has.

Perhaps the most important software element is its capacity. First-generation software can create documents up to 32 pages in length, while second generations handle up to 96 pages. Other features to look for in software are:

- Kerning, or the ability to automatically adjust the amount of space between letters.
- Automatic page numbering.
- Ability to change type styles within a line.
- Ability to change graphic size without distortion.

If a simple newsletter is all that will be produced, a first-generation software program in the $100–$200 range will be adequate. However, if reports, documentation, and brochures will be the main focus of the system, then a sophisticated program costing $500 or more may be necessary.

AVOIDING PITFALLS

Although desktop publishing opens the world of publishing to everyone, not everyone has the innate conceptual ability to use desktop publishing. A major complaint many layout specialists have is the overuse of graphics. Fortunately, most software programs come with a tips section that outlines how to develop publications. More sophisticated programs may require seminars and professional instruction. See Figure 1 for typical business uses of desktop publishing.

FIGURE 1   10 Typical Business Uses for Desktop Publishing

- Internal employee newsletter.
- External customer newsletter.
- Business forms, such as invoices and purchase orders.
- Product documentation, such as owner manuals and instructions.
- Company capability brochures.
- Product sales brochures.
- Product price lists.
- Magazines.
- Meeting information packets.
- Sales kits.

Reading 8–4

DESKTOP PUBLISHING: PROFESSIONAL-LOOKING DOCUMENTS FROM THE OFFICE MICRO

By Christopher Wolfe, *CPA*, and Kent T. Fields, *CPA*

Accountants create and disseminate a wide variety of printed materials, including

- Client financial statements.
- Newsletters.
- Reports.
- Business and tax forms.
- Presentation aids, such as slides and transparency masters.
- Tax calendars and updates.

Reprinted with permission from *The Journal of Accountancy,* © 1988 by American Institute of CPAs. Opinions of the authors are their own and do not necessarily reflect policies of the AICPA.

Until recently, accountants had two options when producing higher-quality printed material: The documents could be either typewritten or typeset.

Typewritten documents from a typewriter or personal computer printer, however, do not create a quality image in the minds of most clients. For this reason, accountants have traditionally sent all critical documents to a print shop for a slow and expensive, albeit professional, job.

Desktop publishing provides a solution to this dilemma. Using a personal computer, accountants can produce high-quality printed material quickly and economically.

BASIC QUESTIONS

Several important questions should be asked by firms or practitioners considering a desktop publishing system:

- What is desktop publishing?
- What software is needed?
- What hardware is needed?
- How much expertise is necessary?
- Is investing in a desktop publishing system worthwhile?

These will each be dealt with below.

WHAT IS DESKTOP PUBLISHING?

To begin with, desktop publishing is the use of a PC system to generate documents comparable to those produced by a professional printer.

In general, this involves "pouring" text (produced on a word processor) and graphics (produced from graphics software) into desktop publishing software. The publishing software then allows you to cut and paste the text and graphics to an electronic layout sheet—much the same as a layout artist would cut and paste to a paper layout sheet. Once the electronic layout has been specified, the desktop publishing software sends the layout to a laser printer, which produces the high-quality output desired.

WHAT SOFTWARE IS NEEDED?

Desktop publishing has become a generic term, with a number of software packages using the label. True desktop publishing software should be able to combine text and graphics in a single document. It should generate a layout screen for the text and graphics that is essentially a what-you-see-is-what-you-get (also called "WYSIWYG") view of the printed page.

It should also be possible to use the publishing software to edit the text and graphics extensively on the layout screen. Finally, the desktop publishing software should support sophisticated, high-resolution laser printers.

True desktop publishing software is very difficult to develop. The package must support different word processor formats for entering text and different graphics formats for entering graphics. In addition, all type styles, type sizes and typesetting design tools must be available to the page designer for editing documents. And the desktop publishing software must interface with page-design languages built into the sophisticated laser printers used in desktop publishing.

The complexity of developing true publishing software still limits the number of packages available to accountants. Exhibit 1, below, provides a listing of desktop publishing packages that meet the above requirements.

Much software that bills itself as desktop publishing software does not meet all the criteria given above. These packages often lack the WYSIWYG screen display or the ability to edit with a wide variety of type styles, type

EXHIBIT 1   Full-Featured Desktop Publishing Software

DOS-based software		Apple Macintosh software	
Program	*Price**	*Program*	*Price**
Pagemaker Aldus Corp. 411 First Avenue, #200 Seattle, Washington 98104 (206) 622-5500	$695	*Pagemaker* Aldus Corp. 411 First Avenue, #200 Seattle, Washington 98104 (206) 622-5500	$495
Ventura Publisher Xerox Corp. 101 Continental Boulevard El Segundo, California 90245 (800) 822-8221	$895	*MacPublisher III* Boston Publishing Systems 1260 Boylston Street Boston, Massachusetts 02215 (617) 267-4747	$295
GEM Desktop Publisher Digital Research Inc. 60 Garden Court P.O. Box DRI Monterey, California 93942 (408) 649-3896	$395	*Quark XPress* Quark Inc. 2525 West Evans Suite 220 Denver, Colorado 80219 (303) 934-2211	$695
The Office Publisher Laser Friendly Inc. 930 Benicia Avenue Sunnyvale, California 94086 (408) 730-1921	$995	*Ready, Set, Go!* Letraset USA 40 Eisenhower Drive Paramus, New Jersey 07653 (201) 845-6100	$495

*Manufacturer's suggested retail price.

sizes, and typesetting features. Graphics displays are severely limited in lower-level programs, which allow only certain types of graphs and little or no control of graph sizing from within the publishing software. Lower-level packages also have highly varied, and typically limited, levels of laser-printer support.

In the same vein, better word processors, such as Word Perfect, can print graphics and text in columnar form on a laser printer. But this isn't true desktop publishing either. A word processing system just can't provide all the multiple type styles, typesetting features, and graphic design tools that together create a highly polished document.

The shortcomings of lower-level publishing packages (or high-end word processors) do not make these products useless for desktop publishing tasks. However, they are better suited to small jobs that don't need the professional touch available from full-featured desktop publishing software. (See exhibit 2 for a listing of lower-level DOS-based publishing software.)

Most accountants would best be served by a full-featured desktop publishing package. Given the relatively small price differential between full-featured and lower-level packages, it's wise to purchase software that can grow to take on new publishing tasks.

EXHIBIT 2 Lower-Level DOS-Based Desktop Publishing Software

Program	Price*	Program	Price*
PFS: First Publisher	$129	*NewsMaster*	$99.95
Software Publishing Corp.		Unison World	
1901 Landings Drive		2150 Shattuck Avenue, #902	
Mountain View, California 94039		Berkeley, California 94704	
(415) 962-8910		(415) 848-6666	
Printrix	$165	*Power Test Formatter*	$149.95
Fontrix	$155	Beaman Porter Inc.	
Data Transforms Inc.		417 Halstead Avenue	
616 Washington Street		Harrison, New York 10528	
Denver, Colorado 80203		(800) 431-0007	
(303) 832-1501		(914) 835-3156	
Fancy Font	$180	*Byline*	$295.00
SoftCraft Inc.		Ashton-Tate Corp.	
16 North Carroll Street		20101 Hamilton Avenue	
Madison, Wisconsin 53703		Torrance, California 90502	
(800) 351-0500		(800) 437-4329	
(608) 257-3300		(303) 799-4900	

*Manufacturer's suggested retail price.

WHAT HARDWARE IS NEEDED?

Desktop publishing can be carried out with either IBM and compatible systems (which use the MS-DOS operating environment) or with Apple Computer's powerful Macintosh. The merits of both systems are examined below.

IBM AND COMPATIBLE HARDWARE

An overwhelming number of accountants already use IBM or IBM-compatible microcomputers that, when properly equipped, can be the basis for a desktop publishing system.

The desktop publishing environment demands the speed of an IBM PC AT class microcomputer (i.e., 80286 microprocessor). Also, at least 512K of random access memory (RAM) is needed for publishing jobs. A hard-disk drive is required to handle the text files, graphics files, and actual publishing files, along with the application software.

Hardware that is somewhat unique to desktop publishing includes graphics cards, monitors, mice and laser printers. Graphics capabilities are needed to display different typefaces, type sizes, and pictorial representations in a WYSIWYG screen display of the printed page. These require a graphics card and graphics monitor on an IBM or compatible. Many DOS-based microcomputers come with graphics capabilities, including IBM's new (and much heralded) PS/2 line.

New 19-inch color displays that can show two magazine-size pages on one screen are state-of-the-art in desktop publishing monitors. Although a standard 12-inch graphics monitor is acceptable, high-volume desktop publishers are opting for the bigger screens.

Finally, a mouse is a great advantage for producing quality documents, although it must be purchased as an aftermarket accessory to most IBM and compatible microcomputers. About the size of a pack of cigarettes, the mouse is an input device that can be used to move an icon on the computer's screen. This icon, often an arrow, can point and execute specific commands from on-screen menus.

For example, a large graphic imported into publishing software can be moved to its appropriate spot on the layout screen by using a mouse, first pointing to the graphic, then pointing to its destination and finally pointing to the move command. Desktop publishing software is designed to be used with a mouse as a data input device.

APPLE HARDWARE

What has helped the IBM and its compatibles in business microcomputing is hurting them in desktop publishing. The PC is a very flexible machine and a number of vendors offer a multitude of hardware and software products for different system environments. But in order for desktop publishing software to operate effectively, it must be designed for a specific hardware–software configuration.

Because of Apple Computer's powerful graphics capabilities, standard file formats and hardware (which includes a mouse as standard equipment rather than an add-on), the Apple Macintoshes are better suited to desktop publishing. The Macintosh has a friendly, standardized operating environment, and desktop publishing on the Mac appeared on the market approximately a year and a half ahead of the DOS crowd.

Moreover, Apple produces the LaserWriter, the quintessential desktop publishing laser printer. The Apple system is the market-share leader in desktop publishing.

As the desktop publishing market matures, however, hardware will become less of an issue. For example, Pagemaker, the most popular publishing software, has an Apple version and a DOS version that operate almost identically. Firmwide software compatibility appears to be the critical issue in hardware selection. That is, a firm should use the desktop publishing system designed for its microcomputer system.

LASER PRINTERS

Laser printers operate on something of the same principle as photocopiers. A dry ink, referred to as toner, is attracted to a light-sensitive print drum. The print drum is marked with very small beams of light generated by a laser. The laser beam produces very small dots on the print drum in the form of characters and images. Since the print drum is light-sensitive, the toner is magnetically attracted to the areas etched by the laser beam.

The print quality of laser printers is unmatched by any other microcomputer printer. However, the price of laser printers is also unmatched by other microcomputer printers. Top-of-the-line laser printers run approximately $6,000, and the lower-level models are priced around $2,000.

A higher-priced, higher-quality laser printer offers the desktop publisher several advantages. Top-end printers are faster and produce a better looking, higher-resolution output. However, the main advantage of laser printers aimed specifically at desktop publishing is their built-in page description language.

The standard page description language is Adobe Systems' Postscript. A Postscript laser printer produces multiple typefaces in the same document and very sophisticated page layouts. The desktop publishing software works with the page description language to produce this sophisticated output. All full-featured desktop publishing software packages support Postscript laser printers.

HOW MUCH EXPERTISE IS NECESSARY?

A relatively sophisticated PC configuration is needed to do desktop publishing. The ability to handle and maintain this hardware is the first type of expertise needed. This is common among accountants who use powerful microcomputer systems.

The other area for which expertise is needed is page design. Desktop publishing puts a very powerful page layout toolbag in the hands of its user.

If you have not mastered the rudiments of basic page design, a low-grade output is all you will be able to produce, regardless of your system's capabilities. Some skill is required to blend different typefaces, type sizes and graphics into a professional document. Most firms, however, have at least one person who has shown an interest in, and a talent for, producing well-designed reports in a word processing environment. Such people are good candidates for further training in desktop publishing.

IS INVESTING IN A DESKTOP PUBLISHING SYSTEM WORTHWHILE?

Desktop publishing can be valuable because it performs a service currently provided to many accounting firms by print shops. For these firms, the major advantages of desktop publishing are that

1. A large part of printing costs become fixed.
2. The firm retains complete control of the printing process.

Desktop publishing is easily justified by the printing costs it eliminates.

Since most accounting firms already have microcomputer systems in place, the move to desktop publishing may involve a minimal incremental investment. Furthermore hardware purchased for desktop publishing can be used for other tasks. This is especially true of laser printers, which can enhance the appearance of all printed material.

The cost benefits of desktop publishing to accounting firms are, for the most part, intangible. Clients and potential clients will receive higher-quality documents. A quality image is important to accountants, although it can be hard to put a price tag on quality.

GOOD RETURN ON THE INVESTMENT

Desktop publishing is, in short, an excellent way to reduce publishing costs and enhance your firm's professional image. The micro-based publishing workstation is a quick, high-quality tool for disseminating accounting information. The return on the relatively modest investment necessary to become a desktop publisher should encourage many accounting firms to implement desktop publishing systems in the near future.

Expert Systems—Taking an Expert to the Field

Neil Frude indicated that "the ideal companion machine would not only look, feel, and sound friendly but would also behave in a congenial manner." A computer with a congenial personality may be the ultimate achievement of "user friendly." So far, this particular machine exists only in episodes of Star Trek. However, in recent years, much progress has been made in the field of artificial intelligence, particularly in the subfield of expert systems. To appreciate the recent advances made in this field, one has only to recall that the term *expert system* did not even appear in the accounting literature until the early 1980s. While authors of many articles on expert systems feel obliged to list the limitations of such software, it is important to recognize the potential of future expert systems applications.

Today, expert systems are widely used in all areas of business. The benefits of this recent innovation include improved products or services, increased productivity, improved quality of employee output, and a wider distribution of expertise. Expert systems are employed in manufacturing, research and development, marketing, management information systems, accounting, and finance. The failure to use expert systems could leave a business at a serious competitive disadvantage. The ability of business managers to apply the latest technologies, including expert systems, is an increasingly valuable skill. Familiarity with the spreadsheet and other basic software is no longer considered adequate computer skills.

Among the four readings on expert systems, the first is appropriately titled "Expert Systems: Machines that Think Like You—Sometimes Better." Three areas in which the judgment of financial executives can be aided are illustrated and discussed. In the second article, "The Development of Accounting Expert Systems," an overview of the development of accounting expert systems is presented. "A Sample Expert System for Financial Statement Analysis" describes the steps in the development process of an expert system.

The fourth and final article, "Expert Systems as Decision Aids: Issues and Strategies," indicates that expert systems are appropriate when qualitative reasoning is required, and decision making is structured and repetitive. For nonstructured decision making, human experts are still necessary.

CHAPTER 9 READINGS

1. Grover L. Porter, "Expert Systems: Machines that Think Like You—Sometimes Better," *Financial Executive,* May/June 1988, pp. 44–46.
2. James A. Sena and L. Murphy Smith, "The Development of Accounting Expert Systems," *Journal of Accounting and EDP,* Summer 1987, pp. 9–14.
3. James A. Sena and L. Murphy Smith, "A Sample Expert System for Financial Statement Analysis," *Journal of Accounting and EDP,* Summer 1987, pp. 15–22.
4. Ting-peng Liang, "Expert Systems as Decision Aids: Issues and Strategies," *Journal of Information Systems,* Spring 1988, pp. 41–50.

CHAPTER 9 QUESTIONS

Article 1

1. Define artificial intelligence and expert systems.
2. Discuss the four-step decision-making process. What are three areas of expert systems?

Article 2

3. Describe the components of an expert system.
4. Discuss the fundamental characteristics of an expert system.
5. In what areas of accounting are expert systems being developed?
6. Describe some practical uses of expert systems.

Article 3

7. How does the expert system for financial statement analysis interact with the user?
8. Discuss Expert Edge.

Article 4

9. Describe the initial applications of expert systems.
10. Discuss the potential benefit of expert systems.

Reading 9–1

EXPERT SYSTEMS: MACHINES THAT THINK LIKE YOU—SOMETIMES BETTER

By Grover L. Porter

Artificial intelligence (AI) is one of the most exciting and promising developments of the computer age. An oversimplified, but reasonably accurate, description of AI is that it is the attempt to build machines that think. One of the main categories of AI is expert systems, which capture in computer programs the reasoning and decision-making processes of human experts, providing, in effect, computerized consultants. To do this, an expert system applies rules of thumb, gained from a human expert, to analyze a problem and make recommendations. Most expert systems can also explain how they arrived at a particular conclusion.

Financial executives can use expert systems in a number of ways. For example, a financial analyst could use an expert system as a means of "second guessing" his own review of financial data when performing a financial analysis of, say, a company that has requested an extension of credit. Or the executive could use such a system to evaluate the financial statements of an acquisition candidate. Other uses include evaluating the financial soundness of a major supplier or any company the executive's firm may have a significant contractual relationship with; reviewing a draft of financial statements before submitting them to higher management; and reviewing financial reports from subsidiaries and affiliates.

As an example of one use of expert systems for financial analysis, we use the data for a hypothetical business firm, Company X. Assume a financial executive is reviewing this data in considering a significant 10-year contract with the company. The executive naturally is wary of entering the contract with any company that is not stable and reliable, and therefore potentially unable to service his products and services properly throughout the contract. The executive is thus evaluating the financial strength of Company X, as one aspect of the overall review. The information surrounding the financial data explains how expert systems can facilitate this financial executive's analysis task.

DIFFERENT TYPES OF EXPERT SYSTEMS

In response to the increased demand for expert systems for financial analysis, a small number of expert systems have been introduced in recent years. They

Used by permission from *Financial Executive*, May/June 1988, copyright 1988 by Financial Executives Institute.

come in different sizes, at different costs, and for different uses within the framework of financial analysis.

Expert systems have been developed for mainframe computers, minicomputers, and microcomputers. The mainframe and minicomputer versions are relatively expensive, typically custom-designed for a particular company or a particular application, and relatively little is published about them. Microcomputer types of systems, on the other hand, have a much broader and more significant impact on decision making by financial executives, and the development of expert systems is generally heading in the direction of microcomputer applications.

It is useful in discussing these expert systems to start with some distinctions. We categorize expert systems for financial analysis into three areas in which the judgment of the financial executive can be aided. These areas are related to the four-step process executives use for decision making: gather *data* to develop *analyses* from which specific *insights* are drawn about an entity and a *decision* is made. These three areas are:

- Insight-facilitating
- Decision-facilitating
- Decision-making

INSIGHT-FACILITATING SYSTEMS

Systems that are insight facilitating have the objective to simply produce relevant analyses—usually financial statement ratios and graphs. These ratios and graphs are useful to the financial executive in developing insights into the financial condition and prospects of a given entity, as well as any required management action. The first two of the four steps of financial analysis—data gathering and analysis—are thus completed by these systems.

We call these systems insight facilitating because they are intended to help the executive develop specific insightful observations. However, the degree of expertise in the insights depends directly upon the degree of expertise of the user. For this reason, these systems are sometimes called "expert-like" systems, or they may not be labeled as expert systems at all, in that they do not actually embody the expertise of a given expert or group of experts.

Three examples of insight-facilitating systems are INSIGHT by Layered, Inc., a firm out of Boston; NEWVIEWS by Q. W. Page Associates, Inc., in Toronto; and REFLEX by Borland International of Scotts Valley, Calif. Of the three systems, INSIGHT and NEWVIEWS are quite similar. Both offer integrated accounting systems for reporting and analyzing financial data. For example, NEWVIEWS performs the accounting applications for accounts receivable, accounts payable, inventory, and payroll in an interactive format and then permits a spreadsheet type of analysis of the data in the system. In effect, it is an integrated accounting/spreadsheet system that allows regular accumulation and reporting of financial data, as well as access to specific analyses in the form of ratios, trends, and graphs.

INSIGHT offers the same features as NEWVIEWS except that it is designed for the Macintosh computer. Additionally, it provides definitions of 12 key financial ratios and suggests interpretations for these ratios.

REFLEX is a simpler system in that it does not include an integrated accounting system. Instead, it is a RAM-based data base system with integrated spreadsheet analysis and graphics tools.

These systems might analyze the data for Company X by producing a listing of key financial ratios.

DECISION-FACILITATING SYSTEMS

The second category of systems is decision facilitating, so-called because it accesses a financial knowledge base to retrieve insights about an entity. In contrast to the above systems, which require the user to develop the insightful observations from the analyses presented, this type of system analyzes the data *and* provides the insights.

Like the insight-facilitating systems, the decision facilitators provide reports of financial analyses containing trends and ratios as well as graphs, but they also contain decision rules which "trigger" relevant insights about the data under analysis. In effect, the systems produce "exception reports" of insights that are relevant to the specific entity under analysis. Therefore, these systems provide the first three of the four steps of analysis—data gathering, analysis, and insight generation. The only widely available system of this type is ANSWERS, a product of Financial Audit Systems out of Raleigh, N.C.

DECISION-MAKING SYSTEMS

The third category of expert systems is the most complete of all, the decision-making system. Many would call this the true expert system, in that it is the only type that produces a judgment. At this time, there are no widely available financial analysis systems of this type for the microcomputer. Those now available run on mainframe and minicomputers. However, it is possible to design your own expert system for a micro using a system such as EXPERT-EASE, produced by Human Edge Software in Palo Alto, Calif., or 1st-CLASS, by Programs in Motion, Inc., of Wayland, Massachusetts.

EXPERT-EASE and 1st-CLASS elicit example decisions from an expert decision maker for a number of hypothetical case situations and, using a logic designed into the software, produce a system that a nonexpert can use. The resulting expert system queries the nonexpert for answers to related questions, and the logic of the system operates on these answers to recommend a decision. These systems can be used to produce decision-making tools for a number of decision problems facing the financial executive. For example, one such expert system described in the EXPERT-EASE tutorial provides advice on certain investment decisions. Remember, however, that these systems—EXPERT-EASE and 1st-CLASS—do not contain an expert knowledge base;

this is added by the expert system designer. These systems simply provide the logic component.

EXPERT SYSTEMS—QUO VADIS?

Expert systems are allowing financial executives to enhance their performance in the management arena today. A survey conducted by Coopers & Lybrand revealed, for example, that expert systems are currently being used to improve business operations, for a competitive edge, and for a strategic advantage. Most companies surveyed said they have derived such benefits from expert systems technology as improved products or services, increased productivity, and improved quality of employee output. A fourth benefit, especially among companies' top-level executives, is the broader distribution of expertise that comes with expert systems.

A second survey, by the University of Minnesota, confirmed that expert systems are currently being used in such areas as manufacturing, research and development, marketing, management information systems, and finance. In the area of finance, expert systems help most frequently in planning, diagnosis, and control.

In the future, expert systems will make many decisions that are now made by humans. To paraphrase David Shpilberg, Coopers & Lybrand's expert on expert systems: Expert systems won't replace financial executives; they aim at enhancing the advice people provide rather than merely automating a process. But, unless financial executives are young-minded enough to use state-of-the-art information management technology to enhance decision making in their organizations, an executive runs the risk of losing his position as the chief adviser to the chief executive officer.

Reading 9–2

THE DEVELOPMENT OF ACCOUNTING EXPERT SYSTEMS

By James A. Sena and L. Murphy Smith

Artificial intelligence (AI) is emerging from the laboratory and is being implemented in the business world. AI, and expert systems (ESs) in particular, will change the way that managers and staff interact with and use computer resources in the accounting field. This article describes ESs, discusses their operating mechanisms, and examines current and future applications in auditing, taxation, and management accounting.

Expert systems can be defined as sophisticated computer programs that manipulate knowledge to solve problems efficiently and effectively in a narrow problem domain.[1] They are composed of two basic components:

- *An explicit and accessible body of knowledge.* This is known as the knowledge base and includes the rules and facts applicable to a particular domain or range of acceptable values.

- *An inference engine.* This allows the application of the rules and facts in the knowledge base to a problem.

These two components combine to give true ESs the following fundamental characteristics:

- *Expertise.* An ES should exhibit expert performance, have a high level of skill, and possess adequate depth and breadth in a subject.

- *Symbolic reasoning.* The system should represent knowledge symbolically (not mathematically) and should be able to reformulate arbitrary symbolic knowledge into mathematical computer language with which it can work.

- *Self-knowledge.* The system should be able to examine and explain its own reasoning and apply rules to check the accuracy, consistency, and plausibility of its conclusions.

Most ESs display each of these features to some degree.

An ES attempts to solve problems like an expert in a particular domain. Like all experts, it produces the correct answer most of the time and incorrect answers some of the time. A true ES does not require human involvement. For example, a decision support system aids in human decision making but does not actually make decisions; an ES attempts to make decisions in its particular domain. Currently, however, ES users maintain human involvement because human expertise is better in certain areas and cannot be completely duplicated. Humans are more creative, can learn in difficult domains, can comprehend an entire situation, and have common sense. Therefore, many ESs are like decision support systems because they still act as consultants in certain domains.

MECHANISMS FOR ES OPERATION

There are many ways to build ESs, but all systems have two principal components: a knowledge base and an inference engine. The knowledge base represents the expert's knowledge about a specific problem area and the

EXHIBIT 1   The Inner Workings of an Expert System

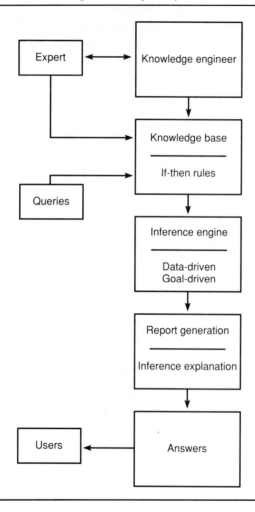

inference engine provides a method for reasoning within that body of knowledge. Exhibit 1 presents the inner workings of an ES.

Rule-Based ESs

In most ESs, the knowledge base is a rule-based system that consists of a series of if-then rules concerning pertinent objects and events. The *if* part of the rule presents the situation, and the *then* part is the response. An example of such a premise is: "If evidence indicates liquidity deterioration, then the liquidity status needs improvement." Such rules, which are known as the

ES's heuristics, can be added to or deleted from the system as the program is used. This is one of the advantages of an ES: the system can be refined continually. A true ES usually needs at least 20 rules to effectively cover its subject, but most systems have more than 100 rules and others have more than 1,000. Exhibit 2 illustrates a nested set of rules for the liquidity problem. The probability figures given in the exhibit are established by the expert accountant and are used to draw inferences from the evidence. The top figure indicates the likelihood that the evidence is true when the conclusion is true, and the bottom figure indicates the likelihood that the evidence is true when the conclusion is false.

Example-Based ESs

Another type of ES is the example-based system. Instead of rules, these systems are based on recorded examples. Using the liquidity problem illustrated in Exhibit 2, the system would contain the statement: "Bad ratios and slow turnovers denote liquidity deterioration." When a sufficient number of examples are entered into the knowledge base, the system can induce a rule that is stated in an if-then construction.

Inference Methods

Rules or examples alone constitute nothing more than a data base. What makes an ES expert is the way the rules are processed by the system and the way they are acted on; this is the inference engine. The two most common inference methods are backward chaining, which is goal driven, and forward chaining, which is data driven. As the name implies, backward chaining starts with the *then* part of an if-then statement—a goal or result; the system then searches for an appropriate *if* clause. For example, using the scenario presented in Exhibit 2, if it is known that a firm has an unsatisfactory current ratio, the system can search for the appropriate *if*—which in this case is: if the current ratio is below 13. Forward chaining works in reverse order.

Whether the system uses forward chaining, backward chaining, or a combination of the two, several *if* or *then* clauses may be true at the same time. The system must decide which is more important or meaningful for a given problem and must show the user how the decision was reached. In most ESs, a combination of techniques is employed. The most important part of an ES is the analysis of how human experts reach a conclusion and which facts are most useful in the process.

ACCOUNTING ESs

Accounting ESs are being developed in three accounting fields: auditing, taxation, and management accounting. They are applied to such specific accounting-related problems as evaluating internal controls, analyzing a firm's

EXHIBIT 2   Example of Expert System—Nested Rules

Knowledge base name		Liquidity analysis	
Rule name	Liquid	Rule type	Inquiry
Probability	Evidence	Question answer help	
(NA)	Financial statement analysis	Q. Liquidity analysis	
Question answer help	Probability	Evidence	
	NA	Liquidity deteriorated	

Knowledge base name		Liquidity analysis	
Rule name	Liquid	Rule type	Answer
Probability	Evidence	Question answer help	
(NA)	Liquidity analysis	A. Liquidity status needs improvement	
Question answer help	Probability	Evidence	
Q. Is the company under protection?	5 / 5	The company is under Chapter 11	
	70 / 10	Ratios are bad	
	70 / 10	Turnovers are slow	

Knowledge base name		Liquidity analysis	
Rule name	Ratio	Rule type	Answer
Probability	Evidence	Question answer help	
(NA)	Ratios are bad	A. Poor liquidity observed	
Question answer help	Probability	Evidence	
Q. Is current ratio below 1.3?	75 / 10	Current ratio is below 1.3	
Q. Is acid test ratio below 0.8?	70 / 10	Acid test ratio is below 0.8	

Knowledge base name		Liquidity analysis	
Rule name	Turnover	Rule type	Answer
Probability	Evidence	Question answer help	
(NA)	Turnovers are slow	A. Poor turnover rate observed	
Question answer help	Probability	Evidence	
Q. Is inventory turnover one standard error below industry average?	85 / 5	Inventory turnover is one standard error below industry average	
Q. Is accounts receivable turnover one standard error below industry average?	85 / 5	Accounts receivable turnover is one standard error below industry average	

Note:
NA Not applicable

allowance for bad debts, auditing advanced DP systems, and evaluating tax-related problems.

Audit-Related ESs

A study was conducted using the ES approach to resolve two audit problems: designing an appropriate, sufficient, and economical audit plan to evaluate an internal control system; and finding a decision rule for terminating the audit process.[2] One conclusion was that DP systems are usually more explicitly and rigorously defined than manual systems and therefore facilitate a more comprehensive and systematic approach to audit planning. As internal control systems become more sophisticated, comprehensive automated audit approaches will be required to efficiently audit these systems. Although simulation models can also be used to analyze manual systems, they are especially useful for analyzing automated systems. Several examples of audit-related ESs follow:

The first audit-related ES dealt with the auditor's evaluation of a commercial client's allowance for bad debts[3] and used Michie's rule-based AL/X system.[4]

The Internal Control Monitor (TICOM)[5] analyzes the flow of documents and effectiveness of controls, recommends additional controls, and points out potential weaknesses. An auditor using TICOM first completes a traditional review of the internal control system and then employs TICOM to model the system. TICOM is superior to traditional internal control evaluation methods in the following ways:

- The evaluation can be more extensive.
- The documentation of the system can be more thorough.
- The auditor can probe and test controls by using the query-processing portion of TICOM.

Another approach is an events-based model of an accounting system.[6] Each of the model's simulation building blocks can represent many individual processing and control steps (e.g., shipping, billing, or accounts-receivable posting); this approach is therefore well suited for high-level analysis. Another proposed simulation approach is designed for the detailed analysis of error and control relationships at a cycle or subcycle level.[7] It provides simulation building blocks that are generalized at a lower level (e.g., processing, control, and branch steps) so that individual processing and control tasks can be modeled in detail and the model can be tailored to diverse applications. Both simulation models can provide auditors and management accountants with decision support to evaluate internal control systems.

Expert Edge (Human Edge Software, Palo Alto, Calif.) and VP-Expert (Paperback Software International, Berkeley, Calif.) are two widely used general-purpose ESs. Both are microcomputer-based systems that can be used on the IBM PC-XT or compatible machines. These packages provide the accountant with the tools necessary to design and install a relatively sophisticated ES. The most appropriate applications for these software packages are well-defined problems that consider two, three, or four options in which the expert decision requires simultaneous evaluation of two or more (usually three to six) decision-relevant factors, particularly when the factors interact in a complex fashion.

An ES currently in use for audit planning is Arthur Young's AY/Decision Support, which is the cornerstone of the firm's auditing software AY/ASQ (Audit Smarter, Quicker).

In one Peat, Marwick, Mitchell & Co.–sponsored study, an ES was developed to assist in the audit of bank loan collectibility;[8] the firm hopes to have it available for use by its auditors in the field.

A common criticism of simulation models, which are used to predict a system's reliability, is that they are usually based on restrictive assumptions about actual accounting environments. An element of all reliability models, which includes simulation models, is a set of assumptions that determine the specifications of discrete probabilities of error distribution that govern the generation of processing errors in the accounting system. A study of simulation models concluded that for accounting systems exhibiting relatively low error rates and effective control procedures (i.e., aggregate error rates of less than 10 percent), the simplifying assumptions provide a close approximation of the overall reliability of a system.[9] Simulations of systems with higher error rates are less accurate.

Research and practical application have demonstrated the usefulness of ESs to auditing. ESs can be used for planning the audit program, analytic review, internal control evaluation, continuous auditing, and system design.

Tax-Related ESs

There have been several attempts to develop ES tax applications. One system, TAX ADVISOR (Robert H. Michaelson, University of Illinois, Champaign), provides estate-planning advice.[10] Another application that is based on ES concepts, but is really a decision support system and not a true expert system, is CORPTAX (Financial Decision Systems, Agoura, Calif.). CORPTAX assists the accountant with Section 302(b) redemptions.[11] Both applications can provide helpful decision support to tax accountants.

Members of several public accounting firms are monitoring the developments of tax-related ESs. The Internal Revenue Service has created an advisory group to evaluate potential applications in the compliance area. Several commercial firms are seeking applications of tax-related ESs.[12] It is anticipated that future research funding in the tax area will be substantially greater than past funding.

Management-Accounting ESs

Management accountants provide a wide variety of services to organizations. In industry, the accounting information system of many firms includes a systems study section. Management accountants in this section evaluate existing financial systems and design and implement new systems. This can also be done by consultants. Whether a systems study is done in-house or by consultants, there is a potential for many expert applications in this area.

POSSIBILITIES FOR THE FUTURE

There are many applications for expert systems in accounting. It is anticipated that the codification of Statements on Auditing Standards (SASs) will serve as a knowledge base for an auditing ES in the near future.[13] This SAS-based ES will probably involve the use of such AI languages as PROLOG or LISP. The SAS-based ES will facilitate the research efforts of practicing CPAs and improve the training techniques of new staff accountants.

Another proposed ES application will simplify the process of preparing financial reports: Expert Systems Corp.'s first application will be general accounting packages that use the Financial Accounting Standards Board (FASB) rules and provide industry standard data organized by Standard Industrial Classification codes. These packages would be tailored to specific industries to assist management accountants in preparing external financial reports.[14]

Many future ES applications will be written by the users themselves. General-purpose expert systems (e.g., Expert Edge) that enable users in various fields (e.g., business, engineering, and medical diagnosis) to create their own expert systems applications are being developed.

BEHAVIOR VARIABLES AND ESs

Designing a useful computer-based information system requires more than just technical knowledge. Incorporating behavior variables into ESs is critical to the system's success. Sensitivity to human needs and behavior is as important a component as specialized technical knowledge. Involving people in the systems development process is therefore crucial. The following description of the ideal computer affirms the need to incorporate behavior variables into computer technology:

> The ideal companion machine would not only look, feel, and sound friendly but would also be programmed to behave in a congenial manner. Those qualities [that] make interaction with other people enjoyable would be simulated as closely as possible, and the machine would appear to be charming, stimulating, and easygoing. . . . It can be articulated that computer systems will be future friends and intimates as well as colleagues.[15]

Expert systems in business may be the first step toward this ideal. If a computer can be programmed to emulate the decision-making abilities of an expert, it could also be programmed to behave in a congenial manner. Users would enjoy interacting with a user-friendly expert that was also personable and easygoing. Indeed, this type of user-system interaction could lead to an even greater acceptance of computers.

The development of accounting ESs is still in the early stages. There are several ESs available for such specialized problems as evaluating a company's allowance for bad debts, evaluating internal controls, or providing estate-planning advice. Accountants can also write their own ESs, using a general-purpose system (e.g, Expert Edge or VP-Expert).

ESs are powerful research tools that can repeatedly update and reevaluate scenarios; sensitivity analyses can be performed on various assumptions of a given model (e.g., relationships and probabilities). There are various practical uses for ESs, including on-the-job decision support. ESs can also be used to train nonexperts (e.g, new staff accountants).

Of all the technological advances made in computer systems, ESs may ultimately have the greatest effect. Easy accessibility to an expert's advice will have a tremendous impact on decision making, problem solving, and overall management performance.

Notes

1. Donald A. Waterman, *A Guide to Expert Systems Readings* (Reading, MA: Addison-Wesley, 1986).
2. Niv Ahituv; Jonathan Halpern; and Hart Will. "Audit Planning: An Algorithmic Approach." *Contemporary Accounting Research,* Fall 1985, pp. 95–110.
3. C. W. Dungan and J. S. Chandler, "Development of Knowledge-Based Expert Systems to Model Auditor's Decision Processes." Research project for Peat, Marwick, Mitchell & Co. (1981).
4. A. Patterson, *AL/X User Manual* (Oxfordshire, England: Intelligent Terminals Ltd., 1981).
5. Andrew D. Bailey, Jr.; G. L. Duke; J. Gerlach; C. Ko; R. Meservy; and A. B. Whinston, "TICOM and the Analysis of Internal Controls." *The Accounting Review,* April 1985, pp. 186–201.
6. W. Robert Knechel, "A Simulation Model for Evaluating Accounting System Reliability." *Auditing: A Journal of Practice and Theory,* Spring 1985, pp. 38–62.
7. C. E. Wiggins and L. Murphy Smith, "A General Audit Simulation Tool for Evaluating the Reliability of Internal Controls." *Contemporary Accounting Research,* Spring 1987.
8. J. Willingham and W. Wright, "Development of a Knowledge-Based System for Auditing the Collectibility of a Commercial Loan." Research proposal (1985).
9. W. Robert Knechel, "An Analysis of Alternative Error Assumptions in Modeling the Reliability of Accounting Systems." *Journal of Accounting Research,* Spring 1985, pp. 194–212.
10. R. Michaelsen and D. Michie, "Expert Systems in Business." *Datamation,* November 1983, pp. 240–246.
11. Michael D. Akers, Grover L. Porter; E. Blocher; and W. G. Mister. "Expert Systems for Management Accountants." *Management Accounting,* March 1986, pp. 30–34.

12. J. A. Booker; R. C. Kick, Jr., and J. C. Gardner, "Expert Systems in Accounting: The Next Generation of Computer Technology." *Journal of Accountancy,* March 1986, pp. 101–104.
13. Booker, Kick, and Gardner, p. 102.
14. Akers et al., p. 34.
15. Neil Frude, "The Affectionate Machine." *Psychology Today,* December 1983, pp. 23–24.

Reading 9–3

A SAMPLE EXPERT SYSTEM FOR FINANCIAL STATEMENT ANALYSIS

By James A. Sena and L. Murphy Smith

"The Development of Accounting Expert Systems," which also appears in this chapter, explains what expert systems (ESs) are and how they operate. This article describes an ES that assists in financial statement analysis. Financial statement analysis involves examining data reported in external financial reports as well as supplementary information from other sources. The primary objectives of financial statement analysis are to identify new or changing trends, amounts (e.g., significant changes in account balances), and relationships between accounts, and to investigate the reasons for these changes.

Financial statement analysis requires an organized approach to select relevant data from financial statements, analyze the data, and interpret the results. The analytical steps are outlined in Exhibit 1. The five major steps depicted in the exhibit are the primary functions of ES analysis. Examples of how the analysis proceeds follow.

- If the auditor's opinion is adverse or results in a disclaimer, financial statement analysis will not proceed.

- If the auditor renders a qualified opinion, analysis might continue beyond Step 1 (this uncertainty is depicted in Exhibit 1 by the dotted line), but the analyst must consider the potential effects of the qualification. For example, a qualification that results from litigation may

EXHIBIT 1   Financial Statement Analysis

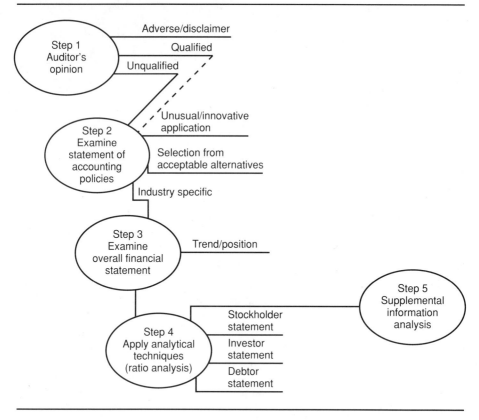

have no effect on a company's financial performance; on the other hand, it may have disastrous financial consequences.

- If the auditor's opinion is not accompanied by qualifications, analysis will proceed to Steps 2 through 5.

Of the five steps outlined in Exhibit 1, Step 4—Apply analytical techniques (also referred to as ratio analysis)—is the most important for financial statement analysis and ES development. The sample ES was developed to perform this particular step of financial statement analysis.

COMPUTING THE RATIOS

Financial statement analysis varies with each industry. The sample ES focuses on the oil and gas industry. Using Standard and Poor's *Industry Surveys*, 16 major oil and gas companies were selected. Ratios were calculated by comparing two accounts or groups of accounts. For example:

$$\frac{\text{Current assets}}{\text{Current liabilities}} = \text{Current ratio}$$

These ratios can then be used as guidelines to evaluate a company's performance. For the sample ES, the ratios were computed from the companies' financial statements over five years and from information obtained from Standard and Poor's *Industry Surveys*. Exhibit 2 lists the industry-specific ratios that were calculated for the sample ES.

SAMPLE SYSTEM DEVELOPMENT

The financial statement analysis ES begins with the question "Is the financial status unsatisfactory?" With the ES, the user can determine whether the financial status of the firm under review is unsatisfactory, based on a comparison with the industry-specific ratios that represent industry norms. The user is guided through a series of questions that require *yes, no,* or *don't know* responses. Exhibit 3 presents the sequence of conclusions made by the ES on the basis of comparisons with the ratios (listed in the exhibit under "Evidence"). The major query ("Financial status unsatisfactory?") is located at the top of the hierarchy. The evidence for that query becomes the next level of inquiry, and the process continues until direct answers can be obtained to determine the answer to the major query. At any stage, the user can ask for help to clarify a question. For example, the question "Is it true that current

EXHIBIT 2   Industry-Specific Ratios Used in the Sample ES

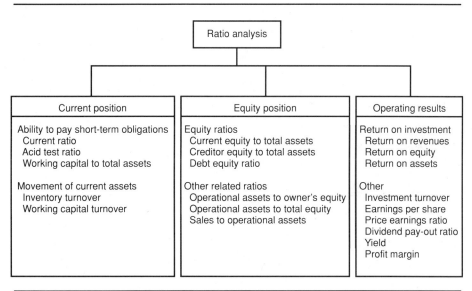

EXHIBIT 3   Sample ES Rules

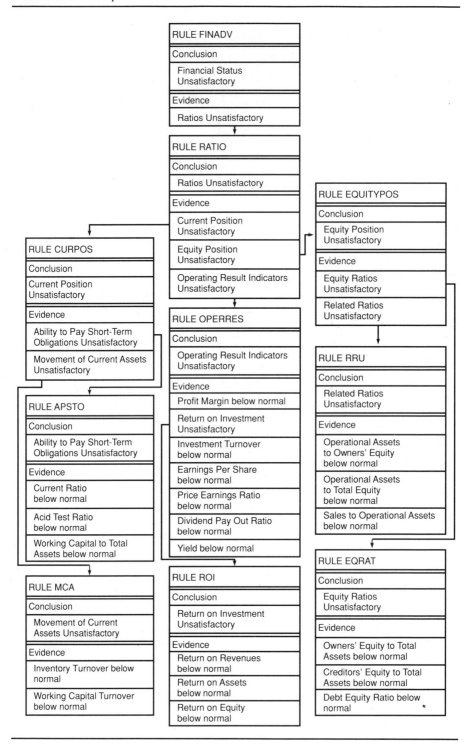

ratio is below normal?" is supplemented by the HELP option that defines below normal as "current ratio < 1.22."

The combination of conclusion and evidence is called a rule. The rules listed in Exhibit 3 present a straightforward approach for determining whether a company's financial statement is within industry norms. The same rules could be used to create queries to identify companies that are within industry norms (satisfactory) or above industry norms (exceptional).

The Expert Edge Package

The rules were entered onto Expert Edge (Human Edge Software, Palo Alto, Calif.), an ES shell used for developing interactive knowledge-based systems. Expert Edge runs on an IBM PC. Its storage and system resource requirements are at the basic level—256K bytes of main storage and two disk drives.

All ratios were entered as equal weights and the queries were structured for positive or negative responses; however, the weights can be changed by adding and modifying the rules. Although Expert Edge can use probabilities and Bayesian statistics to handle uncertainties and lack of complete information, the sample ES uses crisp reasoning—step-by-step reasoning that allows the ES to justify the reasoning for any advice given—and can aid the accounting expert in testing and refining the ES before release for staff (nonexpert) use. If desired, however, the responses can be changed to reply along a probability scale and to include Bayesian probabilities. The probability situation requires greater understanding on the part of the accounting ES builder. Once in place, however, scaled responses can be substituted for the *yes, don't know,* and *no* responses used under the crisp reasoning mode (see Exhibit 4). The scale provides the user with more flexibility when answering queries.

The Expert Edge package accepts the expert's knowledge expressed as rules (see Exhibit 3), and creates an interactive dialogue that leads users through the same decision-making process that an expert would use. The rules can include calculations, equations, logical reasoning, judgment, facts, and uncertainties. Rule building is supported through a natural language interface. Data bases, spreadsheets, and word processors can also be used to enter rules. The developer can request that the package automatically check for rule redundancies and conflicts.

Expert Edge provides a help text to guide the user in responding to system-generated questions. The sample system employs this feature for the lowest-level queries and assists the user by defining below-normal for each ratio.

There are three modes of operation for the ES:

- Advise—Gives the nonexpert advice on a problem situation.
- Learn—Builds the ES and molds or modifies it.
- Demonstrate—Teaches how to operate the ES.

The main screen display for the Expert Edge package is shown in Exhibit 5. The screen is split into six boxes, or windows, that display several types of

EXHIBIT 4   Response Scale for Query

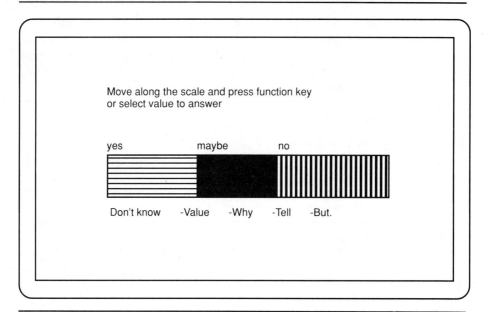

EXHIBIT 5   Expert Edge Main Screen Display

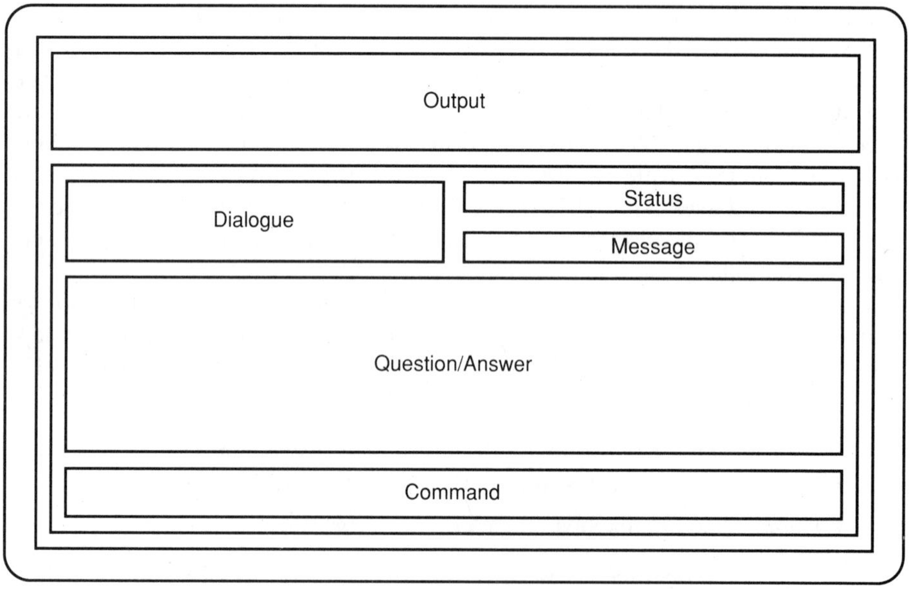

EXHIBIT 6   Entry Screen for the Rule APSTO

Ability to Pay Short-Term Obligations Unsatisfactory	IF -Current Ratio | below | normal
	AND -Acid Test Ratio | below | normal
	AND -Working Capital to Total Assets | below | normal
dialogue window	expert edge 2nd Dec 87 free 93%
	message window
What is the second object (if any):	
Learn: -navigate, -add a rule, or -delete a rule, -rationalize knowledge.	

information on the screen simultaneously. The windows and the types of information displayed in each are:

- Output—The ES's information, conclusions, and progress.
- Dialogue—Questions, answers, and conclusions.
- Question/Answer—Each system question as asked.
- Status—System status data.
- Message—Error messages.
- Command—Choice of commands.

Another window, Help Instruction, overlays the right side of the screen display. Text is entered here by the expert as the system is built. The text helps the user respond to questions.

After the rules are defined, they are entered into the ES shell. The rules are created in an interactive model in which the accounting expert replies to the ES's requests for rule components (i.e., subject, verb, and objects) for conclusions and evidence. The rules are given names, and HELP dialogue and associated entries are added before rule entry is completed. In Expert Edge, the learn mode is used for rule entry. In the sample system, 10 rules were entered. Exhibit 6 depicts the entry of the rule Ability to Pay Short-Term Obligations (APSTO). The conclusion that the ability to pay short-term obligations is unsatisfactory is based on the following evidence:

- Current Ratio below normal.
- Acid Test Ratio below normal.
- Working Capital to Total Assets below normal.

HOW THE SAMPLE SYSTEM OPERATES

After the rules are entered, the system can advise the user. Exhibit 7 presents the inquiry screen for a sample problem that asks: "Financial Status Unsatisfactory?" To invoke analysis, the user responds positively.

If the user answers positively, the ES proceeds to the lowest-level rules (refer to Exhibit 3 to trace the rule hierarchy). Following the arrows, the first evidence would flow from "Current Position Unsatisfactory" to "Ability to Pay Short-Term Obligations Unsatisfactory" to "Current Ratio Below Normal." Exhibit 8 shows the entry screen at this point. The user should now compare the company's various ratios with those entered in the expert system. To determine whether the current ratio is below normal, the user could invoke the HELP function to define normal current ratio. This process is shown in Exhibit 9.

As the arrows indicate in Exhibit 3, the system would then proceed to the other evidence of "Ability to Pay Short-Term Obligations Unsatisfactory": "Acid Test Ratio below normal" and "Working Capital to Total Assets below normal." Following that, the system would return to the other evidence

EXHIBIT 7   Sample Inquiry Screen

output window	
dialogue window	expert edge 2nd Dec 87 free 95%
	message window
Which inquiry would you like me to answer :--	-Financial Status Unsatisfactory.
Main Menu: Please select one of the following commands: -Advise -Learn -Change -Disk.	

EXHIBIT 8   Lowest-Level Rule Interrogation

Financial Status Unsatisfactory.

The acceptance level is currently 70.

The acceptance level is currently 70. Current Ratio below normal.	expert edge 2nd Dec 87 free 92%

Is it true that Current Ratio below normal?
Press function key or select answer.

-yes -don't know -no -why -tell -but,

Main Menu:
Please select one of the following commands: -Advise -Learn -Change -Disk.

EXHIBIT 9   The HELP Function

Financial Status Unsatis	Current Ratio < 1.22
The acceptance level is currently 70.	
The acceptance level is currently 70. Current Ratio below normal Help.	
Is it true that Current Ratio below normal Press function key, or select answer. -yes -don't know -no -why -tell	

Main Menu:
Please select one of the following commands: -Advise -Learn -Change -Disk.

for "Current Position Unsatisfactory": "Movement of Current Assets Unsatisfactory," and the subsequent evidence for it.

After all responses are entered, the ES makes a judgment on the basis of entries made during the dialogue. Exhibit 10 illustrates the final screen. The ratios were unsatisfactory because the next-level sets of evidence were found to be unsatisfactory. The user can ask "why" at any time in the dialogue process, and the system responds with information detailing the logic process in the question/answer window.

The sample system presented here is only the tip of the iceberg for a full-blown financial statement analysis ES. In addition to being adapted to enter such major queries as "satisfactory" and "exceptional," the system can be molded to accept a combination of "satisfactory" and "unsatisfactory" ratios to make intermediate judgments about portions of a company's financial status. The ES developer can also tag on additional messages to system responses to alert the user to related factors, problems, or other situations.

The ES can also be extended to handle the other steps of financial statement analysis presented in Exhibit 1. For example, "Auditor's Opinion" could become another major query or another ES. The process can continue beyond financial statement analysis and extend to other areas of the accountant's decision-making responsibilities.

EXHIBIT 10   Final Response Screen for Query

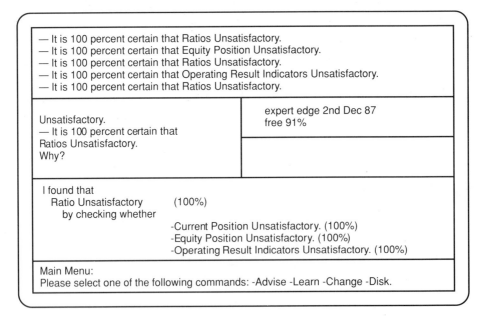

— It is 100 percent certain that Ratios Unsatisfactory.
— It is 100 percent certain that Equity Position Unsatisfactory.
— It is 100 percent certain that Ratios Unsatisfactory.
— It is 100 percent certain that Operating Result Indicators Unsatisfactory.
— It is 100 percent certain that Ratios Unsatisfactory.

Unsatisfactory.
— It is 100 percent certain that Ratios Unsatisfactory.
Why?

expert edge 2nd Dec 87
free 91%

I found that
    Ratio Unsatisfactory   (100%)
        by checking whether
                        -Current Position Unsatisfactory. (100%)
                        -Equity Position Unsatisfactory. (100%)
                        -Operating Result Indicators Unsatisfactory. (100%)

Main Menu:
Please select one of the following commands: -Advise -Learn -Change -Disk.

Reading 9–4

EXPERT SYSTEMS AS DECISION AIDS: ISSUES AND STRATEGIES

By Ting-peng Liang

Abstract. Although expert systems technology that takes advantage of artificial intelligence techniques is very powerful, its application in business domain is not without problems. This article examines issues involved in integrating expert systems and decision support systems and discusses strategies for using this technology. Five general guidelines for developing EDSS are presented. They are (1) selected applications, (2) realistic objectives, (3) validated knowledge, (4) evolutionary design, and (5) risk control.

INTRODUCTION

Expert systems (ES) designed to mimic and replace human experts have drawn considerable attention in the past several years. Although most of the early applications were developed in medical or engineering domains, business applications have become more and more popular [Blanning, 1984; Ernst & Ojha, 1986; Lin, 1986; Michaelsen & Michie, 1983]. Articles presenting existing prototypes have increased dramatically. Many potential benefits have been reported [Fried, 1987]. They include:

- Improved decision making.
- More consistent decision making.
- Reduce design or decision-making time.
- Improved training.
- Operational cost saving.
- Better use of expert time.
- Improved products or service levels.
- Rare or dispersed knowledge captured.

These potential benefits, coupled with research conducted in the decision support systems (DSS) area, have strongly encouraged an integration of ES and DSS technologies. For example, Scott Morton (1984) stated that "DSS as we know them may become obsolete in the foreseeable future. They are being supplanted by expert decision support systems—EDSS. The next generation of DSS will combine existing DSS technology with the capabilities of

Reprinted with permission of *Journal of Information Systems*, Spring 1988, pp. 41–50.

AI." Luconi et al. (1986) argued that "for many of the problems of practical importance in business, we should focus our attention on designing systems that support expert users rather than on replacing them." Turban and Watkins (1986) discussed how to integrate ES programs into a DSS in order to create even more powerful and useful computer-based systems.

Developing EDSS that take advantage of both ES and DSS technologies is certainly promising. Its implementation, unfortunately, is not without problems. ES and DSS have different objectives, different design philosophies, and different architectures [Ford, 1985; Turban & Watkins, 1986]. These differences make this integration difficult. Furthermore, unlike engineering domains, behavioral considerations usually play an important role in the business arena. For a system that focuses on importing outside expertise, the risk of failure would be high. Therefore, before joining the bandwagon of using ES as decision aids, we need to carefully examine potential applications of this technology and to develop a framework that provides guidelines for employing various types of computer-based decision aids. In the remainder of this article, we shall discuss the issues involved in using ES as decision aids and develop strategies for using this technology.

ISSUES IN INTEGRATING ES AND DSS

The basic premise of ES is that in some areas a small group of people (called experts) can perform a particular job significantly better than most of the rest. Since the knowledge (called expertise) of these people is rare and expensive, developing ES that capture and disseminate this expertise will be able to improve the decision performance of nonexperts [Waterman, 1986]. The basic premise of DSS, however, is that for some semistructured problems the decision maker can improve performance by conducting "what-if" type of analysis that takes advantage of the power of computers to speed up data analysis and mathematical calculation. Therefore, the integration of these two technologies have the following problems.

First, ES and DSS have different objectives. DSS focus on supporting decision makers in semistructured or unstructured problems, whereas ES concentrate on replacing human decision makers in structured and narrow problem domains. This difference has resulted in two completely different design philosophies. In designing a DSS, the designer must always have the user in mind and adapt the system to meet user requirements [Keen & Scott Morton, 1978; Sprague & Carlson, 1982]. In designing an ES, however, the designer (called knowledge engineer) must focus on acquiring knowledge from domain experts who are usually not the user of the system. In other words, the quality of knowledge is the primary concern, users are second. The designer of an integrated system must compromise these two philosophies.

Second, it is not clear whether the focus of integration should be the rule-based approach adopted by ES or the concept of including expert judgment in a system. ES and DSS have different functional capabilities. A typical DSS performs data analysis (called a data-oriented DSS) or model execution assistance (called a model-oriented DSS) for the user. The user is responsible for determining the data to be analyzed and the model to be used. A typical ES, however, further makes judgment based on its built-in knowledge and value systems. Figure 1 illustrates this difference. If an integrated EDSS only takes advantage of the rule-based techniques and still leaves the judgment to the user, then, just like rewriting a COBOL program in PASCAL, there will be no functional difference between EDSS and DSS. The resulting system will not have the anticipated power because it does not have the desired knowledge.

If an EDSS is designed to provide not only data analysis and model execution assistance but also its expert judgment, then the next issue is whose value and judgment functions should be coded into the system? From the DSS perspective, the user's judgment function should be used. Since the user may not be an expert, this approach could result in a useless rule-based system. Even if the user is an expert, duplicating the expertise may provide little assistance. From the ES perspective, judgment functions elicited from a small

FIGURE 1

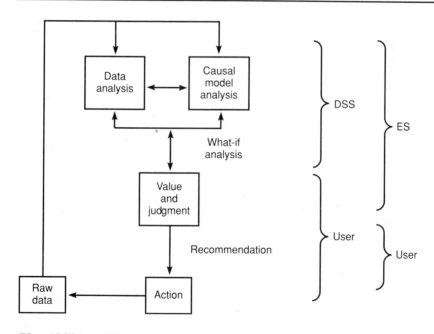

ES and DSS have different functional capabilities. DSS do not have knowledge to make judgments.

group of selected experts are more appropriate. The problem with this approach is that it may generate high resistance—one of the major reasons for DSS to adopt user-oriented design.

Finally, even if the designers successfully implement an EDSS that provides expert judgment, there are chances that in a given situation the EDSS and the user may draw conflicting conclusions. In this case, whose judgment should be adopted? How can we determine whose judgment is correct? Should we bring in another human expert or expert system to make recommendations? If the user's expertise has been proven better than the system's, then why should the user be bothered by the EDSS? If the system is proven better, then how can we allow the user to override the system's judgment?

All these issues suggest that using ES as decision aids is not as simple or as exciting as it seems to be. We need to know where it can be applied and how it can be used appropriately.

SELECTION OF DECISION AIDS

From a broad perspective, all systems, including human expert consultants, are decision aids, because nothing can replace the role of a decision maker who takes full responsibility for the outcome. Different types of decision aids have different characteristics. For example, a human expert has both common sense and professional knowledge in a particular area but is usually less consistent in performance. A DSS provides a strong guidance in the decision process but has high restriction because it lacks common sense. A DSS provides customized support to decision makers but cannot make its own judgment. Figure 2 shows a comparison of four types of decision aids: transaction processing systems (TPS), DSS, ES, and human experts (HE).

With these differences in mind, we must consider at least four factors to select and use a decision aid properly: the task, the nature of knowledge, the system, and the user. The first two factors determine what kind of decision aid is appropriate and the latter two factors determine the strategy for using a selected decision aid.

Selecting a Decision Aid

The first factor that affects decision-aid selection is the nature of the task. There are many ways to differentiate decision problems. Three of them are particularly important:

1. Availability of expertise.
2. Structuredness of the problem.
3. Decision frequency.

If the expertise required for solving the problem is not available, then developing a good decision aid is impossible. If the required expertise exists,

FIGURE 2

	TPS	DSS	ES	HE
System-user interaction	Rare	User-directed	System-directed	Bi-directional
Reasoning model	Quantitative and causal	Quantitative and causal	Qualitative and judgmental	Qualitative and judgmental
System guidance in the decision process	Low	Medium	High	High
System restriction	High	Medium	High	Low
System customization	Low	High	Low	High
Performance consistency	High	High	High	Medium
Common sense reasoning	No	No	No	Yes
Providing judgment	No	No	Yes	Yes

Transaction processing systems (TPS), decision support systems (DSS), expert systems (ES), and human experts (HE) are four types of decision aids. They are different in many aspects.

then we consider whether the problem is structured or unstructured and whether the decision occurs repetitively or only once. The problem structuredness affects the division of labor between the system and the user. In semistructured or unstructured decision making, only the structured portion can be automated because a computer system cannot process a job which human beings do not know how to do. The decision frequency is important in determining whether a particular decision aid is cost effective. For a decision that occurs only once, developing a sophisticated expert system may not be justifiable in terms of development time and costs.

The second factor to be considered is the nature of knowledge processed by the decision aid. It could be qualitative or quantitative. A qualitative reasoning process usually involves judgmental models, whereas a quantitative computation process uses causal models. Transaction processing systems (TPS) and traditional DSS focus on quantitative computation, whereas ES and human experts solve problems by qualitative reasoning.

Taking all these factors into consideration, we find that there is no decision aid that fits all cases. Figure 3 shows the situations where the following decision aids are applicable.

1. **Expert systems.** In a structured domain where qualitative reasoning is crucial to problem solving and expertise is available, developing an ES (or

FIGURE 3

Task / Knowledge	Structured		Unstructured	
	Repetitive	**Ad hoc**	**Repetitive**	**Ad hoc**
Qualitative reasoning	Expert systems	Human experts	Human experts	Human experts
Quantitative reasoning	Transaction processing systems	End-user computing	Decision support systems (institutional)	Decision support systems (ad hoc)

Selecting decision aids must consider the problem structuredness, decision frequency, and reasoning method. When qualitative reason is required, expert systems are appropriate for structured and repetitive decision and human experts must be hired for the rest. When quantitative reasoning is used, transaction processing systems are appropriate for structured and repetitive decisions, end-user computing is appropriate for structured and ad hoc decisions and decision support systems are appropriate for unstructured decisions.

EDSS) to support a repetitive decision in the domain may be appropriate. For example, loan evaluation is a repetitive decision for most banks. Except some special cases, the loan evaluation process and evaluation criteria are clearly defined. Therefore, an ES can reduce the workload of a loan officer and allow the officer to focus on special cases.

2. **Human experts.** If the decision is structured but ad hoc or unstructured by nature, then the assistance an ES can provide is very limited. In this case, human experts must be hired if a support is desired.

3. **Transaction processing systems.** If the desired support is quantitative by nature, and the decision is structured and repetitive, then a traditional transaction processing system that focuses on standard procedures and large amounts of data will be sufficient. For example, providing monthly inventory reports is a repetitive, structured, and quantitative task; a good TPS will make this process much easier.

4. **End-user computing.** When the decision is structured, ad hoc, and quantitative, one technology called end-user computing that encourages decision makers to develop their own ad hoc applications by taking advantage of user-friendly fourth-generation languages (4GLs) is very useful. The key in this case is to provide the user with a powerful 4GL with which an ad hoc application system can be built.

5. **Decision support systems.** For an unstructured domain that needs quantitative support, DSS technology is appropriate. The system performs data

analysis or executes proper models and the user makes judgments. If the decision is repetitive, then an institutional DSS may be developed. Otherwise, the user may develop an ad hoc DSS with a DSS generator and discard the system after successfully making the decision.

From this discussion, we find that ES can support only a small set of decisions. Furthermore, proper use of a particular technology may also be affected by characteristics of the system and the user. This is particularly true when ES are used. As discussed in the previous section, from the same set of facts, ES and the user may draw conflicting conclusions. Therefore, strategies for resolving the conflict are required.

Developing these strategies, we must consider the expertise of the user and the quality of the system. Users who use ES may have different levels of expertise varying from beginner to expert. The quality of ES may also vary from a rule-based toy to a real expert. There are many ES that do not demonstrate the desired expertise; but there are also systems that outperform human experts. For example, MYCIN, one of the earliest ES designed to diagnose infections and to recommend appropriate treatment, has been reported better than human physicians [Yu et al., 1979]. In the experiment, MYCIN had a 65 percent success rate in prescribing correct medication, while physicians had an average success rate of 55.5 percent (ranging from 62.5 percent to 42.5 percent).

By comparing the quality of the system and the expertise of the user, four strategies for using ES technology can be developed: ignore, revise, follow, and synthesize (Figure 4).

1. **Ignore.**   If only a toy ES is available and the user is also not an expert, then the contribution of the system is virtually none and it should not be used.

FIGURE 4

		Quality of User	
		Nonexpert	**Expert**
Quality of System	Toy	Ignore	Revise
	Expert	Follow	Synthesize

Quality of user and quality of system determine the strategy for using EDSS. If neither the user nor the system has adequate expertise, then the system must be ignored. If the user is an expert but the system is not, then the user can revise the system to improve its knowledge base. If the system has expertise but the user is a beginner, then the user should follow the system's recommendation. If both are experts, then the best strategy is to synthesize two judgments to find synergy.

2. **Revise.** If the system is a toy but the user is an expert, then the user may want to improve the system by revising its knowledge base. This strategy is appropriate only when the user has an intention to disseminate expertise. In other words, the enhanced system can be a good decision aid to other nonexpert users. The resulting system may also work as a checklist for the user to avoid mistakes caused by ignorance in the decision process.

3. **Follow.** The follow strategy applies when the user is not an expert but the system has a real expertise. In this case, the user must trust the system and take actions based on the expert system's recommendation. For example, when consulting with MYCIN, a patient should not overlook the system's prescription.

4. **Synthesize.** When both the user and the ES are at the expert level, the best strategy is to find synergy. The ES must be treated as an independent consultant. The decision process will be similar to a group decision-making process. Potential benefits in this case include reducing obvious mistakes and expanding the scope of consideration by complementing each other.

In summary, we have presented various strategies for selecting and using ES as decision aids in this section. To avoid misapplication of this powerful technology and to alleviate the problems addressed in the previous section, the following general guidelines must be followed: (1) focus on appropriate applications, (2) set up realistic objectives, (3) validate expert knowledge, (4) implement evolutionary design, and (5) control system risk.

GUIDELINES FOR DEVELOPING EDSS

1. Selected Application

One of the obvious dangers involved in using EDSS is called the law of the hammer—give a child a hammer and he will use it on everything encountered [Hopple, 1986]. Therefore, to use ES technology constructively, we must carefully evaluate every application. We have known that an ES is appropriate only when the problem domain is structured, the decision is repetitive, and the knowledge involves qualitative reasoning. In addition, there are several functional categories appropriate for this technology. These include interpretation, prediction, diagnosis, design, planning, monitoring, debugging, repair, instruction, and control [Hayes-Roth et al., 1983]. As long as an application falls into one of these categories, ES may be considered.

To further evaluate an application, the following questions must be asked:

- Does the application have a clear boundary? Current ES technology does not allow the system to have much creativity. Therefore, unless the application needs only a finite set of known knowledge, the support an ES can provide will be limited. For example, tax advising is a bounded domain, but new product development is not.

- Does the application have standard cases from which knowledge can be derived and validated? If these cases do not exist, then knowledge acquisition will be very difficult and the resulting system may not be reliable.

- Is there any expert who can provide knowledge in the domain? The expert must have expertise and also have the willingness and time to cooperate with knowledge engineers in the knowledge acquisition process. If such an expert is not available, developing an ES for the application will not be possible.

- Is the size of the knowledge base reasonable? The complexity of the system is an exponential function of the size of the knowledge base. Therefore, developing a system that needs a huge amount of knowledge may be too costly and error-prone.

- Is a conventional system adequate for this application? Because ES technology is still in its infancy, using a conventional approach may solve the problem quickly and at a lower cost.

2. Realistic Objective

If ES technology is found appropriate for an application, then a realistic objective for system development must be established. This can help us avoid the danger of omniscience that expects an ES to do something we don't know how to do. There are many unsolved (or unsolvable) problems in developing and using DSS. Unfortunately, using ES as a substitute is not the solution. ESs are not super-DSS or super-humans. They are just other types of systems focusing on other types of problems. An ES cannot do anything that no one else knows how to do. In most domains, ES cannot perform even close to a real expert. Therefore, attention should be focused on strong economic benefits or knowledge dissemination, rather than unrealistic expectations.

3. Validated Knowledge

Another important fact about ES is that the power of an ES is derived from the knowledge it possesses, not from the particular formalisms and inference schemes it employs. Therefore, thorough validation of the knowledge base is essential to the reliability of the system. The validation should start from the selection of experts and continue throughout the system development and utilization process.

- Before developing the system, qualified experts must be located. Those experts must have the expertise and also have time to work with knowledge engineers. They may not be the user of the system.

- Knowledge acquired from the experts must be validated before coding into the system. Standard cases may be used at this stage to find inconsistency, and indicate incomplete knowledge.

- A complete validation must be connected before applying the system to any real-world problem.

- During system utilization, the knowledge base must be continuously revised to meet the changing environment.

If the system is purchased from a third-party vendor rather than developed in-house, then the system must be evaluated by a group of experts. In addition, it is important to make sure that the knowledge contained in the system can be either revised by the organization or updated by the vendor.

4. Evolutionary Design

Since the user usually does not trust a decision aid until it shows reliable performance, an evolutionary approach that requires the designer first to develop a simple system and then to revise the system under the guidance of the user has been a major approach for DSS design. In order to support the user with an ES, a similar approach must be adopted. This process will include three major steps.

First, when a system is developed or is purchased from a software vendor, the knowledge base already contains a set of basic knowledge. However, it may not have the specific knowledge that is useful only in that particular organization. Therefore, the system must be considered as a rule-based checklist; the user's judgment still plays a major role in the decision process. The user evaluates the reliability of the system and asks experts to revise the knowledge base if appropriate. The system at this stage may be called a rule-based DSS.

After the first stage, the user has found the strengths and offset the limitations of the system. The reliability of the system increases and the user starts trusting the system. In this case, the system makes judgments, but the user still keeps an eye on the system and overrides the system's judgment. This system is called a human-aided ES.

Finally, the system becomes very reliable after a certain time period. At this time, the system makes most of the judgments and the user only focuses on special cases that cannot be handled by the system. If the system and the user draw conflicting conclusions for a particular problem, a careful examination of the conflict may be required. Unless there is a good reason, the user should avoid changing the system's recommendation.

This process allows a system to evolve from a rule-based DSS, human-aided ES to a valuable ES. It can reduce the possible resistance from the user and also gradually improve the reliability of the system.

5. Risk Control

In addition to the technical issues, another important consideration is to control risks. Both financial and technological risks may occur if EDSS are used.

Financial Risks.   Developing ES is very expensive and time-consuming. A recent survey indicated that the average cost for developing a system was $700.00 per rule—excluding the costs of hardware, software tools, and the time experts contributed to the knowledge base [Fried, 1987]. Therefore, an ES project could be a financial disaster unless the management is fully aware of this fact.

Technological Risks.   Because current ES technology is pretty young, it is very likely that a system developed today will be obsolete in a few years. In addition, it is sometimes difficult to know who is the real expert in a domain. Knowledge acquired from a nonexpert may mislead the user. For example, some lawyers also provide tax-advising service usually provided by accountants. It would be difficult to determine whether they are qualified experts. Finally, no reliable tool for knowledge acquisition is currently available. The development of ES is still more an art than a science. This may significantly restrict the reliability of the system.

CONCLUDING REMARKS

The term *expert system* has been controversial. On the one hand, it creates high expectation and has been used as a buzzword for funding and a flag to wave for all sorts of projects [Bobrow et al., 1986]. On the other hand, many people have criticized its feasibility. For example, Dreyfus and Dreyfus (1986) stated that "we believe that trying to capture more sophisticated skills within the realm of logic—skills involving not only calculation but also judgment—is a dangerously misguided effort and is ultimately doomed to failure."

In fact, ESs are neither the solution to all problems, nor the solution to none. We need to understand where it can be applied and how to use it appropriately. This has been the main focus of this article. In summary, we have first examined the problems involved in using ES as decision aids. Then, strategies for using various types of decision aids have been addressed. Finally, five general guidelines for developing EDSS have been presented.

References

Blanning, R. W. "Management Applications of Expert Systems." *Information & Management,* 7, 1984, pp. 311–316.

Bobrow, D. G.; S. Mittal; and M. J. Stefik. "Expert Systems: Perils and Promise." *Communications of the ACM,* 29:9, 1986, pp. 880–894.

Dreyfus, H. L., and S. E. Dreyfus. "Why Expert Systems Do Not Exhibit Expertise." *IEEE Expert,* 1:2, 1986, pp. 86–90.

Ernst, M. L., and H. Ojha. "Business Applications of Artificial Intelligence Knowledge-Based Expert Systems." *Future Generations Computer System,* 2, 1986, pp. 173–185.

Ford, F. N. "Decision Support Systems and Expert Systems: A Comparison." *Information & Management,* 8, 1985, pp. 21–26.

Fried, L. "The Dangers of Dabbling in Expert System." *Computerworld,* June 29, 1987, pp. 65–72.

Hayes-Roth, F.; D. A. Waterman; and D. B. Lenat. *Building Expert Systems* (Reading, Mass.: Addison-Wesley, 1983).

Hopple, G. W. "Decision Aiding Dangers: The Law of the Hammer and Other Maxims." *IEEE Transactions on Systems, Man, and Cybernetics,* 16:6, 1986, pp. 834–843.

Keen, P. G. W., and M. S. Scott Morton. *Decision Support Systems: An Organizational Perspective* (Reading, Mass.: Addison-Wesley, 1978).

Lin, E. "Expert Systems for Business Applications: Potential and Limitations." *Journal of Systems Management,* July 1986, pp. 18–21.

Luconi, F. L.; T. W. Malone; and M. S. Scott Morton. "Expert Systems: The Next Challenge for Managers." *Sloan Management Review,* Summer 1986, pp. 3–14.

Michaelsen, R. H., and D. Michie. "Expert Systems in Business." *Datamation,* November 1983, pp. 240–246.

Scott Morton, M. S. "Expert Decision Support Systems." Paper Presented at the Special DSS Conference, Planning Executive Institute and Information Technology Institute, New York, NY, May 21–22, 1984, p. 12.

Sprague, R. H., Jr., and E. D. Carlson. *Building Effective Decision Support Systems* (Englewood Cliffs, NJ: Prentice-Hall, 1982).

Turban, E., and P. R. Watkins. "Integrating Expert Systems and Decision Support Systems." *MIS Quarterly,* 10:2, 1986, pp. 121–136.

Waterman, D. A. *A Guide to Expert Systems* (Reading, Mass.: Addison-Wesley, 1986), pp. 24–31.

Yu, V. L., et al. "Antimicrobial Selection by Computers: A Blinded Evaluation of Infectious Disease Experts." *Journal of the American Medical Association,* 242:21, 1970, pp. 1279–1282.

CHAPTER 10

Microcomputers

The first microcomputers were developed in the early 1970s as "garage" projects by electronic hobbyists. Until the late 1970s these primitive machines were largely ignored by the business world. This indifference was due to the high prices of these early PCs and, perhaps more critically, the lack of useful business software. In these early days the microcomputer environment was most unfriendly, and typically required the user to write a separate BASIC program for each individual application. This was not an attractive proposition for most businessmen, who were not and did not wish to invest the time required to become proficient BASIC programmers.

The attitude of business towards microcomputers changed dramatically in 1978, the year in which the initial electronic spreadsheet program for microcomputers was introduced. This program, called VisiCalc, was originally designed to run on Apple microcomputers and was warmly received by the business community. Finally, software which made the microcomputer a useful business tool had been brought to market. As microcomputer hardware prices began to decline in the early 1980s, an increasing number of accounting, tax, and auditing organizations began to use PCs in their everyday operations. Many organizations purchased machines in order to run VisiCalc alone. The business potential of microcomputers became more apparent as new software packages, such as data base management systems and word processors, were developed specifically for business applications. With the introduction of the IBM-PC in 1981, the microcomputer revolution took hold.

Perhaps no other recent development has had as great an impact on the day-to-day activities of business as has the introduction of microcomputers. The business community has invested heavily in microcomputer hardware, software, and training, and microcomputers have penetrated almost all aspects of business activity. The number of PCs in use has increased from fewer than a million in 1980 to over 50 million less than 10 years later. Given their traditional spreadsheet orientation, it is not surprising that tax, accounting, and auditing organizations were among the first to implement the new technology. Numerous accounting, tax, and auditing tasks were found to be compatible with application tools such as spreadsheets, word processors, data base management systems, data communications packages, and desktop publishing. This integration of microcomputers into routine tasks has produced significant benefits and savings.

The benefits attributed to microcomputer integration are many. Numerous organizations have reported significant gains in productivity, cost reductions, and increases in overall effectiveness. Other often-cited advantages include reductions in staffing requirements, more timely and reliable information, less dependence on the entity's data processing center, speedier development of new systems, opportunities for decentralizing operations, and enhanced planning, control, and coordination of activities. Profitability has also been enhanced by the use of point-of-sale retail systems, a reduction in production times, computer models to improve inventory management, and electronic data interchange—all made possible by microcomputer technology.

It should also be noted that the impact of PCs probably will not be limited to positives such as those mentioned above. PCs have the potential to produce permanent changes in the organizations which use them. Integration of microcomputers may alter such basic factors as an entity's organizational structure, degree of capital intensiveness, staff entry requirements, and typical career paths. PCs represent new assets which must be both protected and controlled. They also provide new challenges as potential tools and new targets for computer crime.

The readings included in this chapter further explore the impact of PCs on the accounting and auditing profession. The initial reading, "Impact of Microcomputers on Accounting Systems," discusses the key elements which are affected when a manual accounting system is converted to a microcomputer-based accounting system. The second reading, "Microcomputers in Auditing: A Primer," describes the ways that microcomputers are being used to facilitate many tasks within the audit process. The third reading, "An Overview of Computer Viruses," examines the computer virus phenomenon. Computer viruses represent a growing threat to microcomputer security and serve to remind us that microcomputers also provide new risks and exposures. The final reading, "Microcomputer Accounting Graphics, Why and How to Use Them," concerns the use of graphical presentations, specifically for accounting purposes.

CHAPTER 10 READINGS

1. John T. Overbey, Jo Ann C. Carland, and James W. Carland, "Impact of Microcomputers on Accounting Systems," *Journal of Systems Management,* June 1987, pp. 20–27.
2. Casper E. Wiggins, Jr., and Christopher Wolfe, "Microcomputers in Auditing: A Primer," *Journal of Accounting and EDP,* Spring 1988, pp. 47–50.
3. Jon William Toigo, "An Overview of Computer Viruses," *Journal of Accounting and EDP,* Summer 1989, pp. 21–29.
4. L. Murphy Smith, and Katherine T. Smith, "Microcomputer Accounting Graphics: Why and How to Use Them," *Today's CPA,* January/February 1988, pp. 28–32.

CHAPTER 10 QUESTIONS

Article 1

1. Discuss the principal areas of difference between PC-based accounting systems and their manual counterparts.
2. Distinguish between the modular and the integrated approaches to automated accounting systems.

Article 2

3. Describe the primary audit tasks which have been facilitated by microcomputer integration.
4. Discuss the implications of microcomputer integration for the auditing profession.

Article 3

5. Briefly describe the major types of computer viruses.
6. Describe countermeasures which are available to combat virus infection.

Article 4

7. List the different types of output devices.
8. What are the most commonly used types of graphs?
9. Briefly describe the advantages and disadvantages of using graphical presentations.

Reading 10–1

IMPACT OF MICROCOMPUTERS ON ACCOUNTING SYSTEMS

By John T. Overbey, Ph.D.; Jo Ann C. Carland, Ph.D.; and James W. Carland, Ph.D.

In the past 20 years, computers have increasingly penetrated the sphere of accounting. The first computers were large and expensive and, therefore, had little impact on small businesses or on most practicing accountants. With the

Reprinted with permission from *Journal of Systems Management*, June 1987, pp. 20–27.

advent of the inexpensive microcomputers, this situation has changed. The smallest business today can have its own computer. In addition, in large businesses the micro finds increasing usage as a stand-alone unit or as part of a distributed processing system. As a result of the proliferation of micros, it has become important for the designer, user, and auditor of the accounting systems used or accessed by these microcomputers to understand how such systems differ from their manual predecessors. The main areas of difference are: source document generation; order of the accounting cycle; journal/ledger structure; and techniques of internal control. This article will describe the approaches taken with regard to these areas in manual accounting systems and in microcomputer accounting systems.

MANUAL ACCOUNTING SYSTEM

The heart of a manual accounting system consists of the journal and the general ledger. The journal is the book of original entry, and provides a chronological record of all transactions. The journal is an important link in the audit trail. From the journal, the transactions are posted to the general ledger which summarizes all transactions affecting a given account. Special journals, such as the purchases journal and the cash disbursements journal, provide a refinement of the basic format, but do not affect the order of data flow or the basic underlying theoretical structure. Special journals and their summary postings do provide two important advantages. Their use reduces bookkeeping work and facilitates internal control by separation of duties: One bookkeeper can record purchase transactions while another bookkeeper can record cash disbursement transactions.

Another important part of a manual accounting system is the subsidiary ledgers. Subsidiary ledgers are maintained for any account in the general ledger for which detail beyond the summary data is required. Subsidiary ledgers require separate posting and must be kept in balance with respective controlling accounts in the general ledger. Certain columns in the special journals are posted in total to the general ledger but in detail to the subsidiary ledger. For example, the payments-on-account column in the cash disbursements journal is posted in total to the accounts-payable account in the general ledger, but in detail to the accounts-payable ledger which shows the organization's transactions with and obligations to each creditor. An illustration of the components of a simple manual accounting system and the flow of transactions is shown in Figure 1.

As Figure 1 demonstrates, the source document triggers the recording of a transaction and initiates the accounting cycle. The source document is assumed to have been prepared by an individual outside the firm, as in the case of a bill or statement, or by an individual in authority inside the firm, as in the case of a purchase order or payment voucher. Internal control procedures involving the handling and preparation of source documents are designed to ensure that such documents are indeed genuine, properly prepared and autho-

FIGURE 1   A Manual Accounting System

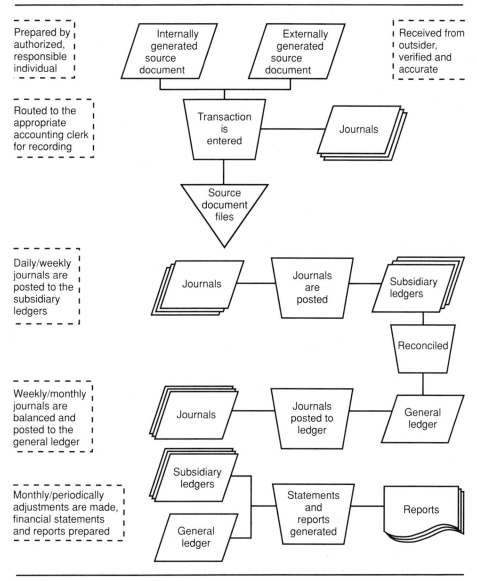

rized by individuals in authority before they are posted to the journal. Thereafter, internal controls are designed to ensure that errors of commission or
omission do not occur in the posting of documents to journals, the posting of
journals to ledgers, the reconciling of ledgers, and the preparation of financial
statements and reports. The controls utilized are the traditional ones of as-

signment of responsibility to competent individuals and the rotation of duties, the separation of responsibility for related operations, the separation of custody and recordkeeping, proofs and security measures, and independent review.

AUTOMATED ACCOUNTING SYSTEM

An automated accounting system has no specific base. It may be designed around a general ledger or it may be designed around a transaction log, or many other imaginable approaches. Microcomputers need no work-saving device and can actually post transactions more efficiently directly to the ledgers or storage logs involved rather than by following a cyclic approach such as that employed in the manual system.

Microcomputer accounting systems generally follow one of two formats with regard to their organization and functioning. The most prevalent type of system, and generally the less expensive system, is modular. This type of system is designed around program and data file modules which have specialized functions. Examination of a typical modular micro accounting system will reveal a transaction log in which each posting entry and information about that transaction is kept, and a data file which can be considered to be a general ledger in which summary balances are kept for each account in the system. The system will typically contain additional data files which function as subsidiary ledgers and which capture the desired detail about specific accounts. The data in the transaction log is usually sufficient to permit the construction of special journals and a detailed trial balance for a specified period. Such constructions are not required by the system, but are provided by the systems' designers to make the packages more acceptable to accountants who, for the most part, continue to view microsystems as automated manual systems. An illustration of the components of a typical, modular microcomputer accounting system and the flow of transactions is shown in Figure 2.

As Figure 2 demonstrates, the source document may be received in the same fashion as that of the manual system if it is generated externally. If the source document is internally generated, as in the case of a purchase order or a check, then the document is frequently generated by the system itself as a by-product of the entry of the transaction. As an internal control step, the operator may be required to perform some identity or access check such as the entry of a password, after which a transaction will be posted to the transaction log. At some future time, usually on a daily or weekly basis, the transactions stored in the transaction log are transferred to the appropriate ledgers through a separate posting routine.

In the second system format, this procedure does not occur. In integrated systems, the transaction entering process results in the direct posting of affected ledgers without the requirement for a separate updating routine. Figure 3 shows an example of an integrated system. Such systems are generally more expensive than modular systems, but are superior in terms of re-

FIGURE 2   A Modular Automated Accounting System

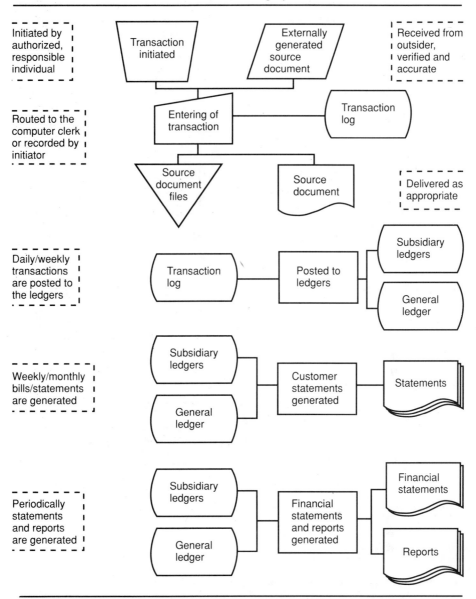

sponsiveness and ease of use. Unfortunately, the potential damage in the event of misuse is greater in this type of system because the general ledger and subsidiary ledger files are available to the system at the time of transaction posting. This also makes internal control more difficult.

FIGURE 3 An Integrated Automated Accounting System

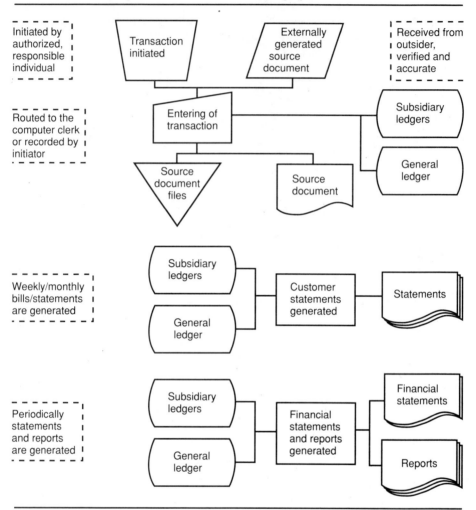

DIFFERENCES IN APPROACH

A comparison of Figures 1, 2, and 3 will reveal striking differences. Initially, the traditional role of source documents, as original evidence showing that transactions have been properly captured, does not hold in microsystems. Externally generated source documents continue to be available in some transactions, but internal control procedures must recognize that anyone with access to the computer and a little knowledge can generate internal source documents as a by-product of recording transactions. Protective steps which limit access, such as passwords, will help in this regard, but the accounting system should incorporate additional tools to prevent abuse and ensure accuracy in the preparation of source documents. For example, a voucher system requiring approval signatures by responsible parties is invaluable as a control over check generation. Most small businesses have avoided vouchers because of the added complexity and other factors, but if a small business employs a micro system which generates checks, the voucher question should be reevaluated. It may well prove to be justifiable from the standpoint of security alone.

The second area of difference between the automated and manual systems is the order of the accounting cycle. The manual system's flow is transaction to journal, journal to subsidiary ledger, journal to general ledger, reconciliation of ledgers, and generation of statements and reports from the ledgers. The microsystems have but a single entry point. In the case of the modular system the entry is to a transaction log. Thereafter, automated routines manipulate the transactions to produce the general and subsidiary ledgers. In the case of the integrated system, the entry is directly to the ledgers. In both system formats, automated routines generate financial statements and reports. If initial internal control steps have been employed to ensure that the automated routines do in fact function properly, then further system flow concerns revolve around the scheduling of program runs and control over data and program files. For the accountant these differences mean that one of the most effective of all control procedures, the separation of responsibility for related operations, is virtually impossible in a microsystem. Instead, controls must be developed which ensure the integrity of the programs themselves, schedule the running of the programs, secure the output resulting from each run and protect data files in the system.

Manual and automated systems differ with regard to structure also. The traditional concept of journals does not hold in a microsystem. Journals do not reduce workloads, do not illustrate account activity, nor provide audit trails. In a microsystem the journals are generated as a result of other records. It would be wiser for accountants to abandon their reliance on journals entirely so that focus on the real records of a system might be developed. The transaction log is often the heart of a modular system. Its location, structure, and maintenance should be the primary concern of the accountant in a microsystem. Account analysis using a detailed trial balance is not an acceptable tool for this purpose either, because the detailed trial balance is generated from the transaction log. Controls must be developed to ensure the accuracy and integrity of the transaction log directly. In an integrated system the ledgers themselves are typically the heart. In order to exert control over these files, accountants must ensure that sufficient detail is captured in the files to provide an audit trail to the transaction entering process and that controls over that entering process exist which are effective.

INTERNAL CONTROL DIFFERENCES

The traditional aspects of internal control are: assignment of responsibility to competent individuals; the rotation of duties; the separation of responsibility for related operations; the separation of custody and recordkeeping; proofs and security measures; and independent review. The first of these control steps is equally valid in either manual systems or microsystems. However, there is a major problem with microcomputers which relates to physical security. In manual systems, journals and ledgers are afforded physical security. In mainframe computer systems access to the computer and its software are restricted. However, companies which employ microcomputers frequently afford such machines no physical security at all. This may be a function of the requirement for quick access or a result of the multiple applications of the equipment (word processing, etc.), but it invites tampering by unauthorized personnel. If the microsystem employs diskettes for record storage, then physical security should be extended to the diskettes as well. If the system employs 'hard' disks which are continuously on-line, other control procedures must be employed to restrict access to the accounting programs and records stored on those disks. Passwords are not effective in micro applications. They help, but not only is it easy in the normal course of transaction processing for unauthorized individuals to discover passwords, it is easy to discover what the passwords are themselves with relatively minor technical skills. The same problem plagues access logs and similar devices. Such technical skills are increasingly present as the society seeks and attains computer literacy. This also means that program integrity is increasingly endangered from the same sources. There is no 'quick fix' for this problem which will intensify as systems knowledge is enhanced. Accountants should pay close attention to the security/access issue and independent reviewers should make it a major factor in audits.

The rotation of duties and the separation of responsibility for related operations do not constitute strong control features for microsystems. The underlying theory of record inspection by new/different people will not suffice in a microsystem because other data files themselves are not viewed in the normal course of affairs, and because those files are subject to direct manipulation, given sufficient technical competency. The separation theory of maintaining the parts of transactions in separate places is also violated by the recording of all transactions in the same place. This issue of direct manipulation is not trivial. In a microsystem an individual with sufficient technical skill can destroy, change, or distort original records. One review tool which can be used to check for such manipulations is the making of transaction data copies or tapes or diskettes at various times and dates. As part of the internal audit and/or independent review, these copies can be checked against transaction records currently in the system. Such verifications can be done with the computer itself. The requirement is for control over the duplication process and custody of the record copies. This should not be a major issue, since backup record-making should already be a part of the daily processing.

Separation of asset custody from recordkeeping continues to be a viable internal control procedure. However, the system access question discussed above reemerges. In the absence of effective access restrictions, individuals with custody of assets could obtain entry to records. Effective access controls make separation of custody and recordkeeping viable.

The use of proofs of various types has long been a major tool of control in mainframe computer systems. Such controls are of less value in a microcomputer system because it is 'live.' Data is not entered in 'batches' nor is data necessarily entered in any given sequence. In a microsystem a purchase order might be generated, followed by a check, followed by the recording of a sale and back to a purchase order. This means that other control steps must be developed to ensure accuracy and validity of data input. If the programs have been well-designed, entry errors can be minimized by controls internal to the computer system itself. Such controls take the form of range and reasonableness tests, balance requirements, transaction completeness limits, etc. For optimum use of these features, they should, of course, be verified by the accountant as part of the design/review process, and the integrity of the programs assured thereafter. Development of other control steps to ensure validity of entries is a repetition of the access problem. The issue is a major one which must be attacked in each company on an individual basis.

SUMMARY

Integrity in manual systems is a constant ongoing concern. The same is true in microcomputer accounting systems. The problem is that the traditional control procedures do not apply. New processes must be developed constantly and reviewed constantly. In order for microsystems to function as desired, accountants must not assume that they are automated manual systems. Resolution of the vagaries in source document generation, order of the accounting cycle, journal/ledger structure, and internal control must be sought by the accountant/auditor as systems become more prevalent in the realm of small business accounting. Accountants must develop an understanding of accounting information systems just as they had to develop an understanding of the manual predecessor.

Reading 10–2

MICROCOMPUTERS IN AUDITING: A PRIMER

By Casper E. Wiggins, Jr., and Christopher Wolfe

Microcomputer software has had a dramatic impact on the auditing profession. A study by the Computer Audit Committee of the President's Council of Integrity and Efficiency found that microcomputers can reduce the time required for most audit tasks by 24 percent to 75 percent. The integration of microcomputers into the auditing process has been responsible for increased productivity and is likely to cause changes in the organizational structure, capital intensiveness, professional training programs, and staffing requirements for accounting organizations. This article addresses the ways microcomputer technology is currently employed in auditing, presents an audit scenario for auditing with a microcomputer, and explores the implications of widespread computerization for the accounting organization of the future.

Staff accountants, who less than five years ago carried footlockers full of working papers, now carry portable microcomputers and disks to audit sites. Spreadsheet, data base, word processing, communications, and graphics software have become mainstays in the audit environment. Specialized audit software is also available for microcomputers and is currently being used in the field. Data management, data access, data analysis, and data manipulation are all facilitated by microcomputers.

DATA MANAGEMENT

Data management is greatly enhanced by the automation of workpapers. The columnar format of spreadsheet packages (e.g., Lotus 1-2-3, Symphony, SuperCalc, and Framework) allows auditors to develop and maintain audit workpapers on the micro. These workpapers may then be easily stored to and retrieved from disks. This process greatly facilitates the organization, indexing, referencing, transport, storage, and retrieval of workpapers. In addition, spreadsheets can be combined, subdivided, and interrelated. Simple commands allow new spreadsheets to be formed from extracted portions of other spreadsheets. Supporting detail can be automatically carried forward to lead schedules, and lead-schedule balances can be transferred to consolidated schedules.

Many auditors initially believed, however, that electronic spreadsheets might be detrimental because errors could become embedded in the spreadsheets and thus be hidden from the managers who review the workpapers. In fact, workpaper accuracy and integrity are often enhanced by internal checks that can be designed into spreadsheets. Internal checks call attention to errors that commonly occur in spreadsheets. For example, range tests can be included to check an entire spreadsheet for data items whose values do not fall within a specified range of values. These checks also indicate the violation of certain logical relationships that should be present in the spreadsheet (e.g., debits that don't equal credits, assets that don't equal liabilities plus stockholders' equity, cross-footed and footed balances that don't match, and bank reconciliations that don't reconcile properly).

DATA ACCESS

Microcomputers offer new channels for data access. With communications software, financial records can be transferred directly from the client's computer to the auditor's microcomputer. In effect, the auditor has direct access to the client's files. By downloading client files to the auditor's microcomputer, data gathering is less disruptive to the client, faster, and free of input errors. Furthermore, once the data is obtained by the auditor, it is usually in a form suitable for testing on the microcomputer. If the client has a microcomputer, however, communications software may not be necessary. In many instances, a client's disks can be processed directly on the auditor's micro. In essence, these capabilities allow the auditor to perform an audit without relying heavily on the client. Special software and cables are also available to permit auditors to access data files that were written by virtually any microcomputer and data format.

DATA ANALYSIS

With the development of spreadsheet models and templates, data analysis can be performed more efficiently. Calculations for depreciation schedules, earnings per share, note and bond amortization, and prepaid expenses are routine for the microcomputer. In addition, analytical review procedures (e.g., ratio analysis, sensitivity analysis, and statistical regression) are easily accomplished with standard spreadsheet commands. Almost all quantitative calculations can also be performed quickly and accurately.

The proliferation of such templates has prompted many large accounting firms to establish firmwide clearinghouses that monitor templates developed by individual employees. These clearinghouses make templates available to all auditors by linking a micro to the firm's central template library and allow the testing of templates that are likely to be widely used before they are disseminated.

DATA MANIPULATION

Data base management software provides data manipulation capabilities (e.g., sorting, alphabetizing, and searching) and performs complex queries and extracts. Once a data base has been searched, any extracted files can be transferred to spreadsheet or word processing programs. For example, an auditor can download accounts-receivable data into a data base program, use the data base program to extract certain receivables for confirmation, and use a word processing program to print the confirmations and address envelopes.

SPECIAL AUDIT SOFTWARE

The specialized software that is now available includes statistical packages that stratify samples, develop statistical data profiles, and calculate statistical confidence levels. Planning and scheduling are facilitated by PERT programs and Gantt charts, and graphics packages clarify confusing statistical tables.

Expert systems on the micro perform internal control evaluation, going-concern analysis, and materiality judgments. Expert systems that can apply the knowledge and experience of an expert senior partner to many audit problems are also being perfected.

Aside from acting as a field audit tool, microcomputers are facilitating the administrative and reporting functions that surround an audit. Automated time budgets keep a running account of audit progress, calendar programs act as ticklers for important financial reporting and taxation dates, and micro-computers can transmit notes and balances to the home office for final word processing. And, at an audit's completion, advanced desktop publishing systems can prepare print-quality reports for clients.

AN AUDIT SCENARIO

With a microcomputer in the auditor's tool bag, several alternatives to the traditional audit approach arise. The following audit scenario reflects the manner in which microcomputers are affecting traditional audit steps.

1. **The auditor gathers or makes copies of last year's data files, which are stored on disks.** The previous year's workpapers and most audit documentation are stored in either spreadsheet files, data base files, or word processor files. These file formats allow analysis of the previous audit and provide templates for current-year workpapers.

2. **The auditor retrieves a copy of the audit plan from a word processor file.** A copy of the audit plan is printed to allow an analysis of the audit steps. Industry data bases and the firm's own auditing data base are accessed to determine whether the specific audit steps need modification. When changes are necessary, the auditor accesses the audit plan file, updates the file, prints it, and sends it to a partner for review.

3. **Once the auditor joins the client, information from critical accounts is downloaded into the auditor's microcomputer.** A statistics program is then used to perform regression and ratio analyses and to produce graphs of these accounts. Analytical review procedures key the auditor to unusual trends or problems. Controls are reviewed through prior years' flowcharts

(stored in a graphics file). The flowcharts are updated as necessary when systems are reviewed and compliance tests are performed. The results of the control analysis and the analytical review help the auditor reevaluate the audit program.

4. **Current-year client financial data is now downloaded into the auditor's microcomputer.** Using last year's workpapers as templates when possible, audit work is performed and documented.

5. **Adjusting and reclassifying entries are made directly to an electronic spreadsheet.** This spreadsheet automatically keeps track of the schedules to which the entries are related.

6. **Most workpaper review is done at the firm's office by sending the workpaper files to the managers, who then review them on their systems.**

7. **A report file is telecommunicated to the accounting firm's office.** Financial statements and the accompanying notes and opinions are printed on a laser printer for client distribution.

As the audit scenario discussion suggests, the microcomputer supports the auditor in every phase of the audit (see Exhibit 1 for a list of audit steps and their specific microcomputer applications).

IMPLICATIONS FOR THE AUDITING PROFESSION

Initially, productivity gains are offset by the complexities of auditing new computerized client systems. Once companies are past the start-up costs and time needed for the development of audit programs for these systems, however, the time involved to complete an audit usually decreases. Because staff accountants now perform many of the tasks that can be automated, they will be freed for other responsibilities.

Procedural changes at one level of an organization often affect other levels and divisions. Audit-based accounting organizations are likely to require fewer managers and staff auditors and more senior supervisors. As audit complexity increases, a higher skill level will be required for auditors and, with routine tasks being computerized, auditors will concentrate on more difficult and significant client issues. In an automated environment, the senior or mid-level auditor becomes the backbone of the audit organization. The clarity and efficiency of a computerized audit should lessen the burden of the audit review for management.

Audit computerization may also bring nonaccountants onto the audit team—computer specialists who can offer high-level systems aid in the audit and paraprofessionals who can perform routine audit tasks. Computer specialists are necessary to audit advanced computer operating systems and to analyze programs written in low-level programming languages. Paraprofessionals fill two needs. First, as routine audit tasks are computerized, performing these tasks has little training value for staff auditors. Second, the

EXHIBIT 1 Audit Steps and Microcomputer Applications

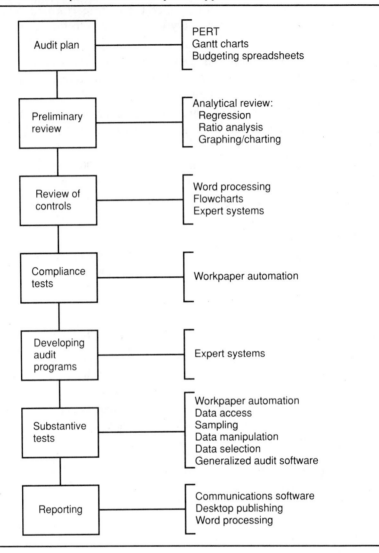

audit team needs a stable group of employees that will not be moving into management.

Even with the use of computer specialists, a more computer-adept audit staff is necessary. Entry-level auditors must possess good microcomputer skills and a good understanding of automated accounting information systems. In all likelihood, auditors' computer knowledge will be as important as their accounting and auditing knowledge. Regardless of the auditors' backgrounds, however, increased and higher-level training will be necessary within the audit organization. Because of the computerization of routine tasks, the audit itself will no longer provide the fertile training ground to bring an entry-level person up to the senior level. Therefore, audit firms are going to have to continually train their personnel.

Training is not the only increased expense audit firms will face because of computerization. Capital outlays for microcomputer hardware and software will also rise, making auditing a much more capital-intensive service. The cost, maintenance, and replacement of microcomputer systems will become a significant expense for audit firms. Upgrading existing software and purchasing new software add to the capital outlays necessary to operate a computerized audit. Overall, hardware and software expenditures, training, and a larger contingent of senior-level personnel will offset cost savings from increased audit productivity.

CONCLUSION

When technology matches a given task as well as microcomputers and auditing match, this technology has a large impact on the performance of that task. Microcomputers are affecting the auditing profession by providing the following enhancements:

- More efficient data management.
- New channels for data access.
- Improved data analysis.
- Fast and efficient data manipulation.
- Specialized audit software.
- New tools for audit planning, administration, and reporting.
- Aids to audit decision making.

This relatively recent and important scenario is changing the face of the traditional audit and audit department. Playing by the new rules will change the look and strategy of audit organizations. Successful organizations will have to effectively integrate and manipulate technology into the audit process.

Reading 10–3

AN OVERVIEW OF COMPUTER VIRUSES

By Jon William Toigo

Computer viruses are a threat to data security. These malicious software programs can lie dormant in a system for weeks, months, or years before manifesting symptoms, then suddenly activate their destructive routines. Thus, critical systems, data, and backup copies may be destroyed simultaneously by the same virus. This article reviews the history of computer viruses, categorizes viruses by type, and offers recommendations for reducing the chance of system infection. Sources of expert advice and specialized tools are also provided.

Accountants are justifiably concerned about the computer virus threat to established security and disaster recovery techniques. Viruses are becoming more sophisticated; they are more difficult to anticipate, prevent, and detect. To complicate the problem, each new type of virus must be fully analyzed before a reliable prevention tool can be developed. Viruses have become an issue of concern to DP insurers, many of whom have disclaimed policy coverage for virus-related data loss. The recommendations in this article are responses only to known virus programs. Unfortunately, experts expect that new generations of viruses will be able to circumvent current prophylactic measures, necessitating continued awareness and preventive efforts.

A BRIEF HISTORY

The computer virus was first unveiled at an IFIP Security conference several years ago by its creator, Fred Cohen of the University of Southern California. Cohen called the threat a computer virus because of its infective behavior, similar to biological viruses. Cohen's virus could remain undetected in a computer for many years, then become active and infect vital programs and data files by modifying them to include some version of itself. According to Cohen, these viruses could be introduced surreptitiously, leave few traces in most systems, act effectively against modern security controls, and require only a minimum of specialized knowledge to implement.

Viruses have since become a growing concern for accountants; many professional journal articles, workshops, and even a Computer Virus Industry

Association (primarily for antivirus software and computer security product vendors and services) have resulted. Sporadic reports of computer virus infections sustained interest in this topic, and, in September 1988, concern about viruses spread to nontechnical business managers when a cover story on computer viruses appeared in *Time* magazine.[1]

The *Time* article stimulated both a fierce rebuttal from several computer trade journals and a boost in the sales of antivirus software. Several popular computer magazines asserted that the *Time* article exaggerated the threat. One cited numerous cases in which system dysfunction thought to be caused by a virus proved to be the result of hardware or user errors.[2]

As these articles were reaching the newsstands, a computer virus attack was making national headlines. In November 1988, nearly 85,000 computers on the Internet network and its 1,200 member networks (serving universities, federal government agencies, and military contractors) were brought down by one, relatively benign computer virus for a period ranging from a few hours to several days. Although the virus did not destroy any files, the cost of the disruption has been estimated conservatively at $97 million.

THE SCOPE OF THE PROBLEM

Since 1983, several university computer centers, government and business computers connected to electronic mail networks, and private microcomputers (especially those accessing public electronic bulletin boards) have fallen prey to viruses. The Internet virus, infecting at least 6,200 UNIX-based computers and disrupting the work of more than eight million programmers and other MIS personnel, is the most damaging incident reported to date.

Viruses target networked systems for several reasons. University computer environments, electronic networks, and bulletin board systems are relatively unprotected and often allow user anonymity. This easy access makes them targets for computer criminals who wish to propagate viruses. These environments are sometimes referred to as social because of the ease of access to shared information. After a virus is planted in such an environment, virus-contaminated software is unintentionally disseminated by the network's users, spreading infection in a geometric progression.

Inevitably, viruses have reached business systems. Reports have begun to circulate about virus-related damage in nearly all sectors of the business community. However, few companies have publicly admitted suffering a virus-related disaster. Understandably, in the corporate environment there is an incentive to keep such matters quiet. Publicizing the vulnerabilities of a company's system may lead to additional attacks as well as customer dissatisfaction and fear.

Several cases have been reported that help to define the scope of businesses' vulnerability to computer virus attacks. One victim was the Miami branch of the Bank of South Carolina; a disgruntled employee placed a virus that was intended to slow the recording of deposits from .5 to 3 seconds per transaction in the bank computer system. The virus could have placed the bank one month behind in bookkeeping within one week had it not been purged after being discovered during a routine audit.

A Fort Worth case, which became public with the prosecution of the virus's author, involved a fired employee of USPA & IRA. The employee hacked into the insurance company's IBM System/38 and planted a virus program that deleted 168,000 employee records.

In another case, the Providence Journal Company was infected by a virus in early 1988 that spread to several microcomputers, destroying nearly $10,000 worth of data and equipment by rendering hard disk drives unusable. That experience pointed to another aspect of the virus dilemma: the amount of insurance coverage needed for virus-related losses. Insurance is often viewed as the stopgap between failed disaster prevention and total disaster; yet existing insurance policies did not cover the losses to Providence Journal. Accrued dollar losses totaled less than the company's DP insurance deductible. Furthermore, many insurers are reconsidering whether they will cover virus-related damages at all. Insurance vendors question whether the loss of data can be reasonably valued and insured.

Government computers have also been infected by viruses. In 1988, the Navy Regional Data Automation Center in Jacksonville, Fla., was infected by a virus disguised as a public domain data archiving program that was downloaded from a bulletin board system. Operating the software caused the data on the hard disk of the host microcomputer to be irreparably damaged. Other agencies, including the Environmental Protection Agency, NASA, the Department of Defense, and the CIA, have been plagued by viruses that have destroyed data on IBM and Macintosh microcomputers and VAX/VMS, Unisys, and IBM mainframes.

Some observers attribute the great damage potential of computer viruses to the decentralization of computing and the associated lack of centralized management and monitoring. However, the vast majority of cases have involved microcomputers, lax security, and a lack of standards for computer use. In most cases, viruses were transmitted with public domain software or were deliberately introduced with malicious intent. There are confirmed instances of virus programs debilitating systems on most hardware platforms, on networks, and even within microprocessors.

TYPES OF VIRUSES

The targets of computer viruses are typically nonspecific. Often, a virus infecting an organization's computer is not originally intended for that computer, though viruses can be directed and effective. Here is a summary of three of the most common types of computer viruses.

Boot Infectors

Boot infectors are viruses that attach themselves to a diskette or hard disk at sector 0, the boot sector (containing the bootstrap loader program). The virus is activated when the system is booted and often will infect any diskette that is used with the infected system, even when a warm boot, or reinitialization is performed. The virus writes itself to the boot sectors of any diskettes that are used with an infected system.

The most notorious boot infector is the Pakistani Brain virus. This prepenned virus is believed to have reached the United States from Pakistan by way of universities in the United Kingdom. In fact, the names and addresses of the virus's authors in Lahore, Pakistan, appear at the beginning of the program together with the recommendation that victims contact them for a cure. Originally conceived as a protection scheme, the virus code was designed to debilitate unlicensed duplicates of application software developed by the authors. However, somewhere along its journey from Asia to the United States, the virus code was altered to become the malicious and highly infectious virus it is today.

This particular virus damages a disk by embedding itself in the boot sector, then scrambling data. It creates three successive clusters in six sectors of a DOS-formatted disk and marks them as bad sectors. The code then copies the file allocation tables and jumbles numbers, destroying the boot sector and the file allocation tables and rendering the data on the disk unusable. The Pakistani Brain virus received its name from a signature it left on an infected disk, which appeared as the volume label of the disk.

This virus, which infected Providence Journal computers, recently spread to the University of Delaware, where employees of 480 of the Fortune 500 companies attend computer classes. Many of these employees are permitted to use company computers to perform homework assignments. This policy may have introduced the Brain virus to several of those companies.

Systems' Infectors

A second type of virus (as classified by the Computer Virus Industry Association) is identified by its ability to attach itself to system files and remain memory-resident. These viruses make subtle changes to the infected system over a period of time (such as gradually increasing transaction processing times or changing system error or informational messages). Sometimes they are designed to monitor system variables, such as the system clock, and activate their destructive mechanisms when a certain condition is met, such as a date or time.

A virus can be programmed to create havoc at a specific time, as was demonstrated on May 13, 1988, at Hebrew University in Israel. The Fridaythe-13th virus was written and introduced into the university computers by a Palestinian student as a political act. The program was timed to activate on the date that corresponded to the 40th anniversary of the Palestinian state before the formation of the state of Israel. Presumably, the virus program was linked to the system's internal clock.

Such virus time bombs are particularly challenging for traditional data protection. If virus-infected programs are backed up, there is every chance that reloading the backup software following a virus-related system failure will result in a repetition of the failure. Virus programs can remain dormant for as long as their authors wish, potentially infecting many generations of backup tapes and disks.

Executable-File Infectors

According to the Computer Virus Industry Association, viruses infecting executable files (with the file name extensions .COM or .EXE) are the most dangerous. They infect other systems by attaching duplicates of themselves to specific executable files located on any disk that comes into contact with the virus-infected host. Infection may occur during direct exposure (e.g., when a diskette is used) or through a network connection.

How viruses spread from one disk to another, or across networks, or over data communications lines is a matter of considerable concern. The Lehigh University virus illustrates one common method of virus transmission.

This virus that infected several microcomputers on the Lehigh campus was discovered in 1987. The virus was in the stack spaces of the COMMAND.COM program on an infected diskette. Because the virus used empty but allocated storage space, the size of the COMMAND.COM file was not increased. By reading the COMMAND.COM program each time a DOS command was executed against another disk, the virus spread to the subject disk.

The Lehigh virus destroyed disks by erasing them. Erasure did not occur immediately after infection; a counter in the virus program recorded the number of DOS command calls, and when the counter reached 4, the virus erased the disk on which it resided. The newly infected disks similarly self-destructed after they infected four more disks.

The selection of 4 as the counter value appears to have been arbitrary; it could have been 40 or 400.

A VIRUS PROGRAMMING PRIMER

Many virus types use different hiding places, time delay functions, and sophisticated camouflage techniques, but a highly infectious executable-file virus basically operates in the following manner (see Exhibit 1).

The virus program code replaces the first program instruction of a host program with an instruction to jump to the memory location following the last instruction in the host program. The virus program code is inserted at

EXHIBIT 1 How Viruses Work

Step 1

The virus code replaces first program instruction with a jump to the memory location following the last program instruction.

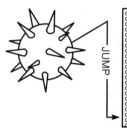

```
00000              HOST PROGRAM
00010 FIRST INSTRUCTION




00B12 LAST INSTRUCTION
```

Step 2

The virus code is inserted at that memory location.

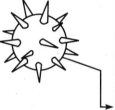

```
00000              HOST PROGRAM
00010  FIRST INSTRUCTION




00B12 LAST INSTRUCTION VIRUS
```

Step 3

The virus simulates the host program instruction replaced by the jump.

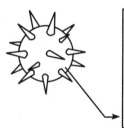

```
00000              HOST PROGRAM
00010  FIRST INSTRUCTION




00B12 LAST INSTRUCTION
       VIRUS CODE
```

Step 4

The virus jumps back to the host's second program instruction.

```
00000              HOST PROGRAM
00010  FIRST INSTRUCTION
00200  SECOND INSTRUCTION




00B12 LAST INSTRUCTION
       VIRUS CODE
```

Step 5

Every time the host program is run, the virus will infect another program, then run the host program.

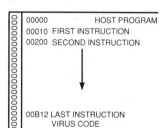

```
00000              HOST PROGRAM
00010  FIRST INSTRUCTION
00200  SECOND INSTRUCTION




00B12 LAST INSTRUCTION
       VIRUS CODE
```

that memory location. Next, the virus simulates the instruction replaced by the jump. The virus program then jumps back to the second instruction in the host program, and the balance of the host program is executed. In this way, every time the host program is run, the virus will infect another program, then run the host program.

This is the most common method by which a virus spreads. Unfortunately, it does so at a phenomenal speed. In tests at the University of Southern California, Cohen introduced viruses into computer systems. None of the viruses took more than an hour to infect the entire system. Some took as little as five minutes. Later tests, directed against a Univac 1108 system equipped with security software that restricted data flow and program access according to user access levels, allowed Cohen (as a user with a low security clearance) to infect all programs and data on the system, even those files restricted to users with high-level security clearances.

With many viruses, damage to systems and data is the result not of virus transmission but of the activation of some part of the virus program that is designed to debilitate the system. After it has infected files on the disk, a virus usually responds to a trigger (e.g., a counter or a clock), or it goes immediately to work performing its programmed function (e.g., file deletion or cluster reallocation). In this way, the computer virus resembles a Trojan horse program, but one with a sophisticated means for penetrating and propagating within a computer before debilitating it.

COUNTERACTING VIRUSES

Many businesses and government organizations have instituted standards and procedures to prevent computer viruses from infecting their systems. However, in many medium-sized and small businesses, there is still a dearth of information about computer viruses, how to prevent them, and how to detect them. Two organizations that disseminate information to concerned professionals are:

Software Development Council
PO Box 61031
Palo Alto CA 94306
(415) 854–7219

Computer Virus Industry Association
4423 Cheeney St
Santa Clara CA 95054
(408) 988–3832

Together with professional computer journals, these resources can help to keep you apprised of developments in virus prevention.

Virus prevention begins with the analysis of the current computer systems with which a company is working. These systems need to be verified as virus-free before any controls can be established that will help prevent and detect a newly introduced virus.

Detecting computer viruses can be complicated and time-consuming. Often, viruses hide where their presence cannot be detected except by bit-level file comparison. Here are some indications that a virus may have contaminated a system:

- Programs take longer to load.
- Disk access time seems excessive for even simple tasks.
- Unusual error messages occur with increasing frequency.
- Indicators are lit on devices that are not being accessed.
- Less memory is available than usual; some larger programs won't load.
- Program or data files are erased.
- Disk space is less than seems reasonable.
- Executable files (those with .EXE or .COM file name extensions) have changed size.
- Unfamiliar hidden files have appeared.

Such indicators as longer-than-usual program loading delays or excessive disk access may only be perceptible to those who use the system on a regular basis, so the users' impressions are extremely important.

Some computer virus detection products also provide canary programs (named for the canaries that miners used to send into shafts to check for poisonous gas) that may be loaded, run, and then examined for signs of virus contamination. While not completely reliable for all types of viruses, these programs can be useful indicators of contamination.

After a system has been examined and, with reasonable certainty, deemed virus-free, a global snapshot, or system status log, may be created. (Several of the antivirus software products provide this capability.) This snapshot includes the boot sectors of the disk, system interrupt vector addresses and code, system files, and all .EXE and .COM files. Because it is unusual for these items to be updated frequently, a periodic comparison of a new global snapshot to the original should reveal the presence of a virus. A number of antivirus products provide utilities for performing such a comparison automatically during boot-up and even following a restart. Exhibit 2 provides a partial listing of antivirus software packages.

Some of these products can detect viruses before they cause damage. However, virus programmers will constantly upgrade the elements of their programs to conceal their viruses and elude detection. These programmers will usually be aware of which prophylactic measures are implemented on a targeted system.

In addition to the methods already described, there are some common-sense steps that can be taken to help guard systems against viruses. Many are drawn from established security practices.

EXHIBIT 2 Antivirus Software Vendors

Product Name	Environment	Vendor	Function
Antidote	IBM PC and PS/2	Quaid Software Ltd 45 Charles St Toronto Ontario Canada M4Y 1S2	Examines files for alteration during boot-up.
Antigen	IBM PC	Digital Dispatch 1580 Rice Creek Rd Minneapolis MN 55432	Attaches itself to programs, detects modifications, and stops virus program execution once detected.
C–4/Retro V	IBM PC	Interpath 4423 Cheeny St Santa Clara CA 95054	Claims to filter out all 39 known virus programs.
Data Physician	IBM PC	Digital Dispatch *(see above)*	Blocks viruses during downloading; monitors write-to-disk commands. User can set up list of protected files and directories that will be monitored for changes.
Disk Watcher	IBM PC	RG Software Systems 2300 Computer Ave Suite 1–51 Willow Grove PA 19090	Contains virus protection software (Release 2.0).
Dr. Panda Utilities	IBM PC	Panda Systems 801 Wilson Rd Wilmington DE 19803	Three programs: Physical, Monitor, and Labtest protect against reformatting of the hard disk, re-writing the boot sector, writing the stack space of file allocation tables, and formatting of diskettes and hard disks.
Electronic Filter	IBM Information Network	IBM authorized dealers	Prohibits the transfer of programs within an IBM system.
Flu Shot Plus	IBM PC	Ross M. Greenberg Software Concepts Design 594 Third Ave New York NY 10016	Filters out virus program code.

Name	Platform	Company	Description
Immunize	IBM PC through mainframe	Remote Technologies 3612 Cleveland Ave St Louis MO 63110	Is a low-level antiviral program.
Interferon	IBM PC and Apple	Sirtech 10 Spruce La Ithaca NY 14850	Detects and recognizes signals that viruses give off when they are present; code at the end of an application or changes in common system files.
Mace Vaccine	IBM PC	Paul Mace Software 400 Williamson Way Ashland OR 97520	Protects system files, hard disk boot sector, and partition tables from virus infection.
NoVirus	IBM PC	Digital Dispatch (*see above*)	Is a memory resident virus checker.
Vaccinate	IBM PC	Sophco PO Box 7430 Boulder CO 80306	Is itself a virus that uses a program called SYRINGE to innoculate programs and a program called CANARY for sacrificial use with suspect programs.
Vaccine	Bulletin Board System Operators	CE Software Co 1854 Fuller Rd West Des Moines IA 50265	Alerts system operators to virus activity.
VC-Immune VC-Shield	IBM PC	Villarreal Consulting 4633 Capitola Ave San Jose CA 95111	Immune keeps track of file sizes and other characteristics; Shield prohibits anyone from performing certain functions without authorization.
VirALARM	IBM PC	Lasertrieve Inc 395 Main St Metuchen NJ 08840	Protects programs by erecting a barrier.
Virusafe	IBM PC	ComNet Co 29 Olcott Sq Bernardsville NJ 07924	Checks program for infections. (Memory-resident program.)
Virus RX	Apple	Apple Computer Inc via Applelink or BBS	Informs the user of any infections; user reloads from backup software.

Microcomputer Virus Countermeasures

Here is a list of techniques that will help prevent viruses in a microcomputer environment:

- The use of public domain or shareware programs should be restricted or eliminated, or every such program should be thoroughly reviewed and tested before use.
- Production software should be subjected to nondestructive testing before use. Include shrink-wrapped software and all updates and revisions.
- Microcomputers should be isolated and delegated to specific users. Software sharing should be restricted.
- The use of modems should be controlled, and communication with bulletin boards should be confined to a single, stand-alone microcomputer. All shareware should be tested before use.
- Regular examination of disk boot records should be performed. Viruses often reveal themselves through odd changes in byte number or quizzical messages.
- Critical and sensitive files and programs should be write-protected.
- A schedule of backups and removal of backups from the facility where they originated should be strictly enforced. Monthly backups should be retained for at least one year.
- The user community should have access to information on computer viruses and related security issues. Users should be aware of the signs of possible contamination.
- In-house programmers should be able to attend training seminars that teach techniques for developing virus-resistant program code.
- The boot should always be done with an approved boot diskette, if a boot diskette is used.
- Volume labels on all fixed disks and diskettes should be meaningful and should be inspected regularly.
- The disk containing the file to be printed should not be bootable and should not contain system files when a second microcomputer is used for printing.

Network Virus Countermeasures

Network manufacturers, including Novell, ADI, Elgar, and Datapoint, met in Vail, Colo., in September 1988 to draft a set of recommendations for combating viruses in LAN environments. Here is a list of their suggestions:

- The countermeasures for microcomputer environments should also be observed with network nodes and workstations.

- A network should be disconnected if a virus is detected. All workstations should be tested for viruses before reconnection.
- Network security procedures should be enforced to ensure that unauthorized access is not possible. (There is considerable information to suggest that the Internet virus would not have been so successful if proper user ID and password measures had been enforced.)
- Shareware or bulletin board downloads should not be filed in common file-server directories where they can be accessed by all nodes.

Mainframe Virus Countermeasures

The following preventive measures are effective against viruses in mainframe environments:

- Interfaces should be designed so that direct access is restricted to mainframes from communications networks.
- Users should be prevented from performing direct terminal-to-mainframe updates. Batch updates should be performed when possible.
- Terminal emulation software should be stored in a separate subdirectory. Executable files should not be stored in the same directory as emulator software.

In addition to these countermeasures, standard security procedures still apply. Exposure of computer systems to viruses can be greatly reduced by following the general-use procedures described.

Recovery Techniques

When a virus has contaminated a system, recovering from the infection with minimum data loss is difficult. A major obstacle is the identification of the virus.

Viruses often destroy themselves when they become active. Even if remnants of the virus are still present, they can be difficult to collect from damaged media. As with the Internet virus, the virus remnant must be taken apart and analyzed. In the Internet case, Lawrence Livermore Laboratories needed 16 hours to develop a fix program. They detected the virus, dropped the connection with the Internet network, eliminated the virus from their systems, reconnected to the network, and were promptly reinfected. Finally, they dropped the connection and developed a fix program to prevent reinfection.

The Computer Virus Industry Association recommends the following steps for recovering from a virus infection in a microcomputer or LAN environment:

1. Power down equipment.
2. Seek professional help.

3. Reboot from original (write-protected) system diskette.

4. Back up all nonexecutable files.

5. Perform a low-level format on the disk.

6. Replace system and executable files.

7. Restore data from backup.

A more detailed procedure for recovering from an infection is available from the association.

CONCLUSION

The computer virus is a threatening reality. However, the threat posed by viruses is inversely proportional to the security awareness of the end-user and programming population and to the quality of preventive programs that a company employs. The reported statistics on viruses, often cited by those who want to minimize the threat, indicate that 94 percent of reported virus events are not actually caused by viruses. Of the remaining 6 percent, most are nonclassifiable, presumably because the virus has destroyed all traces of itself. Often a virus is mistaken for a hardware or software bug. However, there are clear-cut indications of computer viruses in about 3 percent of the reported incidents. The Internet incident was one such case and caused more than $97 million in damage.

In light of the potential magnitude of such a disastrous event, the importance of undertaking a program of prevention is well worth the small cost of a reliable antivirus software package and extra attention.

Notes

1. P. Elmer-Dewit, "Invasion of the Data Snatchers," *Time,* September 26, 1988.
2. J. Getts, "Viruses and Trojans Strike—But Very Rarely," *PC World* 6, no. 10, October 1988.

Reading 10–4

MICROCOMPUTER ACCOUNTING GRAPHICS:
WHY AND HOW TO USE THEM

By L. Murphy Smith, CPA, DBA, and Katherine T. Smith, DBA

In a world filled with information, we still hear the hue and cry for the need to communicate. What is the real message? A thirst for even more information? Probably not. The nation already suffers from "information overload." We believe the challenge is to communicate more effectively.

For CPAs, the challenge is even more difficult to meet. As accountants, we have the responsibility to explain complicated financial information in a manner which clients and employees can understand easily. Presenting facts and figures in a visual or graphic manner is one of the most effective ways to communicate with our audience.

Graphics are one of the most effective communication media available to CPAs who wish to convey information to facilitate financial analysis and management decision making. Many accounting reports can be communicated better via properly prepared graphics.

In recent years there has been substantial development in computer technology. Today there is a wide variety of microcomputer graphics hardware and software choices. This paper discusses:

- Microcomputer software and hardware for preparing graphics.
- Types of graphics commonly used.
- Advantages and disadvantages of graphical presentations.

MICROCOMPUTER SOFTWARE

Microcomputer graphics software or programs may be generally categorized as either stand-alone, dedicated programs or integrated programs. Stand-alone programs require the accountant to enter (key-in) the appropriate tabular information into a program file which is then used to create the graphics. Stand-alone programs include PC chart, GSS-Chart, Graphwriter, Chart-Master, and Graph-in-the-Box.

Integrated programs include several subprograms such as electronic spreadsheets, personal data managers, word processors, and/or graphics in one software package. Because of their flexibility, integrated programs are the most commonly used by accountants.

Reprinted with permission from *Today's CPA*, January/February 1988, pp. 28–32.

In the accounting field, popular integrated packages include Lotus 1-2-3, Symphony, SuperCalc, and Twin Classic. Lotus, for example, is principally an electronic spreadsheet offering a number of sophisticated built-in functions (e.g., present value and regression analysis), as well as graphics capability. The advantage of integrated programs is that the data needed for the graphics presentation may already exist from some previous application, thus saving time in preparing the graphics. The accountant simply retrieves the appropriate data from an existing file and uses the graphics functions (subprograms) to create new graphics.

Integrated software, though satisfactory for most accounting applications, may be too limited for some users. Generally, integrated software does not offer the wide range of graph choices and options of stand-alone software. For example, these programs usually include only a limited number of graph types, labeling options, and formats. A comparison of features of integrated programs and stand-alone programs is provided in Table 1.

MICROCOMPUTER HARDWARE

A basic microcomputer system typically consists of four principal components:

- A microcomputer (CPU), which includes a keyboard for data input.
- A disk drive for secondary storage.
- A monitor (VDT/CRT/Screen) for visual display.
- A printer.

The software usually should be selected before the hardware. In other words, the accountant should determine what types of graphs will be needed and select the software which will prepare (process) those graphs. After selecting the software, the accountant would then acquire the hardware which will run the software. However, if the accountant already owns a microcomputer system, this approach may not be economically feasible. Whichever position the buyer is in, the system and programs should always be tested prior to purchase. Be sure the hardware and the software line up to the sales pitch.

Generally, a microcomputer must have a graphics board (video controller board) to permit viewing of graphics on the monitor. Some microcomputers come with this feature built-in; in other cases, the graphics board is an optional component and must be purchased separately.

Monitors, monochrome or color, are offered in a wide range of quality. Enhanced color monitors offer the best graphics displays but are relatively expensive.

In addition to visually displaying graphics on a monitor, most accounting applications require a hardcopy (e.g., paper) output. Among a wide choice of output devices, the most commonly used is the dot matrix printer which also

TABLE 1   Integrated and Stand-Alone Microcomputer Graphics Software

Name	*System Requirements*	*Supports*	*List Price*
Integrated programs:			
Lotus 1-2-3 Lotus Development Corp. 55 Cambridge Parkway Cambridge, MA 02142	256K RAM 1 Disk Drive DOS 2.0 or later	IBM Monochrome Adapter, CGA, EGA; Hercules monochrome/graphics card. Dot matrix, ink jet, and laser printers; plotters.	$495
Symphony Lotus Development Corp. 55 Cambridge Parkway Cambridge, MA 02142	384K RAM 1 Disk Drive DOS 2.0 or later	IBM Monochrome Adapter, CGA, and EGA; Hercules monochrome/graphics card. Dot matrix, ink jet, and laser printers; plotters.	$895

SuperCalc4
Computer Associates
   International, Inc.
2195 Fortune Dr.
San Jose, CA 95131
	256K RAM
	2 Disk Drives or
	   Hard Disk
	DOS 2.0 or later
	   for a PC or XT
	DOS 3.0 for an
	   AT
		IBM Monochrome Adapter, CGA, and EGA; Hercules monochrome/graphics card. Dot matrix, ink jet, and laser printers; plotters. Polaroid Palette image recorder.	$495

Twin Classic Mosaic Software, Inc. 1972 Massachusetts Ave. Cambridge, MA 02140	320K RAM 2 Disk Drives DOS 2.0 or later	IBM Monochrome Adapter and CGA; Hercules monochrome/graphics card. Dot matrix, ink jet, and laser printers; plotters.	$99

TABLE 1   *(continued)*

Name	*System Requirements*	*Supports*	*List Price*
Stand-alone programs:			
Graph-in-the-Box New England Software, Inc. Greenwich Office Park, #3 Greenwich, CT 06831	256K RAM 1 Disk Drive DOS 2.0 or later	IBM Mono- chrome Adapter, CGA, and EGA; Hercules mono- chrome/graphics card. Dot matrix, ink jet, and laser printers; plotters.	Protected $98 Not protected $148
Chart-Master Ashton-Tate 25 Sylvan Rd. Westport, CT 06880	256K RAM (320K RAM with printer or Polaroid Pal- ette output) 1 Disk Drive DOS 2.0 or later	IBM Mono- chrome Adapter, CGA, and EGA; Hercules mono- chrome/graphics card. Dot matrix, ink jet, and laser printers; plotters. Polaroid Palette and HP 7510A image recorders.	$375
Graphwriter Lotus Development Corp. 55 Cambridge Parkway Cambridge, MA 02142	256K RAM 2 Disk Drives DOS 2.0 or later	IBM Mono- chrome Adapter and CGA; Her- cules mono- chrome/graphics card. Dot matrix and ink jet print- ers; HP Laser jet; plotters. Po- laroid Palette im- age recorder.	$495
GSS-Chart Graphic Software Systems, Inc. 9590 Southwest Gemini Dr. Beaverton, OR 97005	512K RAM 2 Disk Drives DOS 2.1 or later	IBM CGA, EGA, and PGA; Her- cules mono- chrome/graphics card. Dot matrix, ink jet, and laser printers; plotters. Polaroid Palette image recorder.	$295

TABLE 1 (*concluded*)

Name	System Requirements	Supports	List Price
Stand-alone programs:			
PCchart Aztek, Inc. 17 Thomas Irvine, CA 92718	448K RAM 2 Disk Drives DOS 2.0 or later	IBM Mono- chrome Adapter, CGA, EGA, and PGA; Hercules monochrome/ graphics card. Polaroid Palette and other image recorders.	$695

can be used for printing text (i.e., regular reports). Whatever output device is used, it is critical that it be compatible with the graphics software.

In addition to dot matrix printers, there are laser printers, ink jet printers, and plotters. Daisy-wheel printers cannot do graphics. Dot matrix printers are least expensive. The most economical may be purchased for about $200.

Laser printers, like dot matrix printers, offer the advantage of producing text as well as relatively distortion-free graphics. Laser printers are much more expensive, generally starting at $2,000 for a desktop style. Typically, laser and dot matrix printers print in only one color of ink and, thus, cannot create color graphics.

Plotters and ink jet printers often are dedicated to graphics output. Ink jet printers create output by spraying ink. Plotters are output devices that use mechanical arms (with pens) to draw graphs. Both plotters and ink jet printers may be used to create color graphics.

Unlike other output devices, plotters cannot produce text. Nor can they compete with the speed of laser printers. However, plotters can provide striking color graphics. During the past year, plotter prices declined substantially while better interfaces with popular microcomputer software were developed. Consequently, more firms now may acquire plotters for producing improved accounting graphics. Nevertheless, it is still important that the accountant be sure that the graphics software can drive (run) the plotter. Table 2 provides a list of several plotters and their respective features.

Another hardware device useful with some hardware and software is a "mouse." The mouse, typically featuring a steel ball (that fits under the palm of the hand) and a couple of buttons, facilitates creation of freehand drawings.

TABLE 2   Microcomputer Color Plotters

Vendor	Plotter	Supports	*List* *Price*

Arden Systems
12335 Santa Monica Blvd.
  Suite 240
Los Angeles, CA 90025
(213) 479-6707
	Houston
	Instruments
	PC 595
		RS-232 port; 4
		  pens
			$545

Hewlett-Packard
9606 Arrow Dr.
San Diego, CA 92123
(619) 279-3200
	HP 7475A
	
	HP 7550A
		RS-232 port; 6
		  pens
		Same systems; 8
		  pens
			$1,895
			
			$3,900

PC Source
12303-G Technology Blvd.
Austin, TX 78727
(800) 643-0992 (Texas resi-
  dents (512) 331-6700)
	HP 7440A	RS-232 port; 8
		  pens
			$999

Roland DG
7200 Dominion Circle
Los Angeles, CA 90040
(213) 685-5141
	DXY 880
	
	DXY 980
		Serial and parallel
		  ports; 8 pens
		Same systems; 8
		  pens; electro-
		  static paper hold
			$1,395
			
			$1,795

Tekgraf
6721 Portwest, Suite 100
Houston, TX 77024
(713) 868-9330
	Houston Instru-
	  ments
	PC 695A
	DMP-56A
		Apple micros, RS-
		  232 port; 4 pens
		
		RS-232 port; 1 pen
			$799
			
			$5,995

Other output devices allow the creation of slides, transparencies, and paper copies.

It is not necessary to purchase specialized (and expensive) graphics hardware. The best choice when only limited graphics output is needed may be to have a computer service center produce your graphics on a fee basis.

TYPES OF GRAPHS

A wide variety of graphs is available for business and accounting applications. Modern computer systems can generate almost any type of graph imaginable. The most commonly used are as follows:

- Line graphs.
- Bar graphs.
- Pie graphs.

Different types of graphs are well suited for various presentation or analysis needs. For example, the line graph is especially helpful for evaluating trends (e.g., sales over time) as shown in Figure 1.

Figure 1 clearly shows that Tracy's Toy Emporium is experiencing a general upward trend in sales and net income, with the exception of a decline in 1986. An investigation into the cause of the decline in 1986 sales might be warranted as a result of this graphical analysis. Another type of financial analysis facilitated by graphics is provided in Figure 2; a line graph is used to examine cost-volume-profit relationships (sometimes referred to as break-even analysis). The area between the "sales" and "total cost" curves (lines) represents profit.

As shown in Figure 3, the decline in 1986 sales corresponds to a decline in sales by salesperson Bert Taken. A review of personnel data might reveal that Bert, the firm's top salesperson, was on an extended vacation for most of that year.

Pie graphs also are useful for analyzing the components of some overall amount. Figure 4 provides a breakdown of 1987 doll sales by type. Tracy's Toy Emporium offers seven types of dolls, the big-seller "Willie Walker" gen-

FIGURE 1   Tracy's Toy Emporium

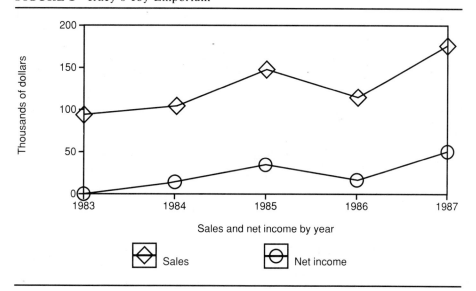

FIGURE 2   Cost-Volume Profit Analysis

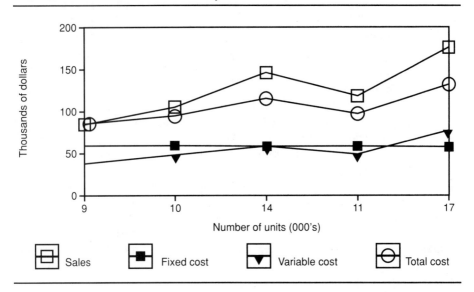

FIGURE 3   Tracy's Toy Emporium

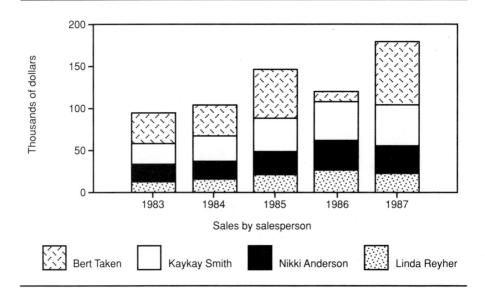

FIGURE 4   Tracy's Toy Emporium

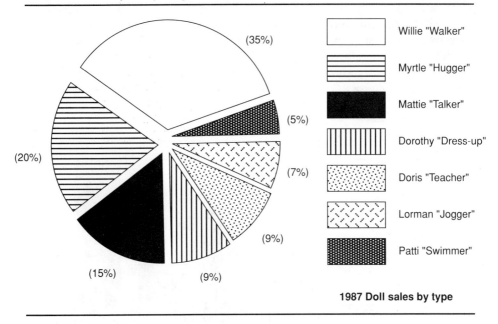

1987 Doll sales by type

erating 35 percent of sales revenues from dolls. Product lines that are not selling well may be discontinued.

ADVANTAGES AND DISADVANTAGES

Graphs are effective communication devices. Recent studies have shown that persons using graphical presentation materials were perceived as being more professional and more likely to have their cases accepted. Vision is usually the dominant human sense. People remember things they see longer than things they read or hear.

Important trends and/or relationships, that might be overlooked in a textual or tabular presentation, may become clear and obvious via a graphical presentation. Most people would rather look at a picture or graph than a page of text or numbers.

However, graphical presentations have an important disadvantage. Depending on how graphs are set up, they may deceive the viewer. The accounting process depends upon effective communication of financial information; the proper and nondeceptive presentation of information is critical to that process.

In his book, *The Visual Display of Quantitative Information* (1982), Edward R. Tufte refers to the ability of graphs to mislead as a "lie factor." The lie factor can be measured as follows: Lie Factor = [(Size of Effect in Graphical Presentation)/(Size of Effect in Data)]. For example, using the sales data for Tracy's Toy Emporium, a bar graph showing sales by year could be deceptive, depending on the starting point (bottom axis) for measuring sales. As shown, the change in sales does not look as dramatic in Figure 6 as in Figure 5.

Figure 6 clearly shows the 88.8 percent change in sales. Figure 5, however, gives the impression that the change is much greater because the bottom

FIGURE 5   Tracy's Toy Emporium

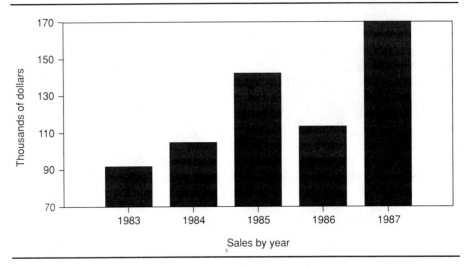

FIGURE 6   Tracy's Toy Emporium

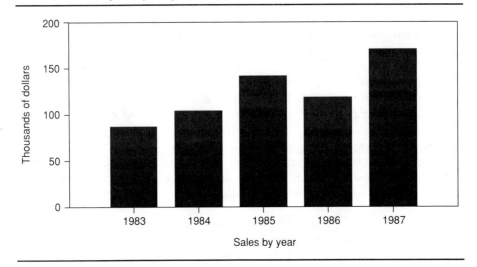

axis is $70,000, not $-0-$. The lie factor for Figure 5 would be computed as follows: Lie factor $= [(400\%)/(88.8\%)] = 4.5$.

Tufte says that a lie factor greater than 1.05 or less than 0.95 indicates substantial distortion far beyond minor inaccuracies in plotting. Thus, a lie factor of 4.5 indicates substantial distortion.

Some people might argue that the graph is clearly labeled and that any distortion is the fault of the reader and not the graph. This argument alone, however, may not be adequate defense for misleading or deceptive graphs. For instance, in the advertising field, previous research by Dr. Katherine T. Smith (*An Analysis of Distortion in the Processing of Advertising by Consumers and Its Effect on Comprehension of Advertising Information,* Louisiana Tech University, Dissertation, 1986) indicated that the Federal Trade Commission's (FTC) criterion for deception in advertising is that the message possesses the tendency or capacity to deceive a substantial portion of the public. Thus, the FTC need not find actual deception, only its potential.

Research has shown that improperly prepared graphs possess a tendency to distort or deceive. In designing graphs, accountants must be careful to avoid potential distortion or deception.

CONCLUSIONS

Graphical presentations can assist greatly the CPAs' communications responsibilities by illustrating activities and trends that might be overlooked using other types of presentations. However, graphs can be misleading. It is critical that they be properly prepared in order to avoid distortion of the data.

A wide variety of microcomputer graphics hardware and software is available. Generally the best rule to follow in acquiring a microcomputer graphics system is to acquire the software before the hardware.

This article has presented features and list prices for some graphics hardware and software. Other sources of information are computer vendors and publications such as *PC Magazine* and *PC Week*. Also, there are now several computer-oriented accounting publications such as *The Journal of Information Systems* and *Financial and Accounting Systems* (formerly *Journal of Accounting and EDP*).

As microcomputer hardware and software have evolved, graphics systems have been developed that can produce a variety of useful graphics displays. Computer-generated accounting graphics are an exciting new way for effectively communicating financial information.

APPENDIX A:

Microcomputer Spreadsheets

This appendix is provided to permit students with little or no knowledge of microcomputer spreadsheet software to quickly acquire a working knowledge. An article on the ABCs of spreadsheet preparation discusses the basic guidelines that should be followed in preparing spreadsheets. Following the article are six short exercises which a student may use to self-teach basic spreadsheet techniques, such as file manipulation, macros, and graphics.

THE ABCs OF SPREADSHEET PREPARATION

By L. Murphy Smith

Microcomputer spreadsheets have had a dramatic impact on the accounting profession. Most firms today use spreadsheets to prepare worksheets, build models, and perform various types of financial analysis. Knowledge of spreadsheet software, particularly Lotus 1-2-3, is increasingly important to accountants and students. Employers expect higher degrees of microcomputer skills in order to remain competitive in an increasingly high-tech business environment. This article provides guidelines for spreadsheet preparation and explores the characteristics of several spreadsheet packages.

The popularity of Lotus 1-2-3 has led to the development of several Lotus compatibles. These Lotus compatibles include, among others, VP-Planner by Paperback Software International and The Twin Classic by Mosaic Software Inc. These compatibles may be used to retrieve and manipulate files that were created using Lotus. In addition to Lotus compatibles, there are other spreadsheet software packages that are not compatible with Lotus (e.g., SuperCalc). All spreadsheets provide the user with a preformatted screen, which consists of rows and columns in which data (text and mathematical expressions) is entered, and a series of special functions (e.g., print, copy, and file).

GUIDELINES FOR SPREADSHEET DESIGN

The following general guidelines should be considered when using Lotus, Lotus compatibles, or any other spreadsheet package:

1. Outline spreadsheet requirements (i.e., input/output).
2. Create a file identification area.
3. Establish data input areas separate from output areas.
4. Input data in rows or columns, but not both.
5. Use manual recalculation when working with large files.
6. Create backup files.
7. Test the spreadsheet.

Requirements Outline. The first guideline in creating any spreadsheet is to outline the spreadsheet requirements. What input is necessary to solve the problem at hand (i.e., to run the spreadsheet)? What output is required (i.e., the spreadsheet's objectives)? These requirements should be determined before beginning the program. For example, assume that a user is creating a template that projects income statements for the next two years based on a constant growth rate in sales revenue. In addition, the cost of goods sold is assumed to be a constant percentage of sales and operating expenses are assumed to be a fixed amount each year. In this case, the following input is required:

- Current sales amount.
- Sales growth rate.
- Cost of goods sold as a percentage of sales.
- Fixed amount of operating expenses.

For purposes of this example, the income statement is limited to only five line-items. The output requirements would be projected income statements for the next two years (see Exhibit 1).

File ID. A file identification area should be prepared at the top of the spreadsheet. This area should include such pertinent information as the file name, the

EXHIBIT 1   Required Output

	1988	1989
Projected sales	$ xx	$ xx
Cost of goods sold	xx	xx
Gross profit	xx	xx
Operating expenses	xx	xx
Projected net income	$ xx	$ xx

spreadsheet designer's name, the input required, the output generated, and the dates the file was created, modified, and last used (see Exhibit 2).

Data Input and Output. Separate areas should be created for input and output in order to facilitate use of the spreadsheet by users not familiar with it. In the input and output template illustrated in Exhibit 3, the four data items necessary for using the spreadsheets—current sales, growth rate, cost of goods sold as a percentage of sales, and operating expenses—are entered in the second column of the input area. The output area consists of an income statement with five line-items and a

EXHIBIT 2 Spreadsheet Template Identification Area

IDENTIFICATION AREA

Filename: Forecast
Designer: Nick Morgan
Input Required:
  a. Current Sales Amount
  b. Sales Growth Rate
  c. Cost of Goods Sold as % of Sales
  d. Operating Expenses
Output: Projected Income Statements
File Created: March 26, 1987
File Modified: June 20, 1987
Last Used: July 20, 1987

EXHIBIT 3 Spreadsheet Template Input and Output Areas

Input Area

Current sales ($):	1,000
Growth rate as % of sales:	12
Cost of goods sold as % of sales	60
Operating expenses ($):	100

Output Area
Projected Income Statements for Next Two Years

	1988	*1989*
Sales	1120	1254
Cost of goods sold	672	753
Gross profit	448	501
Operating expenses	100	100
Projected net income	348	401

separate column for each of the two years projected. Nothing is entered in this area. The output area is totally formula driven based on figures previously entered into the input area.

Input Alignment.   For maximum efficiency, the input cells should be aligned vertically (in a column) or horizontally (in a row), but not both. Fewer mistakes should occur if the user doesn't have to steer the cursor through a maze of input cells. In Exhibit 3 the input area is aligned vertically so that the user can easily move from the first to the last input cell by using the down-arrow key.

Manual Recalculation.   Manual recalculation must be used with large spreadsheet files. Usually, the spreadsheet automatically recalculates mathematical expressions when values are modified or added. Data cannot, however, be entered while the recalculations are taking place. The time involved is inconsequential for small spreadsheets but can become a burden for large spreadsheets. It is simple to change from automatic recalculation to manual recalculation. The Lotus 1-2-3 command is /WGRM (W for worksheet, G for global, R for recalculation, and M for manual). After entering this command, the F9 key must be pressed for the recalculation to be completed.

Backup Files.   Backup copies should be continually updated and stored in more than one place. When creating a spreadsheet, the user should periodically (every 15–30 minutes) save the spreadsheet file in case of a power outage or other event that may cause erasure of the file and the loss of hours of work.

Testing.   Any new spreadsheet should be manually tested. If formulas are involved, the user must test the spreadsheet results against an example that is already proven correct.

COMMON PITFALLS

Many inexperienced users do not properly plan the objective of the spreadsheet template. As a result, the designer may have spent hours creating a spreadsheet with no logical flow and a labyrinth of input areas. Or worse, after meandering through the spreadsheet, the original objectives may not even be accomplished. Without an outline, speadsheets are often illogical, inaccurate, and useless and the designer might actually be confused by the finished product.

An equally common pitfall (and perhaps the most frustrating) is to create a successful spreadsheet template that works but is difficult to locate and retrieve later on. The file identification area alleviates this problem by listing the file name, among other items, at the beginning of the template. This area also lists the designer's name so that subsequent users can bring problems or suggestions to the original designer. In addition, listing the date of file creation or modification informs users of the currency of the spreadsheet.

Another problem may occur when the input and output areas are mixed. This is especially confusing to subsequent users who may be unable to determine where data must be entered. The input area must be separated from the output area in order to avoid confusion and to allow the person entering the data to work as efficiently as possible.

DIFFERENCES AMONG SPREADSHEET PROGRAMS

Lotus 1-2-3 has not always held the superior market position it has now. The first widely used spreadsheet was VisiCalc, which was originally used on the Apple II microcomputer. Another early spreadsheet was SuperCalc, which was written for use on CP/M-based microcomputers. MSDOS versions of both VisiCalc and SuperCalc were developed for use on the IBM PC in 1981 (the year the PC was introduced). Lotus 1-2-3, however, was specifically written for the IBM PC's 8088 microprocessor. Lotus made effective use of the PC's 16-bit chip and its 10 function keys, giving it a jump on its competitors.

Vendor addresses, system requirements, and supports for four popular spreadsheet software packages are shown in Exhibit 4. There are many spreadsheets

EXHIBIT 4   Microcomputer Spreadsheet Software Packages

Name	System Requirements	Supports	Price
Lotus 1-2-3 Lotus Development Corp 55 Cambridge Pkwy Cambridge MA 02142	256K RAM, 1 disk drive, DOS 2.0 or later version	IBM Monochrome Adapter, CGA, and EGA; Hercules monochrome/graphics card. Dot matrix, ink-jet, and laser printers; plotters.	$495
VP-Planner Paperback Software International 2830 Ninth St Berkeley CA 94710	256K RAM, 1 disk drive, DOS 2.0 or later version	IBM Monochrome Adapter, CGA, and EGA; Hercules monochrome/graphics card. Dot matrix, ink-jet, and laser printers; plotters.	$99.95
SuperCalc4 Computer Associates International Inc 2195 Fortune Dr San Jose CA 95131	256K RAM, 2 disk drives or 1 hard disk, DOS 2.0 or later version for an IBM PC or PC XT or DOS 3.0 for a PC AT	IBM Monochrome Adapter, CGA, and EGA; Hercules monochrome/graphics card. Dot matrix, ink-jet, and laser printers; plotters. Polaroid Palette image recorder.	$495
Twin Classic Mosaic Software Inc 1972 Massachusetts Ave Cambridge MA 02140	320K RAM, 2 disk drives, DOS 2.0 or later version	IBM Monochrome Adapter and CGA; Hercules monochrome/graphics card. Dot matrix, ink-jet, and laser printers; plotters.	$99

available that are competitive with Lotus 1-2-3 in quality and performance, and the four spreadsheet packages shown in Exhibit 4 are representative of the overall spreadsheet market.

Twin Classic and VP-Planner are compatible with Lotus. Lotus compatibles can be used to retrieve and manipulate Lotus files using the same basic command structure. The compatibles usually offer some additional features that Lotus does not provide; they also usually lack some Lotus features. SuperCalc4 is a well-designed non-Lotus-compatible spreadsheet. It is a rare example of a spreadsheet introduced before Lotus that is still on the market. SuperCalc4 provides good graphing capability and the graphs look better than Lotus's.

The differences among the spreadsheets may be more important to some users than others. For example, Lotus 1-2-3 offers the widest possible column width, 240 characters, compared with only 127 for SuperCalc4, 72 for Twin Classic, and 72 for VP-Planner. Another difference among spreadsheets is inclusion of a learn mode for macros. This function facilitates the creation of macros. All four packages shown in Exhibit 4 will run Lotus macros, but only VP-Planner and SuperCalc4 offer the learn mode. VP-Planner provides up to six split screens and the other provides for only two.

Graphic capability is another important difference among spreadsheet packages. Lotus offers only five graph types; VP-Planner—five; SuperCalc4—seven; and Twin Classic—eight. Exhibit 5 illustrates the different graph types available with each spreadsheet. Exhibit 6 is a 3-D bar graph of the projected income statement items computed in the earlier example. This graph was created using Twin Classic, which is the only package that provides 3-D bar graphs. Generally, it is easier to create a graph using the non-Lotus packages because a separate printgraph disk must be used with Lotus. This may not be a major concern, however, if graphing

EXHIBIT 5 Graph Types Available among Spreadsheets

	Lotus 1-2-3 Release 2.01	Super-Calc4	Twin Classic	VP-Planner
Bar	X	X	X	X
Stacked Bar	X	X	X	X
3-D Bar			X	
Pie	X	X	X	X
3-D Pie			X	
Pie-Bar			X	
Line	X	X	X	X
X-Y	X	X	X	X
Area		X		
High-Low		X		

EXHIBIT 6   3-D Bar Graph of Projected Income Statement Items—
1988 and 1989

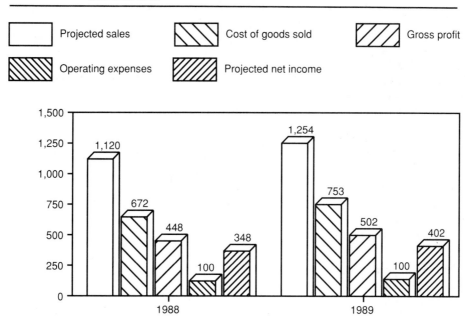

is not important to the user or if a separate stand-alone graph program (e.g., Graph-in-the-Box or Chart-Master) is used to generate graphs from spreadsheet files. Exhibit 7 provides an overall comparison of spreadsheet package features.

CONCLUSION

Spreadsheets are extremely useful for a variety of business applications. The seven guidelines for designing spreadsheet templates provided here apply no matter what spreadsheet software package is being used. Following these basic guidelines will help the inexperienced user design more effective spreadsheets.

Although Lotus 1-2-3 sets the industry standard and dominates the spreadsheet market today, it faces substantial competition from a number of other software vendors. In order to remain the industry leader in this dynamic market, Lotus must be continually revamped to provide improved or additional features. For example, Version 2.0 of Lotus 1-2-3 was released in 1985 and Version 3.0 was released in 1989. The new release provides several enhancements (e.g., improved graphics and the ability to stack spreadsheet files like pages). As existing spreadsheet packages are improved and new ones introduced, spreadsheets will become increasingly helpful in solving business problems.

EXHIBIT 7   Comparison of Speadsheet Features

	The Twin Classic	VP-Planner	Lotus 1-2-3, Release 2.01	SuperCalc4
Size and Speed:				
No. of columns and rows in work area	256 × 8,192	256 × 9,999	256 × 8,192	255 × 9,999
No. of characters in cell/range name	239/15	255/14	240/15	240/32
Column-width range	1-72	1-72	1-240	1-127
Uses math coprocessor	Yes	No	Yes	Yes
Functions and Formulas:				
Math/logic/financial functions	18/8/8	19/5/5	17/7/11	16/16/18
Logical and arithmetic operators	14	15	15	12
Macro Capabilities:				
Learn mode for macros	No	Yes	No	Yes
Runs 1-2-3 macros	Yes	Yes	Yes	Yes
Miscellaneous:				
No. of split screens	2	6	2	2
Cursor keys enter cell data	Yes	Yes	Yes	Yes
Back-step through previous commands	Yes	Yes	Yes	Yes
Cell protection	Yes	Yes	Yes	Yes
Merge contents of spreadsheets	Yes	Yes	Yes	Yes
Graph types	8	5	5	7
Context-sensitive help	Yes	Yes	Yes	Yes

LOTUS 1-2-3 EXERCISE 1

Prepare an income statement using the following format:

Company Name
Income Statement
For the year ended 12/31/XX

Sales
Cost of Sales
Gross Profit
Operating Expense
Net Income

   Assume that your company expects sales of $100,000 for the year ended 12/31/XX. The cost of sales is expected to be 60 percent of sales and operating expenses average 10 percent of sales. Ignore income taxes. Use formulas for all entries except the sales figure.

   After loading the LOTUS program, select 1-2-3 by pressing the Enter key. Then press any key to clear logo.

   When the LOTUS program is first loaded, the column width will be 9 characters. If you need wider columns, use the /wcs command to change the width of specific columns as follows:

/	Command mode
w	Select worksheet
c	Select column
s	Select set width
X	Select width of X characters
Enter	Enter

   Type in the descriptive information, using abbreviations where necessary. With a little practice, you will be able to center headings, by using several columns. Before you do this, be sure that you will not need to change the column width, because unwanted spaces may be introduced.

   When you have completed entering the information and checked the results for accuracy, save your template, using the /fs command.

/	Select command mode
f	Select file
s	Select save
XXXXXXXX	Select filename
Enter	Enter

Print your income statement, using the /p command as follows:

/	Select command mode
p	Select print
p	Select output to printer
r	Select range to be printed (Type cell location of two diagonally opposed corners of range separated by a period; e.g., A1.D10. You can also use pointing—check Help Index (F1)
g	Select go

Use the /fr command to recall your income statement (or any other worksheet you have saved) as follows:

/	Select command mode
f	Select file
r	Select retrieve
XXXXXXXX	Select filename desired
Enter	Enter

When the sheet is loaded, enter various amounts for sales and see how the other values are automatically updated.

Hints:

- Use the Help function (F1) for assistance.
- To retract incorrect commands, simply press the escape key (Esc).

LOTUS 1-2-3 EXERCISE 2

Load the template created and saved in Exercise 1.

Improve the appearance of your income statement by adding rows and lines in the appropriate places, and adding a double line under the net income figure.

To insert a row in your worksheet, use the /wir command:

/	Select command mode
w	Select worksheet
i	Select insert
r	Select row (The new row is inserted above the row containing the cursor.)
Enter	Enter

Lines are created, using the repeating character key (\), the minus sign (-), and the equal sign (=) as follows:

\-   Puts a series of minus signs across the cell; e.g., ----------.

\=   Puts a series of equals signs across the cell; e.g., = = = = = = = = = =.

The repeating character key works with other keys as well. Feel free to experiment.

Expand your report to show projected income for 5 years. Make the necessary changes in the heading and indicate the year above each column. Assume that sales are expected to increase 15 percent each year. Other relationships remain the same.

With the cursor on the Sales row in the second-year column, type a formula for sales. If first-year sales is in B4, your cursor will be in C4 and the formula would be 1.15*B4. Use the /c command to copy the formula in the remaining columns. Cursor should be in C4. To copy a range, do the following:

/   Select command mode

c   Select copy

xx..xx   Identify range if more than one cell

Enter   Enter range to be copied

            Move cursor to cell (or upper right
               corner of range) to be copied to

Enter   Enter

Follow the same procedure to copy formulas from first-year column for remainder of data. To improve the presentation quality of the output (i.e., by aligning the decimal points) use the /RF (Range Format) command (see Exercise 3).

Print your output on one page, using condensed print as follows:

/   Select comand mode

p   Select print

p   Select output to printer

r   Select range to be printed

o   Select options

s   Select setup

\015   Setup string for many common
               printers.
                 If it does not work, check the
                 printer manual for the correct code.

Enter   Set options selected

q   Select quit

g   Select go

Save your template, using /fs.

LOTUS 1-2-3 EXERCISE 3

Calculate the monthly payments needed in the following loan payment plans:

Principal	$100,000	$30,000	$80,000	$20,000	$40,000
Rate	10.0%	5.0%	5.0%	6.0%	12.0%
Years	10	20	15	8	5
Monthly Payment					

Hints:

To create the formats for the principal, interest rate and number of years, use the following commands.

/rfc	Currency format
/rfp	Percentage format
/rff	Fixed number format

To calculate the monthly payments, you need to use the @PMT function:

$$@PMT(principal, interest\ rate/12, year*12)$$

You need to put the cell addresses in the parentheses.

Use the copy command (/c) to copy the @PMT function to each plan. Use the Help Index (F1) to learn how to do this.

LOTUS 1-2-3 EXERCISE 4

A home was bought with a loan of $72,000 at 14.23 percent for a term of 30 years. Assume payments are made in yearly installments.

Required:

Prepare a schedule of payments showing: beginning balance, ending balance, total paid, principal, and interest for each year until the loan is paid off. Finally, compute the total paid in interest, principal, and principal and interest together.

Use the following format:

	A	B	C	D	E	F
1	Principal		xxxx			
2	Interest rate(%)		xx			
3	Term(years)		xx			
4	Payments		@PMT (c1,c2,c3)			
5						

	A	B	C	D	E	F
6	Year	Beg.Bal	End.Bal	Total Pd	Princ.	Interest
7	------	------	------	------	------	------
8	1984	$72,000	+B8-E8	+$C$4	+D8-F8	+B8*$C$2
9	1+A8	+C8	+B9-E9	+$C$4	+D9-F9	+B9*$C$2
10						

One copy command can fill all this in.

37						
38			------	------	------	
39			TOTALS	@SUM(D8..D37)	@SUM(E8..E37)	@SUM(F8..F37)

LOTUS 1-2-3 EXERCISE 5

One powerful feature of Lotus that has not been addressed is the macro. In its simplest form, the macro is a key-stoke saver. It will allow you to reduce a lengthy set of key strokes to two. This is a walk-through exercise in which you will be exposed to the efficiency and convenience of macros.

Required:

Create a macro that will print a prenamed range in condensed print.

Procedures:

1. Create a worksheet to be printed.
    a. In range A1..G8, provide your name, class, section, and the filename.
    b. Starting in cell B15, enter a table of numbers from 1 to 25 in the following format:

			Column		
	A	*B*	*C*	*D*	*E*
Row					
15	1	6	11	16	21
16	2	7	12	17	22
17	3	8	13	18	23
18	4	9	14	19	24
19	5	10	15	20	25

[This table can be quickly created by using the /df command.]

    c. The region to be printed is A1..J36. Using /rnc, name this range EXERCISE5.

2. Create the macro.

    (Note: In creating a macro, you must determine the keys *YOU* would have to press to perform the task desired. These are the strokes that you must incorporate into your macro.)

    a. In cell B24 place \p (remember to make it a label by preceding the backslash-p with a single quote mark).

    b. Starting in cell C24, type the following in columns C and D:

	Strokes:	*Function(s):*
Row	*(C)*	*(D)*
24	/pp	To select print menu and printer.
25	ca	To reset all print settings to their default settings.
26	os\015~	To create setup string to condense printing.
27	ml20~	To set the left margin at 20 (this is ML20 not M120).
28	mr130~	To set the right margin at 130.
29	q	To quit the option menu.
30	rEXERCISE5~	To select range to print. The range to be printed is named "EXERCISE5." The tilde (~) is the symbol for return.
31	a	Align.
32	g	Start printing.
33	p	Page up after printing.
34	q	Quit the print menu.

3. Name the macro.

    Put the cursor in cell B24. Use the /rnlr to name the macro \p (Note: This is a backslash not a slash).

4. Invoke the macro.

    Invoke the macro to print your spreadsheet by typing Alt-P (press the Alt and the P simultaneously).

Comments:

1. The macro should have executed within a few *seconds*. If there are any problems, review the procedures listed above.

2. Be sure you have named the first cell of the macro with a range name as directed in Procedure 3.

3. You cannot have blank cells in your macro. A blank cell must follow the last command of your macro.

4. All the macro cells must be labels.

5. The macro can be put into one cell (up to a limit of about 240 strokes), but it becomes difficult to read and debug. The number of strokes that one puts in any cell, up to the limit, is the operator's choice.

6. The most common cause of errors in macros is omitting a tilde (~).

7. This is only a small example of what macros can do. Feel free to modify the above macro to work in your own spreadsheets. For more information check the Help Index, the Lotus manual, or one of the many Lotus guides written by third parties.

8. "Always check out your macro on something you can afford to lose before using it on important, hard-to-replace information."

—Experience

SPREADSHEET EXERCISE 6

Prepare a pie graph of the division of sales revenue from the data provided in the following income statement:

Company Name
Income Statement
For the Year Ended 19X1

Sales	$100,000
Cost of Sales	60,000
Gross Profit	40,000
Operating Expenses	10,000
Net Income	30,000

Procedure:

This problem is based on VP-Planner because the print graph function is not on a separate disk as is the case with Lotus.

1. Set up a schedule of data to be graphed:

COS	60,000
Op. Expenses	10,000
Net Income	30,000

---

2. Create the graph:

/g	Select the graph menu.
tp	Select the type of graph—pie.
x	Select the range for the pie graph labels. In this case, the range includes COS, Op. Expenses, and Net Income.
a	Select the data range for the pie graph. In this case the range includes 60,000, 10,000, and 30,000.
o	Select the graph options menu.
tf	Enter the first line of the title: Spreadsheet Exercise 6.
ts	Enter the second line of the title: Division of Revenue - 19X1.
q	Quit the print options menu.
nc	Name the graph you have just created so you can select it for future reference from among other graphs you may have. Name the graph SALESX1.
p.	Print the currently selected graph. Be sure to check your printer paper before executing this step.
q	Quit the graph menu. This returns you to the spreadsheet.

---

3. Save your spreadsheet exercise.

Required:

Provide a printout of the graph data schedule and of the graph.

Note: When in the graph menu, the current graph can be viewed by selecting v. The current graph can be viewed while working in the spreadsheet by entering the F10 key.

To print the graph using Lotus: After the nc command above, enter s to save the graph for printing using the Printgraph disk (if you hit "s" in VP Planner, you will get the message "Command not available."). You may save more than one graph as long as the names are unique. Once you have saved all the graphs you need, exit the graph menu. To actually print a graph in Lotus, exit to the Access System, select Printgraph, and follow the instructions on the screen. You will find that Lotus is more complex than VP Planner, but Lotus has more options available.

SOLUTIONS TO EXERCISES

Spreadsheet Exercise 1: Income Statement

```
------------------------------------------
FILE IDENTIFICATION AREA
------------------------
    Name:
    Class:
    Section:
    Filename:  Lotex1
------------------------------------------
            INPUT AREA
            ----------
    Sales:                100000
------------------------------------------
            OUTPUT AREA
            -----------
            Company Name
          Income Statement
For the Year Ended 12/31/XX
Sales                  100000
COS                     60000
GrPr                    40000
OpEx                    10000
NI                      30000
```

Spreadsheet Exercise 2: Five-Year Income Statement

```
-----------------------------------------------------
                  FILE IDENTIFICATION AREA
                  -----------------------
     Name:
     Class:
     Section:
     Filename:  Lotex2
-----------------------------------------------------
                        INPUT AREA
                        ----------
     Sales: 100,000
-----------------------------------------------------
                        OUTPUT AREA
                        -----------
                       Company Name
                     Income Statement
               For the Periods 1/1/X1 through 12/31/X5
     FYE         X1        X2        X3        X4        X5
            ------------------------------------------------
     Sales 100,000  115,000  132,250  152,087  174,901
     COS    60,000   69,000   79,350   91,252  104,940
            ------------------------------------------------
     GrPr   40,000   46,000   52,900   60,835   69,960
     OpEx   10,000   11,500   13,225   15,209   17,490
            ------------------------------------------------
     NI     30,000   34,500   39,675   45,626   52,470
            ================================================
```

Spreadsheet Exercise 3: Monthly Loan Payments

```
------------------------------------------------------------------
              FILE IDENTIFICATION AREA
              ----------------------------

    Name:
    Class:
    Section:
    Filename: Lotex3
------------------------------------------------------------------
                    INPUT AREA
                    ----------

    Not applicable.
------------------------------------------------------------------
                    OUTPUT AREA
                    -----------

Principal: $100,000.00 $30,000.00 $80,000.00 $20,000.00 $40,000.00
Rate:            10.0%       5.0%       5.0%       6.0%      12.0%
Years:              10         20         15          8          5
Monthly
Payment:     $1,321.51    $197.99    $632.63    $262.83    $889.78
```

Spreadsheet Exercise 4: Amortization Schedule

FILE IDENTIFICATION AREA:

Name:
Class:
Section:
Filename: Lotex4

INPUT AREA:

Principal	$72,000.00
Interest Rate	14.23%
Term (years)	30
Payments	$10,438.46

OUTPUT AREA:

Year	Beg.Bal	End.Bal	Total Pd.	Princ.	Interest
1984	$72,000.00	$71,807.14	$10,438.46	$192.86	$10,245.60
1985	$71,807.14	$71,586.85	$10,438.46	$220.30	$10,218.16
1986	$71,586.85	$71,335.20	$10,438.46	$251.65	$10,186.81
1987	$71,335.20	$71,047.74	$10,438.46	$287.46	$10,151.00
1988	$71,047.74	$70,719.38	$10,438.46	$328.36	$10,110.09
1989	$70,719.38	$70,344.30	$10,438.46	$375.09	$10,063.37

Year					
1990	$70,344.30	$69,915.83	$10,438.46	$428.46	$10,009.99
1991	$69,915.83	$69,426.40	$10,438.46	$489.08	$9,949.02
1992	$69,426.40	$68,867.32	$10,438.46	$559.51	$9,879.38
1993	$68,867.32	$68,228.69	$10,438.46	$638.32	$9,799.82
1994	$68,228.69	$67,499.16	$10,438.46	$729.51	$9,708.94
1995	$67,499.16	$66,665.86	$10,438.46	$833.32	$9,605.13
1996	$66,665.86	$65,713.95	$10,438.46	$951.90	$9,486.55
1997	$65,713.95	$64,626.50	$10,438.46	$1,087.36	$9,351.10
1998	$64,626.50	$63,384.50	$10,438.46	$1,242.09	$9,196.36
1999	$63,384.50	$61,965.76	$10,438.46	$1,420.74	$9,019.61
2000	$61,965.76	$60,344.55	$10,438.46	$1,620.77	$8,817.71
2001	$60,344.55	$58,493.72	$10,438.46	$1,851.37	$8,587.08
2002	$58,493.72	$56,378.96	$10,438.46	$2,114.76	$8,323.63
2003	$56,378.96	$53,962.43	$10,438.46	$2,415.76	$8,022.69
2004	$53,962.43	$51,203.46	$10,438.46	$2,759.53	$7,678.93
2005	$51,203.46	$48,450.46	$10,438.46	$3,152.21	$7,286.25
2006	$48,450.46	$44,837.31	$10,438.46	$3,600.77	$6,837.69
2007	$44,837.31	$40,638.85	$10,438.46	$4,113.16	$6,325.30
2008	$40,638.85	$35,271.81	$10,438.46	$4,698.46	$5,740.00
2009	$35,271.81	$30,271.81	$10,438.46	$5,367.05	$5,071.41
2010	$30,271.81	$24,141.03	$10,438.46	$6,130.78	$4,307.68
2011	$24,141.03	$17,137.84	$10,438.46	$7,003.19	$3,435.27
2012	$17,137.84	$9,138.10	$10,438.46	$8,001.74	$2,436.72
2013	$9,138.10	$0.00	$10,438.46	$9,138.10	$1,300.35
Totals			$313,153.65	$72,000.00	$241,153.65

Spreadsheet Exercise 5: Create a Print Macro

```
------------------------------------
        IDENTIFICATION AREA
        -------------------
Name:
Class:
Section:
Filename: Lotex5
------------------------------------
        INPUT AREA/OUTPUT AREA
        ----------------------
     1    6   11   16   21
     2    7   12   17   22
     3    8   13   18   23
     4    9   14   19   24
     5   10   15   20   25
------------------------------------
```

PRINT WORKSHEET:

\p /pp	Select Print menu and printer.
ca	Return all printer print settings to the default mode.
os\015~	Set printer to condensed print.
ml20~	Set left margin to 20 (ML20 not ML20).
mr130~	Set right margin to 130.
q	Quit option menu.
rEXERCISE5~	Select for printing range named ''EXERCISE5''
a	Align.
g	Start printing.
p	Page up after printing.
q	Quit to worksheet.
	<== EMPTY cell indicates end of macro.

Spreadsheet Exercise 6: Pie Graph

```
-----------------------------------------------
FILE IDENTIFICATION AREA
-----------------------
Name:
Class:
Section:
Filename: Lotex6
-----------------------------------------------
INPUT AREA
-----------------
Schedule of data to be graphed:

Cst of Sales              60000
Op. Expenses             10000
Net Income               30000
```

Spreadsheet Exercise 6: Division of Revenue—19X1

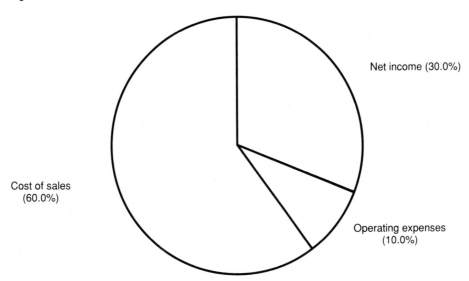

APPENDIX B
DBASE III+

This appendix is provided to permit students with little or no knowledge of micro-computer data base management software to quickly acquire a working knowledge. A brief introductory lesson is followed by three short exercises. Basic procedures are discussed, including: creating files, printing reports, and indexing files.

DBASE III+ INTRODUCTORY LESSON

First, load the DBASE III+ program. Follow the directions included with your software.

After loading DBASE III+, go to the dot (.) prompt by pressing the escape key <esc>. At the dot prompt type: create, then press <enter>. The computer will respond by asking for the name of the data base file. At this point type whatever name you choose to call your data base file and then press <enter>.

The computer will next display the "create" menu screen. This menu is used to create the characteristics of fields (e.g., account name and account number) within your file. The menu screen has four sections: the name section, the type section, the width section, and the decimal section.

The name section contains the name of the field. Enter the name you choose and press <enter>. The type section specifies if the field is to contain character data or numeric data. If this field is character, press <enter>; if this field is numeric, press the "n". The width section specifies the width of the field. Enter the appropriate field width here. If the field is numeric, you then enter the number of decimal places in the field. This is the number of decimal places the number will have. The width field is the total width of the number, including the decimal point and decimal places if decimal places are specified. Enter a 0 (zero) if the number has no decimal places. If the field is character, then you will automatically go to the position to create the next field's description.

EXAMPLE

File name:	Payroll		
Field one:	Emp__name <enter>	=>	field name for field one
	<enter>	=>	this specifies character data
	20	=>	size of field is 20 characters
Field two:	Salary <enter>	=>	field name for field two
	n	=>	numeric data
	7 <enter>	=>	size of field is 7 characters
	2 <enter>	=>	two decimal places

Note: The salary field will be 4 digits before the decimal, the decimal point, and 2 digits after the decimal for a total field length of 7 numeric characters including the decimal point.

The <enter> is pressed to move to the next field position; alternatively, the arrow keys can be used to move about the field positions.

Once all of the fields are created, then press <Ctrl><End> (or <Ctrl> "w") *together* to save the file. The computer will ask if you want to add records now. Type "y" and proceed to enter the data. After entering all your records, once again press <Ctrl><End> to save the file. The arrow keys can be used to move through the records.

TO ADD RECORDS TO AN ALREADY CREATED FILE

To add records at a later date you must first tell the computer to 'use' the data base file to which you want to add records. At the dot prompt, type: use "data base file name here" <enter>. Next, type: Append <enter>.

TO CREATE AND PRINT A REPORT FROM A DBASE III+ FILE

The process of creating a report is menu driven. First, bring up the data base from which you wish to print fields with the 'Use' command (see above). Next, at the dot prompt type: create report <enter>. Next, enter the name of the report, such as "report1".

The computer will respond with the "report form" menu screen. Next, go to the options menu. Under the options menu, go to the "page title" line and press <enter>. Enter the title you wish the report to have in the space provided (up to 4 lines). Next, press <enter> until you get back to the main menu.

From the main menu, go to the columns menu and enter the contents submenu. Press the F10 key. In the box in the left-hand corner of the screen will be a listing of all the field names in your DBASE III+ file. Select the field name you wish to print first and press <enter>. Use the down cursor to move to the heading field in the original box (and press <enter>). Type the heading you want to be printed to describe the field you just selected. To select the next field you wish to print, press the <PgDn> key and repeat the above process until all the fields you wish to print are selected. When you are done, the bottom of the screen will display two large boxes. The top box shows the field names you are printing and the bottom box shows how much line space the fields are using.

Next, use the cursor keys to go to the exit menu to save the report file. At the dot prompt, type: assist <enter> to return to the main menu. Move the cursor to the retrieve menu and select report. The computer will respond with A: B: C: etc. Select the appropriate disk drive. Press <enter>. Retrieve the report form you just created (e.g., "report1") from the list of report forms shown.

After selecting the report form, position the cursor on the submenu field: "Execute the command" and press <enter>. The computer will respond by asking if the output is to be sent to printer. Make sure the printer is ready and paper is aligned, and type "Y". The report will then be printed using the column headings you provided earlier and the data included in the previously selected fields.

Note: In the main menu, press <escape> key to go to dot (.) prompt. At dot prompt, type: assist <enter> to go to the main menu. At dot prompt type: quit <enter> to exit DBASE III+ program

DBASE III+ EXERCISE 1: CREATE A FILE

Load DBASE III+ program and create a payroll file as described in the introductory lesson. Name the file "payroll". Enter five records (type the employee name with the last name first). Create a report form which includes all fields (two) and name it "report1". Print the report.

DBASE III+ EXERCISE 2: ADD A NEW FIELD

Retrieve the payroll file created in Exercise 1 and add a 25-character address field to the existing file. Enter addresses for the five existing records. Create a new report form which includes all fields and name it "report2". Print the report.

To retrieve your data base go to the "set up" menu from the main menu and choose the "data base file" submenu. The screen will respond with a listing of A: B: etc.; select the appropriate disk drive and press <enter>. The display will then ask if the data base is indexed; press "no."

To insert the new address field and edit the existing records, perform the following steps using the menu. Go to the "modify" menu and choose the "data base file" submenu. The screen will then display the structure of your data base. Use the cursor keys to go down to the "salary" field's line. Press the <Ctrl> and "n" keys together. A new field line will be inserted above the "salary" field. Position cursor and enter the new field name, type, etc. Next, press the <Ctrl> and <End> keys together to save the new structure (press the <enter> key to confirm changes when prompted).

Next, go to the "Position" menu and the "Go to record" submenu and choose "top." This will position the internal pointer to the top (record 1) of your data base. Finally, go to the "Update" menu and choose the "Edit" submenu. The screen will respond by displaying record 1. Use the cursor keys to insert the data for the address field and then press the <PgDn> key to go to the next record.

Continue doing this until all the records are updated, at which time you will reach the end-of-file (EOF) and the computer will automatically save your updated records.

DBASE III+ EXERCISE 3: INDEX A FILE

Retrieve the modified payroll file from Exercise 2 and append 5 new records. Index the updated file by alphabetical order, using the employee name field. Use the report form created in Exercise 2 to print the indexed records.

To append records go to the "Update" submenu and choose the "append" submenu. A display will respond with a blank record. Enter the data for the record and use the "down" cursor key to proceed to the next blank record after entering the necessary data. Once all the new records are entered, press the <Ctrl> and <End> keys together to save the new records.

To index the updated file go to the "organize" menu and choose the "Index" submenu. The display will ask which field you wish to index; type: emp_name<enter>. The display will then respond with a drive listing A: B: etc.; select the appropriate drive and press <enter>. Next, the display will prompt you to supply a name for the index. For example, type: empindex.ndx (for employee index). After creating the index go back to the "set up" menu and retrieve your original file but this time enter "yes" when asked if the data base is indexed. The display will show all of the indexes you have created. Choose the index you want (e.g., empindex.ndx) and press <enter>. Now when you print this file it will be printed in the order of the index (i.e., by employee name).

To use a previously created report form, go to the "retrieve" menu and choose the "report" submenu. The display will show a listing of your report forms. Select the appropriate report form. After selection, the computer will respond with another menu. Choose "Execute the command" option, and then send the output to the printer.

ADDITIONAL EXERCISES

The skills you learned in the three exercises above will enable you to complete additional exercises, such as those shown below:

1. Create a more complete payroll file with additional fields.

2. Create an inventory file.

3. Create an accounts receivable file.

4. Create an accounts payable file.

The possibilities are virtually unlimited. Numerous accounting files can be effectively processed using DBASE III+ or other data base manager software.